PENGUIN BOOKS

Orwell's England

'One of the most influential English writers of the twentieth century' Robert McCrum, *Observer*

'A prophet who thought the unthinkable and spoke the unspeakable, even when it offended conventional thought' Peter Grosvenor, *Daily Express*

'He saw through everything because he could also see through himself. Many writers and journalists have tried to imitate his particular kind of clarity without possessing anything like his moral authority' Peter Ackroyd, *The Times*

'Orwell's innocent eye was often devastatingly perceptive . . . a man who looked at his world with wonder and wrote down exactly what he saw, in admirable prose' John Mortimer, *Evening Standard*

'Matchlessly sharp and fresh . . . The clearest and most compelling English prose style this century' John Carey, *Sunday Times*

'It is impossible not to be elated by his literary and political writing – and enraged by what he was up against . . . the most lovable of writers, someone whose books can make the reader long for his company' Geoffrey Wheatcroft, *Spectator*

'His intellectual honesty was a virtue . . . it wasn't just the amount of truth he told but the way he told it, in prose transmuted to poetry by the pressure of his dedication' Clive James, *New Yorker*

'The finest English essayist of his century . . . He made it his business to tell the truth at a time when many contemporaries believed that history had ordained the lie . . . His work endures, as lucid and vigorous as the day it was written' Paul Gray, *Time*

ERIC ARTHUR BLAIR (George Orwell) was born in 1903 in India, where his father worked for the Civil Service. The family moved to England in 1907 and in 1917 Orwell entered Eton, where he contributed regularly to the various college magazines. From 1922 to 1927 he served with the Indian Imperial Police Force in Burma, an experience that inspired his first novel, *Burmese Days* (1934). Several years of poverty followed. He lived in Paris for two years before returning to England, where he worked successively as a private tutor, schoolteacher and bookshop assistant, and contributed reviews and articles to a number of periodicals. *Down and Out in Paris and London* was published in 1933. In 1936 he was commissioned by Victor Gollancz to visit areas of mass unemployment in Lancashire and Yorkshire, and *The Road to Wigan Pier* (1937) is a powerful description of the poverty he saw there. At the end of 1936 Orwell went to Spain to fight for the Republicans and was wounded. *Homage to Catalonia* is his account of the civil war. He was admitted to a sanatorium in 1938 and from then on was never fully fit. He spent six months in Morocco and there wrote *Coming Up for Air*. During the Second World War he served in the Home Guard and worked for the BBC Eastern Service from 1941 to 1943. As literary editor of *Tribune* he contributed a regular page of political and literary commentary, and he also wrote for the *Observer* and later for the *Manchester Evening News*. His unique political allegory, *Animal Farm*, was published in 1945, and it was this novel, together with *Nineteen Eighty-Four* (1949), which brought him world-wide fame.

George Orwell died in London in January 1950. A few days before, Desmond MacCarthy had sent him a message of greeting in which he wrote: 'You have made an indelible mark on English literature . . . you are among the few memorable writers of your generation.'

PETER DAVISON is Research Professor of English at De Montfort University, Leicester. He was born in Newcastle upon Tyne in 1926 and studied for a London External BA (1954) by correspondence course. He edited an Elizabethan text for a London MA (1957) and then taught at Sydney University, where he gained a Ph.D. He was awarded a D.Litt. and an Hon. D. Arts by De Montfort University in 1999. He has written and edited fifteen books as well as the Facsimile Edition of the manuscript of *Nineteen Eighty-Four* and the twenty volumes of Orwell's *Complete Works* (with Ian Angus and Sheila Davison). He is a Past-President of the Bibliographical Society, whose journal he edited for twelve years. He was made an OBE in 1999 for services to literature.

BEN PIMLOTT is Warden of Goldsmiths College, University of London. His books include *Labour and the Left in the 1930s, Hugh Dalton* (Whitbread Prize), *Harold Wilson, Frustrate Their Knavish Tricks* and *The Queen: A Biography of Elizabeth II*. He is a Fellow of the British Academy.

Orwell's England

The Road to Wigan Pier
in the Context of Essays, Reviews, Letters and Poems
selected from The Complete Works of George Orwell

Edited by Peter Davison
Introduction by Ben Pimlott

PENGUIN BOOKS

PENGUIN BOOKS

Published by the Penguin Group
Penguin Books Ltd, 27 Wrights Lane, London w8 5TZ, England
Penguin Putnam Inc., 375 Hudson Street, New York, New York 10014, USA
Penguin Books Australia Ltd, Ringwood, Victoria, Australia
Penguin Books Canada Ltd, 10 Alcorn Avenue, Toronto, Ontario, Canada M4V 3B2
Penguin Books India (P) Ltd, 11 Community Centre, Panchsheel Park, New Delhi – 110 017, India
Penguin Books (NZ) Ltd, Private Bag 102902, NSMC, Auckland, New Zealand
Penguin Books (South Africa) (Pty) Ltd, 5 Watkins Street, Denver Ext 4, Johannesburg 2094, South Africa

Penguin Books Ltd, Registered Offices: Harmondsworth, Middlesex, England

This collection first published 2001
1

The texts in this collection are taken from *The Complete Works of George Orwell*, published by Martin Secker & Warburg Ltd (vols. 1–9 1986, vols. 10–20 1998). *The Road to Wigan Pier* previously published in Penguin Books 1962 and 1989. Some material previously published in different form, in *The Collected Essays, Journalism and Letters of George Orwell, Vols. 1–4*, in Penguin Books 1970

Set in 10/12.5 pt Monotype Columbus
Typeset by Rowland Phototypesetting Ltd, Bury St Edmunds, Suffolk
Printed in England by Clays Ltd, St Ives plc

Contents

Introduction

I have always felt as if I lived in Orwell's England. Like every English child born at the end of the Second World War, I grew up in it. My first memories are American – colourful, plentiful and warm. My first English memories are of London in 1948. By contrast, they are grey and sepia, like a backdrop to *Nineteen Eighty-Four.* I recall a city of bombsites and soot-covered, pock-marked buildings, of gas fires turned low to save fuel and curtains lined with blackout material to keep in the warmth, of sweets on ration, cod-liver oil capsules and undrinkable National Health orange-juice. Germany had been beaten, the Soviet Union was the next enemy, capitalism was on the slide and everybody looked to the state as the provider.

As it happens, I also grew up in Orwell's England in a more personal way. From a very early age, I was aware of a connection with the writer which was no less evocative for being remote. One of my childhood treasures was a christening mug given by my godmother, Gwen O'Shaughnessy, sister-in-law of Orwell's first wife Eileen. George Orwell died of tuberculosis in January 1950, at the age of forty-six. In the mid-1950s, my elder sister and I used to stay with Gwen and her half-sister Doreen Kopp in Norfolk, where Gwen continued to practise as a doctor, and where the two of them brought up a pooled brood of five children. Gwen and Doreen were both widows. It was a happy household, but one that was full of the echoes of dead men.

I remember George as a ghostly presence: a difficult, often exasperating, yet beloved spectre, whose name conjured up muddy boots and dirty finger-nails, adventures in foreign parts, and a stubbornly masculine failure to be practical. For me, Orwell's stern whimsicality has ever since been bound up with a pre-affluent world that no longer exists – of long-faced, heavy-smoking, *New Statesmen & Nation*-reading men (and a few women), who treated the well-to-do with tolerant condescension, and regarded a commitment to history, literature and the public service as taken-for-granted attributes of any civilized human being.

Today – in my mind, at least, but also I think more widely – Orwell's England still conveys a sense of time and place: in particular, the atmosphere of a capital city traumatized by two world wars, London during the threadbare 1930s and the austere 1940s. Sometimes the metropolis is in the foreground. For example, few things Orwell wrote are more grainily evocative of austerity London than *The English People*, a text written during the Second World War as semi-propaganda, though not published until 1947. At other times, what the author writes about seems to have nothing to do with London. But London is there, none the less: *The Road to Wigan Pier* is as much about the mentality of the capital, as it is about the North. Thus, the rootedness of Orwell, the precision of his social comment, make it tempting to see his work as a kind of old-fashioned art movie. England, after all, no longer has coal-mines: and there are probably more wine bars than tripe shops in Wigan.

Yet there is a paradox. On the one hand, Orwell is quintessentially an English writer, carrying into his work many English qualities (suspicion of theory, for example), and his work will always be cited for its representative Englishness. On the other hand – like Boswell's Samuel Johnson, another firmly based Englishman, whom in some ways he resembles – Orwell is the reverse of parochial. Indeed, by one reading, Orwell's England is not a place at all. It is a state of mind. That is why the writings in this volume will continue to be appreciated by people who have only the haziest knowledge of, and only the most limited interest in, the national context in which they were written.

As well as a paradox, there is an irony. Somebody who pitted his satirical talent against the mid-twentieth-century obsession with utopias, appears today – more than fifty years after his death – as one of the most persuasively utopian writers who ever put pen to paper. If Orwell continues to nibble and gnaw at the reader's moral conscience, it is because of the conviction infusing all his work that a satisfactory way of living with neighbours is attainable. Orwell was a socialist – the point needs underlining, for there have been many who have preferred to ignore this fundamental aspect of his life and work. His attacks on other socialists derived, not from a rejection of their goal, but from his own assessment of the vanities and humbug of many of those who self-consciously adopted the label.

Abolishing cant was his aim. What gives him his unique appeal is a passion for honesty which acknowledges that nobody is ever completely honest. If he had a universal message, it was this: a better life can be achieved, not by the repetition of stock phrases, but by examining the actual world we inhabit.

George Orwell was a socialist. Was he also a hero, even a martyr? It is important to get things into perspective. One obstacle to a proper understanding of his work is the posthumous cult that grew up in the years after his death, and especially (another irony) after the publication of Bernard Crick's masterly and not at all reverential biography. The cult focused on the life, presenting the writer as a Christ or John the Baptist, and conveniently dividing the narrative into New Testament segments: youthful promise, followed by retreat into the wilderness and period of obscurity; self-examination in the company of outcasts and the needy; brief, brilliant and controversial ministry; even briefer period of celebrity; early death. The cult apparently solved the problem of Orwell's refusal to be categorized: morally perfect and above reproach, the writer became the property of everybody. As a result, his work is nowadays quoted as scripture, often by people to whom he would not have given the time of day (and, no doubt, vice versa).

Orwell would laugh at this, and so should we. The passage of time ought to enable us to see him today as altogether fallible, struggling for most of his adult life to find a voice and earn his crust. To regard him in this light does not diminish the work but, on the contrary, makes it more remarkable: it helps us to appreciate that author, social inquirer and human being are of a piece. In place of the god or prophet, we discover a 'degenerate modern semi-intellectual' (his self-description) trembling on the edge of failure. We see writing that stems not from a master plan, but from a series of false starts. Indeed, so far from being structured, Orwell's actual life was chaotic. The Orwell we encounter at the beginning of this book is Eric Blair, the Old Etonian drop-out and insecure drifter, more or less on his beam ends. If England is his topic, this is *faute de mieux* – it has less to do with a fascinated interest in his native country, than because it is the material most readily at hand.

By the mid-1930s, the scene has changed. With three published books under his belt and another on the way, he has acquired a literary persona (as well as a name). Yet he remains an eccentric, if by now well-directed, outsider – eking out a meagre existence on the margins of London journalistic and political life. We see an ambitious author who rather pettishly resents the success of his better-organized contemporaries. We see a rebel whose rebellion is more against the caste of left-wing fellow-writers, than against the shabby-genteel stratum which he identifies as his own. We see a vocal critic of social snobbery, whose access to publishing houses and literary journals owes more to doors opened through old-boy connections with people like Cyril Connolly, than he is ever prepared to admit. In such a context, Orwell's famously savage indictment of brutality and conditioning at his prep school ('Such, Such Were the Joys') appears almost ungrateful.

Yet if Orwell in this pre-war period is an aspirant writer like any other, seizing at every opportunity to climb the greasy pole, he stands out from the rest – because of his relationship to his subject. He observes, and he chews at his observations, like a dog with a bone. Orwell is a classic documentary writer, not because experts say he is – stylistically, he breaks practically every rule – but because of his story-teller's instinct for conveying the emotions of a social traveller. Orwell's skill is in convincing his audience that his own non-conventional feelings are actually the same as theirs would be, if they had shared his experience. He is not just a voyeur, peering at the dirty linen and messy lives of people the world prefers not to know about. He is a collusive, seductive voyeur. His achievement is to abolish (or appear to abolish) self-censorship, and to provide in his account an almost embarrassing intimacy: the reader is told to peer into the writer's psyche and see the unpleasant things, as well as the good ones.

In this he differs from many of the philosophers and agitators among his contemporaries who saw themselves as messengers for a higher cause, interpreting or relaying points of view derived from Continental theories. For such people, documentary was political ammunition in a war with set battle-lines. By contrast, Orwell sniffs orthodoxy at a hundred yards: and, having sniffed, seeks to upset its adherents. Nobody was ever more politically incorrect than Orwell – or, on occasion, more illiberal: so far from being a model for twenty-first century progressives, he reveals attitudes (towards 'Nancy poets' of the literary establishment, for example, and 'birth controllers') which, if expressed for the first time today, would get him thrown out of the faculty of an American university. However, he does not claim superior virtue. He admits that many of his own attributes are undesirable. He self-flagellates as much as he flagellates.

The core of this volume is provided by Orwell's most important non-fiction work. *The Road to Wigan Pier* is a sequel to *Down and Out in Paris and London,* the author's first book, which established his distinctive style, and also himself as a social investigator of a particular, Jack London, type. At the same time, it is transitional, marking the writer's move from amateur to professional status. *Wigan Pier* was commissioned by his publisher, Victor Gollancz, in January 1936, just after Orwell had finished the manuscript of his third novel, *Keep the Aspidistra Flying.* Hitherto, he had lived hand to mouth. The commission marked a step forward in his standing as a writer, and signalled a new confidence.

Orwell's brief was to write about the condition of the unemployed in the North of England, much as he had previously written about tramps and social outcasts. Though non-fiction, it contains a literary convention that is fictional. The portrayal of the author as an impecunious scribbler not far removed from those he is observing ('Economically, I belong to the working class'), is unduly modest. Every other aspect of the book, however, is essentially truthful – as the meticulous 'Road to Wigan Pier Diary', included in this volume, shows. Orwell treated the project with the utmost seriousness. For *Down and Out* he himself became a tramp, to find out what it felt like. For *Wigan Pier* he travelled North as a burgeoning writer, armed with letters of introduction from journalists and political activists, making no pretence of joining the ranks of those he sought to observe. At the same time, he was concerned to write as sensitive a description as he could, in the time available.

The book was based on two months (February and March, 1936) with working people and their families in Manchester, Wigan, Barnsley and

Sheffield, together with a spell with his sister and her husband in Leeds, and a visit to Liverpool docks. The author did not seek to be like the people he visited. However, he tried to be more than a typical journalist: he avoided staying in ordinary hotels, adopting instead the style of an anthropologist. After taking a train to Coventry, he made his way to Manchester by bus and on foot through some of the grimmest industrial areas, sleeping in lodging houses and on one occasion in a doss-house. In Manchester, he stayed for four days with a trade union official and his wife, and was directed on to Wigan, a town particularly hard hit by cotton-mill and coal-mine closures. There he lived at a variety of addresses (as his Diary entries record), including lodgings over a tripe shop. He visited homes, attended political meetings, and went down a pit. The fruit of his efforts is a work that combines detailed observation, a matter-of-fact tone, human feeling and political passion. At the same time, the author uses his account of proletarian life as a peg on which to hang what really interested him: not just the lives of working-class people as such, but his own inner dialogue about how middle-class people like himself did and should relate to them.

The Road to Wigan Pier is about class, and its effects. It is not about industry, or the economy. 'I know nothing whatever about the technical side of mining', the author is at pains to point out. 'I am merely describing what I have seen . . . I am not a manual labourer and please God I never shall be one.' The book is about the English as they really were, and possibly still are. It is about contrasts, hypocrisy, and convenient amnesia. Thus, the author drives home the unwelcome truth that, whoever you happen to be, the luxury to do what you do depends on hard, physical work done by others. 'In order that Hitler may march the goose-step', he writes, 'that the Pope may denounce Bolshevism, that the cricket crowds may assemble at Lord's, that the Nancy poets may scratch one another's backs, coal has got to be forthcoming.' Middle-class Southerners are a particular target. There may be, he suggests, 'at least a tinge of truth in that picture of Southern England as one enormous Brighton inhabited by lounge-lizards', who know little about the manual labour they require to be performed.

The first part of *Wigan Pier* (buttressed by photos and simple bits of arithmetic which, alas, the passage of time has rendered quaint, rather than shocking) is a Baedeker's guide to the slums, damp, dirt, disease, accident rates and high mortality that are the consequence of poor wages and bad working conditions. Repeatedly, the author stresses how difficult it is for a middle-class observer to take in what is going on. The conditions of the English proletariat, he indicates, are a foreign country. 'Even when I am on the verge of starvation', he points out, 'I have certain rights attaching to my bourgeois status.' The working class are not so lucky. Juxtaposed are the tragedy of squalid lives ('on the day when there was a full chamber-pot under the breakfast table, I decided to leave'); and the confessional, as the author seeks to explain why, to middle-class eyes and nostrils, working-class conditions are repugnant as well as tragic. It is a shattering book, yet surprisingly not a despairing one. It ends on a positive note: the reader is left with a sense that the task of breaking down social barriers is almost impossible – but not quite. The solution, Orwell argues, is for middle-class wage-earners in Southern England to accept that their future lies in alliance with, not in fearful opposition to, the Northern proletariat. The message is uncompromisingly political. If Socialism becomes something 'large numbers of Englishmen genuinely care about', he declares, then 'the class-difficulty may solve itself more rapidly than now seems thinkable.'

Such an upbeat conclusion may have owed something to the author's concern – in view of his heavy criticisms of socialists early in the book – to make clear which side he is on. The Left–Right struggle was intensifying, and it was not a time for ambiguity. It may also have something to do with an event in the author's private life. In June 1936, Orwell married Eileen O'Shaughnessy. Orwell's friend Geoffrey Gorer once remarked that the only time he ever saw Orwell really happy was in the first year of his marriage. It also happened to be the period when the author was writing up his *Wigan Pier* notes. Whether or not this was a factor, the reader comes away from *The Road to Wigan Pier* horrified by what it describes, but also with a sense of the dignity of those described in it, and of a challenge.

The challenge went beyond England. Orwell wrote *Wigan Pier* just as the attention of radicals at home was moving away from domestic problems to European ones. In March 1936, German troops entered the demilitarized zone of the Rhineland, in violation of the Treaties of Versailles and Locarno. In July, Franco's rebellion against the Republican Government in Spain precipitated a civil war. By the time *The Road to Wigan Pier* was published, its topic had become unfashionable: everybody on the Left was talking about Spain, and Orwell himself had taken time off from writing to arrange to join the Independent Labour Party's expeditionary unit. If the book can be seen as a follow-up to *Down and Out*, it is also a prequel to *Homage to Catalonia* – the final section, on the need to resist creeping fascism, was written against the background of the growing Spanish conflict.

Spain impinged in another way as well. A week after Franco's return to the mainland, Gollancz launched his pioneering Left Book Club, whose monthly 'choices' – selected by a triumvirate of Gollancz himself, John Strachey and Harold Laski – were guaranteed not only a wide but an enthusiastic and committed readership. The Club was a movement as well as a publishing venture. Its primary aim was to whip up support for the Spanish Republican cause and for a pro-Communist, anti-fascist popular front. Most of the 'choices' were by Communists or fellow-travellers. *The Road to Wigan Pier*, with its open scorn for middle-class Marxists, scarcely fitted the Club's mould. Gollancz's publishing instincts, however, were even stronger than his political ones, and as soon as he had read the manuscript he offered the author a place on the LBC list. The book was duly published by the Club in March 1937 – albeit with a preface by the publisher, distancing himself from Orwell's anti-Communist opinions. By then, Orwell was in Spain, and received his copy in the trenches before Huesca. The first edition sold over 47,000 copies.

It is easy to see why *Wigan Pier* made Gollancz both excited and nervous. On the one hand, the descriptions of poverty were grist to the Marxist and 'popular front' mill. On the other, Orwell's attack in the second half of the book on actually existing socialists (which Gollancz urged him to drop), was disconcertingly persuasive. Modern readers may also have difficulty with parts of the book, but for different reasons. Some may be more amused than outraged by a famous passage in which the author provocatively lumps together the many varieties of people he regards as cranks ('One sometimes gets the impression that the mere words "Socialism" and "Communism" draw towards them with magnetic force every fruit-juice drinker, nudist, sandal-wearer, sex maniac, Quaker, "Nature Cure" quack, pacifist and feminist in England'). Harder to take, however, is Orwell's blush-making description of working-class life at its best:

> Especially on winter evenings after tea, when the fire glows in the open range and dances mirrored in the steel fender, when Father, in shirt-sleeves, sits in the rocking chair at one side of the fire reading the racing finals, and Mother sits on the other with her sewing, and the children are happy with a pennorth of mint humbugs, and the dog lolls roasting himself on the rag mat – it is a good place to be in, provided that you can be not only in it but sufficiently *of* it to be taken for granted.

Such passages have been used to lampoon Orwell as a naïve and patronizing sentimentalist. Fortunately there are few of them: and they do little to detract from the author's powerful account of a country morally crippled by class, by a bourgeois urge to keep up appearances, and by ignorance of the working and housing conditions of those whose downtrodden lives support the comforts of the better off.

There is a need for people to know. 'It is a kind of duty', he insists, 'to see and smell such places now and again, especially smell them, lest you should forget that they exist.' Smell plays a critical part. Orwell reminds the reader, self-analytically, that people like him – precariously 'lower-upper-middle-class' – were brought up to believe that 'the lower classes smell'. Things may have changed since his own childhood before and during the Great War, he acknowledges. But he doubts if they have changed much.

Wigan Pier presents one picture of Orwell's England. It is refined, but seldom contradicted, elsewhere in the author's writings. A pattern emerges: England (not Ireland or Scotland or Wales – none of which greatly interests him) is a country where social divisions cause the poor unnecessary suffering; and also where the middle and upper classes are maimed by their upbringing and education. It is an England where, because of class, those on the margins of a particular layer attach themselves desperately, and pathetically, to the values of the one above them. There is a lace-curtain, 'old maids biking to Holy Communion' aspect. There is also militarism. 'Most of the English middle class are trained for war from the cradle onwards', the author observes, and asks, 'how is it that England, with one of the smallest armies in the world, has so many retired colonels?'

People of moderate disposition who imagine that *Orwell's England* may offer them consolation will have to look elsewhere: the author is uncompromising. In *Wigan Pier*, he writes of the need for an 'effective Socialist party . . . with genuinely revolutionary intentions', in order to resist an English form of fascism. The Second World War radicalizes him still further. Who can be relied on? Not the English police, 'the very people who would go over to Hitler once they were certain he had won'. In his wartime essay, 'My Country Right or Left', Orwell does not mince his words. 'Only revolution can save England', he concludes, 'that has been obvious for ten years. I dare say London gutters will have to run with blood.' But if Orwell's England is a country on the brink, its weaknesses can also be saving graces. Thus, the English 'training for war' and public-school system may even have advantages: turning out stiff-upper-lip idealists of the John Cornford type, splendidly equipped for leadership roles as revolutionaries. Meanwhile, if England gets into serious trouble, the loyalty of anybody who has experienced 'the long drilling in patriotism which the middle classes go through' can be relied upon to rally round, regardless of political opinions.

In sum, the England that emerges from this book is a country (and an idea) which Orwell regards with a kind of weary affection and matured respect, even against his own better judgement: an England whose manifold injustices should not obscure its blessings. It is a country where everybody knows everybody else's place. It is an England of tramps on the way down ('homosexuality is a vice which is not unknown to these eternal wanderers'), trade union officials on the way up ('as soon as a working-man gets an official post in the Trade Union or goes into Labour politics, he becomes middle-class whether he wish or no'), of schools like Roedean ('I could feel waves of snobbishness pouring out'), and a socialist bourgeoisie 'most of whom give me the creeps'; an England where red pillar-boxes and suet puddings enter your soul, an England of privacy, an England which is also 'the most class-ridden country under the sun'; an irreligious yet vaguely theistic England that maintains an unusual tradition of people 'not killing one another'; a philistine, xenophobic England of compromises, bad teeth, lack of artistic talent or ability at languages. The

English are 'not intellectual', the author tells us, approvingly – a dig at the 'Nancy poets' and other members of the intelligentsia who 'take their cookery from Paris and their opinions from Moscow'.

Like the writer himself (and, implicitly, the readers he takes into his confidence) Orwell's England is a territory of contradictions – in need of new management, but neither negligible, nor to be disregarded. Orwell indicts the double-standards, lack of warmth and pomposity of the English. No other author dissects his fellow countrymen so pitilessly. But he also refuses to scorn English qualities of common sense, empiricism and toleration.

The books, essays, reviews, articles and jottings contained within this volume do not provide a comprehensive picture of the nation in Orwell's head. What they do capture, however, is a sense of the author's changing world view, with England as his point of reference. *Orwell's England* displays a writer and his subject-matter in varying moods – of depression, fear, doggedness, bereavement, make-do-and-mend. It also provides, for the first time, a gathering impression of an outlook that is questioning, affectionate, critical and hopeful: a non-topographical, abstract Albion.

Will a modern young person – a black or brown Briton, born in Wilson's England or Thatcher's – feel any affinity towards it? Would Eric Blair recognize Tony Blair's England? In some respects he would find it unimaginably different, in others only superficially so. Some characteristic features of Orwell's sepia England have undoubtedly faded. The great work-forces of miners, dockers, metal-workers, ship-builders that dominated mid-century proletarian England no longer exist, and blue-collar workers are now supposedly in a minority. In place of slum-dwelling and the Means Test, problems to do with schooling, crime and family breakup dominate the contemporary social agenda. Among the middle class, stiff upper lips are less in evidence and social distinctions, though still harshly divisive, have blurred at the edges. Yet there are elements of bourgeois culture that remain stubbornly recognizable, down the generations:

> 'How much a year has your father got?'
>
> I told him what I thought it was, adding a few hundred pounds to make it sound better . . .

> 'My father has over two hundred times as much money as yours', he announced with a sort of amused contempt.
>
> That was in 1915 ... I wonder, do conversations of that kind happen at preparatory schools now?

Do they still? It is conceivable. It is equally conceivable that there are people inhabiting what nowadays we call Middle England (not to mention up-market London boroughs where millionaires and beggars live cheek by jowl), who have as small an understanding of those below the poverty line – and as small a wish to know – at the start of the twenty-first century as their counterparts had, at the beginning of the twentieth.

Orwell's account of England endures partly because the modern bourgeoisie, complacent and blinkered as ever, still define the essence of the Englishness the world sees; and partly because the poor (now called the socially excluded), who constitute the invisible England, are ever with us. It endures as an idea because, in our better moments, many of the most bourgeois of us continue to support Orwell's dream – of an England and a world without barriers of any description; and because everything Orwell ever wrote is part of an extended polemic in favour of seeing the truth, however ugly, in ourselves.

Ben Pimlott

Editorial Note

In the main, the items reproduced here are given in the chronological order in which they were written or published. However, the order of events is sometimes better represented by not following this practice. It will be obvious, from dates and item numbers, where the chronological order has not been followed. Letters are typewritten unless stated otherwise. The titles used for Orwell's essays and articles are not always his own but this distinction is not noted unless there is a special reason to do so.

All the items are drawn from *The Complete Works of George Orwell*, edited by Peter Davison, assisted by Ian Angus and Sheila Davison (Secker & Warburg, 1998). Some explanatory headnotes and many footnotes have been added, amplified and modified. The *Complete Works* did not provide biographical notes of authors of books reviewed but, for this selection, these have been added if the author had a link with Orwell or if they might illuminate the context of Orwell's review. Item numbers from the original edition are given in italics within square parentheses, and a list of volumes in which these items can be found is given in the Further Reading.

Where the text was in some way obscure, the original edition does not modify but marks the word or passage with a superior degree sign (°); in most instances such passages have been silently corrected in this edition but in a few instances the degree sign has been retained, for example, where one of Orwell's idiosyncratic spellings occurs: e.g., 'agressive' or 'adress'.

References to items in the *Complete Works* are generally given by volume, forward slash and item number in italic: e.g.: XV/*1953*; page references to *CW* are given similarly except that the page number is in roman: XII/387; page references to this present volume are given as 'p. 57'; references are also made to the companion three volumes: *Orwell in Spain, Orwell and Politics* and *Orwell and the Dispossessed.* References to *The Road to Wigan Pier* are given to this edition by page and, within square brackets, by the *CW* volume number (V) and page (the page numbers in *CW* and Penguin Twentieth-Century Classics are identical for the text): e.g., p. 81 [V/36].

The following works are designated by abbreviated forms:

Complete Works and *CW*: *The Complete Works of George Orwell,* edited by Peter Davison assisted by Ian Angus and Sheila Davison, 20 vols. (1998); volume numbers are given in roman numerals, I to XX. Vols. X–XX of a second, enlarged and amended, edition are being published in paperback from September 2000.

CEJL: *The Collected Essays, Journalism and Letters of George Orwell;* edited by Sonia Orwell and Ian Angus, 4 vols. (1968; paperback, 1970)

Crick: Bernard Crick, *George Orwell: A Life* (1980; 3rd edn, 1992)

A Literary Life: P. Davison, *George Orwell: A Literary Life* (1996)

Orwell Remembered: Audrey Coppard and Bernard Crick, eds., *Orwell Remembered* (1984)

Remembering Orwell: Stephen Wadhams, ed., *Remembering Orwell* (1984)

S&A, *Unknown Orwell*: Peter Stansky and William Abrahams, *The Unknown Orwell* (1972)

S&A, *Transformation*: Peter Stansky and William Abrahams, *Orwell: The Transformation* (1979)

Shelden: Michael Shelden, *Orwell: The Authorised Biography* (1991)

Thompson: John Thompson, *Orwell's London* (1984)

The Thirties: Malcolm Muggeridge, *The Thirties* (1940; 1971); reviewed by Orwell, XII/*615*

A fuller reading list is given in Further Reading.

Peter Davison,
De Montfort University, Leicester

Acknowledgements

George Orwell's (Eric Blair's) work is the copyright of the Estate of the late Sonia Brownell Orwell. Most of the documents in this edition are held by the Orwell Archive (founded by Sonia Orwell in 1960) at University College London. Gratitude is expressed to the Archive, and particularly its Archivist, Gill Furlong, for the help given the editor. Thanks are also gratefully extended to the Henry W. and Albert A. Berg Collection. The New York Public Library, Astor, Lennox and Tilden Foundations, for permission to reproduce Orwell's letters to Jack Common, 16(?) April 1936 and 25 August 1938; and Eileen Blair's letter to him, 20 July 1938.

From Burma to Paris

George Orwell served in the Indian Imperial Police in Burma from 1922 until 1927. He returned to England on leave on 12 July 1927 and, having left his ship in Marseilles and travelled home through France, he arrived back in England in August. While on holiday with his family in Cornwall in September he decided not to return to Burma. His resignation took effect from 1 January 1928 and entailed the loss of almost £140 (approximately £5,500 in today's values). By the time he left Burma he was earning £696 a year (roughly £28,000 today), to which were added bonuses for learning Hindi, Burmese and Shaw-Karen. He would only earn nearly as much again in the next fourteen years when he joined the BBC in 1941 (£640). It is likely, from what we know of clothes he had made for him on his return (see A Literary Life, *36) and from what we know from various sources of the style in which he lived in Paris until he ran out of money, that he had saved a fair amount of his pay. During the rest of his leave he rented a cheap room in the Portobello Road in Notting Hill, London W1. He began to make expeditions to the East End of London in the autumn of 1927. In the spring of 1928, Orwell went to Paris and took a room at 6 rue du Pot de Fer in the Fifth Arrondissement, a working-class district near Monge Métro station. He set himself to becoming a writer and had a modest success in getting articles into small-circulation, left-wing journals. He also wrote either one or two novels and a number of short stories, none of which survives. The article reproduced here, 'A Day in the Life of a Tramp' (translated from the French version by Janet Percival and Ian Willison), is one of three from 'An Inquiry into "Civic Progress" in England: The Plight of the British Workers', published by* Le Progrès Civique *in 1928 and 1929. Another article, 'Unemployment', is reprinted in a companion volume in this series,* Orwell and the Dispossessed. *For each he was paid 225 francs (about £1.80 – some £70 at today's values). He also wrote articles on John Galsworthy, the exploitation of the Burmese people, and on censorship in England, for French journals. They, with an article on 'A Farthing Newspaper' published in England (and reproduced in* Orwell and the Dispossessed*), are an epitome of the interests he would pursue as an essayist: social and political issues, literature, popular culture and imperialism.* The Complete Works *prints all the articles, with their French originals.*

The very short paragraphs are not typical of Orwell. Orwell wrote in English (in a version that has not survived), and the French translator, Raoul Nicole, is almost certainly responsible for breaking Orwell's prose into short bites. It is possible that the divisions marked by asterisks represent Orwell's original paragraphing. For later reworkings of the experiences described here, see 'The Clink', published by The Adelphi, *April 1931 (*X/*104), and chapters 27 and 35 of* Down and Out in Paris and London. *There were once about 750 spikes (casual wards or workhouses); a government order closed the last (at Bishopbriggs, near Glasgow) in 1996. The French text has* asile *for* workhouse *and usually prints* tramp*(*s*) in italic but occasionally translates it as* vagabond*(*s*). There is a note on 'casual ward' in the French translation of* Down and Out in Paris and London *(*CW, I/226, *see note 140/4) that probably derives from Orwell. The square brackets are Orwell's.*

[83]

'A Day in the Life of a Tramp'

Le Progrès Civique, *5 January 1929*

First, what is a *tramp*?

A tramp is a native English species. These are his distinguishing characteristics: he has no money, he is dressed in rags, he walks about twenty kilometres a day and never sleeps two nights together in the same place.

In short, he is a wanderer, living on charity, roaming around on foot day after day for years, crossing England from end to end many times in his wanderings.

He has no job, home or family, no possessions in the world apart from the rags covering his poor body; he lives at the expense of the community.

No one knows how many individuals make up the tramp population.

Thirty thousand? Fifty thousand? Perhaps a hundred thousand in England and Wales when unemployment is particularly bad.

The tramp does not wander for his own amusement, or because he has inherited the nomadic instincts of his ancestors; he is trying first and foremost to avoid starving to death.

It is not difficult to see why; the tramp is unemployed as a result of the state of the English economy. So, to exist, he must have recourse to public or private charity. To assist him, the authorities have created *asiles* (workhouses) where the destitute can find food and shelter.

These places are about twenty kilometres apart, and no-one can stay in any one spike more than once a month. Hence the endless pilgrimages of tramps who, if they want to eat and sleep with a roof over their heads, must seek a new resting-place every night.

That is the explanation for the existence of tramps. Now let us see what sort of life they lead. It will be sufficient to look at just one day, for the days are all the same for these unfortunate inhabitants of one of the richest countries in the world.

*

Let us take one of them as he comes out of the spike at about ten in the morning.

He is about twenty kilometres from the next workhouse. He will probably take five hours to walk that distance, and will arrive at his destination at about three in the afternoon.

He will not rest much on the way, because the police, who look on tramps with a suspicious eye, will make quick work of sending him packing from any town or village where he might try to stop. That is why our man will not tarry on the way.

It is, as we have said, around three o'clock in the afternoon when he turns up at the spike. But the spike does not open until six in the evening. Three weary hours to kill in the company of the other tramps who are already waiting. The herd of human beings, haggard, unshaven, filthy and tattered, grows from minute to minute. Soon there are a hundred unemployed men representing nearly every trade.

Miners and cotton-spinners, victims of the unemployment which is raging in the North of England, form the majority but all trades are represented, skilled or not.

Their age? From sixteen to seventy.

Their sex? There are around two women for every fifty tramps.

Here and there, an imbecile jabbers meaningless words. Some men are so weak and decrepit that one wonders how they could possibly walk twenty kilometres.

Their clothes strike you as grotesque, tattered and revoltingly filthy.

Their faces make you think of the face of some wild animal, not perhaps a dangerous one, but one which has become at once savage and timorous through lack of rest and care.

*

There they wait, lying on the grass or squatting in the dust. The bravest prowl around the butcher's or the baker's, hoping to glean some scrap of food. But this is dangerous, because begging is against the law in England, so for the most part they are content to remain idle, exchanging vague words in a strange slang, the tramps' special language, full of bizarre and picturesque words and phrases which cannot be found in any dictionary.

They have come from all four corners of England and Wales, and tell each other their adventures, discussing without much hope the likelihood of finding work on the way.

Many have met before in some spike at the other end of the country for their tracks cross again and again in their ceaseless wanderings.

These workhouses are miserable and sordid caravanserais where the miserable English pilgrims assemble for a few hours before scattering again in all directions.

All the tramps smoke. As smoking is forbidden inside the spike, they make the most of their waiting hours. Their tobacco consists mainly of cigarette-ends which they pick up in the street. They roll it in paper or stuff it into old pipes.

When a tramp does come by some money, which he has worked for or begged on the way, his first thought is to buy tobacco, but mostly he has to make do with cigarette-ends picked up from the pavement or road. The spike only gives him his board: for the rest, clothes, tobacco etc. he has to shift for himself.

*

But it is nearly time for the gates of the spike to open. The tramps have got up, and are queuing by the wall of the huge building, a vile yellow cube of brick, built in some distant suburb, and which might be mistaken for a prison.[1]

A few more minutes and the heavy gates swing open and the herd of human beings enters.

The resemblance between one of these spikes and a prison is even more striking once you are through the gates. In the middle of an empty yard, surrounded by high brick walls, stands the main building containing bare-walled cells, a bathroom, the administrative offices, and a tiny room furnished with plain deal benches which serves as a dining-room. Everything is as ugly and as sinister as you care to imagine.

The prison atmosphere can be found everywhere. Uniformed officials bully the tramps and push them about, never neglecting to remind them that in coming into the workhouse they have given up all their rights and all their freedom.

The tramp's name and trade are written in a register. Then he is made to have a bath, and his clothes and personal possessions are taken away. Then he is given a coarse cotton workhouse shirt for the night.

If he should happen to have any money, it is confiscated, but if he admits to more than two francs [fourpence] he will not be allowed into the spike and will have to find a bed somewhere else.

As a result those tramps – there are not many of them – who have more than two francs have taken pains to hide their money in the toes of their boots, making sure they are not observed, for this fraud could be punished with imprisonment.

After his bath, the tramp, whose clothes have now been taken away, receives his supper: half a pound of bread with a little margarine and a half-litre of tea.

The bread made specially for tramps is terrible. It is grey, always stale, and has a disagreeable taste which makes one think that the flour it is made from comes from tainted grain.

Even the tea is as bad as it can be, but the tramps drink it gladly, as it warms and comforts them after the exhaustion of the day.

This unappetising meal is gulped down in five minutes. After that, the tramps are ordered into the cells where they will spend the night.

These cells, real prison cells of brick or stone, are about twelve feet by six. There is no artificial light – the only source of light is a narrow barred window very high up in the wall and a spyhole in the door which allows the guards to keep an eye on the inmates.

Sometimes the cell contains a bed, but normally the tramps have to sleep on the floor with only three blankets for bedding.

There are often no pillows, and for this reason the unfortunate inmates are allowed to keep their coats to roll into a sort of cushion for their heads.

Usually the room is terribly cold, and as a result of long use the blankets have become so thin that they offer no protection at all against the severity of the cold.

As soon as the tramps have entered their cells, the doors are firmly bolted on the outside: they will not open until seven o'clock next morning.

Usually there are two inmates in each cell. Walled up in their little prison for twelve weary hours with nothing to keep out the cold but a cotton shirt and three thin blankets, the poor wretches suffer cruelly from the cold and the lack of the most elementary comfort.

The places are nearly always bug-infested, and the tramp, a prey to vermin, his limbs worn out, spends hours and hours tossing and turning in a vain wait for sleep.

If he does manage to fall asleep for a few minutes, the discomfort of sleeping on a hard floor soon wakes him up again.

The wily old tramps who have been living like this for fifteen or twenty years, and have become philosophical as a result, spend their nights talking. They will rest for an hour or two next day in a field, under some hedge which they find more welcoming than the spike. But the younger ones, not yet hardened by familiarity with the routine, struggle and groan in the darkness, waiting impatiently for the morning to bring their release.

And yet, when the sunlight finally shines into their prison, they consider with gloom and desperation the prospect of another day exactly like the one before.

Finally, the cells are unlocked. It is time for the doctor's visit – indeed, the tramps will not be released until this formality is completed.

The doctor is usually late, and the tramps have to wait for his inspection, lined up half-naked in a passage. Then one can get an idea of their physical condition.

What bodies and what faces!

Many of them have congenital malformations. Several suffer from hernias, and wear trusses. Almost everyone has deformed feet covered in sores as a result of lengthy tramping in ill-fitting boots. The old men are nothing but skin and bone. All have sagging muscles, and the wretched look of men who do not get a square meal from one end of the year to the other.

Their emaciated features, premature wrinkles, unshaven beards, everything about them tells of insufficient food and lack of sleep.

But here comes the doctor. His inspection is as rapid as it is cursory. It is designed, after all, merely to detect whether any of the tramps are showing the symptoms of smallpox.

The doctor glances at each of the tramps in turn rapidly up and down, front and back.

Now most of them are suffering from some disease or other. Some of them, almost complete imbeciles, are hardly capable of taking care of themselves. Nevertheless they will be released as long as they are free from the dreaded marks of smallpox.

The authorities do not care whether they are in good or bad health, as long as they are not suffering from an infectious disease.

After the doctor's inspection, the tramps get dressed again. Then, in the cold light of day, you can really get a good look at the clothes the poor devils wear to protect themselves against the ravages of the English climate.

These disparate articles of clothing – mostly begged from door to door – are hardly fit for the dustbin. Grotesque, ill-fitting, too long, too short, too big or too small, their quaintness would make you laugh in any other circumstances. Here, you feel enormous pity at the sight of them.

They have been repaired as far as possible, with all kinds of patches. String does duty for missing buttons. Underclothes are nothing but filthy tatters, holes held together by dirt.

Some of them have no underclothes. Many do not even have socks; after binding their toes in rags, they slide their bare feet into boots whose leather, hardened by sun and rain, has lost all suppleness.

It is a fearful sight watching tramps getting ready.

Once they are dressed, the tramps receive their breakfast, identical to the previous night's supper.

Then they are lined up like soldiers in the yard of the spike, where the guards set them to work.

Some will wash the floor, others will chop wood, break coal, do a variety of jobs until ten o'clock, when the signal to leave is given.

They are given back any personal property confiscated the previous evening. To this is added half a pound of bread and a piece of cheese for their midday meal, or sometimes, but less often, a ticket which can be exchanged at specified cafés along the way for bread and tea to the value of three francs [sixpence].

A little after ten o'clock, the gates of the spike swing open to let loose a crowd of wretched and filthy destitute men who scatter over the countryside.

Each one is making for a fresh spike where he will be treated in exactly the same way.

And for months, years, decades perhaps, the tramp will know no other existence.

*

In conclusion, we should note that the food for each tramp consists, all in all, around 750 grammes [2 pounds] of bread with a little margarine and cheese, and a pint of tea a day; this is clearly an insufficient diet for a man who must cover twenty kilometres a day on foot.

To supplement his diet, to obtain clothing, tobacco and the thousand other things he might need, the tramp must beg when he cannot find work (and he hardly ever finds work) – beg or steal.

Now begging is against the law in England, and many a tramp has become acquainted with His Majesty's prisons because of it.

It is a vicious circle; if he does not beg, he dies of starvation; if he begs, he is breaking the law.

The life of these tramps is degrading and demoralising. In a very short time it can make an active man unemployable and a sponger.

Moreover it is desperately monotonous. The only pleasure for tramps is coming by a few shillings unexpectedly; this gives them the chance to eat their fill for once or to go on a drinking spree.

The tramp is cut off from women. Few women become tramps. For their more fortunate sisters the tramp is an object of contempt. So homosexuality is a vice which is not unknown to these eternal wanderers.

Finally the tramp, who has not committed any crime, and who is, when all is said and done, simply a victim of unemployment, is condemned to live more wretchedly than the worst criminal. He is a slave with a semblance of liberty which is worse than the most cruel slavery.

When we reflect upon his miserable destiny, which is shared by thousands of men in England, the obvious conclusion is that society would be treating him more kindly by shutting him up for the remainder of his days in prison, where he would at least enjoy relative comfort.

E.-A. BLAIR[2]

1. Ironically, some former workhouses are now being converted into luxurious apartments, for example, at Marlborough.

2. The pen-name 'George Orwell' was first used in January 1933 for *Down and Out in Paris and London.* It was not regularly used for reviews and articles until December 1936. Unless the pen-name is used, the form given here for articles and essays is that found in the original publication – E. A. Blair, Eric Blair, E.A.B. or E.B. For much of his time at the BBC (1941–3) Orwell was known as Eric Blair. In correspondence, he tended to sign himself, and be addressed, as Eric or George depending upon whether the correspondent originally knew him as Eric or George. Occasionally, if a secretary typed a letter for him, he would sign Eric Blair over a typed George Orwell.

---

[116]

'Hop-Picking'

New Statesman & Nation,[1] *17 October 1931*

This article was adapted from Orwell's Hop-Picking Diary, see Orwell and the Dispossessed *in this series;* CW I/*111; and* A Clergyman's Daughter, *ch. II, sections 3–6.*

'A holiday with pay.' 'Keep yourself all the time you're down there, pay your fare both ways and come back five quid in pocket.' I quote the words of two experienced hop-pickers, who had been down into Kent almost every season since they were children, and ought to have known better. For as a matter of fact hop-picking is far from being a holiday, and, as far as wages go, no worse employment exists.

I do not mean by this that hop-picking is a disagreeable job in itself. It entails long hours, but it is healthy, outdoor work, and any able-bodied person can do it. The process is extremely simple. The vines, long climbing plants with the hops clustering on them in bunches like grapes, are trained up poles or over wires; all the picker has to do is to tear them down and strip the hops into a bin, keeping them as clean as possible from leaves. The spiny stems cut the palms of one's hands to pieces, and in the early morning, before the cuts have reopened, it is painful work; one has trouble too with the plant-lice which infest the hops and crawl down one's neck, but beyond that there are no annoyances. One can talk and smoke as one works, and on hot days there is no pleasanter place than the shady lanes of hops, with their bitter scent – an unutterably refreshing scent, like a wind blowing from oceans of cool beer. It would be almost ideal if one could only earn a living at it.

Unfortunately, the rate of payment is so low that it is quite impossible for a picker to earn a pound a week, or even, in a wet year like 1931, fifteen shillings.[2] Hop-picking is done on the piece-work system, the pickers being paid at so much a bushel. At the farm where I worked this year, as at most farms in Kent, the tally was six bushels to the shilling – that is, we were paid twopence for each bushel we picked. Now, a good vine yields about half a bushel of hops, and a good picker can strip a vine in ten or fifteen minutes; it follows that an expert picker might, given perfect conditions, earn thirty shillings in a sixty-hour week. But, for a number of reasons, these perfect conditions do not exist. To begin with, hops vary enormously in quality. On some vines they are as large as small pears, on others no bigger than hazel nuts; the bad vines take as long to strip as the good ones – longer, as a rule, for their lower shoots are more tangled – and often five of them will not yield a bushel. Again, there are frequent delays in the work, either in changing from field to field, or on account of rain; an hour or two is wasted in this manner every day, and the pickers are paid no compensation for lost time. And, lastly, the greatest cause of loss, there is unfair measurement. The hops are measured in bushel baskets of standard size, but it must be remembered that hops are not like apples or potatoes, of which one can say that a bushel *is* a bushel and there is an end of it. They are soft things as compressible as sponges, and it is quite easy for the measurer to crush a bushel of them into a quart if he chooses. As the hop-pickers often sing –

When he comes to measure,
He never knows where to stop;

Ay, ay, get in the bin,
And take the bloody lot!

From the bin the hops are put into pokes, which are supposed when full to weigh a hundredweight, and are normally carried by one man. But it often needs two men to handle a full poke, when the measurer has been 'taking them heavy'.

With these working conditions a friend and myself earned, this September, about nine shillings a week each. We were new to the job, but the experienced pickers did little better. The best pickers in our gang, and among the best in the whole camp, were a family of gypsies, five adults and a child; these people, spending ten hours a day in the hop-field, earned just ten pounds between them in three weeks. Leaving the child out of account (though as a matter of fact all the children in the hop-field work) this was an average of thirteen and fourpence a week each. There were various farms nearby where the tally was eight or nine bushels to the shilling, and where even twelve shillings a week would have been hard to earn. Besides these starvation wages, the hop-picker has to put up with rules which reduce him practically to a slave. One rule, for instance, empowers a farmer to sack his employees on any pretext whatever, and in doing so to confiscate a quarter of their earnings; and the picker's earnings are also docked if he resigns his job. It is no wonder that itinerant agricultural labourers, most of whom are in work ten months of the year, travel 'on the toby'[3] and sleep in the casual ward between jobs.

As to the hop-pickers' living accommodation, there is now a whole tribe of Government officials to supervise it, so presumably it is better than it used to be. But what it can have been like in the old days is hard to imagine, for even now the ordinary hop-picker's hut is worse than a stable. (I say this advisedly: on our farm the best quarters, specially set apart for married people, *were* stables.) My friend and I, with two others, slept in a tin hut ten feet across, with two unglazed windows and half a dozen other apertures to let in the wind and rain, and no furniture save a heap of straw: the latrine was two hundred yards away, and the water tap the same distance. Some of these huts had to be shared by eight men – but that, at any rate, mitigated the cold, which can be bitter on September nights when one has no bedding but a disused sack. And, of course, there were all the normal discomforts of camp life; not serious hardships, but enough to make sure that when we were not working or sleeping we were either fetching water or trying to coax a fire out of wet sticks.

I think it will be agreed that these are thoroughly bad conditions of pay and treatment. Yet the curious thing is that there is no lack of pickers, and what is more, the same people return to the hop-fields year after year. What keeps the business going is probably the fact that the Cockneys rather enjoy the trip to the country, in spite of the bad pay and in spite of the discomfort. When the season is over the pickers are heartily glad – glad to be back in London, where you do not have to sleep on straw, and you can put a penny in the gas instead of hunting the firewood, and Woolworth's is round the corner – but still, hop-picking is in the category of things that are great fun when they are over. It figures in the pickers' mind as a holiday, though they are working hard all the time and out of pocket at the end. And besides this there is the piece-work system, which disguises the low rate of payment; for 'six bushels a shilling' sounds much more than 'fifteen shillings a week'. And there is the tradition of the good times ten years ago, when hops were dear and the farmers could pay sixpence a bushel; this keeps alive the tales about 'coming home five quid in pocket'. At any rate, whatever the cause, there is no difficulty in getting people to do the work, so perhaps one ought not to complain too loudly about the conditions in the hop-fields. But if one sets pay and treatment against work done, then a hop-picker is appreciably worse off than a sandwich-man.

ERIC BLAIR

1. The *New Statesman* was founded on 12 April 1913; it incorporated *Nation and Athenaeum*, 28 February 1931. *Nation* had been founded as *The Speaker*, 4 January 1890; the name was changed on 2 March 1907; it absorbed *The Athenaeum*, founded 2 January 1828, on 19 February 1921. Orwell contributed more than twenty items to the *New Statesman & Nation*.
2. A shilling (1/– or 1s) was equivalent to 5p, fifteen shillings (15/– or 15s) to 75p. In value, fifteen shillings in 1931 would now be approximately equivalent to £30.
3. 'The toby' was 'the road' (so 'the high toby' was 'the highway').

[171]

'Summer-like for an instant'

The Adelphi, *May 1933*

Summer-like for an instant the autumn sun bursts out,
And the light through the turning elms is green and clear;
It slants down the path and the ragged marigolds glow
Fiery again, last flames of the dying year.

A blue-tit darts with a flash of wings, to feed
Where the coconut hangs on the pear tree over the well;
He digs at the meat like a tiny pickaxe tapping
With his needle-sharp beak as he clings to the swinging shell.

Then he runs up the trunk, sure-footed and sleek like a mouse,
And perches to sun himself; all his body and brain
Exult in the sudden sunlight, gladly believing
That the cold is over and summer is here again.

But I see the umber clouds that drive for the sun,
And a sorrow no argument ever can make away
Goes through my heart as I think of the nearing winter,
And the transient light that gleams like the ghost of May;

And the bird unaware, blessing the summer eternal,
Joyfully labouring, proud in his strength, gay-plumed,
Unaware of the hawk and the snow and the frost-bound nights,
And of his death foredoomed.

Eric Blair

---

[196]

'On a Ruined Farm near the His Master's Voice Gramophone Factory'

The Adelphi, *April 1934*[1]

As I stand at the lichened gate
With warring worlds on either hand –
To left the black and budless trees,
The empty sties, the barns that stand

Like tumbling skeletons – and to right
The factory-towers, white and clear
Like distant, glittering[2] cities seen
From a ship's rail – as I stand here,

I feel, and with a sharper pang,
My mortal sickness; how I give
My heart to weak and stuffless ghosts,
And with the living cannot live.

The acid smoke has soured the fields,
And browned the few and windworn flowers;
But there, where steel and concrete soar
In dizzy, geometric towers –

There, where the tapering cranes sweep round,
And great wheels turn, and trains roar by
Like strong, low-headed brutes of steel –
There is my world, my home; yet why

So alien still? For I can neither
Dwell in that world, nor turn again
To scythe and spade, but only loiter
Among the trees the smoke has slain.

Yet when the trees were young, men still
Could choose their path – the wingèd soul,
Not cursed with double doubts, could fly,
Arrow-like to a foreseen goal;

And they who planned those soaring towers,
They too have set their spirit free;
To them their glittering world can bring
Faith, and accepted destiny;

But none to me as I stand here
Between two countries, both-ways torn,
And moveless still, like Buridan's donkey[3]
Between the water and the corn.

Eric Blair

1. This version has been checked against Orwell's typescript; see variants in notes 3 and 4. The factory is illustrated in Thompson, 39. The poem was selected for *The Best Poems of 1934*, edited by Thomas Moult.
2. The typescript suggests that Orwell considered using 'glistering' here, probably to avoid repetition, see penultimate stanza. He would have had the chance to make the change in proof, but apparently did not wish to do so. His letter to Eleanor Jaques of 18 February 1933 (X/*161*) suggests that proofs were sent to contributors, but not long before publication.
3. Buridan's ass (rather than donkey) died of starvation because, standing midpoint between two kinds of food, it could not decide which was the more attractive and so stood stockstill. This problem is attributed to Jean Buridan, French scholastic philosopher of the fourteenth century.

---

[245]

To Brenda Salkeld

7 May [1935] *Handwritten postscript*

77 Parliament Hill, Hampstead, NW3

Dearest Brenda,[1]
I am afraid this will not reach St Felix before you do, as I only got your letter this evening – I suppose the posts were late owing to the jubilee.[2] I

went down to Brighton, for the first time in my life, for Sunday and Monday. I went there with disagreeable apprehensions, but consoling myself by thinking that sooner or later I was sure to want to mention a trip to Brighton in a novel. However, I was rather agreeably surprised, and I didn't, in any case, spend much time by the sea shore, but went inland and picked bluebells etc. I found a number of nests, including a bullfinch's with four eggs, and by the way about a week ago I found a tit's nest, but I couldn't get at it, though I saw the bird go off the nest, as it was in the middle of a thorn bush. The crowds in Brighton weren't so bad, but of course it was an awful business getting back on Sunday,[3] the train being so packed that people were hanging out of the windows. On Saturday night I was down in Chelsea, and it took me two hours to get back to Hampstead, the whole centre of London was so blocked with taxis full of drunken people careering round, singing and bellowing 'Long live the King!' What surprised me was that most of them were very young – the last people whom you would expect to find full of patriotic emotion; but I suppose they just welcomed the excuse for making a noise. That night I had been to see Rees,[4] really to borrow some money off him, as I had forgotten Monday was a bank holiday and had not got any money out of the bank, but he was at some sort of Socialist meeting and they asked me in and I spent three hours with seven or eight Socialists harrying me, including a South Wales miner who told me – quite good-naturedly, however – that if he were dictator he would have me shot immediately. I have done quite a lot of work, but oh! what mountains there are to do yet. I don't know that I shall be able to let you have that piece[5] to see in June after all, but I will some time – when it is fit to be seen, I mean. I am now getting to the stage where you feel as though you were crawling about inside some dreadful labyrinth. I don't know that I have read much. I read D. H. Lawrence's *Women in Love*, which is certainly not one of his best. I remember reading it before in 1924 – the unexpurgated version that time – and how very queer it seemed to me at that age. I see now that what he was trying to do was to create characters who were at once symbolical figures and recognizable human beings, which was certainly a mistake. The queer thing is that when he concentrates on producing ordinary human characters, as in *Sons and Lovers* and most of the short stories, he gets his meaning across much better as well as being much more readable. I have also been glancing into some numbers of *The Enemy*, the occasional paper Wyndham Lewis[6] used to run, which we have in the shop. The man is certainly insane. I have hit on a wonderful recipe for a stew, which is the following: half a pound of ox-kidney, chopped up small, half a pound of mushrooms, sliced; one onion chopped very fine, two cloves of garlic, four skinned tomatoes, a slice of lean bacon chopped up, and salt, the whole stewed very gently for about two and a half hours in a very little beef stock. You eat it with sphagetti° or rather coquillettes. It is a good dish to make, as it cooks itself while you are working. I have been deriving a lot of pleasure from some numbers of the *Girl's Own Paper* of 1884 and 1885. In the answers to correspondents two questions crop up over and over again. One, whether it is ladylike to ride a tricycle. The other, whether Adam's immediate descendents° did not have to commit incest in order to carry on the human species. The question of whether Adam had a navel does not seem to have been agitated, however.

I must stop now, as I don't think I have any more news. As to your presentiment, or 'curious feeling' about me, you don't say when exactly you had it. But I don't know that I have been particularly unhappy lately – at least, not more than usual.

With much love and many kisses
Eric

P.S. [at top of first page] Near Brighton I passed Roedean School. It seemed to me that even in holiday time I could feel waves of snobbishness pouring out of it, & also aerial music to the tune of the female version of 'Forty Years On' & the Eton 'Boating Song'.[7] Do you play them at hockey, or did they write to you 'St Felix, who are you?'

1. Brenda Salkeld (1908–99) met Orwell in 1928 when she was working as a gym mistress at St Felix Girls' School, Southwold (where Orwell's parents lived). They remained good friends until Orwell died; she visited him at Cranham Sanatorium in 1949 and he arranged for a copy of *Nineteen Eighty-Four* to be sent to her (XX/*3637*). *See Remembering Orwell*, 39–41, 204, and *Orwell Remembered*, 67–8, for her reminiscences; also Crick, 206; S&A, *Unknown Orwell*, 244–6; Shelden, 157. At the time of writing (2000) the school is still open.

2. The Silver Jubilee of King George V, Monday 6 May 1935. The day was marked by a bank holiday and a royal procession from Buckingham Palace to St Paul's Cathedral.

3. Orwell must mean Monday.

4. Sir Richard Rees (1900–1970), artist and editor of *The Adelphi*, October 1930 to 1937 (1930–32 with Max Plowman), and a good friend of Orwell's from 1930 until Orwell's

death; with Sonia Orwell he served as Orwell's literary executor. He had been an attaché at the British Embassy in Berlin, 1922–3, and Honorary Treasurer and Lecturer, London District of the Workers' Educational Association, 1925–7. He gave Orwell much encouragement and he and Orwell were partners of Barnhill on Jura. Ravelston of *Keep the Aspidistra Flying* owes something to Rees's generous nature. See his *George Orwell: Fugitive from the Camp of Victory* (1961); Crick, 202–5; *Orwell Remembered*, 115–26; S&A, *Unknown Orwell*, 186–7, 248–9; Shelden, 223–4.

5. Presumably a portion of *Keep the Aspidistra Flying*. In his letter to Leonard Moore of 14 May 1935 (X/*246*), Orwell says he intended to write what became a novel as a book of essays; the 'piece' referred to was perhaps one of these essays in process of transformation into a different genre.

6. Percy Wyndham Lewis (1882–1957), painter, novelist and critic. He was a leader of the Vorticist movement in painting and took a very independent line in his critical writing. In the early thirties he supported Hitler. His novels include *Tarr* (1918) and *The Apes of God* (1930). He edited two reviews, *Blast: Review of the Great English Vortex* (two issues, 1914 and 1915) and *The Enemy: A Review of Arts and Literature*, of which three numbers were published in 1927 and 1929.

7. 'Forty Years On', the Harrow School song, was written in 1872 by John Farmer. It was also sung by many girls' schools. Celia Haddon, in her *Great Days and Jolly Days* (1977), lists a wide range of twenty-one girls' schools which adopted this song. It was also sung by coeducational schools such as Eccles Grammar. Haddon gives an excellent, well-illustrated account of this phenomenon that so intrigued Orwell.

---

[249]

Review of Twenty Thousand Streets under the Sky *by Patrick Hamilton;* The Proceedings of the Society *by Katharine M. Williams;* I Lie Alone *by R. G. Goodyear*

New English Weekly, *1 August 1935*

Here are three novels all endeavouring, in very different ways, to present a picture of 'real life'. I think the best way I can deal with them is to mention them in descending order of length – which is also, as it happens, ascending order of merit.

Twenty Thousand Streets under the Sky is an enormous novel – to be exact, it is a trilogy, but bound into one cover – describing the not very complicated relations between a literary young man bartender, a good-hearted barmaid who loves the bartender in vain, and a worthless little prostitute who does the bartender out of his money. Here, I think, is a fair sample:

In their journey from the table to the door Jenny said nothing about Turkish Delight. In fact, she was scrupulously careful not to even *look* Turkish Delight – possibly too careful. At any rate, in Tom's imagination, it seemed that if he did not get Turkish Delight the entire evening was endangered. For it was an axiom that, amid all the varied delights that generous nature showered, to Turkish Delight Jenny was most consistently faithful.

There are 753 pages, all of them round about this level. The style, it will be seen, is what one may call the masticatory style – that is, the style that comments on everything, à la Bennett, instead of making plain statements. Mr. Hamilton's[1] more immediate master, however, is obviously Priestley. He has set out, sincerely enough, to write a novel about 'real life', but with the Priestleyan assumption that 'real life' means lower-middle-class life in a large town and that if you can pack into your novel, say, fifty-three descriptions of tea in a Lyons Corner House,[2] you have done the trick. The result is what one might expect: a huge well-meaning book, as shapeless and inert as a clot of frog-spawn.

However, *Twenty Thousand Streets under the Sky* is good of its rather unappetising kind. It is perfectly self-consistent and contains nothing wilfully cheap or false. And whatever one may think of its quality, there can be no two opinions about its quantity; 753 pages for eight and sixpence is good value. Mr. Priestley contributes an introduction, thus giving the lie to a well-known epigram of Mr. Yeats.[3]

The Proceedings of the Society is shorter, and its subject matter is more genteel. As a matter of fact it is not really a novel, but a series of stories and sketches dealing with the members of a literary society in a South of England watering-place. These people are the most depressing Struldbrugs[4] I have read about for a long time. Without exception they lead lives of unutterable futility, and nearly all of them are so old as to have no active memories later than the reign of King Edward. Personally, I doubt whether even the members of the Bournemouth Literary Society (is it Bournemouth?) are quite as bad as they are pictured here. But Miss Williams has clearly a bias in favour of the depressing. Nothing lurid, of course – no heads stuck in gas ovens or anything of that kind; merely the peaceful, deadly depression of people who are now old and have never even been alive. Over it all there hangs the atmosphere of genteel decay;

residential hotels, fixed annuities, false teeth, galoshes and bath chairs. Life unlived – that is Miss Williams's theme essentially.

It is curious, but the cult of disillusionment in books of this type has a certain resemblance to the old Christian cult of self-mortification. The *ideal rongeur*[5] has merely changed its shape. Instead of being the ideal Christian sanctity, it is now the ideal – equally unattained by most people – of a life fully lived. In Baudelaire's day you woke in the brothel and lamented your lost innocence. Now, on the other hand, you are wheeled in your bath chair down the Bournemouth parade, thinking with mingled desolation and relief of the adultery you failed to commit in '97. It is perhaps a spiritual come-down. But this is a distinctly readable book. It is typically a woman's book (it owes a little to Katherine Mansfield, perhaps) in its mixture of sentimentality and disillusionment. The fourth story, 'Remembering Ethel', is a very good story – excellently conceived and sufficiently well executed.

I Lie Alone is much narrower in its range. In fact, it is hardly more than a full-length portrait of a single character, Lyddie Gossett, a peculiarly graceless and soulless old maid. Lyddie's true character is revealed only by degrees, and rather subtly. At the beginning one imagines that she is going to be the typical dear old hen of fact and fiction – the dear 'motherly' old soul who makes quince jelly and cowslip wine and sews patchwork quilts for the poor. As the story goes on, however, it becomes clearer and clearer that she is an entirely worthless slut whose every thought turns on food or drink, usually food. Throughout the book, on almost every page, she is either devouring, planning or recovering from some sordid 'tasty' meal; or else she is sinking, flannel-nightgowned, into the stuffy embraces of a feather bed. Mr. Goodyear is very ruthless in his descriptions. No *preux chevalier*, I feel, would write like this about a lady:

> Groping in the hot darkness, she belched. 'Cucumber,' she said, and patted her breast.
>
> A warm, fruity perfume spread through the room as she lovingly cut the cake. A faint steam rose from the dark slices.

Towards the end the book becomes more of a narrative, and perhaps deteriorates a little. Lyddie's father, for whom she has kept house all her life, dies, and his pension with him. Of course such a woman as Lyddie is incapable either of saving money or of keeping a job. She sponges on one relative after another, goes to pieces, drinks more and more, and at last dies miserably in the public infirmary. A squalid story, but interesting. After reading it one sees more clearly than before why gluttony was included among the seven deadly sins. The book's originality lies rather in its subject-matter than in its treatment. The actual writing, as can be seen from the extract I have given above, is undistinguished. This book is recommended by the Book Guild.

1. Patrick Hamilton (1904–62), novelist and dramatist. His novels include *Hangover Square, or, The Man with Two Minds – a story of darkest Earl's Court in 1939* (1941; filmed 1945) and *The Slaves of Solitude* (1947). Among his best-remembered plays are *Rope* (1929; filmed 1948), *Gaslight* (1938) and *The Duke in Darkness* (1942).

2. The catering firm of J. Lyons & Co. set up 'Corner Houses' in Coventry Street, Tottenham Court Road, the Strand and at Marble Arch, London, the first in 1908, each with several floors of restaurants and cafés. The restaurants varied in style, some with waitress service (epitomized by the much-advertised 'Nippie'), cafeterias, 'Salad Bowls', at least one 'Vienna Café' (at Coventry Street), where, in the thirties, the waiters were chiefly Jewish refugees, often professional men in their own countries. They sold decent meals at very modest prices. Aldous Huxley in *Antic Hay* (1923) has a reference to an acquaintanceship ripening over the tea-cups on the fifth floor of the Strand Corner House (xii, 179). All have now, alas, closed. Lyons also ran a large number of small, individual cafés.

3. 'But was there ever dog that praised his fleas?' from 'To a Poet, who would have me praise certain bad Poets, Imitators of his and mine'.

4. Struldbrugs: inhabitants of the kingdom of Luggnagg in the third part of *Gulliver's Travels* (1726) by Jonathan Swift. Though immortal they lacked vigour and intellect and as a result were thoroughly miserable.

5. *Rongeur* is French for 'gnawing' or 'fretting'. A *ver rongeur* is a worm that gnaws one from the inside (like a tapeworm). The expression here is close to what in Shakespeare's time was called the worm, or prick, of conscience; today perhaps 'soul-searching' would be appropriate. Queen Margaret tells Richard III that she hopes 'The worm of conscience [will] still [= constantly] begnaw thy soul' (*Richard III*, I.iii.222), because he lacks any ideal of Christian sanctity.

Extracts from The Road to Wigan Pier *Diary*

Orwell was commissioned by his publisher, Victor Gollancz (not the Left Book Club as is often stated), to visit depressed areas of the North of England. He left for Wigan on 31 January 1936 after handing in the typescript of Keep the Aspidistra Flying. *The first advertisement announcing the formation of the Left Book Club appeared in the* New Statesman & Nation *on 29 February 1936. Orwell returned to his cottage in Wallington at the end of March. The first two books published by the Club appeared on 18 May. He handed in the typescript of* The Road to Wigan Pier *on 15 December 1936, and he told his literary agent, Leonard Moore, that he thought his book's chance of selection for the Left Book Club was slim. Orwell left for Spain shortly after seeing Gollancz in London on Monday 21 December, and on 30 December he enlisted in the POUM militia in Barcelona to fight for the Republicans in the Spanish Civil War (see companion volume,* Orwell in Spain*). It was only when Orwell was in Spain that a decision was taken to publish a Left Book Club edition of* The Road to Wigan Pier.

It is frequently stated that Orwell received an advance of £500 (perhaps some £18,000 at today's values) to write this book, a suggestion that emanated originally from Geoffrey Gorer.[1] *That, understandably, has aroused lingering resentment in the parts of the North he visited. Logic and arithmetic show that it must be incorrect. The full details are given in* X/*341 and my article 'Orwell: Balancing the Books' (*The Library, *VI (16 June 1994), 86–8); they are summarized in* Literary Life, *67–9. Suffice here to say that Gollancz's policy was not to give large advances; for* Down and Out in Paris and London *Orwell received an advance of £40 and for* Keep the Aspidistra Flying, *£75; just before going to Spain he received an advance on royalties for* The Road to Wigan Pier *of £100, which, with the supposed £500, would have made a total of £600. Until a Left Book Club edition was agreed (twelve months after that supposed advance had been given), the only edition in prospect was the normal trade edition (sold at 10s 6d), the first printing of which was of 2,000 copies. That would have realized for Orwell £105 in royalties at 10 per cent. A further 150 copies were printed producing (at royalties now of 15 per cent) just under £12. On his return to Wallington, Orwell wrote to his friend Jack Common, on 30 April (*X/*300), telling him he was too hard up to spend £20 on stocking the shelves of his little shop and asking Common whether he thought the wholesalers would advance him credit if he could put down £5. This was hardly a man who had received £500 three months earlier. Though Orwell was a generous man, he was not profligate. As the notes from his Diary show* *(see below) he started with virtually nothing in his pocket. On 4 February 1936 he was down to threepence (1p) and had to pawn his scarf.*

Had Gollancz given Orwell such a large sum, plus an advance on royalties of £100, by the time he had paid booksellers' discounts, he would have been left with a mere £95 to pay the costs of publishing the trade edition, which included thirty-two pages of half-tone plates. In the event, the Left Book Club edition sold 44,039 copies (at 2s 6d – 12½p); 2,150 copies of the trade edition; and 890 copies of Part One on its own; 150 copies were destroyed in an air-raid. Thus, for the Club's twenty-second book, 47,229 copies were printed. Orwell would have received £594 – still below the total of the supposed and known advances. It can only be a guess, but I imagine Orwell may *have had an advance of £50 in expenses for his two months of research and expenses.*

The extracts printed here from Orwell's Diary of his visit to the North require a brief explanation. It has been argued that this is not a diary but something 'worked up afterwards – complete with author's footnotes' to help in the production of the book. Though proposed by a very well-informed scholar (see Crick, 280 and n. 8 on p. 628), I am not convinced. Orwell regularly added footnotes to what we know are diaries; secondly, Orwell himself called this a Diary, giving it that heading; and it was typed using two different typewriters, one of which Orwell had with him in Wigan. It is likely that his wife, Eileen (who had a typewriter), typed up some of her husband's notes from his manuscript on his return home, and that Orwell later added footnotes. The notes Orwell made and typed up about housing conditions, a very short extract of which is reproduced below, also have handwritten notes and one example is included. Only a few extracts of the Diary are given here; for the full text, see Volume X of The Complete Works *and the first volume of* CEJL, *194–243. What was certainly prepared later by Orwell was a sketch map of the journey; this is reproduced in* X/*418).*

For further reading on Orwell's journey to the North, see Crick, 278–94; Literary Life, *67–78;* Orwell Remembered, *127–39; Robert Pearce, 'Revisiting Orwell's* Wigan Pier', History, *82 (July 1997), 410–28;* Remembering Orwell, *59–66; S&A,* The Transformation, *137–48; Shelden, 243–60.*

1. Geoffrey Gorer (1905–85), social anthropologist and author. His books include *Africa Dances* (1935), *The American People: A Study of National Character* (revised, New York, 1964) and *Death, Grief and Mourning in Contemporary Britain* (1965). After he had praised Orwell's novel *Burmese Days* (1934; 'you have done a necessary and important piece of work as well as it could be done') they met, corresponded and remained lifelong friends.

---

[272]

31.1.36: To Coventry by train as arranged, arriving about 4 pm. Bed and Breakfast house, very lousy, 3/6. Framed certificate in hall setting forth that (John Smith) had been elected to the rank of Primo Buffo. Two beds in room – charge for room to yourself 5/–.[1] Smell as in common lodging houses. Half-witted servant girl with huge body, tiny head and rolls of fat at back of neck curiously recalling ham-fat.

1.2.36: Lousy breakfast with Yorkshire commercial traveller. Walked 12 miles to outskirts of Birmingham, took bus to Bull Ring (very like Norwich Market) and arrived 1 pm. Lunch in Birmingham and bus to Stourbridge. Walked 4–5 miles to Clent Youth Hostel. Red soil everywhere. Birds courting a little, cock chaffinches and bullfinches very bright and cock partridge making mating call. Except for village of Meriden, hardly a decent house between Coventry and Birmingham. West of Birmingham the usual villa-civilization creeping out over the hills. Raining all day, on and off.

Distance walked, 16 miles. Spent on conveyances, 1/4. On food, 2/3.

2.2.36: Comfortable night in hostel, which I had to myself. One-storey wooden building with huge coke stove which kept it very hot. You pay 1/– for bed, 2d for the stove and put pennies in the gas for cooking. Bread, milk etc. on sale at hostel. You have to have your own sleeping bag but get blankets, mattress and pillows. Tiring evening because the warden's son, I suppose out of kindness, came across and played ping-pong with me till I could hardly stand on my feet. In the morning long talk with the warden who keeps poultry and collects glass and pewter. He told me how in France in 1918, on the heels of the retreating Germans, he looted some priceless glass which was discovered and looted from him in turn by his divisional general. Also showed me some nice pieces of pewter and some very curious Japanese pictures, showing clear traces of European influence, looted by his father in some naval expedition about 1860.

Left 10 am., walked to Stourbridge, took bus to Wolverhampton, wandered about slummy parts of Wolverhampton for a while, then had lunch and walked 10 miles to Penkridge. Wolverhampton seems frightful place. Everywhere vistas of mean little houses still enveloped in drifting smoke, though this was Sunday, and along the railway line huge banks of clay and conical chimneys ('pot-banks'). Walk from W'ton to Penkridge very dull and raining all the way. Villa-civilization stretches almost unbroken between the two towns. In Penkridge about 4.30 halted for cup of tea. A tiny frouzy parlour with a nice fire, a little wizened oldish man and an enormous woman about 45, with tow-coloured bobbed hair and no front teeth. Both of them thought me a hero to be walking on such a day. Had tea with them en famille. About 5.15 left and walked another couple of miles, then caught buss° the remaining 4 miles to Stafford. Went to Temperance Hotel thinking this would be cheap, but bed and breakfast 5/–. The usual dreadful room and twill sheets greyish and smelly as usual. Went to bathroom and found commercial traveller developing snapshots in bath. Persuaded him to remove them and had bath, after which I find myself very footsore.

Distance walked, about 16 miles. Spent on conveyances, 1/5. On food, 2/8½.

3.2.36: Left 9 am. and took bus to Hanley. Walked round Hanley and part of Burslem. Frightfully cold, bitter wind, and it had been snowing in the night; blackened snow lying about everywhere. Hanley and Burslem about the most dreadful places I have seen. Labyrinths of tiny blackened houses and among them the pot-banks like monstrous burgundy bottles half buried in the soil, belching forth smoke. Signs of poverty everywhere and very poor shops. In places enormous chasms delved out, one of them about 200 yards wide and about as deep, with rusty iron trucks on a chain railway crawling up one side, and here and there on the almost perpendicular face of the other, a few workmen hanging like samphire-gatherers, cutting into the face with their picks apparently aimlessly, but I suppose digging out clay. Walked on to Eldon and lunch at pub there. Frightfully cold. Hilly country, splendid views, especially when one gets further east and hedges give way to stone walls. Lambs here seem much more backward than down south. Walked on to Rudyard Lake.[2]

Rudyard Lake (really a reservoir, supplying the pottery towns) very depressing. In the summer it is a pleasure resort. Cafés, houseboats and pleasure-boats every ten yards, all deserted and flyblown, this being the off-season. Notices relating to fishing, but I examined the water and it did not look to me as though it had any fish in it. Not a soul anywhere and bitter wind blowing. All the broken ice had been blown up to the south end, and the waves were rocking it up and down, making a clank-clank, clank-clank – the most melancholy noise I ever heard. (Mem. to use in novel some time and to have an empty Craven A packet bobbing up and down among the ice.)

Found hostel, about 1 mile further on, with difficulty. Alone again. A most peculiar place this time. A great draughty barrack of a house, built in the sham-castle style – somebody's Folly – about 1860. All but three or four of the rooms quite empty. Miles of echoing stone passages, no lighting except candles and only smoky little oilstoves to cook on. Terribly cold.

Only 2/8d left, so tomorrow must go into Manchester (walk to Macclesfield, then bus) and cash cheque.

Distance walked, 12 miles. Spent on conveyances 1/8. On food, 2/8½d.

4.2.36: Got out of bed so cold that I could not do up any buttons and had to [go] down and thaw my hands before I could dress. Left about 10.30 am. A marvellous morning. Earth frozen hard as iron, not a breath of wind and the sun shining brightly. Not a soul stirring. Rudyard Lake (about 1½ miles long) had frozen over during the night. Wild ducks walking about disconsolately on the ice. The sun coming up and the light slanting along the ice the most wonderful red-gold colour I have ever seen. Spent a long time throwing stones over the ice. A jagged stone skimming across ice makes exactly the same sound as a redshank whistling.

Walked to Macclesfield, 10 or 11 miles, then bus to Manchester. Went and collected letters, then to bank to cash cheque but found they were shut – they shut at 3 pm. here. Very awkward as I had only 3d in hand. Went to Youth Hostel headquarters and asked them to cash cheque, but they refused, then to Police Station to ask them to introduce me to a solicitor who would cash a cheque, but they also refused. Frightfully cold. Streets encrusted with mounds of dreadful black stuff which was really snow frozen hard and blackened by smoke. Did not want to spend night in streets. Found my way to poor quarter (Chester Street), went to pawnshop and tried to pawn raincoat but they said they did not take them any longer. Then it occurred to me my scarf was pawnable, and they gave me 1/11d on it. Went to common lodging house, of which there were three close together in Chester Street.

Long letter from Rees advising me about people to go and see, one of them, luckily, in Manchester.

Distance walked, about 13 miles. Spent on conveyances, 2/–. On food, 10d.

5.2.36: Went and tried to see Meade[3] but he was out. Spent day in common lodging house. Much as in London. 11d for bed, cubicles not dormitories. The 'deputy' a cripple as they seem so often to be. Dreadful method here of making tea in tin bowls. Cashed cheque in morning but shall stay tonight in lodging house and go and see Meade tomorrow.

6–10.2.36: Staying with the Meades at 49 Brynton Rd., Longsight, Manchester. Brynton Rd. is in one of the new building estates. Very decent houses with bathrooms and electric light, rent I suppose about 12/– or 14/–. Meade is some kind of Trade Union Official and has something to do with the editing of *Labour's Northern Voice* – these are the people who do the publishing side of the *Adelphi.* The M.s have been very decent to me. Both are working-class people, speak with Lancashire accents and have worn the clogs in their childhood, but the atmosphere in a place like this is entirely middle-class. Both the M.s were faintly scandalised to hear I had been in the common lodging house in Manchester. I am struck again by the fact that as soon as a working man gets an official post in the Trade Union or goes into Labour politics, he becomes middle-class whether he will or no. ie. by fighting against the bourgeoisie he becomes a bourgeois. The fact is that you *cannot help* living in the manner appropriate and developing the ideology appropriate to your income (in M's case I suppose about £4 a week). The only quarrel I have with the M.s is that they call me 'comrade'. Mrs M., as usual, does not understand much about politics but has adopted her husband's views as a wife ought to; she pronounces the word 'comrade' with manifest discomfort. Am struck by the difference of manners even as far north as this. Mrs M. is surprised and not altogether approving when I get up when she enters the room, offer to help with the washing-up, etc. She says, 'Lads up here expect to be waited on.'

M. sent me across to Wigan to see Joe Kennan, an electrician who takes a prominent part in the Socialist movement. Kennan also lives in a decent

Corporation house (Beech Hill Building Estate) but is more definitely a working man. A very short, stout, powerful man with an extraordinarily gentle, hospitable manner and very anxious to help. His elder child was upstairs in bed (scarlet fever suspected), the younger on the floor playing with soldiers and a toy cannon. Kennan smiles and says, 'You see – and I'm supposed to be a pacifist.' He sent me to the N.U.W.M.[4] shelter with a letter to the secretary asking him to find me a lodging in Wigan. The shelter is a dreadful ramshackle little place but a godsend to these unemployed men as it is warm and there are newspapers etc. there. The secretary, Paddy Grady, an unemployed miner. A tall lean man about 35, intelligent and well-informed and very anxious to help. He is a single man getting 17/– a week and is in a dreadful state physically from years of underfeeding and idleness. His front teeth are almost entirely rotted away. All the men at the N.U.W.M. very friendly and anxious to supply me with information as soon as they heard I was a writer and collecting facts about working-class conditions. I cannot get them to treat me precisely as an equal, however. They call me either 'Sir' or 'Comrade'.

[278]

15.2.36: Went with N.U.W.M. collectors on their rounds with a view to collecting facts about housing conditions, especially in the caravans. Have made notes on these, Q.V.[5] What chiefly struck me was the expression on some of the women's faces, especially those in the more crowded caravans. One woman had a face like a death's head. She had a look of absolutely intolerable misery and degradation. I gathered that she felt as I would feel if I were coated all over with dung. All the people however seemed to take these conditions quite for granted. They have been promised houses over and over again but nothing has come of it and they have got into the way of thinking that a livable house is something absolutely unattainable.

Passing up a horrible squalid side-alley, saw a woman, youngish but very pale and with the usual draggled exhausted look, kneeling by the gutter outside a house and poking a stick up the leaden waste-pipe, which was blocked. I thought how dreadful a destiny it was to be kneeling in the gutter in a back-alley in Wigan, in the bitter cold, prodding a stick up a blocked drain. At that moment she looked up and caught my eye, and her expression was as desolate as I have ever seen; it struck me that she was thinking just the same thing as I was.[6]

Changing lodgings as Mrs H[ornby][7] is ill with some mysterious malady and ordered into hospital. They have found lodgings for me at 22 Darlington Rd.,[8] over a tripe shop where they take in lodgers. The husband an ex-miner (age 58), the wife ill with a weak heart, in bed on sofa in kitchen. Social atmosphere much as at the H.s but house appreciably dirtier and very smelly. A number of other lodgers. An old ex-miner, age about 75, on old age pension plus half a crown weekly from parish (12/6 in all). Another, said to be of superior type and 'come down in the world', more or less bedridden. An Irish ex-miner who had shoulder blade and several ribs crushed by a fall of stone a few years ago and lives on disability pension of about 25/– a week. Of distinctly superior type and started off as a clerk but went 'down pit' because he was big and strong and could earn more as a miner (this was before the War). Also some newspaper-canvassers. Two for *John Bull*,[9] distinctly motheaten, ages about 40 and 55, one quite young and was for four years in rubber firm in Calcutta. Cannot quite make this lad out. He puts on Lancashire accent when talking to the others (he belongs locally) but to me talks in the usual 'educated' accent. The family apart from the Forrests themselves consists of a fat son who is at work somewhere and lives nearby, his wife Maggie who is in the shop nearly all day, their two kids, and Annie, fiancée of the other son who is in London. Also a daughter in Canada (Mrs F. says 'at Canada'). Maggie and Annie do practically the whole work of the house and shop. Annie very thin, overworked (she also works in a dress-sewing place) and obviously unhappy. I gather that the marriage is by no means certain to take place but that Mrs F. treats Annie as a relative all the same and that Annie groans under her tyranny. Number of rooms in the house exclusive of shop premises, 5 or six and a bathroom-W.C. Nine people sleeping here. Three in my room besides myself.

Struck by the astonishing ignorance about and wastefulness of food among the working class people here – more even than in the south, I think. One morning when washing in the H.s' scullery made an inventory of the following food: A piece of bacon about 5 pounds. About 2 pounds of shin of beef. About a pound and a half of liver (all of these uncooked). The wreck of a monstrous meat pie. (Mrs H. when making a pie always made it in an enamelled *basin* such as is used for washing up in. Ditto with puddings.) A dish containing 15 or 20 eggs. A number of small cakes. A flat fruit pie and a 'cake-a-pie' (pastry with currants in it). Various fragments of earlier pies. 6 large loaves and 12 small ones. (I had seen Mrs H. cook these the night before.) Various odds and ends of butter, tomatoes, opened tins of milk etc. There was also more food keeping warm in the oven in the kitchen. Everything except bread habitually left about uncovered and shelves filthy. Food here consists almost entirely of bread and starch. A typical day's meals at the H.s'. Breakfast (about 8 am): Two fried eggs and bacon, bread (no butter) and tea. Dinner (about 12.30 pm): A monstrous plate of stewed beef, dumplings and boiled potatoes (equal to about 3 Lyons[10] portions) and a big helping of rice pudding or suet pudding. Tea (about 5 pm): A plate of cold meat, bread and butter, sweet pastries and tea. Supper (about 11 pm): fish and chips, bread and butter and tea.

16.2.36: Great excitement because a couple who stayed here for a month about Xmas have been arrested (at Preston) as coiners and it is believed they were making their false coins while here. The police inspector here for about an hour asking questions. Mrs F. tells of snooping round their room while they were out and finding a lump of something like solder under the mattress and some little pots like egg-cups only larger. Mrs F. agreed instantly to everything the police inspector suggested, and when he was upstairs searching the room I made two suggestions and she agreed to those too. I could see she had made up her mind they were guilty on hearing they were unmarried. When the inspector had written out her statement it came out that she could not read or write (except her signature), though her husband can read a little.

One of the canvassers' beds is jammed across the foot of mine. Impossible to stretch my legs out straight as if I do so my feet are in the small of his back. It seems a long time since I slept between linen sheets. Twill sheets even at the M.s. Theirs (the M.s') was the only house I have been in since leaving London that did not smell.

17.2.36: The newspaper-canvassers are rather pathetic. Of course it is a quite desperate job. I fancy what *John Bull* do is to take on people who make frantic efforts and work up a little more or less spurious business for a while, then sack them and take on more, and so on. I should judge these men each make £2 or £3 a week. Both have families and one is a grandfather. They are so hard up that they cannot pay for full board but pay something for their rooms and have a squalid little cupboard of food in the kitchen, from which they take out bread, packets of marg. etc. and cook themselves meals in a shamefaced manner. They are allocated so many houses each day and have to knock at every door and book a minimum number of orders. They are at present working some swindle on behalf of *John Bull* by which you get a 'free' tea set by sending two shillings worth of stamps and twenty four coupons. As soon as they have had their food they start filling up blank forms for the next day, and presently the older one falls asleep in his chair and begins snoring loudly.

Am struck, though, by their knowledge of working-class conditions. They can tell you all about housing, rents, rates, state of trade etc. in every town in the north of England.

[285]

24.2.36: Yesterday went down Crippen's mine with Jerry Kennan,[11] another electrician friend of his, two small sons of the latter, two other electricians and an engineer belonging to the pit, who showed us round. The depth to the cage bottom was 300 yards. We went down at 10.30 and came up at 1.30, having covered, according to the engineer who showed us round, about 2 miles.

As the cage goes down you have the usual momentary qualm in your belly, then a curious stuffed-up feeling in your ears. In the middle of its run the cage works up a tremendous speed (in some of the deeper mines they are said to touch 60 mph. or more) then slows down so abruptly that it is difficult to believe you are not going upwards again. The cages are tiny – about 8 feet long by 3½ wide by 6 high. They are supposed to hold 10 men or (I think) about a ton and a half of coal. There were only six of us and two boys, but we had difficulty in packing in and it is important to face in the direction you are going to get out the other end.

Down below it was lighter than I expected, because apart from the lamps we all carried there were electric lights in the main roads. But what I had not expected, and what for me was the most important feature all through, was the lowness of the roof. I had vaguely imagined wandering about in places rather like the tunnels of the Underground; but as a matter of fact there were very few places where you could stand upright. In general the roof was about 4 ft. or 4 ft. 6 ins high, sometimes much lower, with every now and again a beam larger than the others under which you had to duck especially low. In places the walls were quite neatly built up, almost like the stone walls in Derbyshire, with slabs of shale. There were pit-props, almost all of wood, every yard or so overhead. They are made of small larch trees sawn to the appropriate length (from the quantity used I see now why people laying down plantations almost always plant larch) and are simply laid on the ends of the upright props, which are laid on slabs of wood, and not fixed in any way. The bottom slabs gradually sink into the floor, or, as the miners put it, 'the floor comes up', but the weight overhead keeps the whole thing in place. By the way the steel girders used here and there instead of wooden props had buckled, you got an idea of the weight of the roof. Underfoot is thick stone dust and the rails, about 2½ ft. wide, for the trolleys. When the path is down hill miners often slide down these on their clogs, which, being hollow underneath, more or less fit onto the rails.

After a few hundred yards of walking doubled up and once or twice having to crawl, I began to feel the effects in a violent pain all down my thighs. One also gets a bad crick in the neck, because though stooping one has to look up for fear of knocking into the beams, but the pain in the thighs is the worst. Of course as we got nearer the coal face the roads tended to get lower. Once we crawled through a temporary tunnel which was like an enlarged rat hole, with no props, and in one place there had been a fall of stone during the night – 3 or 4* tons of stuff, I should judge. It had blocked up the entire road except for a tiny aperture near the roof which we had to crawl through without touching any timber. Presently I had to stop for a minute to rest my knees, which were giving way, and then after a few hundred yards more we came to the first working. This was only a small working with a machine worked by two men, much like an enlarged version of the electric drills[12] used for street mending. Nearby was the dynamo (or whatever it is called) which supplied the power through cables to this and the other machines; also the comparatively small drills (but they weigh

* Jerry Kennan said 20 or 30. I don't know which of us would be best judge [Orwell's handwritten footnote].

50 lbs. each and have to be hoisted onto the shoulder) for drilling holes for blasting charges; also bundles of miners' tools locked together on wires like bundles of keys, which is always done for fear of losing them.

We went a few hundred yards further and came to one of the main workings. The men were not actually working here, but a shift was just coming down to start work about 250 yards further on. Here there was one of the larger machines which have a crew of 5 men to work them. This machine has a revolving wheel on which there are teeth about a couple of inches long set at various angles; in principle it is rather like an immensely thickened circular saw with the teeth much further apart, and running horizontally instead of vertically. The machine is dragged into position by the crew and the front part of it can be swivelled round in any direction and pressed against the coal face by the man working it. Two men called 'scufters' shovel the coal onto a rubberbelt conveyor which carries it through a tunnel to the tubs on the main road, where it is hauled by steam haulage to the cages. I had not realised before that the men operating the coal-cutter are working in a place rather less than a yard high. When we crawled in under the roof to the coal face we could at best kneel, and then not kneel upright, and I fancy the men must do most of their work lying on their bellies. The heat also was frightful – round about 100 degrees F. so far as I could judge. The crew keep burrowing into the coal face, cutting a semi-circular track, periodically hauling the machine forward and propping as they go. I was puzzled to know how that monstrous machine – flat in shape, of course, but 6 or 8 feet long and weighing several tons, and only fitted with skids, not wheels – could have been got into position through that mile or so of passages. Even to drag the thing forward as the seam advances must be a frightful labour, seeing that the men have to do it practically lying down. Up near the coal face we saw a number of mice, which are said to abound there. They are said to be commonest in pits where there are or have been horses. I don't know how they get down into the mine in the first place. Probably in the cages, but possibly by falling down the shaft, as it is said that a mouse (owing to its surface area being large relative to its weight) can drop any distance uninjured.

On the way back my exhaustion grew so great that I could hardly keep going at all, and towards the end I had to stop and rest every fifty yards.

The periodical effort of bending and raising oneself at each successive beam was fearful, and the relief when one could stand upright, usually owing to a hole in the roof, was enormous. At times my knees simply refused to lift me after I had knelt down. It was made worse by the fact that at the lowest parts the roof is usually on a slope, so that besides bending you have to walk more or less sideways. We were all pretty distressed except the engineer taking us round, who was used to it, and the two small boys, who did not have to bend to any extent; but I was by a good deal the worst, being the tallest. I would like to know whether any miners are as tall as I am, and if so, whether they suffer for it. The few miners whom we met down the pit could move with extraordinary agility, running about on all fours among the props almost like dogs.

After we had at last emerged and washed off the more obtrusive dirt and had some beer, I went home and had dinner and then soaked myself for a long time in a hot bath. I was surprised at the quantity of dirt and the difficulty of getting it off. It had penetrated to every inch of my body in spite of my overalls and my clothes underneath those. Of course very few miners have baths in their homes – only a tub of water in front of the kitchen fire. I should say it would be quite impossible to keep clean without a proper bathtub.

In the room where we changed our clothes there were several cages of canaries. These have to be kept there by law, to test the air in cases of explosion. They are sent down in the cage, and, if they do not faint, the air is all right.

The Davy lamps give out a fair amount of light. There is an air intake at the top but the flame is cut off from this by a fine gauze. Flame cannot pass through holes of less than a certain diameter. The gauze therefore lets the air in to sustain the flame but will not let the flame out to explode dangerous gases. Each lamp when full will burn for 8–12 hours, and they are locked, so that if they go out down the pit they cannot be relighted. Miners are searched for matches before going down the pit.[13]

[294]

16.3.36: Last night to hear Mosley[14] speak at the Public Hall, which is in structure a theatre. It was quite full – about 700 people I should say. About

100 Blackshirts on duty, with two or three exceptions weedy-looking specimens, and girls selling *Action*[15] etc. Mosley spoke for an hour and a half and to my dismay seemed to have the meeting mainly with him. He was booed at the start but loudly clapped at the end. Several men who tried at the beginning to interject questions were thrown out, one of them – who as far as I could see was only trying to get a question answered – with quite unnecessary violence, several Blackshirts throwing themselves upon him and raining blows on him while he was still sitting down and had not attempted any violence. M. is a very good speaker. His speech was the usual claptrap – Empire free trade, down with the Jew and the foreigner, higher wages and shorter hours all round etc. etc. After the preliminary booing the (mainly) working-class audience was easily bamboozled by M. speaking from as it were a Socialist angle, condemning the treachery of successive governments towards the workers. The blame for everything was put upon mysterious international gangs of Jews who are said to be financing, among other things, the British Labour Party and the Soviet. M.'s statement re. the international situation: 'We fought Germany before in a British quarrel; we are not going to fight them now in a Jewish one' was received with loud applause. Afterwards there were questions as usual, and it struck me how easy it is to bamboozle an uneducated audience if you have prepared beforehand a set of repartees with which to evade awkward questions. eg. M. kept extolling Italy and Germany, but when questioned about concentration camps etc. always replied, 'We have no foreign models; what happens in Germany need not happen here.' To the question, 'How do you know that your own money is not used to finance cheap foreign labour?' (M. having denounced the Jewish financiers who are supposed to do this), M. replied, 'All my money is invested in England,' and I suppose comparatively few of the audience realised that this means nothing.

At the beginning M. said that anyone ejected would be charged under the public meetings act. I don't know whether this was actually done, but presumably the power to do so exists. In connection with this the fact that there are no police on duty *inside the building* is of great importance. Anyone who interrupts can be assaulted and thrown out and then charged into the bargain, and of course the stewards, ie. M. himself, are the judges of what constitutes an interuption.° Therefore one is liable to get both a hammering and a fine for asking a question which M. finds it difficult to answer.

At the end of the meeting a great crowd collected outside, as there was some public indignation about the men who had been thrown out. I waited for a long time in the crowd to see what would happen, but M. and party did not emerge. Then the police managed to split the crowd and I found myself at the front, whereupon a policeman ordered me away, but quite civilly. I went round to the back of the crowd and waited again, but still M. did not appear and I concluded he had been sneaked out by a back door, so went home. In the morning at the *Chronicle* office, however, I was told that there had been some stone-throwing and two men had been arrested and remanded.

G.[16] changed this morning onto the early morning shift. He gets up at 3.45 am. and has to be at work, ie. at the coal face, at 6. He gets home about 2.30 pm. His wife does not get up to get his breakfast and he says few miners will allow their wives to do so. Also that there are still some miners who if they meet a woman on their way to work will turn back and go home. It is considered bad luck to see a woman before going to work. I presume this only applies to the early morning shift.

1. Figures such as 3/6 and 5/– stand for shillings and pence in pre-decimal currency. Thus, 3/6 = three shillings and sixpence and 5/– = five shillings. There were 240 old pence to £1 and 12 old pence to one shilling (therefore twenty shillings to £1). Thus, in decimal currency, 1p is approximately equivalent to 2½ old pence; one shilling is approximately equivalent to 5p. Thus, 3/6 = 17½p and 5/– = 25p. It is only possible to give approximate value equivalences to mid-thirties' prices (because different items have not increased in cost with inflation at the same rates), but a rough approximation can be given by multiplying Orwell's figures by thirty-five. Thus 5/– would now be roughly £8.75. Ellis Firth's 'weekly budget' of £1 12s to keep an unemployed miner, his wife and two small children (see *Road to Wigan Pier*, pp. 118–19 [*CW*, V/85–6]) is roughly equivalent to £56 at the end of the twentieth century. Orwell attached to his Diary for 5 March a cutting from the *News of the World* of 1 March (reproduced in *The Road to Wigan Pier*, p. 120 [*CW*, V/87]) which reported that Mr W. Leach of Lilford Road, London, SE, managed on a budget for food of 3s 11½d a week (very slightly less than 20p – perhaps about £7 at contemporary values). For this he could buy three wholemeal loaves; half a pound each of margarine and dripping; one pound each of cheese, onions, carrots and broken biscuits; two pounds of dates; one tin of evaporated milk and ten oranges. Mr Leach said he would prefer to cook the carrots rather than eat them raw, 'but, of course, to boil the water would cost too much'. This detail prompts doubt as to the genuineness of the letter. When the

editor priced these in London in November 1993 they cost £8.80. Orwell pointed out that this did not allow for fuel, clothes and tobacco (to which one should add rent); he did comment, 'Whether the letter was genuine or a hoax does not matter for the moment', but found it useful to compare it with Ellis Firth's budget. See *CW*, V/84–93 and X/448 and 450–51.

2. A lake in Staffordshire. The derivation of Rudyard is uncertain but may mean a pool where rudd, a freshwater fish, is found.

3. Frank Meade was an official of the Amalgamated Society of Woodworkers. He ran the Manchester office of *The Adelphi* and was business manager of *Labour's Northern Voice*, organ of the Independent Socialist Party. For a valuable corrective to the Diary and book, see Robert Pearce's 'Revisiting Orwell's *Wigan Pier*', referred to at the end of the headnote, above.

4. National Unemployed Workers' Movement.

5. 'Which see'. Orwell is referring to his notes on caravan dwellers, reproduced in X/546 and 548. See *Road to Wigan Pier*, pp. 96–8 [*CW*, V/56–9].

6. For a more sophisticated version of this 'epiphany', see *The Road to Wigan Pier*, p. 66 [*CW*, V/14–15], where Orwell describes himself as seeing the woman from a train bearing him away from the 'monstrous scenery of slag-heaps'.

7. Orwell left 72 Warrington Lane on 15 February 1936 and Mrs Hornby was taken to hospital. The lodgings run by the Forrests (Mrs F.) found for Orwell were over the infamous tripe shop, described in *The Road to Wigan Pier*, p. 59 [*CW*, V/5–6].

8. 'Rd.' typed in error for Street.

9. *John Bull* was a popular weekly founded in 1906 and initially edited by Horatio Bottomley (1860–1933), who, describing himself during World War I as 'The Soldier's Friend', campaigned for Ramsay MacDonald (later prime minister) to be imprisoned; but it was Bottomley who was imprisoned, for fraud. His journal specialized in sensationalism and competitions for relatively large prizes. Publication ceased in 1960.

10. J. Lyons & Co., see n. 2 to review of *Twenty thousand Streets under the Sky*, above.

11. Joe ('Jerry') Kennan (dates unknown) was an unemployed collier at this time and an activist in the Independent Labour Party. He maintained that the lodgings at 72 Warrington Lane were spotlessly clean, despite Orwell's strictures and 'that Orwell left it for the tripe shop in order to find something worse' (headnote to 'With the Wigan Miners', Joe Kennan's memories in *Orwell Remembered*, 130). Whether spotless or not, Orwell's hurried departure tallies with Mrs Hornby's illness as reported by Orwell. Kennan, perhaps understandably, resented not being sent an autographed copy of *The Road to Wigan Pier*.

12. Orwell presumably had in mind pneumatic drills.

13. Orwell describes the experience he underwent in *The Road to Wigan Pier*, pp. 68–73 [*CW*, V/18–25]. Crick (284) records Jerry Kennan's account of Orwell's journey underground, first given for a BBC 'Omnibus' programme in 1970. When Orwell did not duck quickly enough to avoid an overhead beam, he was knocked 'flat out' and had to be revived. By the time they got to the coal face, 'Orwell was unquestionably exhausted' – and he still had to get back to the surface. On three such occasions (not only this Crippen visit), Orwell 'was completely out'. When Orwell got back to his lodgings at 22 Darlington Street, he found a list of changes required for *Keep the Aspidistra Flying*, a book he thought already passed for printing before he left for Wigan. He sent the alterations to Gollancz (X/*284*) and, doubtless

weary from his day down the pit and exasperated by the contrast between what he had seen there and the triviality of what he was being asked to do, wrote an angry letter to his agent, Leonard Moore, expressing his annoyance: 'they asked me to make the alterations when the book was in type and asked me to equalise the letters' (in the days of hot-metal printing, unless line lengths were left unchanged, much consequential re-setting was called for). He went on, 'In general a passage of prose or even a whole chapter revolves round one or two key phrases, and to remove these, as was done in this case, knocks the whole thing to pieces.' He asked that in future arrangements be made with Gollancz for alterations to be made 'while the book is in typescript' (X/*284*). See Textual Note to *Keep the Aspidistra Flying*, CW, IV/279–87; and 'A Note on the Text', Penguin Twentieth-Century Classics, edition, pp. v–viii.

14. Sir Oswald Mosley, Bt. (1896–1980), politician, successively Conservative, Independent and Labour MP. In 1931 he broke away from the Labour Party to form the New Party. He became a fanatical supporter of Hitler and his party became the British Union of Fascists, the uniformed members of which were known as Blackshirts. He was interned during the war.

15. *Action* was the journal of the British Union of Fascists. On 9 July 1936, Orwell was asked by Mrs Hastings Bonora if she could quote from the Trafalgar Square scene of *A Clergyman's Daughter* in a review of *Victoria of England* she was writing for *Action*. She hoped he was not violently anti-Fascist and would 'consequently say CERTAINLY NOT'. Evidently that was what Orwell did say, because on 14 July she wrote to him, 'Even if you disapprove of the Fascist ideal, you must still recognise the point we all have in common – the welfare of the unfortunate "Down and Outs".' In a final letter, 24 July, she claimed that her party at least had a programme, 'but you have never put forward a single suggestion for ameliorating the lot of our "Misérables" '.

16. Mr Grey, a miner aged about forty-five, lived at 4 Agnes Terrace, Barnsley, with his wife, some ten years younger, and two daughters, Doreen and Irene, aged ten and eleven. Orwell lodged there and he noted that their house was 'very clean and decent'. See X/453–4.

---

[347]

Extracts from Orwell's 'Notes on Houses', Barnsley

Orwell's preparation for the writing of The Road to Wigan Pier *went much further than his visit to the North. He dug out information from newspapers, books and Town Halls; he spent time in Wigan Reference Library and he did some research in the British Museum (now the British Library). His typed-up notes, miners' pay-slips and some of his newspaper cuttings have survived; they are held by the Orwell Archive, University College London. Volume X of* The Complete Works *devotes an Appendix to summarizing and reproducing this material (pp. 538–84). Below are his notes on six of the nine houses in Barnsley that he described, with two of his drawings.*

No. 12 Albert Street East.[1] 3 up 2 down. Front room (parlour type) 15′ by 12′, back room (kitchen) about 12′ by 10′. Back room has kitchener[2] but is almost uninhabitable owing to damp. Front room rather damp also. Cellar. No cupboard under stairs. Outside WC. Door between two downstairs rooms has fallen off hinges. Two of upstairs rooms very damp. One has no gasjet, one has gasjet not in working order. Rent 9/0½d. Family, parents and two kids age 2 years 5 months and 10 months. Total income 32/– plus some baby food from Infants Welfare Clinic. No coal allowance as income is from U.A.B. not P.A.C.[3] Family possesses two beds but not enough bedding to cover them in winter, so sleep all four in one bed. Gas (for lighting only) reckoned as 1/3 a week. Through friend in work family are able to purchase coal at 9d a cwt.

Spring Gardens, Mapplewell. 2 up 1 down. Living room about 14′ by 12′. Kitchener. Sink in living room. 1 cupboard. Gas lighting (1d in slot). Plaster cracking and in places has peeled off walls. No shelves in oven. Gas said to leak slightly.

Upstairs. Two rooms each 10′ by 8′, arranged thus: Stairs have no banister at side marked AB, so that by stepping carelessly out of bed one may fall 10 feet onto stones. Dry. Dryrot in planks through which one can see into downstairs rooms. One bedroom has gasjet, one not. Four beds altogether (for 6 persons) but 'one bed does nowt', presumably for lack of bedclothes. Only old overcoats etc on bed.

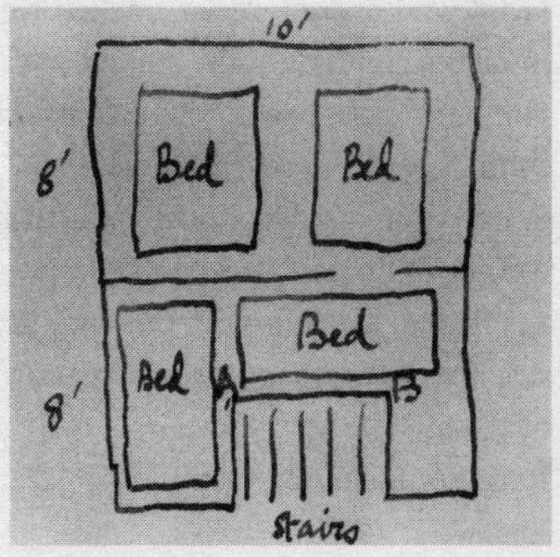

House infested with bugs, but 'I keeps 'em down with sheep-dip'. Reasonably clean and tidy as far as can be in circumstances. 6 persons in house, all adults, two working. Rent 5/–. About £11 in arrears ('strike rent') and for some weeks

past have been paying extra 1/– a week towards arrears. Landlord (woman) now refuses this and has served order to quit. Tenants have been in house 22 years.
Earth road past these cottages like a muckheap and said to be almost impassable in winter. Tiny garden. Stone lavatories at ends of gardens in semi-ruinous condition.

Another, two doors away. 2 up 2 down. Living room with sink and kitchener about 16′ by 12′. Scullery about one third of size of this, without ceiling – only rafters. These let in water to such an extent as to make the room useless except as lumber room. All woodwork of kitchen rotting away and doors loose on hinges.
2 upstairs rooms in much the same condition.
Rent 5/3. Tenant has been 23 years in house, now under orders to quit for arrears ('strike rent').
House in indescribable state of filth (tenant's own doing) and furniture falling to pieces.

Wortley Street. 2 up 1 down.
Downstairs. Living room about 12 by 10 with kitchener, sink and copper. Sink worn almost flat and constantly overflowing. Coal hole under stairs extending into a sort of tiny outhouse, semi-ruinous. Walls not too sound. Room very dark. Gas estimated at 4d a day.
Upstairs. Really 1 large room partitioned into two. Room nearest stairs has no door. Gas light in both rooms, fireplace in one. Walls in very bad state. Front wall of back room cracked right through. Window frames coming to pieces and have to be stuffed with bits of wood. 3 beds in these rooms. No bedclothes except overcoats, miscellaneous rags etc. Rain comes through walls in several places.
Sewer runs under house and stinks in summer. Corporation 'says they can't do nowt'. 6 people in house, 2 parents and 4 children aged 15, 14, 8 and 6. Youngest but one attending Queen's Rd. Hospital, TB. suspected. Bugs very bad – 'We can't sleep in summer, there's that many of them.'
Rent 5/3 including rates.

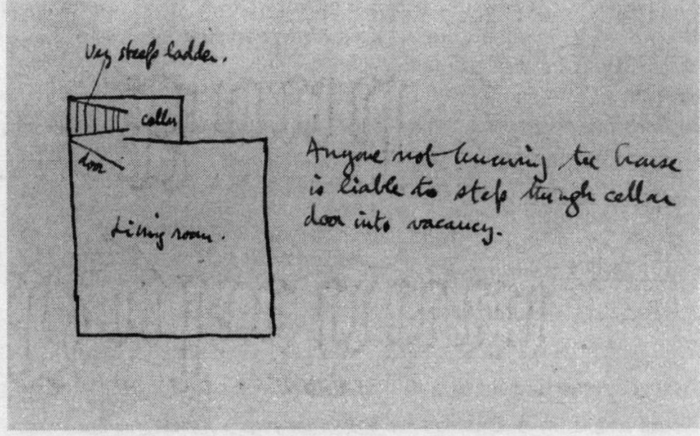
Very steep ladder.
cellar
door
Living room.
Anyone not knowing the house
is liable to step through cellar
door into vacancy.

[Orwell's handwritten note and drawing on verso of typed notes]

Haig's Yard, Providence Street. 1 up and 1 down and cellar.
Downstairs. Living room about 16′ by 10′ with kitchener, copper and sink. Walls fairly dry. Almost too dark to read by daylight. Gas estimated at 3d a day. Cellar door extremely dangerous.
Rent 5/– including rates. Landlord not bad. 3 persons in house, 2 adults (men) and 1 child.

Peel Street (Worsboro' Common). Back to Back. 2 up 2 down.
Living room about 10 feet square with kitchener, copper and sink. Other room about same size, perhaps intended as parlour, used as bedroom. Large cellar.* 70 yards walk to lavatory. Living room very dark, the other a little less so. Used 16/6 worth of gas in 6 weeks, or about 4½d a day.
Size of upstairs room as below. 3 beds. No bedding except old coats etc.
Bugs very bad – 'You can't keep 'em down when it's 'ot.'
Rent 5/7½ including rates. Landlord not complained of.
8 people in house. (4 beds altogether), 2 parents, 2 adult girls, (eldest 27), 1 young man and 3 children. Father and mother have 1 bed, son has another and remaining 5 share the other two.
It is said that there is always someone ill in this family. Indescribable squalor in downstairs rooms and smell of upstairs rooms almost unbearable.

* These are one-time weavers' houses [Orwell's footnote].

1. Ellis Firth's house. Firth's weekly budget is given by Orwell in *The Road to Wigan Pier*, pp. 118–19 [*CW*, V/85–6]; the original handwritten document is reproduced in X/565, and transcribed and explained on p. 566.
2. Cooking stove.
3. Unemployment Assistance Board and Public Assistance Committee (of the local authority).

---

[300]

To Jack Common

Thursday, [16? April 1936]

Orwell rented The Stores, 2 Kits Lane, Wallington, from a Mr Dearman from 2 April 1936. Dearman had bought the cottage from Agrar Ltd when it went bankrupt in the 1920s. The firm had run a small general store and post office from the front room. There was no other shop in Wallington. It was fairly primitive and its chimney smoked badly. See Shelden, 260–61. One attraction for Orwell was its very low rent and that it had land attached on which he could grow food and keep hens and goats; a picture of Orwell with Muriel, his favourite goat, is reproduced by Crick (plate 19). It was the Orwells' home until May 1940.

The Stores, Wallington, near Baldock

Dear Common,[1]
Thanks for yours. I have now seen my landlord and it is O.K. about the rent, so I have definitely decided to open the shop and have spread the news among the villagers to some extent. I should certainly be very obliged if you would find out about the wholesalers.[2] I didn't know you had your shop still. I believe there are some wholesalers of the kind at Watford, Kingford or Kingston or some such name. I don't know whether, seeing that I shall only want tiny amounts at a time (apart from the smallness of the village I haven't much storage room), they will make any trouble about delivery. I intend, at first at any rate, to stock nothing perishable except children's sweets. Later on I might start butter and marg. but it would mean getting a cooler. I am not going to stock tobacco because the pubs here (two to about 75 inhabitants!) stock it and I don't want to make enemies, especially as one pub is next door to

me. I am beginning to make out lists, though whether any one wholesaler will cover the lot I am not certain. I suppose what I shall start off [with] will be about twenty quids' worth of stuff. Are these people good about giving credit? What I would like to do would be to give a deposit of about £5 and then pay quarterly. I suppose my bank would give me a reference. It is a pity in view of this that I have just changed my branch because the Hampstead branch were getting quite trustful and told me I could overdraw, though I never asked them. I shall want besides stock one or two articles of shop equipment, such as scales, a bell etc. There are some that go with this place but my landlord has them and he is the sort of person who takes a year before he hands anything over. I have got to tidy up the shop premises and repaint, but if I can click with the wholesalers I should be ready to open up in about 3 weeks.

Yes, this business of class-breaking is a bugger. The trouble is that the socialist bourgeoisie, most of whom give me the creeps, will not be realistic and admit that there are a lot of working-class habits which they don't like and don't want to adopt. E.g. the typical middle-class socialist not only doesn't eat with his knife but is still slightly horrified by seeing a working man do so. And then so many of them are the sort of eunuch type with a vegetarian smell who go about spreading sweetness and light and have at the back of their minds a vision of the working class all T.T.,[3] well washed behind the ears, readers of Edward Carpenter[4] or some other pious sodomite and talking with B.B.C. accents. The working classes are very patient under it all. All the two months I was up north, when I spent my entire time in asking people questions about how much dole they got, what they had to eat etc., I was never once socked on the jaw and only once told to go to hell, and then by a woman who was deaf and thought I was a rate-collector. This question has been worrying me for a long time and part of my next book is to be about it.

I will get over when I have a bike or something. If you come over here, either let me know so that there shall be food, or take your chance – but there'll always be *something*, of course. The garden is still Augean (I have dug up twelve boots in two days) but I am getting things straight a little. It is awful to think that for nearly three months I have not done a stroke of work. Getting and spending we lay waste our powers.[5] However

I have wads of notes which give me the illusion of not having wasted my time.

Yours

Eric A. Blair

1. Jack Common (1903–68) worked in a solicitor's office, a shoe shop and as a mechanic. He was co-editor of *The Adelphi*, 1935–6. Crick calls him 'one of the few authentic English proletarian writers', and describes Common's first meeting with Orwell (204). Though there was a certain tension between the two men, they remained friends. Common's books include *The Freedom of the Streets* (1938), described by Crick as 'straight-talking or garrulous polemic' (354), *Kiddar's Luck* (1951) and *The Ampersand* (1954). A manuscript, 'Orwell at Wallington', written in the 1950s, was found among his papers; see *Orwell Remembered*, 139–43. It concludes, 'Years later I realised that no pub ever knew my friend as "Eric", let alone "George".'

2. Although he retained the tenancy, Orwell rarely visited the cottage (which was by then no longer a shop) from 1940 to 1942. He let Lydia Jackson (1899–1983; pen-name Elisaveta Fen) use the cottage with her flatmate, Patricia Donohue. On 28 July 1947, Orwell wrote to Lydia Jackson to say he had been given notice to quit (XIX/*3250*). He was now committed to Barnhill on Jura, and Lydia could not legally take a tenancy. In 1997 the cottage, much refurbished, with two bedrooms and a detached studio, was offered for sale at £195,000. Part of its attraction (and price) was that Orwell had lived there.

3. Tuberculin-tested (milk). Here meaning 'absolutely pure'. TT also means teetotal.

4. Edward Carpenter (1844–1929) was a socialist writer and social reformer whose works include *Towards Democracy* (1883) and *The Intermediate Sex: A Study of Some Transitional Types of Men and Women* (1908).

5. Line 2 of Wordsworth's sonnet, the first line of which is 'The world is too much with us; late and soon' (1807).

---

[331]

Review of Walls Have Mouths: A Record of Ten Years' Penal Servitude *by W. F. R. Macartney, with Prologue, Epilogue and Comments on the Chapters by Compton Mackenzie*

The Adelphi, *November 1936*

This very valuable and absorbingly interesting book – a record of ten years' penal servitude in Parkhurst Prison – brings out two facts about prison life which are not generally appreciated. The first is that the evil thing about the English prison system is not the abuses but the system itself. When you talk to a man who has been in prison, he generally lays emphasis on the bad food, the petty injustices, the cruelty of individual warders, etc., giving the impression that if these minor evils were rectified our prisons would become tolerable, supposing that any prisons could be that. Actually, the cold, rigid discipline of a modern English jail, the solitude, the silence, the everlasting lock-and-key (all of it the work of prison reformers, among the first of whom was Torquemada[1]), is more cruel and far more demoralising than the barbarous punishments of the Middle Ages. Worse than the loss of liberty, worse even than sexual deprivation, is boredom. Mr. Macartney has a good eye for significant detail, and he rubs this fact well home. It is quite usual, he says, at the week-end, to be left in utter solitude for forty-four hours with nothing to read. As a result, the tiniest distractions assume colossal importance. Apparently many of the men in Parkhurst Prison used to procure scraps of glass and secretly grind them into lenses – this must take months to do – and then, with tubes of brown paper, make telescopes with which to look out of their cell windows. Only men who were half mad with boredom would take all that trouble, incidentally risking bread and water for doing so.

The other fact Mr. Macartney makes clear is that in our prison system, as in other departments of English life, all real power is in the hands of one-eyed, permanent officials, who take no notice either of the Government of the moment or of public opinion. Even a prison governor, apparently, is almost powerless against the 'screws' who have inherited a brutal system and go on administering it by rule of thumb. It is rather amusing to read about the efforts of the Parkhurst officials to censor the prison library. They were desperately anxious to prevent the convicts getting hold of 'subversive' literature, but were far too illiterate to know which books were 'subversive' and which were not. The only Home Secretary who seems ever to have made a fight against the cruel inertia of the prison system is Winston Churchill. Clynes,[2] the Labour Home Secretary, actually exerted himself to take away a few of the convicts' privileges. No wonder that most long-term convicts are Tories!

The most dreadful chapter in this book is the one entitled 'Notes on Prison Sex Life'. It gave me a shock when I read it, for it suddenly revealed to me the meaning of a conversation of years earlier. I once asked a Burmese criminal why he disliked going to jail. He answered with a look of disgust and the single word, 'Sodomy.' I thought then that he merely meant that among the convicts there were a few homosexuals who pestered the others, but what Mr. Macartney makes clear is that in prison, after a few years, almost *every* man becomes homosexual, in spite of putting up a fight against it. He gives a horrible account of the way in which homosexuality gradually overwhelmed himself, first of all through the medium of his dreams. In a convict prison homosexuality is so general that even the jailors are infected by it, and there are actually cases of jailors and convicts competing for the favours of the same nancy-boy. As for masturbation, it is 'referred to openly and indifferently'. That is what you condemn a man to when you send him to prison for a long term. And this is the achievement of the dear good reformers (see Charles Reade's *It Is Never Too Late To Mend*[3]) who did away with the promiscuity of the eighteenth century jails.

This is a remarkable book. It is formless and badly written, but packed full of the kind of details that matter. The author is an exceptionally brave, sharp-witted and good-tempered person. He is a Communist (he was given his savage sentence for some ineffectual espionage in the service of the Soviet Government), but not, I fancy, a very orthodox one; he will perhaps not be pleased when I say that he is too decent a human being to be 'ideologically' sound. Mr. Compton Mackenzie's prologue and comments might appear at first sight to be unnecessary, but actually they have the effect of pulling the book together and supplying useful corroboration.[4] Probably without Mr. Mackenzie's help the book would not have been published, in which case everyone who cares for decency must be deeply grateful to him.

1. Tomás de Torquemada (1420–98), Dominican confessor to Queen Isabella I and King Ferdinand V of Spain. He became Inquisitor General of Castile, Aragon and other areas of Spain in 1483. He founded the Spanish Inquisition and his cruelty became legendary. He has been held responsible for burning at the stake about 2,000 people. He was also responsible for the expulsion of Jews from Spain in 1492, almost 170,000 being expelled.

2. John Robert Clynes (1869–1949) was Home Secretary in Ramsay MacDonald's Labour administration of June 1929 to August 1931. As Home Secretary, he refused to allow Trotsky to seek refuge in England.

3. Charles Reade (1814–84) published this book in 1856. Much of it is set in Australia and describes the perils of a goldminer's life. A parallel story enables Reade to expose the brutality of British prisons. He wrote a five-act drama on the same subject, *Gold!* (1853).

4. Compton Mackenzie (1883–1972), prolific novelist. He founded *The Gramophone* in 1923 and edited it for many years. It is still the most important British journal of its kind.

Publication of The Road to Wigan Pier
8 March 1937

On Saturday, 19 December, Victor Gollancz telegraphed Orwell at Wallington to say that it was 'exceedingly important' that they should meet, because 'I think we can make Left Book Club[1] *Choice'. He asked Orwell to see him on Monday (the 21st) at any time except 11.30. At this meeting it was decided to illustrate* The Road to Wigan Pier. *On Tuesday, Norman Collins sent the first of a series of letters to those who might provide photographs, indicating that it was Clough Williams-Ellis, an architect and founder of Portmeirion, who provided some of the names. The names had been written by Gollancz on a piece of blotting paper, which, by a quirk of chance, survives* *(see p. 48)**. It was originally intended that there would be forty-eight illustrations, not the thirty-two issued. Orwell's agent, Leonard Moore, was informed of the result of the meeting in a letter from Gollancz, 24 December 1936 (addressed to 'Gerald' Moore): 'It is highly probable that it will be the Left Book Club Choice for March.'*

The Road to Wigan Pier *is in two parts. As Crick explains, 'Gollancz first tried to persuade Orwell's agent to allow a small public edition of both halves to appear in hard covers, and the large Left Book Club edition to be simply the descriptive first half on Wigan . . . Moore and Eileen refused to allow this denaturing of the book; and Orwell himself had had time for a preliminary talk with a worried Gollancz. . . Gollancz got round the difficulty by himself writing an extraordinary introduction to the book' (307–8). Hodges does not mention this in her history of the publishing house. Edwards*[2] *states in her biography of Gollancz, 'Victor could not bear to reject it, even though his suggestion that the "repugnant" second half should be omitted from the Club edition was turned down. On this occasion Victor, albeit nervously, did overrule C[ommunist] P[arty] objections in favour of his publishing instinct. His compromise was to publish the book with what Orwell's biographer, Bernard Crick, rightly calls "an extraordinary introduction", full of good criticism, unfair criticism and half-truths' (246–7).*

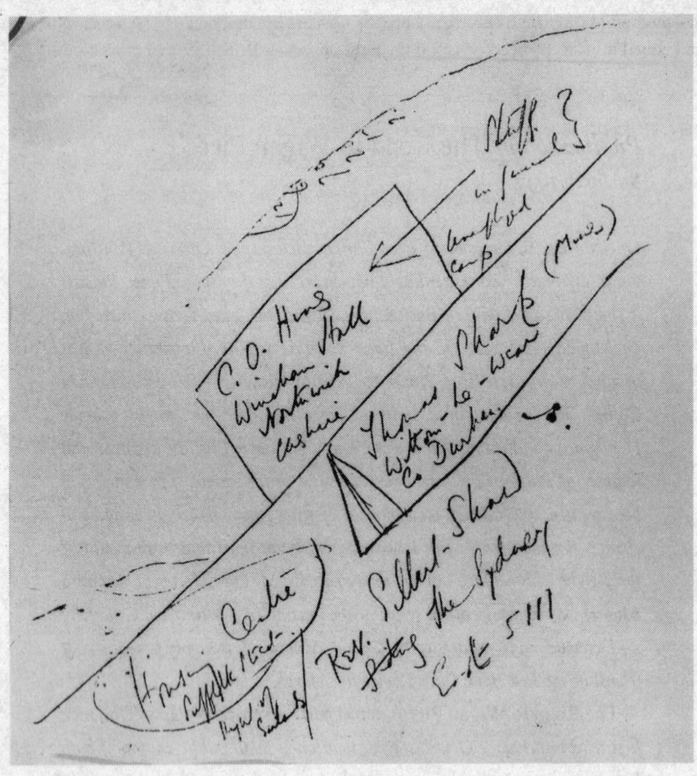

Corner of Victor Gollancz's desk blotter with the names, in his handwriting, of those who might be asked for photographs to illustrate *The Road to Wigan Pier.* When writing to the Reverend Gilbert Shaw, Norman Collins mistakenly addressed the letter to the Reverend Gilbert Sharp – the name noted above Shaw. Reduced to about half of original size.

In the event, a short run of Part One on its own was issued but only 890 copies were sold, compared to 2,150 copies of the hard-back trade edition and 44,039 copies of the Left Book Club edition. For details of Orwell's commission, advance royalty, publishing details and receipts, see pp. 22–3 above.

On 20 August 1937, Orwell wrote to Victor Gollancz about an antagonistic review of The Road to Wigan Pier *by Harry Pollitt,*[3] *leader of the*

*Communist Party of Great Britain (*XI/*390). This said, among other things, that Orwell had stated that the working classes smell. Orwell pointed out that what he had said was that middle-class people were brought up to* believe *that the working classes smell (he actually wrote 'the lower classes': see* V/119*). Attacks on Orwell had 'only begun after it became known to the Communist Party that I was serving with the P.O.U.M. militia'. He asked Gollancz to take this up with the Communists (which he did). There was, said Orwell, 'A campaign of organised libel [by the Communist Party] going on against people who were serving with the P.O.U.M. in Spain'. After Gollancz's intervention the immediate attacks ceased, though they still recur to this day.*

1. The Left Book Club, advertised for the first time in the *New Statesman & Nation*, 29 February 1936, was designed for those 'who desire to play an intelligent part in the struggle *for* World Peace and a better social and economic order, and *against* Fascism'. Books that would normally be sold at from 7s 6d to 25s od were to be sold to members at 5s od; all books would be original. The three selectors were Victor Gollancz; John Strachey, closely aligned to the Communist Party, though not a member; and Harold Laski, a member of the National Executive of the Labour Party and Professor of Political Science at the London School of Economics, University of London. The Left Book Club was the first of its kind in Britain and was modelled on the Book Society and Collins's Crime Club. Its first two books were published on 18 May 1936, when the club's membership was 9,000; by October 1936 there were 28,000 members. A monthly brochure, *Left Book News*, was issued to members, but was also available, free of charge, to non-members. The club ran for twelve years; its last book was offered in October 1948. See Sheila Hodges, *Gollancz: The Story of a Publishing House 1928–1978*, 117–43, 151, and 124–5 for an illustration of the first advertisement; Ruth Dudley Edwards, *Victor Gollancz: A Biography*, in which each issue of the *News* is noted.

2. For details of the Hodges and Edwards books referred to, see n. 1, above.

3. Harry Pollitt (1890–1906), Lancashire boiler-maker and founder-member of the Communist Party of Great Britain, 1920. He became its General Secretary in 1929 and, with Rajani Palme Dutt (1896–1974), led the party until his death. He adversely reviewed *The Road to Wigan Pier* in the *Daily Worker*, 17 March 1937.

The Road to Wigan Pier

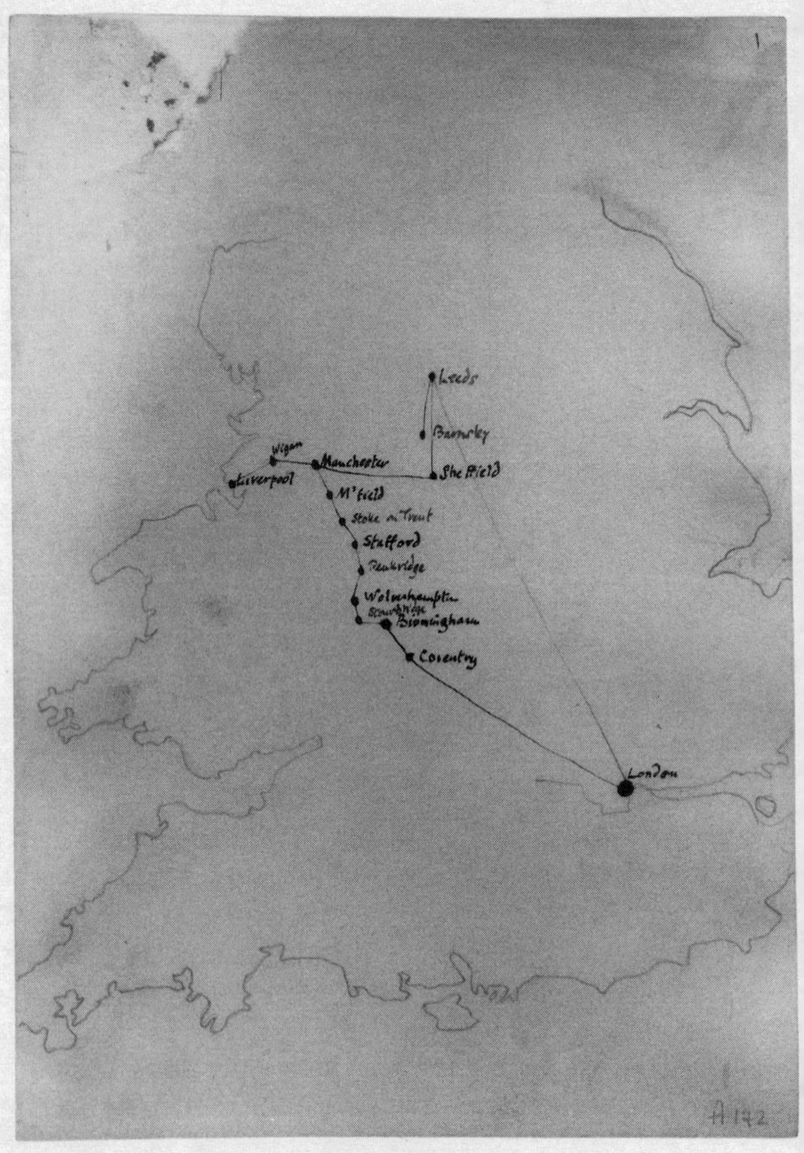

Orwell's sketch-map of his journey to the North

A Note on the Text

George Orwell was commissioned by Victor Gollancz to write on the depressed areas of the North of England and, having handed in his typescript of *Keep the Aspidistra Flying* for publication, he gave up his part-time job as a bookshop assistant in Hampstead and travelled north. He left London on 30 January 1936 and spent two months in Lancashire and Yorkshire. On his return to Wallington on 2 April he set about writing *The Road to Wigan Pier.* He delivered the manuscript on 15 December and it was published on 8 March 1937 in a Left Book Club edition and simultaneously in a higher-priced trade edition. Part I was also issued separately in May 1937 by the Left Book Club as a supplementary volume for 'propaganda distribution'. By 28 November 1939, 44,039 copies of the Left Book Club edition, 2,150 trade copies, and 890 copies of Part I only had been printed: a total of 47,079. A further 150 copies were destroyed in an air-raid. *The Road to Wigan Pier* was not reissued in Orwell's lifetime although a daily newspaper, the *News Chronicle,* published a short section in a series it ran devoted to 'young writers already famous among critics, less well-known by the public' on 10 June 1937. Harcourt, Brace published it in New York in 1958 and it was included in Secker & Warburg's Uniform Edition in 1959; Penguin Books first published *The Road to Wigan Pier* in 1962.

The Road to Wigan Pier was published without being proof-read by either Orwell (who was by then fighting in the Spanish Civil War) or his wife, Eileen. She was offered one day in which she might see the proofs at the publisher's office, such was the pressure to get the book out. Orwell sent a message asking for one change to be made. On page 67, lines 19–20 (*CW*, V/16) he had written 'rooks copulating'. Gollancz had changed this to 'courting'; Orwell asked for it to be altered to 'treading', and the text was amended. The original has now been restored.

The original edition of *The Road to Wigan Pier* was illustrated with a section of 32 plates. Harcourt, Brace reproduced these in 1958, but no later edition did so until the *Complete Works* edition was published in 1986. Orwell did not in fact choose the illustrations and the idea for their inclusion may not have been his. Gollancz telegraphed him to call at his office on 21 December 1936, a day or two before he was due to leave for Spain. Also present at their meeting was the architect Clough Williams-Ellis, best remembered for his work at Portmeirion, but who was also interested in social problems. It may have been Ellis's idea to include illustrations and it was almost certainly Ellis who suggested likely sources. These Gollancz noted down on his blotting pad (see p. 48 above), from which he tore off sections which he handed to Norman Collins (later head of ATV) to process. The inclusion of these illustrations in the new editions of *The Road to Wigan Pier* is important, even if something of their original clarity is lost because they have had to be reproduced from the plates in the first edition. These illustrations reinforce the place of *The Road to Wigan Pier* in the English documentary tradition, as comparison with Edgar Anstey's film, *Housing Problems* (1935), will demonstrate.[1] Victor Gollancz was uneasy about the second part of Orwell's book and he therefore wrote a foreword. This is not reprinted here but can be found in the *Complete Works* edition, V/216–25.

Orwell first saw *The Road to Wigan Pier* when he returned to Barcelona on leave from the front line at the end of April or early in May 1937. On 9 May he wrote to Gollancz to thank him for contributing his foreword. He said he liked the introduction very much though, of course, he could have answered some of Gollancz's criticisms. Whether he was simply being polite, or was a trifle naïve, has been a matter of debate. Perhaps the fact that he wrote against a background of street-fighting in Barcelona must be taken into account. Discussion 'of what one is really talking about', as he put it, must have seemed very civilized by contrast. Orwell never shrank from being direct, so his response was probably quite

[1] For a fuller account of the use of illustrations in *The Road to Wigan Pier*, see the General Introduction to the Complete Works edition, I, pages xxxii–xxxv (Secker & Warburg, 1986).

straightforward. Later, in conversation with Sonia Orwell, he was to see Gollancz's foreword in a different light.

The most important 'textual variant' of *The Road to Wigan Pier*, if it can be so termed, is the omission of illustrations from so many editions. In addition, Secker & Warburg omitted item 3 on page 90 (lines 22–3; *CW*, V/48, lines 25–7) from their Uniform Edition and Penguin Books followed suit; Penguin then incorrectly renumbered the sequence. Orwell himself miscalculated some of the miners' wages and deductions on pages 82–3 (V/38), but, since the pay-slips he used have survived, the correct calculations have now been made. Orwell's error had the effect of making the average weekly earnings appear slightly more than, in fact, they were.

Numbered footnotes are Orwell's.

Part I

1

The first sound in the mornings was the clumping of the mill-girls' clogs down the cobbled street. Earlier than that, I suppose, there were factory whistles which I was never awake to hear.

There were generally four of us in the bedroom, and a beastly place it was, with that defiled impermanent look of rooms that are not serving their rightful purpose. Years earlier the house had been an ordinary dwelling-house, and when the Brookers had taken it and fitted it out as a tripe-shop and lodging-house, they had inherited some of the more useless pieces of furniture and had never had the energy to remove them. We were therefore sleeping in what was still recognisably a drawing-room. Hanging from the ceiling there was a heavy glass chandelier on which the dust was so thick that it was like fur. And covering most of one wall there was a huge hideous piece of junk, something between a sideboard and a hall-stand, with lots of carving and little drawers and strips of looking-glass, and there was a once-gaudy carpet ringed by the slop-pails of years, and two gilt chairs with burst seats, and one of those old-fashioned horsehair armchairs which you slide off when you try to sit on them. The room had been turned into a bedroom by thrusting four squalid beds in among this other wreckage.

My bed was in the right-hand corner on the side nearest the door. There was another bed across the foot of it and jammed hard against it (it had to be in that position to allow the door to open) so that I had to sleep with my legs doubled up; if I straightened them out I kicked the occupant of the other bed in the small of the back. He was an elderly man named Mr Reilly, a mechanic of sorts and employed 'on top' at one of the coal-pits. Luckily he had to go to work at five in the morning, so I could uncoil my legs and have a couple of hours' proper sleep after he was gone.

In the bed opposite there was a Scotch miner who had been injured in a pit accident (a huge chunk of stone pinned him to the ground and it was a couple of hours before they could lever it off), and had received five hundred pounds compensation. He was a big handsome man of forty, with grizzled hair and a clipped moustache, more like a sergeant-major than a miner, and he would lie in bed till late in the day, smoking a short pipe. The other bed was occupied by a succession of commercial travellers, newspaper-canvassers and hire-purchase touts who generally stayed for a couple of nights. It was a double bed and much the best in the room. I had slept in it myself my first night there, but had been manoeuvred out of it to make room for another lodger. I believe all newcomers spent their first night in the double bed, which was used, so to speak, as bait. All the windows were kept tight shut, with a red sandbag jammed in the bottom, and in the morning the room stank like a ferret's cage. You did not notice it when you got up, but if you went out of the room and came back, the smell hit you in the face with a smack.

I never discovered how many bedrooms the house contained, but strange to say there was a bathroom, dating from before the Brookers' time. Downstairs there was the usual kitchen living-room with its huge open range burning night and day. It was lighted only by a skylight, for on one side of it was the shop and on the other the larder, which opened into some dark subterranean place where the tripe was stored. Partly blocking the door of the larder there was a shapeless sofa upon which Mrs Brooker, our landlady, lay permanently ill, festooned in grimy blankets. She had a big, pale yellow, anxious face. No one knew for certain what was the matter with her; I suspect that her only real trouble was over-eating. In front of the fire there was almost always a line of damp washing, and in the middle of the room was the big kitchen table at which the family and all the lodgers ate. I never saw this table completely uncovered, but I saw its various wrappings at different times. At the bottom there was a layer of old newspapers stained by Worcester Sauce; above that a sheet of sticky white oil-cloth; above that a green serge cloth; above that a coarse linen cloth, never changed and seldom taken off. Generally the crumbs from breakfast were still on the table at supper. I used to get to know individual crumbs by sight and watch their progress up and down the table from day to day.

The shop was a narrow, cold sort of room. On the outside of the window a few white letters, relics of ancient chocolate advertisements, were scattered like stars. Inside there was a slab upon which lay the great white folds of tripe, and the grey flocculent stuff known as 'black tripe', and the ghostly translucent feet of pigs, ready boiled. It was the ordinary 'tripe and pea' shop, and not much else was stocked except bread, cigarettes and tinned stuff. 'Teas' were advertised in the window, but if a customer demanded a cup of tea he was usually put off with excuses. Mr Brooker, though out of work for two years, was a miner by trade, but he and his wife had been keeping shops of various kinds as a side-line all their lives. At one time they had had a pub, but they had lost their licence for allowing gambling on the premises. I doubt whether any of their businesses had ever paid; they were the kind of people who run a business chiefly in order to have something to grumble about. Mr Brooker was a dark, small-boned, sour, Irish-looking man, and astonishingly dirty. I don't think I ever once saw his hands clean. As Mrs Brooker was now an invalid he prepared most of the food, and like all people with permanently dirty hands he had a peculiarly intimate, lingering manner of handling things. If he gave you a slice of bread-and-butter there was always a black thumb-print on it. Even in the early morning when he descended into the mysterious den behind Mrs Brooker's sofa and fished out the tripe, his hands were already black. I heard dreadful stories from the other lodgers about the place where the tripe was kept. Black-beetles were said to swarm there. I do not know how often fresh consignments of tripe were ordered, but it was at long intervals, for Mrs Brooker used to date events by it. 'Let me see now, I've had in three lots of froze (frozen tripe) since that happened,' etc. etc. We lodgers were never given tripe to eat. At the time I imagined that this was because tripe was too expensive; I have since thought that it was merely because we knew too much about it. The Brookers never ate tripe themselves, I noticed.

The only permanent lodgers were the Scotch miner, Mr Reilly, two old-age pensioners and an unemployed man on the PAC named Joe – he was the kind of person who has no surname. The Scotch miner was a bore when you got to know him. Like so many unemployed men he spent too much time reading newspapers, and if you did not head him off he would discourse for hours about such things as the Yellow Peril, trunk murders, astrology, and the conflict between religion and science. The old-age pensioners had, as usual, been driven from their homes by the Means Test. They handed their weekly ten shillings over to the Brookers and in return got the kind of accommodation you would expect for ten shillings; that is, a bed in the attic and meals chiefly of bread-and-butter. One of them was of 'superior' type and was dying of some malignant disease – cancer, I believe. He only got out of bed on the days when he went to draw his pension. The other, called by everyone Old Jack, was an ex-miner aged seventy-eight who had worked well over fifty years in the pits. He was alert and intelligent, but curiously enough he seemed only to remember his boyhood experiences and to have forgotten all about the modern mining machinery and improvements. He used to tell me tales of fights with savage horses in the narrow galleries underground. When he heard that I was arranging to go down several coal mines he was contemptuous and declared that a man of my size (six feet two and a half) would never manage the 'travelling'; it was no use telling him that the 'travelling' was better than it used to be. But he was friendly to everyone and used to give us all a fine shout of 'Good night, boys!' as he crawled up the stairs to his bed somewhere under the rafters. What I most admired about Old Jack was that he never cadged; he was generally out of tobacco towards the end of the week, but he always refused to smoke anyone else's. The Brookers had insured the lives of both old-age pensioners with one of the tanner-a-week companies. It was said that they were overheard anxiously asking the insurance-tout 'how long people lived when they'd got cancer'.

Joe, like the Scotchman, was a great reader of newspapers and spent almost his entire day in the public library. He was the typical unmarried unemployed man, a derelict-looking, frankly ragged creature with a round, almost childish face on which there was a naïvely naughty expression. He looked more like a neglected little boy than a grown-up man. I suppose it is the complete lack of responsibility that makes so many of these men look younger than their ages. From Joe's appearance I took him to be about twenty-eight, and was amazed to learn that he was forty-three. He had a love of resounding phrases and was very proud of the astuteness with which he had avoided getting married. He often said to me, 'Matrimonial chains is a big item', evidently feeling this to be a very subtle and portentous remark. His total income was fifteen shillings a week, and he paid out six or seven to the Brookers for his bed. I sometimes used to see him making himself a cup of tea over the kitchen fire, but for the rest he got his meals somewhere out of doors; it was mostly slices of bread-and-marg. and packets of fish and chips, I suppose.

Besides these there was a floating clientele of commercial travellers of the poorer sort, travelling actors – always common in the North because most of the larger pubs hire variety artists at the week-ends – and newspaper-canvassers. The newspaper-canvassers were a type I had never met before. Their job seemed to me so hopeless, so appalling that I wondered how anyone could put up with such a thing when prison was a possible alternative. They were employed mostly by weekly or Sunday papers, and they were sent from town to town, provided with maps and given a list of streets which they had to 'work' each day. If they failed to secure a minimum of twenty orders a day, they got the sack. So long as they kept up their twenty orders a day they received a small salary – two pounds a week, I think; on any order over the twenty they drew a tiny commission. The thing is not so impossible as it sounds, because in working-class districts every family takes in a twopenny weekly paper and changes it every few weeks; but I doubt whether anyone keeps a job of that kind long. The newspapers engage poor desperate wretches, out-of-work clerks and commercial travellers and the like, who for a while make frantic efforts and keep their sales up to the minimum; then as the deadly work wears them down they are sacked and fresh men are taken on. I got to know two who were employed by one of the more notorious weeklies. Both of them were middle-aged men with families to support, and one of them was a grandfather. They were on their feet ten hours a day, 'working' their appointed streets, and then busy late into the night filling in blank forms for some swindle their paper was running – one of those schemes by which you are 'given' a set of crockery if you take out a six weeks' subscription and send a two-shilling postal order as well. The fat one, the grandfather, used to fall asleep with his head on a pile of forms. Neither of them could afford the pound a week which the Brookers charged for full board. They used to pay a small sum for their beds and make shamefaced meals in a corner of the kitchen off bacon and bread-and-margarine which they stored in their suitcases.

The Brookers had large numbers of sons and daughters, most of whom had long since fled from home. Some were in Canada – 'at Canada', as Mrs Brooker used to put it. There was only one son living near by, a large pig-like young man employed in a garage, who frequently came to the house for his meals. His wife was there all day with the two children, and most of the cooking and laundering was done by her and by Emmie, the fiancée of another son who was in London. Emmie was a fair-haired, sharp-nosed, unhappy-looking girl who worked at one of the mills for some starvation wage, but nevertheless spent all her evenings in bondage at the Brookers' house. I gathered that the marriage was constantly being postponed and would probably never take place, but Mrs Brooker had already appropriated Emmie as a daughter-in-law, and nagged her in that peculiar watchful, loving way that invalids have. The rest of the housework was done, or not done, by Mr Brooker. Mrs Brooker seldom rose from her sofa in the kitchen (she spent the night there as well as the day) and was too ill to do anything except eat stupendous meals. It was Mr Brooker who attended to the shop, gave the lodgers their food and 'did out' the bedrooms. He was always moving with incredible slowness from one hated job to another. Often the beds were still unmade at six in the evening, and at any hour of the day you were liable to meet Mr Brooker on the stairs, carrying a full chamber-pot which he gripped with his thumb well over the rim. In the mornings he sat by the fire with a tub of filthy water, peeling potatoes at the speed of a slow-motion picture. I never saw anyone who could peel potatoes with quite such an air of brooding resentment. You could see the hatred of this 'bloody woman's work', as he called it, fermenting inside him, a kind of bitter juice. He was one of those people who can chew their grievances like a cud.

Of course, as I was indoors a good deal, I heard all about the Brookers' woes, and how everyone swindled them and was ungrateful to them, and how the shop did not pay and the lodging-house hardly paid. By local standards they were not so badly off, for, in some way I did not understand, Mr Brooker was dodging the Means Test and drawing an allowance from the PAC, but their chief pleasure was talking about their grievances to anyone who would listen. Mrs Brooker used to lament by the hour, lying on her sofa, a soft mound of fat and self-pity, saying the same things over and over again. 'We don't seem to get no customers nowadays, I don't know 'ow it is. The tripe's just a-laying there day after day – such beautiful tripe it is, too! It does seem 'ard, don't it now?' etc. etc. etc. All Mrs Brooker's laments ended with 'It does seem 'ard, don't it now?' like the refrain of a ballade. Certainly it was true that the shop did not pay. The whole place had the unmistakable dusty, flyblown air of a business that is going down. But it would have been quite useless to explain to them *why* nobody came to the shop, even if one had had the face to do it; neither was capable of understanding that last year's dead bluebottles supine in the shop window are not good for trade.

But the thing that really tormented them was the thought of those two old-age pensioners living in their house, usurping floor-space, devouring food and paying only ten shillings a week. I doubt whether they were really losing money over the old-age pensioners, though certainly the profit on ten shillings a week must have been very small. But in their eyes the two old men were a kind of dreadful parasite who had fastened on them and were living on their charity. Old Jack they could just tolerate, because he kept out-of-doors most of the day, but they really hated the bedridden one, Hooker by name. Mr Brooker had a queer way of pronouncing his name, without the H and with a long U – 'Uker'. What tales I heard about old Hooker and his fractiousness, the nuisance of making his bed, the way he 'wouldn't eat' this and 'wouldn't eat' that, his endless ingratitude and, above all, the selfish obstinacy with which he refused to die! The Brookers were quite openly pining for him to die. When that happened they could at least draw the insurance money. They seemed to feel him there, eating their substance day after day, as though he had been a living worm in their bowels. Sometimes Mr Brooker would look up from his potato-peeling, catch my eye and jerk his head with a look of inexpressible bitterness towards the ceiling, towards old Hooker's room. 'It's a b——, ain't it?' he would say. There was no need to say more; I had heard all about old Hooker's ways already. But the Brookers had grievances of one kind and another against all their lodgers, myself included, no doubt. Joe, being on the PAC, was practically in the same category as the old-age pensioners. The Scotchman paid a pound a week, but he was indoors most of the day and they 'didn't like him always hanging round the place', as they put it. The newspaper-canvassers were out all day, but the Brookers bore them a grudge for bringing in their own food, and even Mr Reilly, their best lodger, was in disgrace because Mrs Brooker said that he woke her up when he came downstairs in the mornings. They couldn't, they complained perpetually, get the kind of lodgers they wanted – good-class 'commercial gentlemen' who paid full board and were out all day. Their ideal lodger would have been somebody who paid thirty shillings a week and never came indoors except to sleep. I have noticed that people who let lodgings nearly always hate their lodgers. They want their money but they look on them as intruders and have a curiously watchful, jealous attitude which at bottom is a determination not to let the lodger make himself too much at home. It is an inevitable result of the bad system by which the lodger has to live in somebody else's house without being one of the family.

The meals at the Brookers' house were uniformly disgusting. For breakfast you got two rashers of bacon and a pale fried egg, and bread-and-butter which had often been cut overnight and always had thumb-marks on it. However tactfully I tried, I could never induce Mr Brooker to let me cut my own bread-and-butter; he *would* hand it to me slice by slice, each slice gripped firmly under that broad black thumb. For dinner there were generally those threepenny steak puddings which are sold ready-made in tins – these were part of the stock of the shop, I think – and boiled potatoes and rice pudding. For tea there was more bread-and-butter and frayed-looking sweet cakes which were probably bought as 'stales' from the baker. For supper there was the pale flabby Lancashire cheese and biscuits. The Brookers never called these biscuits biscuits. They always referred to them reverently as 'cream crackers' – 'Have another cream cracker, Mr Reilly. You'll like a cream cracker with your cheese' – thus glozing over the fact that there was only cheese for supper. Several bottles of Worcester Sauce and a half-full jar of marmalade lived permanently on the table. It was usual to souse everything, even a piece of cheese, with Worcester Sauce, but I never saw anyone brave the marmalade jar, which was an unspeakable mass of stickiness and dust. Mrs Brooker had her meals separately but also took snacks from any meal that happened to be going, and manoeuvred with great skill for what she called 'the bottom of the pot', meaning the strongest cup of tea. She had a habit of constantly wiping her mouth on one of her blankets. Towards the end of my stay she took to tearing off strips of newspaper for this purpose, and in the morning the floor was often littered with crumpled-up balls of slimy paper which lay there for hours. The smell of the kitchen was dreadful, but, as with that of the bedroom, you ceased to notice it after a while.

It struck me that this place must be fairly normal as lodging-houses in the industrial areas go, for on the whole the lodgers did not complain. The only one who ever did so to my knowledge was a little black-haired sharp-nosed Cockney, a traveller for a cigarette firm. He had never been in the North before, and I think that till recently he had been in better employ and was used to staying in commercial hotels. This was his first glimpse of really low-class lodgings, the kind of place in which the poor tribe of touts and canvassers have to shelter upon their endless journeys. In the morning as we were dressing (he had slept in the double bed, of course) I saw him look round the desolate room with a sort of wondering aversion. He caught my eye and suddenly divined that I was a fellow-Southerner.

'The filthy bloody bastards!' he said feelingly.

After that he packed his suit-case, went downstairs and, with great strength of mind, told the Brookers that this was not the kind of house he was accustomed to and that he was leaving immediately. The Brookers could never understand why. They were astonished and hurt. The ingratitude of it! Leaving them like that for no reason after a single night! Afterwards they discussed it over and over again, in all its bearings. It was added to their store of grievances.

On the day when there was a full chamber-pot under the breakfast table I decided to leave. The place was beginning to depress me. It was not only the dirt, the smells and the vile food, but the feeling of stagnant meaningless decay, of having got down into some subterranean place where people go creeping round and round, just like black beetles, in an endless muddle of slovened jobs and mean grievances. The most dreadful thing about people like the Brookers is the way they say the same things over and over again. It gives you the feeling that they are not real people at all, but a kind of ghost for ever rehearsing the same futile rigmarole. In the end Mrs Brooker's self-pitying talk – always the same complaints, over and over, and always ending with the tremulous whine of 'It does seem 'ard, don't it now?' – revolted me even more than her habit of wiping her mouth with bits of newspaper. But it is no use saying that people like the Brookers are just disgusting and trying to put them out of mind. For they exist in tens and hundreds of thousands; they are one of the characteristic by-products of the modern world. You cannot disregard them if you accept the civilisation that produced them. For this is part at least of what industrialism has done for us. Columbus sailed the Atlantic, the first steam engines tottered into motion, the British squares stood firm under the French guns at Waterloo, the one-eyed scoundrels of the nineteenth century praised God and filled their pockets; and this is where it all led – to labyrinthine slums and dark back kitchens with sickly, ageing people creeping round and round them like black beetles. It is a kind of duty to see and smell such places now and again, especially smell them, lest you should forget that they exist; though perhaps it is better not to stay there too long.

The train bore me away, through the monstrous scenery of slag-heaps, chimneys, piled scrap-iron, foul canals, paths of cindery mud criss-crossed by the prints of clogs. This was March, but the weather had been horribly cold and everywhere there were mounds of blackened snow. As we moved slowly through the outskirts of the town we passed row after row of little grey slum houses running at right angles to the embankment. At the back of one of the houses a young woman was kneeling on the stones, poking a stick up the leaden waste-pipe which ran from the sink inside and which I suppose was blocked. I had time to see everything about her – her sacking apron, her clumsy clogs, her arms reddened by the cold. She looked up as the train passed, and I was almost near enough to catch her eye. She had a round pale face, the usual exhausted face of the slum girl who is twenty-five and looks forty, thanks to miscarriages and drudgery; and it wore, for the second in which I saw it, the most desolate, hopeless expression I have ever seen. It struck me then that we are mistaken when we say that 'It isn't the same for them as it would be for us', and that people bred in the slums can imagine nothing but the slums. For what I saw in her face was not the ignorant suffering of an animal. She knew well enough what was happening to her – understood as well as I did how dreadful a destiny it was to be kneeling there in the bitter cold, on the slimy stones of a slum backyard, poking a stick up a foul drain-pipe.

But quite soon the train drew away into open country, and that seemed strange, almost unnatural, as though the open country had been a kind of park; for in the industrial areas one always feels that the smoke and filth must go on for ever and that no part of the earth's surface can escape them. In a crowded, dirty little country like ours one takes defilement almost for granted. Slag-heaps and chimneys seem a more normal, probable landscape than grass and trees, and even in the depths of the country when you drive your fork into the ground you half expect to lever up a broken bottle or a rusty can. But out here the snow was untrodden and lay so deep that only the tops of the stone boundary-walls were showing, winding over the hills like black paths. I remembered that D. H. Lawrence, writing of this same landscape or another near by, said that the snow-covered hills rippled away into the distance 'like muscle'. It was not the simile that would have occurred to me. To my eye the snow and the black walls were more like a white dress with black piping running across it.

Although the snow was hardly broken the sun was shining brightly, and behind the shut windows of the carriage it seemed warm. According to the almanac this was spring, and a few of the birds seemed to believe it. For the first time in my life, in a bare patch beside the line, I saw rooks copulating. They did it on the ground and not, as I should have expected, in a tree. The manner of courtship was curious. The female stood with her beak open and the male walked round her and appeared to be feeding her. I had hardly been in the train half an hour, but it seemed a very long way from the Brookers' back-kitchen to the empty slopes of snow, the bright sunshine and the big gleaming birds.

The whole of the industrial districts are really one enormous town, of about the same population as Greater London but, fortunately, of much larger area; so that even in the middle of them there is still room for patches of cleanness and decency. That is an encouraging thought. In spite of hard trying, man has not yet succeeded in doing his dirt everywhere. The earth is so vast and still so empty that even in the filthy heart of civilisation you find fields where the grass is green instead of grey; perhaps if you looked for them you might even find streams with live fish in them instead of salmon tins. For quite a long time, perhaps another twenty minutes, the train was rolling through open country before the villa-civilisation began to close in upon us again, and then the outer slums, and then the slag-heaps, belching chimneys, blast-furnaces, canals and gasometers of another industrial town.

II

Our civilisation, *pace* Chesterton, *is* founded on coal, more completely than one realises until one stops to think about it. The machines that keep us alive, and the machines that make the machines, are all directly or indirectly dependent upon coal. In the metabolism of the Western world the coal-miner is second in importance only to the man who ploughs the soil. He is a sort of grimy caryatid upon whose shoulders nearly everything that is *not* grimy is supported. For this reason the actual process by which coal is extracted is well worth watching, if you get the chance and are willing to take the trouble.

When you go down a coal-mine it is important to try and get to the coal face when the 'fillers' are at work. This is not easy, because when the mine is working visitors are a nuisance and are not encouraged, but if you go at any other time, it is possible to come away with a totally wrong impression. On a Sunday, for instance, a mine seems almost peaceful. The time to go there is when the machines are roaring and the air is black with coal dust, and when you can actually see what the miners have to do. At those times the place is like hell, or at any rate like my own mental picture of hell. Most of the things one imagines in hell are there – heat, noise, confusion, darkness, foul air, and, above all, unbearably cramped space. Everything except the fire, for there is no fire down there except the feeble beams of Davy lamps and electric torches which scarcely penetrate the clouds of coal dust.

When you have finally got there – and getting there is a job in itself: I will explain that in a moment – you crawl through the last line of pit props and see opposite you a shiny black wall three or four feet high. This is the coal face. Overhead is the smooth ceiling made by the rock from which the coal has been cut; underneath is the rock again, so that the gallery you are in is only as high as the ledge of coal itself, probably not much more than a yard. The first impression of all, overmastering everything else for a while, is the frightful, deafening din from the conveyor belt which carries the coal away. You cannot see very far, because the fog of coal dust throws back the beam of your lamp, but you can see on either side of you the line of half-naked kneeling men, one to every four or five yards, driving their shovels under the fallen coal and flinging it swiftly over their left shoulders. They are feeding it onto the conveyor belt, a moving rubber belt a couple of feet wide which runs a yard or two behind them. Down this belt a glittering river of coal races constantly. In a big mine it is carrying away several tons of coal every minute. It bears it off to some place in the main roads where it is shot into tubs holding half a ton, and thence dragged to the cages and hoisted to the outer air.

It is impossible to watch the 'fillers' at work without feeling a pang of envy for their toughness. It is a dreadful job that they do, an almost superhuman job by the standards of an ordinary person. For they are not only shifting monstrous quantities of coal, they are also doing it in a position that doubles or trebles the work. They have got to remain kneeling all the while – they could hardly rise from their knees without hitting the ceiling – and you can easily see by trying it what a tremendous effort this means. Shovelling is comparatively easy when you are standing up, because you can use your knee and thigh to drive the shovel along; kneeling down, the whole of the strain is thrown upon your arm and belly muscles. And the other conditions do not exactly make things easier. There is the heat – it varies, but in some mines it is suffocating – and the coal dust that stuffs up your throat and nostrils and collects along your eyelids, and the unending rattle of the conveyor belt, which in that confined space is rather like the rattle of a machine gun. But the fillers look and work as though they were made of iron. They really do look like iron – hammered iron statues – under the smooth coat of coal dust which clings to them from head to foot. It is only when you see miners down the mine and naked that you realise what splendid men they are. Most of them are small (big men are at a disadvantage in that job) but nearly all of them have the most noble bodies; wide shoulders tapering to slender supple waists, and small pronounced buttocks and sinewy thighs, with not an ounce of waste flesh anywhere. In the hotter mines they wear only a pair of thin drawers, clogs and knee-pads; in the hottest mines of all, only the clogs and knee-pads. You can hardly tell by the look of them whether they are young or old. They may be any age up to sixty or even sixty-five, but when they are black and naked they all look alike. No one could do their work who had not a young man's body, and a figure fit for a guardsman at that; just a few pounds of extra flesh on the waist-line, and the constant bending would be impossible. You can never forget that spectacle once you have seen it – the line of bowed, kneeling figures, sooty black all over, driving their huge shovels under the coal with stupendous force and speed. They are on the job for seven and a half hours, theoretically without a break, for there is no time 'off'. Actually they snatch a quarter of an hour or so at some time during the shift to eat the food they have brought with them, usually a hunk of bread and dripping and a bottle of cold tea. The first time I was watching the 'fillers' at work I put my hand upon some dreadful slimy thing among the coal dust. It was a chewed quid of tobacco. Nearly all the miners chew tobacco, which is said to be good against thirst.

Probably you have to go down several coal-mines before you can get much grasp of the processes that are going on round you. This is chiefly because the mere effort of getting from place to place makes it difficult to notice anything else. In some ways it is even disappointing, or at least is unlike what you have expected. You get into the cage, which is a steel box about as wide as a telephone box and two or three times as long. It holds ten men, but they pack it like pilchards in a tin, and a tall man cannot stand upright in it. The steel door shuts upon you, and somebody working the winding gear above drops you into the void. You have the usual momentary qualm in your belly and a bursting sensation in the ears, but not much sensation of movement till you get near the bottom, when the cage slows down so abruptly that you could swear it is going upwards again. In the middle of the run the cage probably touches sixty miles an hour; in some of the deeper mines it touches even more. When you crawl out at the bottom you are perhaps four hundred yards under ground. That is to say, you have a tolerable-sized mountain on top of you; hundreds of yards of solid rock, bones of extinct beasts, subsoil, flints, roots of growing things, green grass and cows grazing on it – all this suspended over your head and held back only by wooden props as thick as the calf of your leg. But because of the speed at which the cage has brought you down, and the complete blackness through which you have travelled, you hardly feel yourself deeper down than you would at the bottom of the Piccadilly tube.

What *is* surprising, on the other hand, is the immense horizontal distances that have to be travelled underground. Before I had been down a mine I had vaguely imagined the miner stepping out of the cage and getting to work on a ledge of coal a few yards away. I had not realised that before he even gets to his work he may have to creep through passages as long as from London Bridge to Oxford Circus. In the beginning, of course, a mine shaft is sunk somewhere near a seam of coal. But as that seam is worked out and fresh seams are followed up, the workings get further and further from the pit bottom. If it is a mile from the pit bottom to the coal face, that is probably an average distance; three miles is a fairly normal one; there are even said to be a few mines where it is as much as five miles. But these distances bear no relation to distances above ground. For in all that mile or three miles as it may be, there is hardly anywhere outside the main road, and not many places even there, where a man can stand upright.

You do not notice the effect of this till you have gone a few hundred yards. You start off, stooping slightly, down the dim-lit gallery, eight or ten feet wide and about five high, with the walls built up with slabs of shale, like the stone walls in Derbyshire. Every yard or two there are wooden props holding up the beams and girders; some of the girders have buckled into fantastic curves under which you have to duck. Usually it is bad going underfoot – thick dust or jagged chunks of shale, and in some mines where there is water it is as mucky as a farmyard. Also there is the track for the coal tubs, like a miniature railway track with sleepers a foot or two apart, which is tiresome to walk on. Everything is grey with shale dust; there is a dusty fiery smell which seems to be the same in all mines. You see mysterious machines of which you never learn the purpose, and bundles of tools slung together on wires, and sometimes mice darting away from the beam of the lamps. They are surprisingly common, especially in mines where there are or have been horses. It would be interesting to know how they got there in the first place; possibly by falling down the shaft – for they say a mouse can fall any distance uninjured, owing to its surface area being so large relative to its weight. You press yourself against the wall to make way for lines of tubs jolting slowly towards the shaft, drawn by an endless steel cable operated from the surface. You creep through sacking curtains and thick wooden doors which, when they are opened, let out fierce blasts of air. These doors are an important part of the ventilation system. The exhausted air is sucked out of one shaft by means of fans, and the fresh air enters the other of its own accord. But if left to itself the air will take the shortest way round, leaving the deeper workings unventilated; so all short cuts have to be partitioned off.

At the start to walk stooping is rather a joke, but it is a joke that soon wears off. I am handicapped by being exceptionally tall, but when the roof falls to four feet or less it is a tough job for anybody except a dwarf or a child. You have not only got to bend double, you have also got to keep your head up all the while so as to see the beams and girders and dodge them when they come. You have, therefore, a constant crick in the neck, but this is nothing to the pain in your knees and thighs. After half a mile it becomes (I am not exaggerating) an unbearable agony. You begin to wonder whether you will ever get to the end – still more, how on earth you are going to get back. Your pace grows slower and slower. You come to a stretch of a couple of hundred yards where it is all exceptionally low and you have to work yourself along in a squatting position. Then suddenly the roof opens out to a mysterious height – scene of an old fall of rock, probably – and for twenty whole yards you can stand upright. The relief is overwhelming. But after this there is another low stretch of a hundred yards and then a succession of beams which you have to crawl under. You go down on all fours; even this is a relief after the squatting business. But when you come to the end of the beams and try to get up again, you find that your knees have temporarily struck work and refuse to lift you. You call a halt, ignominiously, and say that you would like to rest for a minute or two. Your guide (a miner) is sympathetic. He knows that your muscles are not the same as his. 'Only another four hundred yards,' he says encouragingly; you feel that he might as well say another four hundred miles. But finally you do somehow creep as far as the coal face. You have gone a mile and taken the best part of an hour; a miner would do it in not much more than twenty minutes. Having got there, you have to sprawl in the coal dust and get your strength back for several minutes before you can even watch the work in progress with any kind of intelligence.

Coming back is worse than going, not only because you are already tired out but because the journey back to the shaft is probably slightly up hill. You get through the low places at the speed of a tortoise, and you have no shame now about calling a halt when your knees give way. Even the lamp you are carrying becomes a nuisance and probably when you stumble you drop it; whereupon, if it is a Davy lamp, it goes out. Ducking the beams becomes more and more of an effort, and sometimes you forget to duck. You try walking head down as the miners do, and then you bang your backbone. Even the miners bang their backbones fairly often. This is the reason why in very hot mines, where it is necessary to go about half naked, most of the miners have what they call 'buttons down the back' – that is, a permanent scab on each vertebra. When the track is down hill the miners sometimes fit their clogs, which are hollow underneath, onto the trolley rails and slide down. In mines where the 'travelling' is very bad all the miners carry sticks about two and a half feet long, hollowed out below the handle. In normal places you keep your hand on top of the stick and in the low places you slide your hand down into the hollow. These sticks are a great help, and the wooden crash-helmets – a comparatively recent invention – are a godsend. They look like a French or Italian steel helmet, but they are made of some kind of pith and very light, and so strong that you can take a violent blow on the head without feeling it. When finally you get back to the surface you have been perhaps three hours underground and travelled two miles, and you are more exhausted than you would be by a twenty-five-mile walk above ground. For a week afterwards your thighs are so stiff that coming downstairs is quite a difficult feat; you have to work your way down in a peculiar sidelong manner, without bending the knees. Your miner friends notice the stiffness of your walk and chaff you about it. ('How'd ta like to work down pit, eh?' etc.) Yet even a miner who has been long away from work – from illness, for instance – when he comes back to the pit, suffers badly for the first few days.

It may seem that I am exaggerating, though no one who has been down an old-fashioned pit (most of the pits in England are old-fashioned) and actually gone as far as the coal face, is likely to say so. But what I want to emphasise is this. Here is this frightful business of crawling to and fro, which to any normal person is a hard day's work in itself; and it is not part of the miner's work at all, it is merely an extra, like the City man's daily ride in the Tube. The miner does that journey to and fro, and sandwiched in between there are seven and a half hours of savage work. I have never travelled much more than a mile to the coal face; but often it is three miles, in which case I and most people other than coal-miners would never get there at all. This is the kind of point that one is always liable to miss. When you think of a coal-mine you think of depth, heat, darkness, blackened figures hacking at walls of coal; you don't think, necessarily, of those miles of creeping to and fro. There is the question of time, also. A miner's working shift of seven and a half hours does not sound very long, but one has got to add on to it at least an hour a day for 'travelling', more often two hours and sometimes three. Of course, the 'travelling' is not technically work and the miner is not paid for it; but it is as like work as makes no difference. It is easy to say that miners don't mind all this. Certainly, it is not the same for them as it would be for you or me. They have done it since childhood, they have the right muscles hardened, and they can move to and fro underground with a startling and rather horrible agility. A miner puts his head down and *runs,* with a long swinging stride, through places where I can only stagger. At the workings you see them on all fours, skipping round the pit props almost like dogs. But it is quite a mistake to think that they enjoy it. I have talked about this to scores of miners and they all admit that the 'travelling' is hard work; in any case when you hear them discussing a pit among themselves the 'travelling' is always one of the things they discuss. It is said that a shift always returns from work faster than it goes; nevertheless the miners all say that it is the coming away, after a hard day's work, that is especially irksome. It is part of their work and they are equal to it, but certainly it is an effort. It is comparable, perhaps, to climbing a smallish mountain before and after your day's work.

When you have been down two or three pits you begin to get some grasp of the processes that are going on underground. (I ought to say, by the way, that I know nothing whatever about the technical side of mining: I am merely describing what I have seen.) Coal lies in thin seams between enormous layers of rock, so that essentially the process of getting it out is like scooping the central layer from a Neapolitan ice. In the old days the miners used to cut straight into the coal with pick and crowbar – a very slow job because coal, when lying in its virgin state, is almost as hard as rock. Nowadays the preliminary work is done by an electrically-driven coal-cutter, which in principle is an immensely tough and powerful band-saw, running horizontally instead of vertically, with teeth a couple of inches long and half an inch or an inch thick. It can move backwards or forwards on its own power, and the men operating it can rotate it this way and that. Incidentally it makes one of the most awful noises I have ever heard, and sends forth clouds of coal dust which make it impossible to see more than two or three feet and almost impossible to breath. The machine travels along the coal face cutting into the base of the coal and undermining it to the depth of five feet or five feet and a half; after this it is comparatively easy to extract the coal to the depth to which it has been undermined. Where it is 'difficult getting', however, it has also to be loosened with explosives. A man with an electric drill, like a rather smaller version of the drills used in street-mending, bores holes at intervals in the coal, inserts blasting powder, plugs it with clay, goes round the corner if there is one handy (he is supposed to retire to twenty-five yards distance) and touches off the charge with an electric current. This is not intended to bring the coal out, only to loosen it. Occasionally, of course, the charge is too powerful, and then it not only brings the coal out but brings the roof down as well.

After the blasting has been done the 'fillers' can tumble the coal out, break it up and shovel it onto the conveyor belt. It comes out at first in monstrous boulders which may weigh anything up to twenty tons. The conveyor belt shoots it onto tubs, and the tubs are shoved into the main road and hitched on to an endlessly revolving steel cable which drags them to the cage. Then they are hoisted, and at the surface the coal is sorted by being run over screens, and if necessary is washed as well. As far as possible the 'dirt' – the shale, that is – is used for making the roads below. All that cannot be used is sent to the surface and dumped; hence the monstrous 'dirt-heaps', like hideous grey mountains, which are the characteristic scenery of the coal areas. When the coal has been extracted to the depth to which the machine has cut, the coal face has advanced by five feet. Fresh props are put in to hold up the newly exposed roof, and during the next shift the conveyor belt is taken to pieces, moved five feet forward and re-assembled. As far as possible the three operations of cutting, blasting and extraction are done in three separate shifts, the cutting in the afternoon, the blasting at night (there is a law, not always kept, that forbids its being done when there are other men working near by), and the 'filling' in the morning shift, which lasts from six in the morning until half past one.

Even when you watch the process of coal-extraction you probably only watch it for a short time, and it is not until you begin making a few calculations that you realise what a stupendous task the 'fillers' are performing. Normally each man has to clear a space four or five yards wide. The cutter has undermined the coal to the depth of five feet, so that if the seam of coal is three or four feet high, each man has to cut out, break up and load onto the belt something between seven and twelve cubic yards of coal. This is to say, taking a cubic yard as weighing twenty-seven hundredweight, that each man is shifting coal at a speed approaching two tons an hour. I have just enough experience of pick and shovel work to be able to grasp what this means. When I am digging trenches in my garden, if I shift two tons of earth during the afternoon, I feel that I have earned my tea. But earth is tractable stuff compared with coal, and I don't have to work kneeling down, a thousand feet underground, in suffocating heat and swallowing coal dust with every breath I take; nor do I have to walk a mile bent double before I begin. The miner's job would be as much beyond my power as it would be to perform on the flying trapeze or to win the Grand National. I am not a manual labourer and please God I never shall be one, but there are some kinds of manual work that I could do if I had to. At a pinch I could be a tolerable road-sweeper or an inefficient gardener or even a tenth-rate farm hand. But by no conceivable amount of effort or training could I become a coal-miner; the work would kill me in a few weeks.

Watching coal-miners at work, you realise momentarily what different universes different people inhabit. Down there where coal is dug it is a sort of world apart which one can quite easily go through life without ever hearing about. Probably a majority of people would even prefer not to hear about it. Yet it is the absolutely necessary counterpart of our world above. Practically everything we do, from eating an ice to crossing the Atlantic, and from baking a loaf to writing a novel, involves the use of coal, directly or indirectly. For all the arts of peace coal is needed; if war breaks out it is needed all the more. In time of revolution the miner must go on working or the revolution must stop, for revolution as much as reaction needs coal. Whatever may be happening on the surface, the hacking and shovelling have got to continue without a pause, or at any rate without pausing for more than a few weeks at the most. In order that Hitler may march the goose-step, that the Pope may denounce Bolshevism, that the cricket crowds may assemble at Lord's, that the Nancy poets may scratch one another's backs, coal has got to be forthcoming. But on the whole we are not aware of it; we all know that we 'must have coal', but we seldom or never remember what coal-getting involves. Here am I, sitting writing in front of my comfortable coal fire. It is April but I still need a fire. Once a fortnight the coal cart drives up to the door and men in leather jerkins carry the coal indoors in stout sacks smelling of tar and shoot it clanking into the coal-hole under the stairs. It is only very rarely, when I make a definite mental effort, that I connect this coal with that far-off labour in the mines. It is just 'coal' – something that I have got to have; black stuff that arrives mysteriously from nowhere in particular, like manna except that you have to pay for it. You could quite easily drive a car right across the north of England and never once remember that hundreds of feet below the road you are on the miners are hacking at the coal. Yet in a sense it is the miners who are driving your car forward. Their lamp-lit world down there is as necessary to the daylight world above as the root is to the flower.

It is not long since conditions in the mines were worse than they are now. There are still living a few very old women who in their youth have worked underground, with a harness round their waists and a chain that passed between their legs, crawling on all fours and dragging tubs of coal. They used to go on doing this even when they were pregnant. And even now, if coal could not be produced without pregnant women dragging it to and fro, I fancy we should let them do it rather than deprive ourselves of coal. But most of the time, of course, we should prefer to forget that they were doing it. It is so with all types of manual work; it keeps us alive, and we are oblivious of its existence. More than anyone else, perhaps, the miner can stand as the type of the manual worker, not only because his work is so exaggeratedly awful, but also because it is so vitally necessary and yet so remote from our experience, so invisible, as it were, that we are capable of forgetting it as we forget the blood in our veins. In a way it is even humiliating to watch coal-miners working. It raises in you a momentary doubt about your own status as an 'intellectual' and a superior person generally. For it is brought home to you, at least while you are watching, that it is only because miners sweat their guts out that superior persons can remain superior. You and I and the editor of the *Times Lit. Supp.*, and the Nancy poets and the Archbishop of Canterbury and Comrade X, author of *Marxism for Infants* – all of us *really* owe the comparative decency of our lives to poor drudges underground, blackened to the eyes, with their throats full of coal dust, driving their shovels forward with arms and belly muscles of steel.

III

When the miner comes up from the pit his face is so pale that it is noticeable even through the mask of coal dust. This is due to the foul air that he has been breathing, and will wear off presently. To a Southerner, new to the mining districts, the spectacle of a shift of several hundred miners streaming out of the pit is strange and slightly sinister. Their exhausted faces, with the grime clinging in all the hollows, have a fierce, wild look. At other times, when their faces are clean, there is not much to distinguish them from the rest of the population. They have a very upright square-shouldered walk, a reaction from the constant bending underground, but most of them are shortish men and their thick ill-fitting clothes hide the splendour of their bodies. The most definitely distinctive thing about them is the blue scars on their noses. Every miner has blue scars on his nose and forehead, and will carry them to his death. The coal dust of which the air underground is full enters every cut, and then the skin grows over it and forms a blue stain like tattooing, which in fact it is. Some of the older men have their foreheads veined like Roquefort cheeses from this cause.

As soon as the miner comes above ground he gargles a little water to get the worst of the coal dust out of his throat and nostrils, and then goes home and either washes or does not wash according to his temperament. From what I have seen I should say that a majority of miners prefer to eat their meal first and wash afterwards, as I should do in their circumstances. It is the normal thing to see a miner sitting down to his tea with a Christy-minstrel face, completely black except for very red lips which become clean by eating. After his meal he takes a largish basin of water and washes very methodically, first his hands, then his chest, neck and armpits, then his forearms, then his face and scalp (it is on the scalp that the grime clings thickest), and then his wife takes the flannel and washes his back. He has only washed the top half of his body and probably his navel is still a nest of coal dust, but even so it takes some skill to get passably clean in a single basin of water. For my own part I found I needed two complete baths after going down a coal-mine. Getting the dirt out of one's eyelids is a ten minutes' job in itself.

At some of the larger and better appointed collieries there are pithead baths. This is an enormous advantage, for not only can the miner wash himself all over every day, in comfort and even luxury, but at the baths he has two lockers where he can keep his pit clothes separate from his day clothes, so that within twenty minutes of emerging as black as a Negro he can be riding off to a football match dressed up to the nines. But it is only comparatively few mines that have baths, partly because a seam of coal does not last for ever, so that it is not necessarily worth building a bath every time a shaft is sunk. I cannot get hold of exact figures, but it seems likely that rather less than one miner in three has access to a pithead bath. Probably a large majority of miners are completely black from the waist down for at least six days a week. It is almost impossible for them to wash all over in their own homes. Every drop of water has got to be heated up, and in a tiny living-room which contains, apart from the kitchen range and a quantity of furniture, a wife, some children and probably a dog, there is simply not room to have a proper bath. Even with a basin one is bound to splash the furniture. Middle-class people are fond of saying that the miners would not wash themselves properly even if they could, but this is nonsense, as is shown by the fact that where pithead baths exist practically all the men use them. Only among the very old men does the belief still linger that washing one's legs 'causes lumbago'. Moreover the pithead baths, where they exist, are paid for wholly or partly by the miners themselves, out of the Miners' Welfare Fund. Sometimes the colliery company subscribes, sometimes the Fund bears the whole cost. But doubtless even at this late date the old ladies in Brighton boarding-houses are saying that 'if you give those miners baths they only use them to keep coal in'.

As a matter of fact it is surprising that miners wash as regularly as they do, seeing how little time they have between work and sleep. It is a great mistake to think of a miner's working day as being only seven and a half hours. Seven and a half hours is the time spent actually on the job, but, as I have already explained, one has got to add onto this time taken up in 'travelling', which is seldom less than an hour and may often be three hours. In addition most miners have to spend a considerable time in getting to and from the pit. Throughout the industrial districts there is acute shortage of houses, and it is only in the small mining villages, where the village is grouped round the pit, that the men can be certain of living near their work. In the larger mining towns where I have stayed, nearly everyone went to work by bus; half a crown a week seemed to be the normal amount to spend on fares. One miner I stayed with was working on the morning shift, which was from six in the morning till half-past one. He had to be out of bed at a quarter to four and got back somewhere after three in the afternoon. In another house where I stayed a boy of fifteen was working on the night shift. He left for work at nine at night and got back at eight in the morning, had his breakfast and then promptly went to bed and slept till six in the evening; so that his leisure time amounted to about four hours a day – actually a good deal less, if you take off the time for washing, eating and dressing.

The adjustments a miner's family have to make when he is changed from one shift to another must be tiresome in the extreme. If he is on the night shift he gets home in time for breakfast, on the morning shift he gets home in the middle of the afternoon, and on the afternoon shift he gets home in the middle of the night; and in each case, of course, he wants his principal meal of the day as soon as he returns. I notice that the Rev W. R. Inge, in his book *England*, accuses the miners of gluttony. From my own observation I should say that they eat astonishingly little. Most of the miners I stayed with ate slightly less than I did. Many of them declare that they cannot do their day's work if they have had a heavy meal beforehand, and the food they take with them is only a snack, usually bread-and-dripping and cold tea. They carry it in a flat tin called a snap-can which they strap to their belts. When a miner gets back late at night his wife waits up for him, but when he is on the morning shift it seems to be the custom for him to get his breakfast for himself. Apparently the old superstition that it is bad luck to see a woman before going to work on the morning shift is not quite extinct. In the old days, it is said, a miner who happened to meet a woman in the early morning would often turn back and do no work that day.

Before I had been in the coal areas I shared the widespread illusion that miners are comparatively well paid. One hears it loosely stated that a miner is paid ten or eleven shillings a shift, and one does a small multiplication sum and concludes that every miner is earning round about £3 a week or £150 a year. But the statement that a miner receives ten or eleven shillings a shift is very misleading. To begin with, it is only the actual coal 'getter' who is paid at this rate; a 'dataller', for instance, who attends to the roofing, is paid at a lower rate, usually eight or nine shillings a shift. Again, when the coal 'getter' is paid piecework, so much per ton extracted, as is the case in many mines, he is dependent on the quality of the coal; a breakdown in the machinery or a 'fault' – that is, a streak of rock running through the coal seam – may rob him of his earnings for a day or two at a time. But in any case one ought not to think of the miner as working six days a week, fifty-two weeks a year. Almost certainly there will be a number of days when he is 'laid off'. The average earning per shift worked for every mine-worker, of all ages and both sexes, in Great Britain in 1934, was 9*s.* 1¾*d.*[1] If everyone were in work all the time, this would mean that the mine-worker was earning a little over £142 a year, or nearly £2 15*s.* a week. His real income, however, is far lower than this, for the 9*s.* 1¾*d.* is merely an average calculation on shifts actually worked and takes no account of blank days.

I have before me five pay-checks belonging to a Yorkshire miner, for five weeks (not consecutive) at the beginning of 1936. Averaging them up, the gross weekly wage they represent is £2 15*s.* 2*d.*; this is an average of nearly 9*s.*2½*d.* a shift. But these pay-checks are for the winter, when nearly all mines are running full time. As spring advances the coal trade slacks off and more and more men are 'temporarily stopped', while others still technically in work are laid off for a day or two in every week. It is obvious therefore that £150 or even £142 is an immense over-estimate for the mine-worker's yearly income. As a matter of fact, for the year 1934 the average gross earnings of all miners throughout Great Britain was

[1] From the *Colliery Year Book and Coal Trades Directory* for 1935.

only £115 11*s*. 6*d*. It varied considerably from district to district, rising as high as £133 2*s*. 8*d*. in Scotland, while in Durham it was a little under £105 or barely more than £2 a week. I take these figures from *The Coal Scuttle*, by Mr Joseph Jones, Mayor of Barnsley, Yorkshire. Mr Jones adds:

> These figures cover the earnings of youths as well as adults and of the higher as well as the lower-paid grades . . . any particularly high earning would be included in these figures, as would the earnings of certain officials and other higher-paid men as well as the higher amounts paid for overtime work . . .
>
> *The figures, being averages, fail . . . to reveal the position of thousands of adult workers whose earnings were substantially below the average and who received only* 30*s. to* 40*s. or less per week.*

Mr Jones's italics. But please notice that even these wretched earnings are *gross* earnings. On top of this there are all kinds of stoppages which are deducted from the miner's wages every week. Here is a list of weekly stoppages which was given me as typical in one Lancashire district:

	s.	*d.*
Insurance (unemployment and health)	1	5
Hire of lamp		6
For sharpening tools		6
Check-weighman		9
Infirmary		2
Hospital		1
Benevolent Fund		6
Union fees		6
Total	4	5

Some of these stoppages, such as the Benevolent Fund and the union fees, are, so to speak, the miner's own responsibility, others are imposed by the colliery company. They are not the same in all districts. For instance, the iniquitous swindle of making the miner pay for the hire of his lamp (at sixpence a week he buys the lamp several times over in a single year) does not obtain everywhere. But the stoppages always seem to total up to about the same amount. On the Yorkshire miner's five pay-checks, the average gross earning per week is £2 15*s*. 2*d*.; the average net earning, after the stoppages have come off, is only £2 10*s.* 6½*d.* – a reduction of 4*s.* 7½*d.* a week. But the pay-check, naturally, only mentions stoppages which are imposed by or paid through the colliery company; one has got to add the union fees, bringing the total reduction up to something over four shillings. Probably it is safe to say that stoppages of one kind and another cut four shillings or thereabouts from *every* adult miner's weekly wage. So that the £115 11*s.* 6*d.* which was the mine-worker's average earning throughout Great Britain in 1934 should really be something nearer £105. As against this, most miners receive allowances in kind, being able to purchase coal for their own use at a reduced rate, usually eight or nine shillings a ton. But according to Mr Jones, quoted above, 'the average value of all allowances in kind for the country as a whole is only fourpence a day'. And this fourpence a day is offset, in many cases, by the amount the miner has to spend on fares in getting to and from the pit. So, taking the industry as a whole, the sum the miner can actually bring home and call his own does not average more, perhaps slightly less, than two pounds a week.

Meanwhile, how much coal is the average miner producing?

The tonnage of coal raised yearly per person employed in mining rises steadily though rather slowly. In 1914 every mine-worker produced, on an average, 253 tons of coal; in 1934 he produced 280 tons.[1] This of course is an average figure for mine-workers of all kinds; those actually working at the coal face extract an enormously greater amount – in many cases, probably, well over a thousand tons each. But taking 280 tons as a representative figure, it is worth noticing what a vast achievement this is. One gets the best idea of it by comparing a miner's life work with somebody else's. If I live to be sixty I shall probably have produced thirty novels, or enough to fill two medium-sized library shelves. In the same period the average miner produces 8,400 tons of coal; enough coal to pave Trafalgar Square nearly two feet deep or to supply seven large families with fuel for over a hundred years.

Of the five pay-checks I mentioned above, no less than three are rubber-stamped with the words 'death stoppage'. When a miner is killed

[1] *The Coal Scuttle.* The *Colliery Year Book and Coal Trades Directory* gives a slightly higher figure.

at work it is usual for the other miners to make up a subscription, generally of a shilling each, for his widow, and this is collected by the colliery company and automatically deducted from their wages. The significant detail here is the *rubber stamp*. The rate of accidents among miners is so high, compared with that in other trades, that casualties are taken for granted almost as they would be in a minor war. Every year one miner in about nine hundred is killed and one in about six is injured; most of these injuries, of course, are petty ones, but a fair number amount to total disablement. This means that if a miner's working life is forty years the chances are nearly seven to one against his escaping injury and not much more than twenty to one against his being killed outright. No other trade approaches this in dangerousness; the next most dangerous is the shipping trade, one sailor in a little under 1,300 being killed every year. The figures I have given apply, of course, to mine-workers as a whole; for those actually working underground the proportion of injuries would be very much higher. Every miner of long standing that I have talked to had either been in a fairly serious accident himself or had seen some of his mates killed, and in every mining family they tell you tales of fathers, brothers or uncles killed at work. ('And he fell seven hundred feet, and they wouldn't never have collected t'pieces only he were wearing a new suit of oilskins,' etc. etc. etc.) Some of these tales are appalling in the extreme. One miner, for instance, described to me how a mate of his, a 'dataller', was buried by a fall of rock. They rushed to him and managed to uncover his head and shoulders so that he could breathe, and he was alive and spoke to them. Then they saw that the roof was coming down again and had to run to save themselves; the 'dataller' was buried a second time. Once again they rushed to him and got his head and shoulders free, and again he was alive and spoke to them. Then the roof came down a third time, and this time they could not uncover him for several hours, after which, of course, he was dead. But the miner who told me the story (he had been buried himself on one occasion, but he was lucky enough to have his head jammed between his legs so that there was a small space in which he could breathe) did not think it was a particularly appalling one. Its significance, for him, was that the 'dataller' had known perfectly well that the place where he was working was unsafe, and had gone there in daily expectation of an accident. 'And it worked on his mind to that extent that he got to kissing his wife before he went to work. And she told me afterwards that it were over twenty year since he'd kissed her.'

The most obviously understandable cause of accidents is explosions of gas, which is always more or less present in the atmosphere of the pit. There is a special lamp which is used to test the air for gas, and when it is present in at all large quantities it can be detected by the flame of an ordinary Davy lamp burning blue. If the wick can be turned up to its full extent and the flame is still blue, the proportion of gas is dangerously high; it is, nevertheless, difficult to detect, because it does not distribute itself evenly throughout the atmosphere but hangs about in cracks and crevices. Before starting work a miner often tests for gas by poking his lamp into all the corners. The gas may be touched off by a spark during blasting operations, or by a pick striking a spark from a stone, or by a defective lamp, or by 'gob fires' – spontaneously generated fires which smoulder in the coal dust and are very hard to put out. The great mining disasters which happen from time to time, in which several hundred men are killed, are usually caused by explosions; hence one tends to think of explosions as the chief danger of mining. Actually, the great majority of accidents are due to the normal everyday dangers of the pit; in particular, to falls of roof. There are, for instance, 'potholes' – circular holes from which a lump of stone big enough to kill a man shoots out with the promptitude of a bullet. With, so far as I can remember, only one exception, all the miners I have talked to declared that the new machinery, and 'speeding up' generally, have made the work more dangerous. This may be partly due to conservatism, but they can give plenty of reasons. To begin with, the speed at which the coal is now extracted means that for hours at a time a dangerously large stretch of roof remains unpropped. Then there is the vibration, which tends to shake everything loose, and the noise, which makes it harder to detect signs of danger. One must remember that a miner's safety underground depends largely on his own care and skill. An experienced miner claims to know by a sort of instinct when the roof is unsafe; the way he puts it is that he 'can feel the weight on him'. He can, for instance, hear the faint creaking of the props. The reason why wooden props are still generally preferred to iron girders is that a wooden prop which is about to collapse gives warning by creaking, whereas a girder flies out unexpectedly. The devastating noise of the machines makes it impossible to hear anything else, and thus the danger is increased.

When a miner is hurt it is of course impossible to attend to him immediately. He lies crushed under several hundredweight of stone in some dreadful cranny underground, and even after he has been extricated it is necessary to drag his body a mile or more, perhaps, through galleries where nobody can stand upright. Usually when you talk to a man who has been injured you find that it was a couple of hours or so before they got him to the surface. Sometimes, of course, there are accidents to the cage. The cage is shooting several hundred yards up or down at the speed of an express train, and it is operated by somebody on the surface who cannot see what is happening. He has very delicate indicators to tell him how far the cage has got, but it is possible for him to make a mistake, and there have been cases of the cage crashing into the pit-bottom at its very maximum speed. This seems to me a dreadful way to die. For as that tiny steel box whizzes through the blackness there must come a moment when the ten men who are locked inside it *know* that something has gone wrong; and the remaining seconds before they are smashed to pieces hardly bear thinking about. A miner told me he was once in a cage in which something went wrong. It did not slow up when it should have done, and they thought the cable must have snapped. As it happened they got to the bottom safely, but when he stepped out he found that he had broken a tooth; he had been clenching his teeth so hard in expectation of that frightful crash.

Apart from accidents miners seem to be healthy, as obviously they have got to be, considering the muscular efforts demanded of them. They are liable to rheumatism and a man with defective lungs does not last long in that dust-impregnated air, but the most characteristic industrial disease is nystagmus. This is a disease of the eyes which makes the eyeballs oscillate in a strange manner when they come near a light. It is due presumably to working in half-darkness, and sometimes results in total blindness. Miners who are disabled in this way or any other way are compensated by the colliery company, sometimes with a lump sum, sometimes with a weekly pension. This pension never amounts to more than twenty-nine shillings a week; if it falls below fifteen shillings the disabled man can also get something from the dole or the PAC. If I were a disabled miner I should very much prefer the lump sum, for then at any rate I should know that I had got my money. Disability pensions are not guaranteed by any centralised fund, so that if the colliery company goes bankrupt that is the end of the disabled miner's pension, though he does figure among the other creditors.

In Wigan I stayed for a while with a miner who was suffering from nystagmus. He could see across the room but not much further. He had been drawing compensation of twenty-nine shillings a week for the past nine months, but the colliery company were now talking of putting him on 'partial compensation' of fourteen shillings a week. It all depended on whether the doctor passed him as fit for light work 'on top'. Even if the doctor did pass him there would, needless to say, be no light work available, but he could draw the dole and the company would have saved itself fifteen shillings a week. Watching this man go to the colliery to draw his compensation, I was struck by the profound differences that are still made by *status.* Here was a man who had been half blinded in one of the most useful of all jobs and was drawing a pension to which he had a perfect right, if anybody has a right to anything. Yet he could not, so to speak, *demand* this pension – he could not, for instance, draw it when and how he wanted it. He had to go to the colliery once a week at a time named by the company, and when he got there he was kept waiting about for hours in the cold wind. For all I know he was also expected to touch his cap and show gratitude to whomever paid him; at any rate he had to waste an afternoon and spend sixpence in bus fares. It is very different for a member of the bourgeoisie, even such a down-at-heel member as I am. Even when I am on the verge of starvation I have certain rights attaching to my bourgeois status. I do not earn much more than a miner earns, but I do at least get it paid into my bank in a gentlemanly manner and can draw it out when I choose. And even when my account is exhausted the bank people are still passably polite.

This business of petty inconvenience and indignity, of being kept waiting about, of having to do everything at other people's convenience, is inherent in working-class life. A thousand influences constantly press a working man down into a *passive* rôle. He does not act, he is acted upon. He feels himself the slave of mysterious authority and has a firm conviction that 'they' will never allow him to do this, that and the other. Once when

I was hop-picking I asked the sweated pickers (they earn something under sixpence an hour) why they did not form a union. I was told immediately that 'they' would never allow it. Who were 'they'? I asked. Nobody seemed to know; but evidently 'they' were omnipotent.

A person of bourgeois origin goes through life with some expectation of getting what he wants, within reasonable limits. Hence the fact that in times of stress 'educated' people tend to come to the front; they are no more gifted than the others and their 'education' is generally quite useless in itself, but they are accustomed to a certain amount of deference and consequently have the cheek necessary to a commander. That they *will* come to the front seems to be taken for granted, always and everywhere. In Lissagaray's *History of the Commune* there is an interesting passage describing the shootings that took place after the Commune had been suppressed. The authorities were shooting the ringleaders, and as they did not know who the ringleaders were, they were picking them out on the principle that those of better class would be the ringleaders. An officer walked down a line of prisoners, picking out likely-looking types. One man was shot because he was wearing a watch, another because he 'had an intelligent face'. I should not like to be shot for having an intelligent face, but I do agree that in almost any revolt the leaders would tend to be people who could pronounce their aitches.

IV

As you walk through the industrial towns you lose yourself in labyrinths of little brick houses blackened by smoke, festering in planless chaos round miry alleys and little cindered yards where there are stinking dustbins and lines of grimy washing and half-ruinous wcs. The interiors of these houses are always very much the same, though the number of rooms varies between two and five. All have an almost exactly similar living-room, ten or fifteen feet square, with an open kitchen range; in the larger ones there is a scullery as well, in the smaller ones the sink and copper are in the living-room. At the back there is the yard, or part of a yard shared by a number of houses, just big enough for the dustbin and the wc. Not a single one has hot water laid on. You might walk, I suppose, through literally hundreds of miles of streets inhabited by miners, every one of whom, when he is in work, gets black from head to foot every day, without ever passing a house in which one could have a bath. It would have been very simple to install a hot-water system working from the kitchen range, but the builder saved perhaps ten pounds on each house by not doing so, and at the time when these houses were built no one imagined that miners wanted baths.

For it is to be noted that the majority of these houses are old, fifty or sixty years old at least, and great numbers of them are by any ordinary standard not fit for human habitation. They go on being tenanted simply because there are no others to be had. And that is the central fact about housing in the industrial areas: not that the houses are poky and ugly, and insanitary and comfortless, or that they are distributed in incredibly filthy slums round belching foundries and stinking canals and slag-heaps that deluge them with sulphurous smoke – though all this is perfectly true – but simply that there are not enough houses to go round.

'Housing shortage' is a phrase that has been bandied about pretty freely since the war, but it means very little to anyone with an income of more than £10 a week, or even £5 a week for that matter. Where rents are high the difficulty is not to find houses but to find tenants. Walk down any street in Mayfair and you will see 'To Let' boards in half the windows. But in the industrial areas the mere difficulty of getting hold of a house is one of the worst aggravations of poverty. It means that people will put up with anything – any hole and corner slum, any misery of bugs and rotting floors and cracking walls, any extortion of skinflint landlords and blackmailing agents – simply to get a roof over their heads. I have been into appalling houses, houses in which I would not live a week if you paid me, and found that the tenants had been there twenty and thirty years and only hoped they might have the luck to die there. In general these conditions are taken as a matter of course, though not always. Some people hardly seem to realise that such things as decent houses exist and look on bugs and leaking roofs as acts of God; others rail bitterly against their landlords; but all cling desperately to their houses lest worse should befall. So long as the housing shortage continues the local authorities cannot do much to make existing houses more liveable. They can 'condemn' a house, but they cannot order it to be pulled down till the tenant has another house to go to; and so the condemned houses remain standing and are all the worse for being condemned, because naturally the landlord will not spend more than he can help on a house which is going to be demolished sooner or later. In a town like Wigan, for instance, there are over two thousand houses standing which have been condemned for years, and whole sections of the town would be condemned *en bloc* if there were any hope of other houses being built to replace them. Towns like Leeds and Sheffield have scores of thousands of 'back to back' houses which are all of a condemned type but will remain standing for decades.

I have inspected great numbers of houses in various mining towns and villages and made notes on their essential points. I think I can best give an idea of what conditions are like by transcribing a few extracts from my notebook, taken more or less at random. They are only brief notes and they will need certain explanations which I will give afterwards. Here are a few from Wigan:

1. House in Wallgate quarter. Blind back type. One up, one down. Living-room measures 12 ft. by 10 ft., room upstairs the same. Alcove under stairs measuring 5 ft. by 5 ft. and serving as larder, scullery and coal hole. Windows will open. Distance to lavatory 50 yards. Rent 4*s.* 9*d.*, rates 2*s.* 6*d.*, total 7*s.* 3*d.*

2. Another near by. Measurements as above, but no alcove under stairs, merely a recess two feet deep containing the sink – no room for larder, etc. Rent 3*s.* 2*d.*, rates 2*s.*, total 5*s.* 2*d.*

3. Another as above but with no alcove at all, merely sink in living-room just inside front door. Rent 3*s.* 9*d.*, rates 3*s.*, total 6*s.* 9*d.*

4. House in Scholes quarter. Condemned house. One up, one down. Rooms 15 ft. by 15 ft. Sink and copper in living-room, coal hole under stairs. Floor subsiding. No windows will open. House decently dry. Landlord good. Rent 3*s.* 8*d.*, rates 2*s.* 6*d.*, total 6*s.* 2*d.*

5. Another near by. Two up, two down and coal hole. Walls falling absolutely to pieces. Water comes into upstairs rooms in quantities. Floor lopsided. Downstairs windows will not open. Landlord bad. Rent 6*s.*, rates 3*s.* 6*d.*, total 9*s.* 6*d.*

6. House in Greenough's Row. One up, two down. Living-room 13 ft. by 8 ft. Walls coming apart and water comes in. Back windows will not open, front one will. Ten in family with eight children very near together in age. Corporation are trying to evict them for overcrowding but cannot find another house to send them to. Landlord bad. Rent 4*s.*, rates 2*s.* 3*d.*, total 6*s.* 3*d.*

So much for Wigan. I have pages more of the same type. Here is one from Sheffield – a typical specimen of Sheffield's several score thousand 'back to back' houses:

House in Thomas Street. Back to back, two up, one down (i.e. a three-storey house with one room on each storey). Cellar below. Living-room 14 ft. by 10 ft., and rooms above corresponding. Sink in living-room. Top floor has no door but gives on open stairs. Walls in living-room slightly damp, walls in top rooms coming to pieces and oozing damp on all sides. House is so dark that light has to be kept burning all day. Electricity estimated at 6*d.* a day (probably an exaggeration). Six in family, parents and four children. Husband (on PAC) is tuberculous. One child in hospital, the others appear healthy. Tenants have been seven years in this house. Would move, but no other house available. Rent 6*s.* 6*d.*, rates included.

Here are one or two from Barnsley:

1. House in Wortley Street. Two up, one down. Living-room 12 ft. by 10 ft. Sink and copper in living-room, coal hole under stairs. Sink worn almost flat and constantly overflowing. Walls not too sound. Penny in slot, gas-light. House very dark and gas-light estimated at 4*d.* a day. Upstairs rooms are really one large room partitioned into two. Walls very bad – wall of back room cracked right through. Window-frames coming to pieces and have to be stuffed with wood. Rain comes through in several places. Sewer runs under house and stinks in summer but Corporation 'says they can't do nowt'. Six people in house, two adults and four children, the eldest aged fifteen. Youngest but one attending hospital – tuberculosis suspected. House infested by bugs. Rent 5*s.* 3*d.*, including rates.

2. House in Peel Street. Back to back, two up, two down and large cellar. Living-room 10 ft. square with copper and sink. The other downstairs room the same size, probably intended as parlour but used as bedroom. Upstairs rooms the same size as those below. Living-room very dark. Gas-light estimated at 4½*d.* a day. Distance to lavatory 70 yards. Four beds in house for eight people – two old parents, two adult girls (the eldest aged twenty-seven), one young man and three children. Parents have one bed, eldest son another, and remaining five people share the other two. Bugs very bad – 'You can't keep 'em down when it's 'ot.' Indescribable squalor in downstairs room and smell upstairs almost unbearable. Rent 5*s.* 7½*d.*, including rates.

3. House in Mapplewell (small mining village near Barnsley). Two up, one down. Living-room 14 ft. by 12 ft. Sink in living-room. Plaster cracking and coming off walls. No shelves in oven. Gas leaking slightly. The upstairs rooms each 10 ft. by 8 ft. Four beds (for six persons, all adult), but 'one bed does nowt', presumably for lack of bedclothes. Room nearest stairs has no door and stairs have no banister, so that when you step out of bed your foot hangs in vacancy and you may fall ten feet onto stones. Dry rot so bad that one can see through the floor into the room below. Bugs, but 'I keeps 'em down with sheep dip'. Earth road past these cottages is like a muck-heap and said to be almost impassable in winter. Stone lavatories at ends of gardens in semi-ruinous condition. Tenants have been twenty-two years in this house. Are £11 in arrears with rent, and have been paying an extra 1*s.* a week to pay this off. Landlord now refuses this and has served orders to quit. Rent 5*s.*, including rates.

And so on and so on and so on. I could multiply examples by the score – they could be multiplied by the hundred thousand if anyone chose to make a house to house inspection throughout the industrial districts. Meanwhile some of the expressions I have used need explaining. 'One up, one down' means one room on each storey – i.e. a two-roomed house. 'Back to back' houses are two houses built in one, each side of the house being somebody's front door, so that if you walk down a row of what is apparently twelve houses you are in reality seeing not twelve houses but twenty-four. The front houses give on the street and the back ones on the yard, and there is only one way out of each house. The effect of this is obvious. The lavatories are in the yard at the back, so that if you live on the side facing the street, to get to the lavatory or the dust-bin you have to go out of the front door and walk round the end of the block – a distance that may be as much as two hundred yards; if you live at the back, on the other hand, your outlook is onto a row of lavatories. There are also houses of what is called the 'blind back' type, which are single houses, but in which the builder has omitted to put in a back door – from pure spite, apparently. The windows which refuse to open are a peculiarity of old mining towns. Some of these towns are so undermined by ancient workings that the ground is constantly subsiding and the houses above slip sideways. In Wigan you pass whole rows of houses which have slid to startling angles, their windows being ten or twenty degrees out of the horizontal. Sometimes the front wall bellies outward till it looks as though the house were seven months gone in pregnancy. It can be refaced, but the new facing soon begins to bulge again. When a house sinks at all suddenly its windows are jammed for ever and the door has to be refitted. This excites no surprise locally. The story of the miner who comes home from work and finds that he can only get indoors by smashing down the front door with an axe is considered humorous. In some cases I have noted 'Landlord good' or 'Landlord bad', because there is great variation in what the slum-dwellers say about their landlords. I found – one might expect it, perhaps – that the small landlords are usually the worst. It goes against the grain to say this, but one can see why it should be so. Ideally, the worst type of slum landlord is a fat wicked man, preferably a bishop, who is drawing an immense income from extortionate rents. Actually, it is a poor old woman who has invested her life's savings in three slum houses, inhabits one of them and tries to live on the rent of the other two – never, in consequence, having any money for repairs.

But mere notes like these are only valuable as reminders to myself. To me as I read them they bring back what I have seen, but they cannot in themselves give much idea of what conditions are like in those fearful northern slums. Words are such feeble things. What is the use of a brief phrase like 'roof leaks' or 'four beds for eight people'? It is the kind of thing your eye slides over, registering nothing. And yet what a wealth of misery it can cover! Take the question of overcrowding, for instance. Quite often you have eight or even ten people living in a three-roomed house. One of these rooms is a living-room, and as it probably measures about a dozen feet square and contains, besides the kitchen range and the sink, a table, some chairs and a dresser, there is no room in it for a bed. So there are eight or ten people sleeping in two small rooms, probably in at most four beds. If some of these people are adults and have to go to work, so much the worse. In one house, I remember, three grown-up girls shared the same bed and all went to work at different hours, each disturbing the others when she got up or came in; in another house a young miner working on the night shift slept by day in a narrow bed in which another member of the family slept by night. There is an added difficulty when there are grown-up children, in that you cannot let adolescent youths and girls sleep in the same bed. In one family I visited there were a father and mother and a son and daughter aged round about seventeen, and only two beds for the lot of them. The father slept with the son and the mother with the daughter; it was the only arrangement that ruled out the danger of incest. Then there is the misery of leaking roofs and oozing walls, which in winter makes some rooms almost uninhabitable. Then there are bugs. Once bugs get into a house they are in it till the crack of doom; there is no sure way of exterminating them. Then there are the windows that will not open. I need not point out what this must mean, in summer, in a tiny stuffy living-room where the fire, on which all the cooking is done, has to be kept burning more or less constantly. And there are the special miseries attendant upon back to back houses. A fifty yards' walk to the lavatory or the dust-bin is not exactly an inducement to be clean. In the front houses – at any rate in a side-street where the Corporation don't interfere – the women get into the habit of throwing their refuse out of the front door, so that the gutter is always littered with tea-leaves and bread crusts. And it is worth considering what it is like for a child to grow up in one of the back alleys where its gaze is bounded by a row of lavatories and a wall.

In such places as these a woman is only a poor drudge muddling among an infinity of jobs. She may keep up her spirits, but she cannot keep up her standards of cleanliness and tidiness. There is always something to be done, and no conveniences and almost literally not room to turn round. No sooner have you washed one child's face than another's is dirty; before you have washed the crocks from one meal the next is due to be cooked. I found great variation in the houses I visited. Some were as decent as one could possibly expect in the circumstances, some were so appalling that I have no hope of describing them adequately. To begin with, the smell, the dominant and essential thing, is indescribable. But the squalor and the confusion! A tub full of filthy water here, a basin full of unwashed crocks there, more crocks piled in any odd corner, torn newspaper littered everywhere, and in the middle always the same dreadful table covered with sticky oilcloth and crowded with cooking pots and irons and half-darned stockings and pieces of stale bread and bits of cheese wrapped round with greasy newspaper! And the congestion in a tiny room where getting from one side to the other is a complicated voyage between pieces of furniture, with a line of damp washing getting you in the face every time you move and the children as thick underfoot as toadstools! There are scenes that stand out vividly in my memory. The almost bare living-room of a cottage in a little mining village, where the whole family was out of work and everyone seemed to be underfed; and the big family of grown-up sons and daughters sprawling aimlessly about, all strangely alike with red hair, splendid bones and pinched faces ruined by malnutrition and idleness; and one tall son sitting by the fireplace, too listless even to notice the entry of a stranger, and slowly peeling a sticky sock from a bare foot. A dreadful room in Wigan where all the furniture seemed to be made of packing cases and barrel staves and was coming to pieces at that; and an old woman with a blackened neck and her hair coming down denouncing her landlord in a Lancashire-Irish accent; and her mother, aged well over ninety, sitting in the background on the barrel that served her as a commode and regarding us blankly with a yellow, cretinous face. I could fill up pages with memories of similar interiors.

Of course the squalor of these people's houses is sometimes their own fault. Even if you live in a back to back house and have four children and a total income of thirty-two and sixpence a week from the PAC, there is no *need* to have unemptied chamber-pots standing about in your living-room. But it is equally certain that their circumstances do not encourage self-respect. The determining factor is probably the number of children. The best-kept interiors I saw were always childless houses or houses where there were only one or two children; with, say, six children in a three-roomed house it is quite impossible to keep anything decent. One thing that is very noticeable is that the worst squalors are never downstairs. You might visit quite a number of houses, even among the poorest of the unemployed, and bring away a wrong impression. These people, you might reflect, cannot be so badly off if they still have a fair amount of furniture and crockery. But it is in the rooms upstairs that the gauntness of poverty really discloses itself. Whether this is because pride makes people cling to their living-room furniture to the last, or because bedding is more pawnable, I do not know, but certainly many of the bedrooms I saw were fearful places. Among people who have been unemployed for several years continuously I should say it is the exception to have anything like a full set of bedclothes. Often there is nothing that can be properly called bedclothes at all – just a heap of old overcoats and miscellaneous rags on a rusty iron bedstead. In this way overcrowding is aggravated. One family of four persons that I knew, a father and mother and two children, possessed two beds but could only use one of them because they had not enough bedding for the other.

Anyone who wants to see the effects of the housing shortage at their very worst should visit the dreadful caravan-dwellings that exist in numbers in many of the northern towns. Ever since the war, in the complete impossibility of getting houses, parts of the population have overflowed into supposedly temporary quarters in fixed caravans. Wigan, for instance, with a population of about 85,000, has round about 200 caravan-dwellings with a family in each – perhaps somewhere near 1,000 people in all. How many of these caravan-colonies exist throughout the industrial areas it would be difficult to discover with any accuracy. The local authorities are reticent about them and the census report of 1931 seems to have decided to ignore them. But so far as I can discover by enquiry they are to be found in most of the larger towns in Lancashire and Yorkshire, and perhaps further north as well. The probability is that throughout the north of England there are some thousands, perhaps tens of thousands of *families* (not individuals) who have no home except a fixed caravan.

But the word 'caravan' is very misleading. It calls up a picture of a cosy gypsy-encampment (in fine weather, of course) with wood fires crackling and children picking blackberries and many-coloured washing fluttering on the lines. The caravan-colonies in Wigan and Sheffield are not like that. I had a look at several of them. I inspected those in Wigan with considerable care, and I have never seen comparable squalor except in the Far East. Indeed when I saw them I was immediately reminded of the filthy kennels in which I have seen Indian coolies living in Burma. But, as a matter of fact, nothing in the East could ever be quite as bad, for in the East you haven't our clammy, penetrating cold to contend with, and the sun is a disinfectant.

Along the banks of Wigan's miry canal are patches of waste ground on which the caravans have been dumped like rubbish shot out of a bucket. Some of them are actually gypsy caravans, but very old ones and in bad repair. The majority are old single-decker buses (the rather smaller buses of ten years ago) which have been taken off their wheels and propped up with struts of wood. Some are simply wagons with semi-circular slats on top, over which canvas is stretched, so that the people inside have nothing but canvas between them and the outer air. Inside, these places are usually about five feet wide by six high (I could not stand quite upright in any of them) and anything from six to fifteen feet long. Some, I suppose, are inhabited by only one person, but I did not see any that held less than two persons, and some of them contained large families. One, for instance, measuring fourteen feet long, had seven people in it – seven people in about 450 cubic feet of space; which is to say that each person had for his entire dwelling a space a *good deal* smaller than one compartment of a public lavatory. The dirt and congestion of these places is such that you cannot well imagine it unless you have tested it with your own eyes and more particularly your nose. Each contains a tiny cottage kitchener and such furniture as can be crammed in – sometimes two beds, more usually one, into which the whole family have to huddle as best they can. It is almost impossible to sleep on the floor, because the damp soaks up from below. I was shown mattresses which were still wringing wet at eleven in the morning. In winter it is so cold that the kitcheners have to be kept burning day and night, and the windows, needless to say, are never opened. Water is got from a hydrant common to the whole colony, some of the caravan-dwellers having to walk 150 or 200 yards for every bucket of water. There are no sanitary arrangements at all. Most of the people construct a little hut to serve as a lavatory on the tiny patch of ground surrounding their caravan, and once a week dig a deep hole in which to bury the refuse. All the people I saw in these places, especially the children, were unspeakably dirty, and I do not doubt that they were lousy as well. They could not possibly be otherwise. The thought that haunted me as I went from caravan to caravan was, What can happen in those cramped interiors when anybody dies? But that, of course, is the kind of question you hardly care to ask.

Some of the people have been in their caravans for many years. Theoretically the Corporation are doing away with the caravan-colonies and getting the inhabitants out into houses; but as the houses don't get built, the caravans remain standing. Most of the people I talked to had given up the idea of ever getting a decent habitation again. They were all out of work, and a job and a house seemed to them about equally remote and impossible. Some hardly seemed to care; others realised quite clearly in what misery they were living. One woman's face stays by me, a worn skull-like face on which was a look of intolerable misery and degradation. I gathered that in that dreadful pigsty, struggling to keep her large brood of children clean, she felt as I should feel if I were coated all over with dung. One must remember that these people are not gypsies; they are decent English people who have all, except the children born there, had homes of their own in their day; besides, their caravans are greatly inferior to those of gypsies and they have not the great advantage of being on the move. No doubt there are still middle-class people who think that the Lower Orders don't mind that kind of thing and who, if they happened to pass a caravan-colony in the train, would immediately assume that the people lived there from choice. I never argue nowadays with that kind of person. But it is worth noticing that the caravan-dwellers don't even save money by living there, for they are paying about the same rents as they would for houses. I could not hear of any rent lower than five shillings a week (five shillings for 200 cubic feet of space!) and there are even cases where the rent is as high as ten shillings. Somebody must be making a good thing out of those caravans! But clearly their continued existence is due to the housing shortage and not directly to poverty.

Talking once with a miner I asked him when the housing shortage first became acute in his district; he answered, 'When we were told about it', meaning that till recently people's standards were so low that they took almost any degree of overcrowding for granted. He added that when he was a child his family had slept eleven in a room and thought nothing of it, and that later, when he was grown-up, he and his wife had lived in one of the old-style back to back houses in which you not only had to walk a couple of hundred yards to the lavatory but often had to wait in a queue when you got there, the lavatory being shared by thirty-six people. And when his wife was sick with the illness that killed her, she still had to make that two hundred yards' journey to the lavatory. This, he said, was the kind of thing people would put up with 'till they were told about it'.

I do not know whether this is true. What is certain is that nobody *now* thinks it bearable to sleep eleven in a room, and that even people with comfortable incomes are vaguely troubled by the thought of 'the slums'.

Hence the clatter about 're-housing' and 'slum clearance' which we have had at intervals ever since the war. Bishops, politicians, philanthropists and whatnot enjoy talking piously about 'slum clearance', because they can thus divert attention from more serious evils and pretend that if you abolish the slums you abolish poverty. But all this talk has led to surprisingly small results. So far as one can discover, the congestion is no better, perhaps slightly worse, than it was a dozen years ago. There is certainly great variation in the speed at which the different towns are attacking their housing problem. In some towns building seems to be almost at a standstill, in others it is proceeding rapidly and the private landlord is being driven out of business. Liverpool, for instance, has been very largely rebuilt, mainly by the efforts of the Corporation. Sheffield, too, is being torn down and rebuilt pretty fast, though perhaps, considering the unparalleled beastliness of its slums, not quite fast enough.[1]

Why rehousing has on the whole moved so slowly, and why some towns can borrow money for building purposes so much more easily than others, I do not know. Those questions would have to be answered by someone who knows more about the machinery of local government than I do. A Corporation house costs normally somewhere between three and four hundred pounds; it costs rather less when it is built by 'direct labour' than when built by contract. The rent of these houses would average something over twenty pounds a year not counting rates, so one would think that, even allowing for overhead expenses and interest on loans, it would pay any Corporation to build as many houses as could be tenanted. In many cases, of course, the houses would have to be inhabited by people on the PAC, so that the local bodies would merely be taking money out of one pocket and putting it into another – i.e. paying out money in the form of relief and taking it back in the form of rent. But they have got to pay the relief in any case, and at present a proportion of what they pay is being swallowed up by private landlords. The reasons given for the slow rate of building are lack of money and the difficulty of getting hold of sites – for Corporation houses are not erected piecemeal but in 'estates',

[1] The number of Corporation houses in process of construction in Sheffield at the beginning of 1936 was 1,398. To replace the slum areas entirely Sheffield is said to need 100,000 houses.

sometimes of hundreds of houses at a time. One thing that always strikes me as mysterious is that so many of the northern towns see fit to build themselves immense and luxurious public buildings at the same time as they are in crying need of dwelling houses. The town of Barnsley, for instance, recently spent close on £150,000 on a new town hall, although admittedly needing at least 2,000 new working-class houses, not to mention public baths. (The public baths in Barnsley contain *nineteen* men's slipper baths – this in a town of 70,000 inhabitants, largely miners, not one of whom has a bath in his house!) For £150,000 it could have built 350 Corporation houses and still had £10,000 to spend on a town hall. However, as I say, I do not pretend to understand the mysteries of local government. I merely record the fact that houses are desperately needed and are being built, on the whole, with paralytic slowness.

Still, houses *are* being built, and the Corporation building estates, with their row upon row of little red houses, all much liker than two peas (where did that expression come from? Peas have great individuality) are a regular feature of the outskirts of the industrial towns. As to what they are like and how they compare with the slum houses, I can best give an idea by transcribing two more extracts from my diary. The tenants' opinions of their houses vary greatly, so I will give one favourable extract and one unfavourable. Both of these are from Wigan and both are the cheaper 'non-parlour type' houses:

1. House in Beech Hill Estate.

Downstairs. Large living-room with kitchener fireplace, cupboards and fixed dresser, composition floor. Small hallway, largish kitchen. Up-to-date electric cooker hired from Corporation at much the same rate as a gas cooker.

Upstairs. Two largish bedrooms, one tiny one – suitable only for a boxroom or temporary bedroom. Bathroom, wc, with hot and cold water.

Smallish garden. These vary throughout the estate, but mostly rather smaller than an allotment.

Four in family, parents and two children. Husband in good employ. Houses appear well built and are quite agreeable to look at. Various restrictions, e.g. it is forbidden to keep poultry or pigeons, take in lodgers, sublet or start any kind of business without leave from the Corporation. (This is easily granted in the case of taking in lodgers, but not in any of the others.) Tenant very well satisfied with house and proud of it. Houses in this estate all well kept. Corporation are good about repairs, but keep tenants up to the mark with regard to keeping the place tidy, etc.

Rent 11*s.* 3*d.*, including rates. Bus fare into town 2*d.*

2. House in Welly Estate.

Downstairs. Living-room 14 ft. by 10 ft., kitchen a good deal smaller, tiny larder under stairs, small but fairly good bathroom. Gas cooker, electric lighting. Outdoor wc.

Upstairs. One bedroom 12 ft. by 10 ft. with tiny fireplace, another the same size without fireplace, another 7 ft. by 6 ft. Best bedroom has small wardrobe let into wall.

Garden about 20 yards by 10.

Six in family, parents and four children, eldest son nineteen, eldest daughter twenty-two. None in work except eldest son. Tenants very discontented. Their complaints are: House is cold, draughty and damp. Fireplace in living-room gives out no heat and makes room very dusty – attributed to its being set too low. Fireplace in best bedroom too small to be of any use. Walls upstairs cracking. Owing to uselessness of tiny bedroom, 5 are sleeping in one bedroom, 1 (the eldest son) in the other.

Gardens in this estate all neglected.

Rent 10*s.* 3*d.*, inclusive. Distance to town a little over a mile – there is no bus here.

I could multiply examples, but these two are enough, as the types of Corporation houses being built do not vary greatly from place to place. Two things are immediately obvious. The first is that at their very worst the Corporation houses are better than the slums they replace. The mere possession of a bathroom and a bit of garden would outweigh almost any disadvantage. The other is that they are much more expensive to live in. It is common enough for a man to be turned out of a condemned house where he is paying six or seven shillings a week and given a Corporation house where he has to pay ten. This only affects those who are in work or have recently been in work, because when a man is on the PAC his rent is assessed at a quarter of his dole, and if it is more than this he gets an extra allowance; in any case, there are certain classes of Corporation houses to which people on the dole are not admitted. But there are other ways in which life in a Corporation estate is expensive, whether you are in work or out of it. To begin with, owing to the higher rents, the shops in the estate are much more expensive and there are not so many of them. Then again, in a comparatively large, detached house, away from the frowzy huddle of the slum, it is much colder and more fuel has to be burnt. And again there is the expense, especially for a man in work, of getting to and from town. This last is one of the more obvious problems of re-housing. Slum clearance means diffusion of the population. When you rebuild on a large scale, what you do in effect is to scoop out the centre of the town and re-distribute it on the outskirts. This is all very well in a way; you have got the people out of fetid alleys into places where they have room to breathe; but from the point of view of the people themselves, what you have done is to pick them up and dump them down five miles from their work. The simplest solution is flats. If people are going to live in large towns at all they must learn to live on top of one another. But the northern working people do not take kindly to flats; even where flats exist they are contemptuously named 'tenements'. Almost everyone will tell you that he 'wants a house of his own', and apparently a house in the middle of an unbroken block of houses a hundred yards long seems to them more 'their own' than a flat situated in mid-air.

To revert to the second of the two Corporation houses I have just mentioned. The tenant complained that the house was cold, damp, and so forth. Perhaps the house was jerry-built, but equally probably he was exaggerating. He had come there from a filthy hovel in the middle of Wigan which I happened to have inspected previously; while there he had made every effort to get hold of a Corporation house, and he was no sooner in the Corporation house than he wanted to be back in the slum. This looks like mere captiousness but it covers a perfectly genuine grievance. In very many cases, perhaps in half the cases, I found that the people in Corporation houses don't really like them. They are glad to get out of the stink of the slum, they know that it is better for their children to have space to play about in, but they don't feel really at home. The exceptions are usually people in good employ who can afford to spend a little extra on fuel and furniture and journeys, and who in any case are of 'superior' type. The others, the typical slum-dwellers, miss the frowzy warmth of the slum. They complain that 'out in the country', i.e. on the edge of the town, they are 'starving' (freezing). Certainly most Corporation estates are pretty bleak in winter. Some I have been through, perched on treeless clayey hillsides and swept by icy winds, would be horrible places to live in. It is not that slum-dwellers want dirt and congestion for their own sakes, as the fat-bellied bourgeoisie love to believe. (See for instance the conversation about slum-clearance in Galsworthy's *Swan Song*, where the rentier's cherished belief that the slum-dweller makes the slum, and not vice versa, is put into the mouth of a philanthropic Jew.) Give people a decent house and they will soon learn to keep it decent. Moreover, with a smart-looking house to live up to they improve in self-respect and cleanliness, and their children start life with better chances. Nevertheless, in a Corporation estate there is an uncomfortable, almost prison-like atmosphere, and the people who live there are perfectly well aware of it.

And it is here that one comes on the central difficulty of the housing problem. When you walk through the smoke-dim slums of Manchester you think that nothing is needed except to tear down these abominations and build decent houses in their place. But the trouble is that in destroying the slum you destroy other things as well. Houses are desperately needed and are not being built fast enough; but in so far as re-housing is being done, it is being done – perhaps it is unavoidable – in a monstrously inhuman manner. I don't mean merely that the houses are new and ugly. All houses have got to be new at some time, and as a matter of fact the type of Corporation house now being built is not at all offensive to look at. On the outskirts of Liverpool there are what amount to whole towns consisting entirely of Corporation houses, and they are quite pleasing to the eye; the blocks of workers' flats in the centre of the town, modelled, I believe, on the workers' flats in Vienna, are definitely fine buildings. But there is something ruthless and soulless about the whole business. Take, for instance, the restrictions with which you are burdened in a Corporation house. You are not allowed to keep your house and garden as you want them – in some estates there is even a regulation that every garden must have the same kind of hedge. You are not allowed to keep poultry or pigeons. The Yorkshire miners are fond of keeping homer pigeons; they keep them in the back yard and take them out and race them on Sundays. But pigeons are messy birds and the Corporation suppresses them as a matter of course. The restrictions about shops are more serious. The number of shops in a Corporation estate is rigidly limited, and it is said that preference is given to the Co-op. and the chain stores; this may not be strictly true, but certainly those are the shops that one usually sees there. This is bad enough for the general public, but from the point of view of the independent shopkeeper it is a disaster. Many a small shopkeeper is utterly ruined by some rehousing scheme which takes no notice of his existence. A whole section of the town is condemned *en bloc*; presently the houses are pulled down and the people are transferred to some housing estate miles away. In this way all the small shopkeepers of the quarter have their whole clientele taken away from them at a single swoop and receive not a penny of compensation. They cannot transfer their business to the estate, because even if they can afford the move and the much higher rents, they would probably be refused a licence. As for pubs, they are banished from the housing estates almost completely, and the few that remain are dismal sham-Tudor places fitted out by the big brewery companies and very expensive. For a middle-class population this would be a nuisance – it might mean walking a mile to get a glass of beer; for a working-class population, which uses the pub as a kind of club, it is a serious blow at communal life. It is a great achievement to get slum-dwellers into decent houses, but it is unfortunate that, owing to the peculiar temper of our time, it is also considered necessary to rob them of the last vestiges of their liberty. The people themselves feel this, and it is this feeling that they are rationalising when they complain that their new houses – so much better, *as* houses, than those they have come out of – are cold and uncomfortable and 'unhomelike'.

I sometimes think that the price of liberty is not so much eternal vigilance as eternal dirt. There are some Corporation estates in which new tenants are systematically deloused before being allowed into their houses. All their possessions except what they stand up in are taken away from them, fumigated and sent on to the new house. This procedure has its points, for it *is* a pity that people should take bugs into brand new houses (a bug will follow you about in your luggage if he gets half a chance), but it is the kind of thing that makes you wish that the word 'hygiene' could be dropped out of the dictionary. Bugs are bad, but a state of affairs in which men will allow themselves to be dipped like sheep is worse. Perhaps, however, when it is a case of slum clearance, one must take for granted a certain amount of restrictions and inhumanity. When all is said and done, the most important thing is that people shall live in decent houses and not in pigsties. I have seen too much of slums to go into Chestertonian raptures about them. A place where the children can breathe clean air, and women have a few conveniences to save them from drudgery, and a man has a bit of garden to dig in, *must* be better than the stinking back-streets of Leeds and Sheffield. On balance, the Corporation estates are better than the slums; but only by a small margin.

When I was looking into the housing question I visited and inspected numbers of houses, perhaps a hundred or two hundred houses altogether, in various mining towns and villages. I cannot end this chapter without remarking on the extraordinary courtesy and good nature with which I was received everywhere. I did not go alone – I always had some local friend among the unemployed to show me round – but even so, it is an impertinence to go poking into strangers' houses and asking to see the cracks in the bedroom wall. Yet everyone was astonishingly patient and seemed to understand almost without explanation why I was questioning them and what I wanted to see. If any unauthorised person walked into *my* house and began asking me whether the roof leaked and whether I was much troubled by bugs and what I thought of my landlord, I should probably tell him to go to hell. This only happened to me once, and in that case the woman was slightly deaf and took me for a Means Test nark; but even she relented after a while and gave me the information I wanted.

I am told that it is bad form for a writer to quote his own reviews, but I want here to contradict a reviewer in the *Manchester Guardian* who says apropos of one of my books:

> Set down in Wigan or Whitechapel Mr Orwell would still exercise an unerring power of closing his vision to all that is good in order to proceed with his wholehearted vilification of humanity.

Wrong. Mr Orwell was 'set down' in Wigan for quite a while and it did not inspire him with any wish to vilify humanity. He liked Wigan very much – the people, not the scenery. Indeed, he has only one fault to find with it, and that is in respect of the celebrated Wigan Pier, which he had set his heart on seeing. Alas! Wigan Pier has been demolished, and even the spot where it used to stand is no longer certain.

V

When you see the unemployment figures quoted at two millions, it is fatally easy to take this as meaning that two million people are out of work and the rest of the population is comparatively comfortable. I admit that till recently I was in the habit of doing so myself. I used to calculate that if you put the registered unemployed at round about two millions and threw in the destitute and those who for one reason and another were not registered, you might take the number of underfed people in England (for *everyone* on the dole or thereabouts is underfed) as being, at the very most, five millions.

This is an enormous under-estimate, because, in the first place, the only people shown on unemployment figures are those actually drawing the dole – that is, in general, heads of families. An unemployed man's dependants do not figure on the list unless they too are drawing a separate allowance. A Labour Exchange officer told me that to get at the real number of people *living on* (not drawing) the dole, you have got to multiply the official figures by something over three. This alone brings the number of unemployed to round about six millions. But in addition there are great numbers of people who are in work but who, from a financial point of view, might equally well be unemployed, because they are not drawing anything that can be described as a living wage.[1] Allow for these and their dependants, throw in as before the old-age pensioners, the destitute and other nondescripts, and you get an *underfed* population of well over ten millions. Sir John Orr puts it at twenty millions.

Take the figures for Wigan, which is typical enough of the industrial and mining districts. The number of insured workers is round about 36,000 (26,000 men and 10,000 women). Of these, the number unemployed at the beginning of 1936 was about 10,000. But this was in winter when the mines are working full time; in summer it would probably be 12,000. Multiply by three, as above, and you get 30,000 or 36,000.

[1] For instance, a recent census of the Lancashire cotton mills revealed the fact that over 40,000 *full-time* employees receive less than thirty shillings a week each. In Preston, to take only one town, the number receiving *over* thirty shillings a week was 640 and the number receiving *under* thirty shillings was 3,113.

The total population of Wigan is a little under 87,000; so that at any moment more than one person in three out of the whole population – not merely the registered workers – is either drawing or living on the dole. Those ten or twelve thousand unemployed contain a steady core of from four to five thousand miners who have been continuously unemployed for the past seven years. And Wigan is not especially badly off as industrial towns go. Even in Sheffield, which has been doing well for the last year or so because of wars and rumours of war, the proportion of unemployment is about the same – one in three of registered workers unemployed.

When a man is first unemployed, until his insurance stamps are exhausted, he draws 'full benefit', of which the rates are as follows:

	per week
Single man	17*s.*
Wife	9*s.*
Each child below 14	3*s.*

Thus in a typical family of parents and three children of whom one was over 14, the total income would be 32*s.* per week, plus anything that might be earned by the eldest child. When a man's stamps are exhausted, before being turned over to the PAC (Public Assistance Committee), he receives twenty-six weeks' 'transitional benefit' from the UAB (Unemployment Assistance Board), the rates being as follows:

	per week
Single man	15*s.*
Man and wife	24*s.*
Children, 14–18	6*s.*
Children, 11–14	4*s.* 6*d.*
Children, 8–11	4*s.*
Children, 5–8	3*s.* 6*d.*
Children, 3–5	3*s.*

Thus on the UAB the income of the typical family of five persons would be 37*s.* 6*d.* a week if no child was in work. When a man is on the UAB a quarter of his dole is regarded as rent, with a minimum of 7*s.* 6*d.* a week. If the rent he is paying is more than a quarter of his dole he receives an extra allowance, but if it is less than 7*s.* 6*d.*, a corresponding amount is deducted. Payments on the PAC theoretically come out of the local rates, but are backed by a central fund. The rates of benefit are:

	per week
Single man	12*s.* 6*d.*
Man and wife	23*s.*
Eldest child	4*s.*
Any other child	3*s.*

Being at the discretion of the local bodies these rates vary slightly, and a single man may or may not get an extra 2*s.* 6*d.* weekly, bringing his benefit up to 15*s.* As on the UAB, a quarter of a married man's dole is regarded as rent. Thus in the typical family considered above the total income would be 33*s.* a week, a quarter of this being regarded as rent. In addition, in most districts a coal allowance of 1*s.* 6*d.* a week (1*s.* 6*d.* is equivalent to about a hundredweight of coal) is granted for six weeks before and six weeks after Christmas.

It will be seen that the income of a family on the dole normally averages round about thirty shillings a week. One can write at least a quarter of this off as rent, which is to say that the average person, child or adult, has got to be fed, clothed, warmed, and otherwise cared-for for six or seven shillings a week. Enormous groups of people, probably at least a third of the whole population of the industrial areas, are living at this level. The Means Test is very strictly enforced, and you are liable to be refused relief at the slightest hint that you are getting money from another source. Dock-labourers, for instance, who are generally hired by the half day, have to sign on at a Labour Exchange twice daily; if they fail to do so it is assumed that they have been working and their dole is reduced correspondingly. I have seen cases of evasion of the Means Test, but I should say that in the industrial towns, where there is still a certain amount of communal life and everyone has neighbours who know him, it is much harder than it would be in London. The usual method is for a young man who is actually living with his parents to get an accommodation address, so that supposedly he has a separate establishment and draws a separate allowance. But there is much spying and tale-bearing. One man I knew, for instance, was seen feeding his neighbour's chickens while the neighbour was away. It was reported to the authorities that he 'had a job feeding chickens' and he had great difficulty in refuting this. The favourite joke in Wigan was about a man who was refused relief on the ground that he 'had a job carting firewood'. He had been seen, it was said, carting firewood at night. He had to explain that he was not carting firewood but doing a moonlight flit. The 'firewood' was his furniture.

The most cruel and evil effect of the Means Test is the way in which it breaks up families. Old people, sometimes bedridden, are driven out of their homes by it. An old-age pensioner, for instance, if a widower, would normally live with one or other of his children; his weekly ten shillings goes towards the household expenses, and probably he is not badly cared for. Under the Means Test, however, he counts as a 'lodger' and if he stays at home his children's dole will be docked. So, perhaps at seventy or seventy-five years of age, he has to turn out into lodgings, handing his pension over to the lodging-house keeper and existing on the verge of starvation. I have seen several cases of this myself. It is happening all over England at this moment, thanks to the Means Test.

Nevertheless, in spite of the frightful extent of unemployment, it is a fact that poverty – extreme poverty – is less in evidence in the industrial North than it is in London. Everything is poorer and shabbier, there are fewer motor-cars and fewer well-dressed people; but also there are fewer people who are obviously destitute. Even in a town the size of Liverpool or Manchester you are struck by the fewness of the beggars. London is a sort of whirlpool which draws derelict people towards it, and it is so vast that life there is solitary and anonymous. Until you break the law nobody will take any notice of you, and you can go to pieces as you could not possibly do in a place where you had neighbours who knew you. But in the industrial towns the old communal way of life has not yet broken up, tradition is still strong and almost everyone has a family – potentially, therefore, a home. In a town of 50,000 or 100,000 inhabitants there is no casual and as it were unaccounted-for population; nobody sleeping in the streets, for instance. Moreover, there is just this to be said for the unemployment regulations, that they do not discourage people from marrying. A man and wife on twenty-three shillings a week are not far from the starvation line, but they can make a home of sorts; they are vastly better off than a single man on fifteen shillings. The life of a single unemployed man is dreadful. He lives sometimes in a common lodging-house, more often in a 'furnished' room for which he usually pays six shillings a week, finding himself as best he can on the other nine (say six shillings a week for food and three for clothes, tobacco and amusements). Of course he cannot feed or look after himself properly, and a man who pays six shillings a week for his room is not encouraged to be indoors more than is necessary. So he spends his days loafing in the public library or any other place where he can keep warm. That – keeping warm – is almost the sole preoccupation of a single unemployed man in winter. In Wigan a favourite refuge was the pictures, which are fantastically cheap there. You can always get a seat for fourpence, and at the matinée at some houses you can even get a seat for twopence. Even people on the verge of starvation will readily pay twopence to get out of the ghastly cold of a winter afternoon. In Sheffield I was taken to a public hall to listen to a lecture by a clergyman, and it was by a long way the silliest and worst-delivered lecture I have ever heard or ever expect to hear. I found it physically impossible to sit it out; indeed my feet carried me out, seemingly of their own accord, before it was half way through. Yet the hall was thronged with unemployed men; they would have sat through far worse drivel for the sake of a warm place to shelter in.

At times I have seen unmarried men on the dole living in the extreme of misery. In one town I remember a whole colony of them who were squatting, more or less illicitly, in a derelict house which was practically falling down. They had collected a few scraps of furniture, presumably off refuse-tips, and I remember that their sole table was an old marble-topped wash-hand-stand. But this kind of thing is exceptional. A working-class bachelor is a rarity, and so long as a man is married unemployment makes comparatively little alteration in his way of life. His home is impoverished but it is still a home, and it is noticeable everywhere that the anomalous position created by unemployment – the man being out of work while the woman's work continues as before – has not altered the relative status of the sexes. In a working-class home it is the man who is the master and not, as in a middle-class home, the woman or the baby. Practically never, for instance, in a working-class home, will you see the man doing a stroke of the housework. Unemployment has not changed this convention, which on the face of it seems a little unfair. The man is idle from morning to night but the woman is as busy as ever – more so, indeed, because she has to manage with less money Yet so far as my experience goes the women do not protest. I believe that they, as well as the men, feel that a man would lose his manhood if, merely because he was out of work, he developed into a 'Mary Ann'.

But there is no doubt about the deadening, debilitating effect of unemployment upon everybody, married or single, and upon men more than upon women. The best intellects will not stand up against it. Once or twice it has happened to me to meet unemployed men of genuine literary ability; there are others whom I haven't met but whose work I occasionally see in the magazines. Now and again, at long intervals, these men will produce an article or a short story which is quite obviously better than most of the stuff that gets whooped up by the blurb-reviewers. Why, then, do they make so little use of their talents? They have all the leisure in the world; why don't they sit down and write books? Because to write books you need not only comfort and solitude – and solitude is never easy to attain in a working-class home – you also need peace of mind. You can't settle to anything, you can't command the spirit of *hope* in which anything has got to be created, with that dull evil cloud of unemployment hanging over you. Still, an unemployed man who feels at home with books can at any rate occupy himself by reading. But what about the man who cannot read without discomfort? Take a miner, for instance, who has worked in the pit since childhood and has been trained to be a miner and nothing else. How the devil is he to fill up the empty days? It is absurd to say that he ought to be looking for work. There is no work to look for, and everybody knows it. You can't go on looking for work every day for seven years. There are allotments, which occupy the time and help to feed a family, but in a big town there are only allotments for a small proportion of the people. Then there are the occupational centres which were started a few years ago to help the unemployed. On the whole this movement has been a failure, but some of the centres are still flourishing. I have visited one or two of them. There are shelters where the men can keep warm and there are periodical classes in carpentering, boot-making, leather-work, handloom-weaving, basket-work, sea-grass work, etc. etc.; the idea being that the men can make furniture and so forth, not for sale but for their own homes, getting tools free and materials cheaply. Most of the Socialists I have talked to denounce this movement as they denounce the project – it is always being talked about but it never comes to anything – to give the unemployed small-holdings. They say that the occupational centres are simply a device to keep the unemployed quiet and give them the illusion that something is being done for them. Undoubtedly that *is* the underlying motive. Keep a man busy mending boots and he is less likely to read the *Daily Worker*. Also there is a nasty YMCA atmosphere about these places which you can feel as soon as you go in. The unemployed men who frequent them are mostly of the cap-touching type – the type who tells you oilily that he is 'Temperance' and votes Conservative. Yet even here you feel yourself torn both ways. For probably it is better that a man should waste his time even with such rubbish as sea-grass work than that for years upon end he should do absolutely *nothing*.

By far the best work for the unemployed is being done by the NUWM – National Unemployed Workers' Movement. This is a revolutionary organisation intended to hold the unemployed together, stop them black-legging during strikes and give them legal advice against the Means Test. It is a movement that has been built out of nothing by the pennies and efforts of the unemployed themselves. I have seen a good deal of the NUWM, and I greatly admire the men, ragged and underfed like the others, who keep the organisation going. Still more I admire the tact and patience with which they do it; for it is not easy to coax even a penny-a-week subscription out of the pockets of people on the PAC. As I said earlier, the English working class do not show much capacity for leadership, but they have a wonderful talent for organisation. The whole trade union movement testifies to this; so do the excellent working-men's clubs – really a sort of glorified co-operative pub, and splendidly organised – which are so common in Yorkshire. In many towns the NUWM have shelters and arrange speeches by Communist speakers. But even at these shelters the men who go there do nothing but sit round the stove and occasionally play a game of dominoes. If this movement could be combined with something along the lines of the occupational centres, it would be nearer what is needed. It is a deadly thing to see a skilled man running to seed, year after year, in utter, hopeless idleness. It ought not to be impossible to give him the chance of using his hands and making furniture and so forth for his own home, without turning him into a YMCA cocoa-drunkard. We may as well face the fact that several million men in England will – unless another war breaks out – never have a real job this side the grave. One thing that probably could be done and certainly ought to be done as a matter of course, is to give every unemployed man a patch of ground and free tools if he chose to apply for them. It is disgraceful that men who are expected to keep alive on the PAC should not even have the chance to grow vegetables for their families.

To study unemployment and its effects you have got to go to the industrial areas. In the South unemployment exists, but it is scattered and queerly unobtrusive. There are plenty of rural districts where a man out of work is almost unheard-of, and you don't anywhere see the spectacle of whole blocks of cities living on the dole and the PAC. It is only when you lodge in streets where nobody has a job, where getting a job seems about as probable as owning an aeroplane and much *less* probable than winning fifty pounds in the Football Pool, that you begin to grasp the changes that are being worked in our civilisation. For a change *is* taking place, there is no doubt about that. The attitude of the submerged working class is profoundly different from what it was seven or eight years ago.

I first became aware of the unemployment problem in 1928. At that time I had just come back from Burma, where unemployment was only a word, and I had gone to Burma when I was still a boy and the post-war boom was not quite over. When I first saw unemployed men at close quarters, the thing that horrified and amazed me was to find that many of them were *ashamed* of being unemployed. I was very ignorant, but not so ignorant as to imagine that when the loss of foreign markets pushes two million men out of work, those two million are any more to blame than the people who draw blanks in the Calcutta Sweep. But at that time nobody cared to admit that unemployment was inevitable, because this meant admitting that it would probably continue. The middle classes were still talking about 'lazy idle loafers on the dole' and saying that 'these men could all find work if they wanted to', and naturally these opinions percolated to the working class themselves. I remember the shock of astonishment it gave me, when I first mingled with tramps and beggars, to find that a fair proportion, perhaps a quarter, of these beings whom I had been taught to regard as cynical parasites, were decent young miners and cotton-workers gazing at their destiny with the same sort of dumb amazement as an animal in a trap. They simply could not understand what was happening to them. They had been brought up to work, and behold! it seemed as if they were never going to have the chance of working again. In their circumstances it was inevitable, at first, that they should be haunted by a feeling of personal degradation. That was the attitude towards unemployment in those days: it was a disaster which happened to *you* as an individual and for which *you* were to blame.

When a quarter of a million miners are unemployed, it is part of the order of things that Alf Smith, a miner living in the back-streets of Newcastle, should be out of work. Alf Smith is merely one of the quarter million, a statistical unit. But no human being finds it easy to regard himself as a statistical unit. So long as Bert Jones across the street is still at work, Alf Smith is bound to feel himself dishonoured and a failure. Hence that frightful feeling of impotence and despair which is almost the worst evil of unemployment – far worse than any hardship, worse than the demoralisation of enforced idleness, and only less bad than the physical degeneracy of Alf Smith's children, born on the PAC. Everyone who saw Greenwood's play *Love on the Dole* must remember that dreadful moment when the poor, good, stupid working man beats on the table and cries out, 'O God, send me some work!' This was not dramatic exaggeration, it was a touch from life. That cry must have been uttered, in almost those words, in tens of thousands, perhaps hundreds of thousands of English homes, during the past fifteen years.

But, I think not again – or at least, not so often. That is the real point: people are ceasing to kick against the pricks. After all, even the middle classes – yes, even the bridge clubs in the country towns – are beginning to realise that there is such a thing as unemployment. The 'My dear, I don't *believe* in all this nonsense about unemployment. Why, only last week we wanted a man to weed the garden, and we simply couldn't get one. They don't *want* to work, that's all it is!' which you heard at every decent tea-table five years ago, is growing perceptibly less frequent. As for the working class themselves, they have gained immensely in economic knowledge. I believe that the *Daily Worker* has accomplished a great deal here: its influence is out of all proportion to its circulation. But in any case they have had their lesson well rubbed into them, not only because unemployment is so widespread but because it has lasted so long. When people live on the dole for years at a time they grow used to it, and drawing the dole, though it remains unpleasant, ceases to be shameful. Thus the old, independent, workhouse-fearing tradition is undermined, just as the ancient fear of debt is undermined by the hire-purchase system. In the back-streets of Wigan and Barnsley I saw every kind of privation, but I probably saw much less *conscious* misery than I should have seen ten years ago. The people have at any rate grasped that unemployment is a thing they cannot help. It is not only Alf Smith who is out of work now; Bert Jones is out of work as well, and both of them have been 'out' for years. It makes a great deal of difference when things are the same for everybody.

So you have whole populations settling down, as it were, to a lifetime on the PAC. And what I think is admirable, perhaps even hopeful, is that they have managed to do it without going spiritually to pieces. A working man does not disintegrate under the strain of poverty as a middle-class person does. Take, for instance, the fact that the working class think nothing of getting married on the dole. It annoys the old ladies in Brighton, but it is a proof of their essential good sense; they realise that losing your job does not mean that you cease to be a human being. So that in one way things in the distressed areas are not so bad as they might be. Life is still fairly normal, more normal than one really has the right to expect. Families are impoverished, but the family-system has not broken up. The people are in effect living a reduced version of their former lives. Instead of raging against their destiny they have made things tolerable by lowering their standards.

But they don't necessarily lower their standards by cutting out luxuries and concentrating on necessities; more often it is the other way about – the more natural way, if you come to think of it. Hence the fact that in a decade of unparalleled depression, the consumption of all cheap luxuries has increased. The two things that have probably made the greatest difference of all are the movies and the mass-production of cheap smart clothes since the war. The youth who leaves school at fourteen and gets a blind-alley job is out of work at twenty, probably for life; but for two pounds ten on the hire-purchase system he can buy himself a suit which, for a little while and at a little distance, looks as though it had been tailored in Savile Row. The girl can look like a fashion plate at an even lower price. You may have three halfpence in your pocket and not a prospect in the world, and only the corner of a leaky bedroom to go home to; but in your new clothes you can stand on the street corner, indulging in a private daydream of yourself as Clark Gable or Greta Garbo, which compensates you for a great deal. And even at home there is generally a cup of tea going – a 'nice cup of tea' – and Father, who has been out of work since 1929, is temporarily happy because he has a sure tip for the Cesarewitch.

Trade since the war has had to adjust itself to meet the demands of underpaid, underfed people, with the result that a luxury is nowadays almost always cheaper than a necessity. One pair of plain solid shoes costs as much as two ultra-smart pairs. For the price of one square meal you can get two pounds of cheap sweets. You can't get much meat for threepence, but you can get a lot of fish and chips. Milk costs threepence a pint and even 'mild' beer costs fourpence, but aspirins are seven a penny and you can wring forty cups of tea out of a quarter-pound packet. And above all there is gambling, the cheapest of all luxuries. Even people on the verge of starvation can buy a few days' hope ('Something to live for', as they call it) by having a penny on a sweepstake. Organised gambling has now risen almost to the status of a major industry. Consider, for instance, a phenomenon like the Football Pools, with a turnover of about six million pounds a year, almost all of it from the pockets of working-class people. I happened to be in Yorkshire when Hitler re-occupied the Rhineland. Hitler, Locarno, Fascism and the threat of war aroused hardly a flicker of interest locally, but the decision of the Football Association to stop publishing their fixtures in advance (this was an attempt to quell the Football Pools) flung all Yorkshire into a storm of fury. And then there is the queer spectacle of modern electrical science showering miracles upon people with empty bellies. You may shiver all night for lack of bedclothes, but in the morning you can go to the public library and read the news that has been telegraphed for your benefit from San Francisco and Singapore. Twenty million people are underfed but literally everyone in England has access to a radio. What we have lost in food we have gained in electricity. Whole sections of the working class who have been plundered of all they really need are being compensated, in part, by cheap luxuries which mitigate the surface of life.

Do you consider all this desirable? No, I don't. But it may be that the psychological adjustment which the working class are visibly making is the best they could make in the circumstances. They have neither turned revolutionary nor lost their self-respect; merely they have kept their tempers and settled down to make the best of things on a fish-and-chip standard. The alternative would be God knows what continued agonies of despair; or it might be attempted insurrections which, in a strongly governed country like England, could only lead to futile massacres and a régime of savage repression.

Of course the post-war development of cheap luxuries has been a very fortunate thing for our rulers. It is quite likely that fish and chips, art-silk stockings, tinned salmon, cut-price chocolate (five two-ounce bars for sixpence), the movies, the radio, strong tea and the Football Pools have between them averted revolution. Therefore we are sometimes told that the whole thing is an astute manoeuvre by the governing class – a sort of 'bread and circuses' business – to hold the unemployed down. What I have seen of our governing class does not convince me that they have that much intelligence. The thing has happened, but by an unconscious process – the quite natural interaction between the manufacturer's need for a market and the need of half-starved people for cheap palliatives.

VI

When I was a small boy at school a lecturer used to come once a term and deliver excellent lectures on famous battles of the past, such as Blenheim, Austerlitz, etc. He was fond of quoting Napoleon's maxim 'An army marches on its stomach', and at the end of his lecture he would suddenly turn to us and demand, 'What's the most important thing in the world?' We were expected to shout 'Food!' and if we did not do so he was disappointed.

Obviously he was right in a way. A human being is primarily a bag for putting food into; the other functions and faculties may be more godlike, but in point of time they come afterwards. A man dies and is buried, and all his words and actions are forgotten, but the food he has eaten lives after him in the sound or rotten bones of his children. I think it could be plausibly argued that changes of diet are more important than changes of dynasty or even of religion. The Great War, for instance, could never have happened if tinned food had not been invented. And the history of the past four hundred years in England would have been immensely different if it had not been for the introduction of root-crops and various other vegetables at the end of the Middle Ages, and a little later the introduction of non-alcoholic drinks (tea, coffee, cocoa) and also of distilled liquors to which the beer-drinking English were not accustomed. Yet it is curious how seldom the all-importance of food is recognised. You see statues everywhere to politicians, poets, bishops, but none to cooks or bacon-curers or market-gardeners. The Emperor Charles V is said to have erected a statue to the inventor of bloaters, but that is the only case I can think of at the moment.

So perhaps the really important thing about the unemployed, the really basic thing if you look to the future, is the diet they are living on. As I said earlier, the average unemployed family lives on an income of round about thirty shillings a week, of which at least a quarter goes in rent. It is worth considering in some detail how the remaining money is spent. I have here a budget which was made out for me by an unemployed miner and his wife. I asked them to make a list which represented as exactly as possible their expenditure in a typical week. This man's allowance was thirty-two shillings a week, and besides his wife he had two children, one aged two years and five months and the other ten months. Here is the list:

	s.	*d.*
Rent	9	0½
Clothing Club	3	0
Coal	2	0
Gas	1	3
Milk	0	10½
Union fees	0	3
Insurance (on the children)	0	2
Meat	2	6
Flour (2 stone)	3	4
Yeast	0	4
Potatoes	1	0
Dripping	0	10
Margarine	0	10

Bacon		1	2
Sugar		1	9
Tea		1	0
Jam		0	7½
Peas and cabbage		0	6
Carrots and onions		0	4
Quaker oats		0	4½
Soap, powders, blue, etc.		0	10
Total	£1	12	0

In addition to this, three packets of dried milk were supplied weekly for the baby by the Infants' Welfare Clinic.

One or two comments are needed here. To begin with, the list leaves out a great deal – blacking, pepper, salt, vinegar, matches, kindling-wood, razor-blades, replacements of utensils and wear and tear of furniture and bedding, to name the first few that come to mind. Any money spent on these would mean reduction on some other item. A more serious charge is tobacco. This man happened to be a small smoker, but even so his tobacco would hardly cost less than a shilling a week, meaning a further reduction on food. The 'clothing clubs' into which unemployed people pay so much a week are run by big drapers in all the industrial towns. Without them it would be impossible for unemployed people to buy new clothes at all. I don't know whether or not they buy bedding through these clubs. This particular family, as I happen to know, possessed next to no bedding.

In the above list, if you allow a shilling for tobacco and deduct this and the other non-food items, you are left with sixteen and fivepence halfpenny. Call it sixteen shillings and leave the baby out of account – for the baby was getting its weekly packets of milk from the Welfare Clinic. This sixteen shillings has got to provide the entire nourishment, *including fuel*, of three persons, two of them adult. The first question is whether it is even theoretically possible for three persons to be properly nourished on sixteen shillings a week. When the dispute over the Means Test was in progress there was a disgusting public wrangle about the minimum weekly sum on which a human being could keep alive. So far as I remember, one school of dietitians worked it out at five and ninepence, while another school, more generous, put it at five and ninepence half-penny. After this there were letters to the papers from a number of people who claimed to be feeding themselves on four shillings a week. Here is a weekly budget (it was printed in the *New Statesman* and also in the *News of the World*) which I picked out from among a number of others:

	s.	*d.*
3 wholemeal loaves	1	0
½ lb. margarine	0	2½
½ lb. dripping	0	3
1 lb. cheese	0	7
1 lb. onions	0	1½
1 lb. carrots	0	1½
1 lb. broken biscuits	0	4
2 lb. dates	0	6
1 tin evaporated milk	0	5
10 oranges	0	5
Total	3	11½

Please notice that this budget contains *nothing for fuel.* In fact, the writer explicitly stated that he could not afford to buy fuel and ate all his food raw. Whether the letter was genuine or a hoax does not matter at the moment. What I think will be admitted is that this list represents about as wise an expenditure as could be contrived; if you *had* to live on three and elevenpence halfpenny a week, you could hardly extract more food-value from it than that. So perhaps it is possible to feed yourself adequately on the PAC allowance if you concentrate on essential food-stuffs; but not otherwise.

Now compare this list with the unemployed miner's budget that I gave earlier. The miner's family spend only tenpence a week on green vegetables and tenpence halfpenny on milk (remember that one of them is a child less than three years old), and nothing on fruit; but they spend one and nine on sugar (about eight pounds of sugar, that is) and a shilling on tea. The half-crown spent on meat *might* represent a small joint and the materials for a stew; probably as often as not it would represent four or five tins of bully beef. The basis of their diet, therefore, is white bread and margarine, corned beef, sugared tea and potatoes – an appalling diet. Would it not be better if they spent more money on wholesome things like oranges and wholemeal bread or if they even, like the writer of the letter to the *New Statesman*, saved on fuel and ate their carrots raw? Yes, it would, but the point is that no ordinary human being is ever going to do such a thing. The ordinary human being would sooner starve than live on brown bread and raw carrots. And the peculiar evil is this, that the less money you have, the less inclined you feel to spend it on wholesome food. A millionaire may enjoy breakfasting off orange juice and Ryvita biscuits; an unemployed man doesn't. Here the tendency of which I spoke at the end of the last chapter comes into play. When you are unemployed, which is to say when you are underfed, harassed, bored and miserable, you don't *want* to eat dull wholesome food. You want something a little bit 'tasty'. There is always some cheaply pleasant thing to tempt you. Let's have three pennorth of chips! Run out and buy us a twopenny ice-cream! Put the kettle on and we'll all have a nice cup of tea! *That* is how your mind works when you are at the PAC level. White bread-and-marg. and sugared tea don't nourish you to any extent, but they are *nicer* (at least most people think so) than brown bread-and-dripping and cold water. Unemployment is an endless misery that has got to be constantly palliated, and especially with tea, the Englishman's opium. A cup of tea or even an aspirin is much better as a temporary stimulant than a crust of brown bread.

The results of all this are visible in a physical degeneracy which you can study directly, by using your eyes, or inferentially, by having a look at the vital statistics. The physical average in the industrial towns is terribly low, lower even than in London. In Sheffield you have the feeling of walking among a population of troglodytes. The miners are splendid men, but they are usually small, and the mere fact that their muscles are toughened by constant work does not mean that their children start life with a better physique. In any case the miners are physically the pick of the population. The most obvious sign of undernourishment is the badness of everybody's teeth. In Lancashire you would have to look for a long time before you saw a working-class person with good natural teeth. Indeed, you see very few people with natural teeth at all, apart from the children; and even the children's teeth have a frail bluish appearance which means, I suppose, calcium deficiency. Several dentists have told me that in industrial districts a person over thirty with any of his or her own teeth is coming to be an abnormality. In Wigan various people gave me their opinion that it is best to 'get shut of' your teeth as early in life as possible. 'Teeth is just a misery,' one woman said to me. In one house where I stayed there were, apart from myself, five people, the oldest being forty-three and the youngest a boy of fifteen. Of these the boy was the only one who possessed a single tooth of his own, and his teeth were obviously not going to last long. As for the vital statistics, the fact that in any large industrial town the death rate and infant mortality rate of the poorest quarters are always about double those of the well-to-do residential quarters – a good deal more than double in some cases – hardly needs commenting on.

Of course one ought not to imagine that the prevailing bad physique is due solely to unemployment, for it is probable that the physical average has been declining all over England for a long time past, and not merely among the unemployed in the industrial areas. This cannot be proved statistically, but it is a conclusion that is forced upon you if you use your eyes, even in rural places and even in a prosperous town like London. On the day when King George V's body passed through London on its way to Westminster, I happened to be caught for an hour or two in the crowd in Trafalgar Square. It was impossible, looking about one then, not to be struck by the physical degeneracy of modern England. The people surrounding me were *not* working-class people for the most part; they were the shopkeeper-commercial-traveller type, with a sprinkling of the well-to-do. But what a set they looked! Puny limbs, sickly faces, under the weeping London sky! Hardly a well-built man or a decent-looking woman, and not a fresh complexion anywhere. As the King's coffin went by, the men took off their hats, and a friend who was in the crowd at the other side of the Strand said to me afterwards, 'The only touch of colour anywhere was the bald heads.' Even the Guards, it seemed to me – there was a squad of guardsmen marching beside the coffin – were not what they used to be. Where are the monstrous men with chests like barrels and moustaches like the wings of eagles who strode across my childhood's gaze twenty or thirty years ago? Buried, I suppose, in the Flanders mud.

In their place there are these pale-faced boys who have been picked for their height and consequently look like hop-poles in overcoats – the truth being that in modern England a man over six feet high is usually skin and bone and not much else. If the English physique has declined, this is no doubt partly due to the fact that the Great War carefully selected the million best men in England and slaughtered them, largely before they had had time to breed. But the process must have begun earlier than that, and it must be due ultimately to unhealthy ways of living, i.e. to industrialism. I don't mean the habit of living in towns – probably the town is healthier than the country, in many ways – but the modern industrial technique which provides you with cheap substitutes for everything. We may find in the long run that tinned food is a deadlier weapon than the machine gun.

It is unfortunate that the English working class – the English nation generally, for that matter – are exceptionally ignorant about and wasteful of food. I have pointed out elsewhere how civilised is a French navvy's idea of a meal compared with an Englishman's, and I cannot believe that you would ever see such wastage in a French house as you habitually see in English ones. Of course, in the very poorest homes, where everybody is unemployed, you don't see much actual waste, but those who can afford to waste food often do so. I could give startling instances of this. Even the Northern habit of baking one's own bread is slightly wasteful in itself, because an overworked woman cannot bake more than once or, at most, twice a week and it is impossible to tell beforehand how much bread will be wanted, so that a certain amount generally has to be thrown away. The usual thing is to bake six large loaves and twelve small ones at a time. All this is part of the old, generous English attitude to life, and it is an amiable quality, but a disastrous one at the present moment.

English working people everywhere, so far as I know, refuse brown bread; it is usually impossible to buy wholemeal bread in a working-class district. They sometimes give the reason that brown bread is 'dirty'. I suspect the real reason is that in the past brown bread has been confused with black bread, which is traditionally associated with Popery and wooden shoes. (They have plenty of Popery and wooden shoes in Lancashire. A pity they haven't the black bread as well!) But the English palate, especially the working-class palate, now rejects good food almost automatically. The number of people who *prefer* tinned peas and tinned fish to real peas and real fish must be increasing every year, and plenty of people who could afford real milk in their tea would much sooner have tinned milk – even that dreadful tinned milk which is made of sugar and cornflour and has UNFIT FOR BABIES on the tin in huge letters. In some districts efforts are now being made to teach the unemployed more about food-values and more about the intelligent spending of money. When you hear of a thing like this you feel yourself torn both ways. I have heard a Communist speaker on the platform grow very angry about it. In London, he said, parties of Society dames now have the cheek to walk into East End houses and give shopping-lessons to the wives of the unemployed. He gave this as an instance of the mentality of the English governing class. First you condemn a family to live on thirty shillings a week, and then you have the damned impertinence to tell them how they are to spend their money. He was quite right – I agree heartily. Yet all the same it *is* a pity that, merely for the lack of a proper tradition, people should pour muck like tinned milk down their throats and not even know that it is inferior to the product of the cow.

I doubt, however, whether the unemployed would ultimately benefit if they learned to spend their money more economically. For it is only the fact that they are *not* economical that keeps their allowances so high. An Englishman on the PAC gets fifteen shillings a week because fifteen shillings is the smallest sum on which he can conceivably keep alive. If he were, say, an Indian or Japanese coolie, who can live on rice and onions, he wouldn't get fifteen shillings a week – he would be lucky if he got fifteen shillings a month. Our unemployment allowances, miserable though they are, are framed to suit a population with very high standards and not much notion of economy. If the unemployed learned to be better managers they would be visibly better off, and I fancy it would not be long before the dole was docked correspondingly.

There is one great mitigation of unemployment in the North, and that is the cheapness of fuel. Anywhere in the coal areas the retail price of coal is about one and sixpence a hundredweight; in the South of England it is about half a crown. Moreover, miners in work can usually buy coal direct from the pit at eight or nine shillings a ton, and those who have a cellar in their homes sometimes store a ton at a time and sell it (illicitly, I suppose) to those who are out of work. But apart from this there is immense and systematic thieving of coal by the unemployed. I call it thieving because technically it is that, though it does no harm to anybody. In the 'dirt' that is sent up from the pits there is a certain amount of broken coal, and unemployed people spend a lot of time in picking it out of the slag-heaps. All day long over those strange grey mountains you see people wandering to and fro with sacks and baskets among the sulphurous smoke (many slag-heaps are on fire under the surface), prising out the tiny nuggets of coal which are buried here and there. You meet men coming away, wheeling strange and wonderful home-made bicycles – bicycles made of rusty parts picked off refuse-tips, without saddles, without chains and almost always without tyres – across which are slung bags containing perhaps half a hundredweight of coal, fruit of half a day's searching. In times of strikes, when everybody is short of fuel, the miners turn out with pick and shovel and burrow into the slag-heaps, whence the hummocky appearance which most slag-heaps have. During long strikes, in places where there are outcrops of coal, they have sunk surface mines and carried them scores of yards into the earth.

In Wigan the competition among unemployed people for the waste coal has become so fierce that it has led to an extraordinary custom called 'scrambling for the coal', which is well worth seeing. Indeed I rather wonder that it has never been filmed. An unemployed miner took me to see it one afternoon. We got to the place, a mountain range of ancient slag-heaps with a railway running through the valley below. A couple of hundred ragged men, each with a sack and coal-hammer strapped under his coat-tails, were waiting on the 'broo'. When the dirt comes up from the pit it is loaded onto trucks and an engine runs these to the top of another slag-heap a quarter of a mile away and there leaves them. The process of 'scrambling for the coal' consists in getting onto the train while it is moving; any truck which you have succeeded in boarding while it is in motion counts as 'your' truck. Presently the train hove in sight. With a wild yell a hundred men dashed down the slope to catch her as she rounded the bend. Even at the bend the train was making twenty miles an hour. The men hurled themselves upon it, caught hold of the rings at the rear of the trucks and hoisted themselves up by way of the bumpers, five or ten of them on each truck. The driver took no notice. He drove up to the top of the slag-heap, uncoupled the trucks and ran the engine back to the pit, presently returning with a fresh string of trucks. There was the same wild rush of ragged figures as before. In the end only about fifty men had failed to get onto either train.

We walked up to the top of the slag-heap. The men were shovelling the dirt out of the trucks, while down below their wives and children were kneeling, swiftly scrabbling with their hands in the damp dirt and picking out lumps of coal the size of an egg or smaller. You would see a woman pounce on a tiny fragment of stuff, wipe it on her apron, scrutinise it to make sure it was coal and pop it jealously into her sack. Of course, when you are boarding a truck you don't know beforehand what is in it; it may be actual 'dirt' from the roads or it may merely be shale from the roofing. If it is a shale truck there will be no coal in it, but there occurs among the shale another inflammable rock called cannel, which looks very like ordinary shale but is slightly darker and is known by splitting in parallel lines, like slate. It makes tolerable fuel, not good enough to be commercially valuable but good enough to be eagerly sought after by the unemployed. The miners on the shale trucks were picking out the cannel and splitting it up with their hammers. Down at the bottom of the 'broo' the people who had failed to get onto either train were gleaning the tiny chips of coal that came rolling down from above – fragments no bigger than a hazelnut, these, but the people were glad enough to get them.

We stayed there till the train was empty. In a couple of hours the people had picked the dirt over to the last grain. They slung their sacks over shoulder or bicycle, and started on the two-mile trudge back to Wigan. Most of the families had gathered about half a hundredweight of coal or cannel, so that between them they must have stolen five or ten tons of fuel. This business of robbing the dirt trains takes place every day in Wigan, at any rate in winter, and at more collieries than one. It is of course extremely dangerous. No one was hurt the afternoon I was there, but a man had had both his legs cut off a few weeks earlier, and another man lost several fingers a week later. Technically it is stealing but, as everybody knows, if the coal were not stolen it would simply be wasted. Now and again, for form's sake, the colliery companies prosecute somebody for coal-picking, and in that morning's issue of the local paper there was a paragraph saying that two men had been fined ten shillings. But no notice is taken of the prosecutions – in fact, one of the men named in the paper was there that afternoon – and the coal-pickers subscribe among themselves to pay the fines. The thing is taken for granted. Everyone knows that the unemployed have got to get fuel somehow. So every afternoon several hundred men risk their necks and several hundred women scrabble in the mud for hours – and all for half a hundredweight of inferior fuel, value ninepence.

That scene stays in my mind as one of my pictures of Lancashire: the dumpy, shawled women, with their sacking aprons and their heavy black clogs, kneeling in the cindery mud and the bitter wind, searching eagerly for tiny chips of coal. They are glad enough to do it. In winter they are desperate for fuel; it is more important almost than food. Meanwhile all round, as far as the eye can see, are the slag-heaps and hoisting gear of collieries, and not one of those collieries can sell all the coal it is capable of producing. This ought to appeal to Major Douglas.

VII

As you travel northward your eye, accustomed to the South or East, does not notice much difference until you are beyond Birmingham. In Coventry you might as well be in Finsbury Park, and the Bull Ring in Birmingham is not unlike Norwich Market, and between all the towns of the Midlands there stretches a villa-civilisation indistinguishable from that of the South. It is only when you get a little further north, to the pottery towns and beyond, that you begin to encounter the real ugliness of industrialism – an ugliness so frightful and so arresting that you are obliged, as it were, to come to terms with it.

A slag-heap is at best a hideous thing, because it is so planless and functionless. It is something just dumped on the earth, like the emptying of a giant's dust-bin. On the outskirts of the mining towns there are frightful landscapes where your horizon is ringed completely round by jagged grey mountains, and underfoot is mud and ashes and overhead the steel cables where tubs of dirt travel slowly across miles of country. Often the slag-heaps are on fire, and at night you can see the red rivulets of fire winding this way and that, and also the slow-moving blue flames of sulphur, which always seem on the point of expiring and always spring out again. Even when a slag-heap sinks, as it does ultimately, only an evil brown grass grows on it, and it retains its hummocky surface. One in the slums of Wigan, used as a playground, looks like a choppy sea suddenly frozen; 'the flock mattress', it is called locally. Even centuries hence when the plough drives over the places where coal was once mined, the sites of ancient slag-heaps will still be distinguishable from an aeroplane.

I remember a winter afternoon in the dreadful environs of Wigan. All round was the lunar landscape of slag-heaps, and to the north, through the passes, as it were, between the mountains of slag, you could see the factory chimneys sending out their plumes of smoke. The canal path was a mixture of cinders and frozen mud, criss-crossed by the imprints of innumerable clogs, and all round, as far as the slag-heaps in the distance, stretched the 'flashes' – pools of stagnant water that has seeped into the hollows caused by the subsidence of ancient pits. It was horribly cold. The 'flashes' were covered with ice the colour of raw umber, the bargemen were muffled to the eyes in sacks, the lock gates wore beards of ice. It seemed a world from which vegetation had been banished; nothing existed except smoke, shale, ice, mud, ashes and foul water. But even Wigan is beautiful compared with Sheffield. Sheffield, I suppose, could justly claim to be called the ugliest town in the Old World: its inhabitants, who want it to be pre-eminent in everything, very likely do make that claim for it. It has a population of half a million and it contains fewer decent buildings than the average East Anglian village of five hundred. And the stench! If at rare moments you stop smelling sulphur it is because you have begun smelling gas. Even the shallow river that runs through the town is usually bright yellow with some chemical or other. Once I halted in the street and counted the factory chimneys I could see; there were thirty-three of them, but there would have been far more if the air had not been obscured by smoke. One scene especially lingers in my mind. A frightful patch of waste ground (somehow, up there, a patch of waste ground attains a squalor that would be impossible even in London) trampled bare of grass and littered with newspapers and old saucepans. To the right an isolated row of gaunt four-roomed houses, dark red, blackened by smoke. To the left an interminable vista of factory chimneys, chimney beyond chimney, fading away into a dim blackish haze. Behind me a railway embankment made of the slag from furnaces. In front, across the patch of waste ground, a cubical building of red and yellow brick, with the sign 'Thomas Grocock, Haulage Contractor'.

At night, when you cannot see the hideous shapes of the houses and the blackness of everything, a town like Sheffield assumes a kind of sinister magnificence. Sometimes the drifts of smoke are rosy with sulphur, and serrated flames, like circular saws, squeeze themselves out from beneath the cowls of the foundry chimneys. Through the open doors of foundries you see fiery serpents of iron being hauled to and fro by redlit boys, and you hear the whizz and thump of steam hammers and the scream of the iron under the blow. The pottery towns are almost equally ugly in a pettier way. Right in among the rows of tiny blackened houses, part of the street as it were, are the 'pot banks' – conical brick chimneys like gigantic burgundy bottles buried in the soil and belching their smoke almost in your face. You come upon monstrous clay chasms hundreds of feet across and almost as deep, with little rusty tubs creeping on chain railways up one side, and on the other workmen clinging like samphire-gatherers and cutting into the face of the cliff with their picks. I passed that way in snowy weather, and even the snow was black. The best thing one can say for the pottery towns is that they are fairly small and stop abruptly. Less than ten miles away you can stand in undefiled country, on the almost naked hills, and the pottery towns are only a smudge in the distance.

When you contemplate such ugliness as this, there are two questions that strike you. First, is it inevitable? Secondly, does it matter?

I do not believe that there is anything inherently and unavoidably ugly about industrialism. A factory or even a gasworks is not obliged of its own nature to be ugly, any more than a palace or a dog-kennel or a cathedral. It all depends on the architectural tradition of the period. The industrial towns of the North are ugly because they happen to have been built at a time when modern methods of steel-construction and smoke-abatement were unknown, and when everyone was too busy making money to think about anything else. They go on being ugly largely because the Northerners have got used to that kind of thing and do not notice it. Many of the people in Sheffield or Manchester, if they smelled the air along the Cornish cliffs, would probably declare that it had no taste in it. But since the war, industry has tended to shift southward and in doing so has grown almost comely. The typical post-war factory is not a gaunt barrack or an awful chaos of blackness and belching chimneys; it is a glittering white structure of concrete, glass and steel, surrounded by green lawns and beds of tulips. Look at the factories you pass as you travel out of London on the GWR; they may not be aesthetic triumphs but certainly they are not ugly in the same way as the Sheffield gasworks. But in any case, though the ugliness of industrialism is the most obvious thing about it and the thing every newcomer exclaims against, I doubt whether it is centrally important. And perhaps it is not even desirable, industrialism being what it is, that it should learn to disguise itself as something else. As Mr Aldous Huxley has truly remarked, a dark Satanic mill ought to look like a dark Satanic mill and not like the temple of mysterious and splendid gods. Moreover, even in the worst of the industrial towns one sees a great deal that is not ugly in the narrow aesthetic sense. A belching chimney or a stinking slum is repulsive chiefly because it implies warped lives and ailing children. Look at it from a purely aesthetic standpoint and it may have a certain macabre appeal. I find that anything outrageously strange generally ends by fascinating me even when I abominate it. The landscapes of Burma, which, when I was among them, so appalled me as to assume the qualities of nightmare, afterwards stayed so hauntingly in my mind that I was obliged to write a novel about them to get rid of them. (In all novels about the East the scenery is the real subject-matter.) It would probably be quite easy to extract a sort of beauty, as Arnold Bennett did, from the blackness of the industrial towns; one can easily imagine Baudelaire, for instance, writing a poem about a slag-heap. But the beauty or ugliness of industrialism hardly matters. Its real evil lies far deeper and is quite ineradicable. It is important to remember this, because there is always a temptation to think that industrialism is harmless so long as it is clean and orderly.

But when you go to the industrial North you are conscious, quite apart from the unfamiliar scenery, of entering a strange country. This is partly because of certain real differences which do exist, but still more because of the North-South antithesis which has been rubbed into us for such a long time past. There exists in England a curious cult of Northernness, a sort of Northern snobbishness. A Yorkshireman in the South will always take care to let you know that he regards you as an inferior. If you ask him why, he will explain that it is only in the North that life is 'real' life, that the industrial work done in the North is the only 'real' work, that the North is inhabited by 'real' people, the South merely by rentiers and their parasites. The Northerner has 'grit', he is grim, 'dour', plucky, warm-hearted and democratic; the Southerner is snobbish, effeminate and lazy – that at any rate is the theory. Hence the Southerner goes north, at any rate for the first time, with the vague inferiority-complex of a civilised man venturing among savages, while the Yorkshireman, like the Scotchman, comes to London in the spirit of a barbarian out for loot. And feelings of this kind, which are the result of tradition, are not affected by visible facts. Just as an Englishman five feet four inches high and twenty nine inches round the chest feels that as an Englishman he is the physical superior of Carnera (Carnera being a Dago), so also with the Northerner and the Southerner. I remember a weedy little Yorkshireman who would almost certainly have run away if a fox-terrier had snapped at him, telling me that in the South of England he felt 'like a wild invader'. But the cult is often adopted by people who are not by birth Northerners themselves. A year or two ago a friend of mine, brought up in the South but now living in the North, was driving me through Suffolk in a car. We passed through a rather beautiful village. He glanced disapprovingly at the cottages and said:

> Of course most of the villages in Yorkshire are hideous; but the Yorkshiremen are splendid chaps. Down here it's just the other way about – beautiful villages and rotten people. All the people in those cottages there are worthless, absolutely worthless.

I could not help enquiring whether he happened to know anybody in that village. No, he did not know them; but because this was East Anglia they were obviously worthless. Another friend of mine, again a Southerner by birth, loses no opportunity of praising the North to the detriment of the South. Here is an extract from one of his letters to me:

> I am in Clitheroe, Lancs . . . I think running water is much more attractive in moor and mountain country than in the fat and sluggish South. 'The smug and silver Trent,' Shakespeare says; and the South-er the smugger, I say.

Here you have an interesting example of the Northern cult. Not only are you and I and everyone else in the South of England written off as 'fat and sluggish', but even water, when it gets north of a certain latitude, ceases to be H_2O and becomes something mystically superior. But the interest of this passage is that its writer is an extremely intelligent man of 'advanced' opinions who would have nothing but contempt for nationalism in its ordinary form. Put to him some such proposition as 'One Britisher is worth three foreigners', and he would repudiate it with horror. But when it is a question of North versus South, he is quite ready to generalise. *All* nationalistic distinctions – all claims to be better than somebody else because you have a different-shaped skull or speak a different dialect – are entirely spurious, but they are important so long as people believe in them. There is no doubt about the Englishman's inbred conviction that those who live to the south of him are his inferiors; even our foreign policy is governed by it to some extent. I think, therefore, that it is worth pointing out when and why it came into being.

When nationalism first became a religion, the English looked at the map, and, noticing that their island lay very high in the Northern Hemisphere, evolved the pleasing theory that the further north you live the more virtuous you become. The histories I was given when I was a little boy generally started off by explaining in the naïvest way that a cold climate made people energetic while a hot one made them lazy, and hence the defeat of the Spanish Armada. This nonsense about the superior energy of the English (actually the laziest people in Europe) has been current for at least a hundred years. 'Better is it for us,' writes a *Quarterly Reviewer* of 1827, 'to be condemned to labour for our country's good than to luxuriate amid olives, vines and vices.' 'Olives, vines and vices' sums up the normal English attitude towards the Latin races. In the mythology of Carlyle, Creasy, etc., the Northerner ('Teutonic', later 'Nordic') is pictured as a hefty, vigorous chap with blond moustaches and pure morals, while the Southerner is sly, cowardly and licentious. This theory was never pushed to its logical end, which would have meant assuming that the finest people in the world were the Eskimos, but it did involve admitting that the people who lived to the north of us were superior to ourselves. Hence, partly, the cult of Scotland and of Scotch things which has so deeply marked English life during the past fifty years. But it was the industrialisation of the North that gave the North-South antithesis its peculiar slant. Until comparatively recently the northern part of England was the backward and feudal part, and such industry as existed was concentrated in London and the South-East. In the Civil War, for instance, roughly speaking a war of money versus feudalism, the North and West were for the King and the South and East for the Parliament. But with the increasing use of coal industry passed to the North, and there grew up a new type of man, the self-made Northern business man – the Mr Rouncewell and Mr Bounderby of Dickens. The Northern business man, with his hateful 'get on or get out' philosophy, was the dominant figure of the nineteenth century, and as a sort of tyrannical corpse he rules us still. This is the type deified by Arnold Bennett – the type who starts off with half a crown and ends up with fifty thousand pounds, and whose chief pride is to be an even greater boor after he has made his money than before. On analysis his sole virtue turns out to be a talent for making money. We were bidden to admire him because though he might be narrow-minded, sordid, ignorant, grasping and uncouth, he had 'grit', he 'got on'; in other words, he knew how to make money.

This kind of cant is nowadays a pure anachronism, for the Northern business man is no longer prosperous. But traditions are not killed by facts, and the tradition of Northern 'grit' lingers. It is still dimly felt that a Northerner will 'get on', i.e. make money, where a Southerner will fail. At the back of the mind of every Yorkshireman and every Scotchman who comes to London is a sort of Dick Whittington picture of himself as the boy who starts off by selling newspapers and ends up as Lord Mayor. And that, really, is at the bottom of his bumptiousness. But where one can make a great mistake is in imagining that this feeling extends to the genuine working class. When I first went to Yorkshire, some years ago, I imagined that I was going to a country of boors. I was used to the London Yorkshireman with his interminable harangues and his pride in the supposed raciness of his dialect ('"A stitch in time saves nine," as we say in the West Riding'), and I expected to meet with a good deal of rudeness. But I met with nothing of the kind, and least of all among the miners. Indeed the Lancashire and Yorkshire miners treated me with a kindness and courtesy that were even embarrassing; for if there is one type of man to whom I do feel myself inferior, it is a coal-miner. Certainly no one showed any sign of despising me for coming from a different part of the country. This has its importance when one remembers that the English regional snobberies are nationalism in miniature; for it suggests that place-snobbery is not a working-class characteristic.

There is nevertheless a real difference between North and South, and there is at least a tinge of truth in that picture of Southern England as one enormous Brighton inhabited by lounge-lizards. For climatic reasons the parasitic dividend-drawing class tend to settle in the South. In a Lancashire cotton-town you could probably go for months on end without once hearing an 'educated' accent, whereas there can hardly be a town in the South of England where you could throw a brick without hitting the niece of a bishop. Consequently, with no petty gentry to set the pace, the bourgeoisification of the working class, though it is taking place in the North, is taking place more slowly. All the Northern accents, for instance, persist strongly, while the Southern ones are collapsing before the movies and the BBC. Hence your 'educated' accent stamps you rather as a foreigner than as a chunk of the petty gentry; and this is an immense advantage, for it makes it much easier to get into contact with the working class.

But is it ever possible to be really intimate with the working class? I shall have to discuss that later; I will only say here that I do not think it is possible. But undoubtedly it is easier in the North than it would be in the South to meet working-class people on approximately equal terms. It is fairly easy to live in a miner's house and be accepted as one of the family; with, say, a farm labourer in the Southern counties it probably would be impossible. I have seen just enough of the working class to avoid idealising them, but I do know that you can learn a great deal in a working-class home, if only you can get there. The essential point is that your middle-class ideals and prejudices are tested by contact with others which are not necessarily better but are certainly different.

Take for instance the different attitude towards the family. A working-class family hangs together as a middle-class one does, but the relationship is far less tyrannical. A working-man has not that deadly weight of family prestige hanging round his neck like a millstone. I have pointed out earlier that a middle-class person goes utterly to pieces under the influence of poverty; and this is generally due to the behaviour of his family – to the fact that he has scores of relations nagging and badgering him night and day for failing to 'get on'. The fact that the working class know how to combine and the middle class don't is probably due to their different conceptions of family loyalty. You cannot have an effective trade union of middle-class workers, because in times of strikes almost every middle-class wife would be egging her husband on to blackleg and get the other fellow's job. Another working-class characteristic, disconcerting at first, is their plain-spokenness towards anyone they regard as an equal. If you offer a working-man something he doesn't want, he tells you that he doesn't want it; a middle-class person would accept it to avoid giving offence. And again, take the working-class attitude towards 'education'. How different it is from ours, and how immensely sounder! Working-people often have a vague reverence for learning in others, but where 'education' touches their own lives they see through it and reject it by a healthy instinct. The time was when I used to lament over quite imaginary pictures of lads of fourteen dragged protesting from their lessons and set to work at dismal jobs. It seemed to me dreadful that the doom of a 'job' should descend upon anyone at fourteen. Of course I know now that there is not one working-class boy in a thousand who does not pine for the day when he will leave school. He wants to be doing real work, not wasting his time on ridiculous rubbish like history and geography. To the working class, the notion of staying at school till you are nearly grown-up seems merely contemptible and unmanly. The idea of a great big boy of eighteen, who ought to be bringing a pound a week home to his parents, going to school in a ridiculous uniform and even being caned for not doing his lessons! Just fancy a working-class boy of eighteen allowing himself to be caned! He is a man when the other is still a baby. Ernest Pontifex, in Samuel Butler's *Way of All Flesh*, after he had had a few glimpses of real life, looked back on his public-school and university education and found it a 'sickly, debilitating debauch'. There is much in middle-class life that looks sickly and debilitating when you see it from a working-class angle.

In a working-class home – I am not thinking at the moment of the unemployed, but of comparatively prosperous homes – you breathe a warm, decent, deeply human atmosphere which it is not so easy to find elsewhere. I should say that a manual worker, if he is in steady work and drawing good wages – an 'if' which gets bigger and bigger – has a better chance of being happy than an 'educated' man. His home life seems to fall more naturally into a sane and comely shape. I have often been struck by the peculiar easy completeness, the perfect symmetry as it were, of a working-class interior at its best. Especially on winter evenings after tea, when the fire glows in the open range and dances mirrored in the steel fender, when Father, in shirt-sleeves, sits in the rocking chair at one side of the fire reading the racing finals, and Mother sits on the other with her sewing, and the children are happy with a pennorth of mint humbugs, and the dog lolls roasting himself on the rag mat – it is a good place to be in, provided that you can be not only in it but sufficiently *of* it to be taken for granted.

This scene is still reduplicated in a majority of English homes, though not in so many as before the war. Its happiness depends mainly upon one question – whether Father is in work. But notice that the picture I have called up, of a working-class family sitting round the coal fire after kippers and strong tea, belongs only to our own moment of time and could not belong either to the future or the past. Skip forward two hundred years into the Utopian future, and the scene is totally different. Hardly one of the things I have imagined will still be there. In that age when there is no manual labour and everyone is 'educated', it is hardly likely that Father will still be a rough man with enlarged hands who likes to sit in shirt-sleeves and says 'Ah wur coomin' oop street.' And there won't be a coal fire in the grate, only some kind of invisible heater. The furniture will be made of rubber, glass and steel. If there are still such things as evening papers there will certainly be no racing news in them, for gambling will be meaningless in a world where there is no poverty and the horse will have vanished from the face of the earth. Dogs, too, will have been suppressed on grounds of hygiene. And there won't be so many children, either, if the birth-controllers have their way. But move backwards into the Middle Ages and you are in a world almost equally foreign. A windowless hut, a wood fire which smokes in your face because there is no chimney, mouldy bread, 'Poor John', lice, scurvy, a yearly childbirth and a yearly child-death, and the priest terrifying you with tales of Hell.

Curiously enough it is *not* the triumphs of modern engineering, nor the radio, nor the cinematograph, nor the five thousand novels which are published yearly, nor the crowds at Ascot and the Eton and Harrow match, but the memory of working-class interiors – especially as I sometimes saw them in my childhood before the war, when England was still prosperous – that reminds me that our age has not been altogether a bad one to live in.

Part II

VIII

The road from Mandalay to Wigan is a long one and the reasons for taking it are not immediately clear.

In the earlier chapters of this book I have given a rather fragmentary account of various things I saw in the coal areas of Lancashire and Yorkshire. I went there partly because I wanted to see what mass-unemployment is like at its worst, partly in order to see the most typical section of the English working class at close quarters. This was necessary to me as part of my approach to Socialism. For before you can be sure whether you are genuinely in favour of Socialism, you have got to decide whether things at present are tolerable or not tolerable, and you have got to take up a definite attitude on the terribly difficult issue of class. Here I shall have to digress and explain how my own attitude towards the class question was developed. Obviously this involves writing a certain amount of autobiography, and I would not do it if I did not think that I am sufficiently typical of my class, or rather sub-caste, to have a certain symptomatic importance.

I was born into what you might describe as the lower-upper-middle class. The upper-middle class, which had its heyday in the 'eighties and 'nineties, with Kipling as its poet laureate, was a sort of mound of wreckage left behind when the tide of Victorian prosperity receded. Or perhaps it would be better to change the metaphor and describe it not as a mound but as a layer – the layer of society lying between £2,000 and £300 a year: my own family was not far from the bottom. You notice that I define it in terms of money, because that is always the quickest way of making yourself understood. Nevertheless, the essential point about the English class-system is that it is *not* entirely explicable in terms of money. Roughly speaking it is a money-stratification, but it is also interpenetrated by a sort of shadowy caste-system; rather like a jerry-built modern bungalow haunted by medieval ghosts. Hence the fact that the upper-middle class extends or extended to incomes as low as £300 a year – to incomes, that is, much lower than those of merely middle-class people with no social pretensions. Probably there are countries where you can predict a man's opinions from his income, but it is never quite safe to do so in England; you have always got to take his traditions into consideration as well. A naval officer and his grocer very likely have the same income, but they are not equivalent persons and they would only be on the same side in very large issues such as a war or a general strike – possibly not even then.

Of course it is obvious now that the upper-middle class is done for. In every country town in Southern England, not to mention the dreary wastes of Kensington and Earls Court, those who knew it in the days of its glory are dying, vaguely embittered by a world which has not behaved as it ought. I never open one of Kipling's books or go into one of the huge dull shops which were once the favourite haunt of the upper-middle class, without thinking 'Change and decay in all around I see.' But before the war the upper-middle class, though already none too prosperous, still felt sure of itself. Before the war you were either a gentleman or not a gentleman, and if you were a gentleman you struggled to behave as such, whatever your income might be. Between those with £400 a year and those with £2,000 or even £1,000 a year there was a great gulf fixed, but it was a gulf which those with £400 a year did their best to ignore. Probably the distinguishing mark of the upper-middle class was that its traditions were not to any extent commercial, but mainly military, official, and professional. People in this class owned no land, but they felt that they were landowners in the sight of God and kept up a semi-aristocratic outlook by going into the professions and the fighting services rather than into trade. Small boys used to count the plum stones on their plates and foretell their destiny by chanting, 'Army, Navy, Church, Medicine, Law'; and even of these 'Medicine' was faintly inferior to the others and only put in for the sake of symmetry. To belong to this class when you were at the £400 a year level was a queer business, for it meant that your gentility was almost purely theoretical. You lived, so to speak, at two levels simultaneously. Theoretically you knew all about servants and how to tip them, although in practice you had one or, at most, two resident servants. Theoretically you knew how to wear your clothes and how to order a dinner, although in practice you could never afford to go to a decent tailor or a decent restaurant. Theoretically you knew how to shoot and ride, although in practice you had no horses to ride and not an inch of ground to shoot over. It was this that explained the attraction of India (more recently Kenya, Nigeria, etc.) for the lower-upper-middle class. The people who went there as soldiers and officials did not go there to make money, for a soldier or an official does not make money; they went there because in India, with cheap horses, free shooting, and hordes of black servants, it was so easy to play at being a gentleman.

In the kind of shabby-genteel family that I am talking about there is far more *consciousness* of poverty than in any working-class family above the level of the dole. Rent and clothes and school-bills are an unending nightmare, and every luxury, even a glass of beer, is an unwarrantable extravagance. Practically the whole family income goes in keeping up appearances. It is obvious that people of this kind are in an anomalous position, and one might be tempted to write them off as mere exceptions and therefore unimportant. Actually, however, they are or were fairly numerous. Most clergymen and schoolmasters, for instance, nearly all Anglo-Indian officials, a sprinkling of soldiers and sailors and a fair number of professional men and artists, fall into this category. But the real importance of this class is that they are the shock-absorbers of the bourgeoisie. The real bourgeoisie, those in the £2,000 a year class and over, have their money as a thick layer of padding between themselves and the class they plunder; in so far as they are aware of the Lower Orders at all they are aware of them as employees, servants and tradesmen. But it is quite different for the poor devils lower down who are struggling to live genteel lives on what are virtually working-class incomes. These last are forced into close and, in a sense, intimate contact with the working class, and I suspect it is from them that the traditional upper-class attitude towards 'common' people is derived.

And what is this attitude? An attitude of sniggering superiority punctuated by bursts of vicious hatred. Look at any number of *Punch* during the past thirty years. You will find it everywhere taken for granted that a working-class person, as such, is a figure of fun, except at odd moments when he shows signs of being too prosperous, whereupon he ceases to be a figure of fun and becomes a demon. It is no use wasting breath in denouncing this attitude. It is better to consider how it has arisen, and to do that one has got to realise what the working classes look like to those who live among them but have different habits and traditions.

A shabby-genteel family is in much the same position as a family of 'poor whites' living in a street where everyone else is a Negro. In such circumstances you have got to cling to your gentility because it is the only thing you have; and meanwhile you are hated for your stuck-up-ness and for the accent and manners which stamp you as one of the boss class. I was very young, not much more than six, when I first became aware of class-distinctions. Before that age my chief heroes had generally been working-class people, because they always seemed to do such interesting things, such as being fishermen and blacksmiths and bricklayers. I remember the farm hands on a farm in Cornwall who used to let me ride on the drill when they were sowing turnips and would sometimes catch the ewes and milk them to give me a drink; and the workmen building the new house next door, who let me play with the wet mortar and from whom I first learned the word 'b——'; and the plumber up the road with whose children I used to go out bird-nesting. But it was not long before I was forbidden to play with the plumber's children; they were 'common' and I was told to keep away from them. This was snobbish, if you like, but it was also necessary, for middle-class people cannot afford to let their children grow up with vulgar accents. So, very early, the working class ceased to be a race of friendly and wonderful beings and became a race of enemies. We realised that they hated us, but we could never understand why, and naturally we set it down to pure, vicious malignity. To me in my early boyhood, to nearly all children of families like mine, 'common' people seemed almost sub-human. They had coarse faces, hideous accents and gross manners, they hated everyone who was not like themselves, and if they got half a chance they would insult you in brutal ways. That was our view of them, and though it was false it was understandable. For one must remember that before the war there was much more *overt* class-hatred in England than there is now. In those days you were quite likely to be insulted simply for looking like a member of the upper classes;

nowadays, on the other hand, you are more likely to be fawned upon. Anyone over thirty can remember the time when it was impossible for a well-dressed person to walk through a slum street without being hooted at. Whole quarters of big towns were considered unsafe because of 'hooligans' (now almost an extinct type), and the London gutter-boy everywhere, with his loud voice and lack of intellectual scruples, could make life a misery for people who considered it beneath their dignity to answer back. A recurrent terror of my holidays, when I was a small boy, was the gangs of 'cads' who were liable to set upon you five or ten to one. In term time, on the other hand, it was we who were in the majority and the 'cads' who were oppressed; I remember a couple of savage mass-battles in the cold winter of 1916–17. And this tradition of open hostility between upper and lower class had apparently been the same for at least a century past. A typical joke in *Punch* in the 'sixties is a picture of a small, nervous-looking gentleman riding through a slum street and a crowd of street-boys closing in on him with shouts of ''Ere comes a swell! Let's frighten 'is 'oss!'. Just fancy the street-boys trying to frighten his horse now! They would be much likelier to hang round him in vague hopes of a tip. During the past dozen years the English working class have grown servile with a rather horrifying rapidity. It was bound to happen, for the frightful weapon of unemployment has cowed them. Before the war their economic position was comparatively strong, for though there was no dole to fall back upon, there was not much unemployment, and the power of the boss class was not so obvious as it is now. A man did not see ruin staring him in the face every time he cheeked a 'toff', and naturally he did cheek a 'toff' whenever it seemed safe to do so. G. J. Renier, in his book on Oscar Wilde, points out that the strange, obscene bursts of popular fury which followed the Wilde trial were essentially social in character. The London mob had caught a member of the upper classes on the hop, and they took care to keep him hopping. All this was natural and even proper. If you treat people as the English working class have been treated during the past two centuries, you must expect them to resent it. On the other hand the children of shabby-genteel families could not be blamed if they grew up with a hatred of the working class, typified for them by prowling gangs of 'cads'.

But there was another and more serious difficulty. Here you come to the real secret of class distinctions in the West – the real reason why a European of bourgeois upbringing, even when he calls himself a Communist, cannot without a hard effort think of a working man as his equal. It is summed up in four frightful words which people nowadays are chary of uttering, but which were bandied about quite freely in my childhood. The words were: *The lower classes smell.*

That was what we were taught – *the lower classes smell.* And here, obviously, you are at an impassable barrier. For no feeling of like or dislike is quite so fundamental as a *physical* feeling. Race hatred, religious hatred, differences of education, of temperament, of intellect, even differences of moral code, can be got over; but physical repulsion cannot. You can have an affection for a murderer or a sodomite, but you cannot have an affection for a man whose breath stinks – habitually stinks, I mean. However well you may wish him, however much you may admire his mind and character, if his breath stinks he is horrible and in your heart of hearts you will hate him. It may not greatly matter if the average middle-class person is brought up to believe that the working classes are ignorant, lazy, drunken, boorish and dishonest; it is when he is brought up to believe that they are dirty that the harm is done. And in my childhood we *were* brought up to believe that they were dirty. Very early in life you acquired the idea that there was something subtly repulsive about a working-class body; you would not get nearer to it than you could help. You watched a great sweaty navvy walking down the road with his pick over his shoulder; you looked at his discoloured shirt and his corduroy trousers stiff with the dirt of a decade; you thought of those nests and layers of greasy rags below, and, under all, the unwashed body, brown all over (that was how I used to imagine it), with its strong, bacon-like reek. You watched a tramp taking off his boots in a ditch – ugh! It did not seriously occur to you that the tramp might not enjoy having black feet. And even 'lower-class' people whom you knew to be quite clean – servants, for instance – were faintly unappetising. The smell of their sweat, the very texture of their skins, were mysteriously different from yours.

Everyone who has grown up pronouncing his aitches and in a house with a bathroom and one servant is likely to have grown up with these feelings; hence the chasmic, impassable quality of class-distinctions in the West. It is queer how seldom this is admitted. At the moment I can think of only one book where it is set forth without humbug, and that is Mr Somerset Maugham's *On a Chinese Screen.* Mr Maugham describes a high Chinese official arriving at a wayside inn and blustering and calling everybody names in order to impress upon them that he is a supreme dignitary and they are only worms. Five minutes later, having asserted his dignity in the way he thinks proper, he is eating his dinner in perfect amity with the baggage coolies. As an official he feels that he has got to make his presence felt, but he has no feeling that the coolies are of different clay from himself. I have observed countless similar scenes in Burma. Among Mongolians – among all Asiatics, for all I know – there is a sort of natural equality, an easy intimacy between man and man, which is simply unthinkable in the West. Mr Maugham adds:

> In the West we are divided from our fellows by our sense of smell. The working man is our master, inclined to rule us with an iron hand, but it cannot be denied that he stinks: none can wonder at it, for a bath in the dawn when you have to hurry to your work before the factory bell rings is no pleasant thing, nor does heavy labour tend to sweetness; and you do not change your linen more than you can help when the week's washing must be done by a sharp-tongued wife. I do not blame the working man because he stinks, but stink he does. It makes social intercourse difficult to persons of sensitive nostril. The matutinal tub divides the classes more effectually than birth, wealth or education.

Meanwhile, *do* the 'lower classes' smell? Of course, as a whole, they are dirtier than the upper classes. They are bound to be, considering the circumstances in which they live, for even at this late date less than half the houses in England have bathrooms. Besides, the habit of washing yourself all over every day is a very recent one in Europe, and the working classes are generally more conservative than the bourgeoisie. But the English are growing visibly cleaner, and we may hope that in a hundred years they will be almost as clean as the Japanese. It is a pity that those who idealise the working class so often think it necessary to praise every working-class characteristic and therefore to pretend that dirtiness is somehow meritorious in itself. Here, curiously enough, the Socialist and the sentimental democratic Catholic of the type of Chesterton sometimes join hands; both will tell you that dirtiness is healthy and 'natural' and cleanliness is a mere fad or at best a luxury.[1] They seem not to see that they are merely giving colour to the notion that working-class people are dirty from choice and not from necessity. Actually, people who have access to a bath will generally use it. But the essential thing is that middle-class people *believe* that the working class are dirty – you see from the passage quoted above that Mr Maugham himself believes it – and, what is worse, that they are somehow *inherently* dirty. As a child, one of the most dreadful things I could imagine was to drink out of a bottle after a navvy. Once when I was thirteen, I was in a train coming from a market town, and the third-class carriage was packed full of shepherds and pig-men who had been selling their beasts. Somebody produced a quart bottle of beer and passed it round; it travelled from mouth to mouth to mouth, everyone taking a swig. I cannot describe the horror I felt as that bottle worked its way towards me. If I drank from it after all those lower-class male mouths I felt certain I should vomit; on the other hand, if they offered it to me I dared not refuse for fear of offending them – you see here how the middle-class squeamishness works both ways. Nowadays, thank God, I have no feelings of that kind. A working-man's body, as such, is no more repulsive to me than a millionaire's. I still don't like drinking out of a cup or bottle after another person – another man, I mean: with women I don't mind – but at least the question of class does not enter. It was rubbing shoulders with the tramps that cured me of it. Tramps are not really very dirty as English people go, but they have the name for being dirty, and when you have shared a bed with a tramp and drunk tea out of the same snuff-tin, you feel that you have seen the worst and the worst has no terrors for you.

I have dwelt on these subjects because they are vitally important. To get rid of class-distinctions you have got to start by understanding how one class appears when seen through the eyes of another. It is useless to say that the middle classes are 'snobbish' and leave it at that. You get no

[1] According to Chesterton, dirtiness is merely a kind of 'discomfort' and therefore ranks as self-mortification. Unfortunately, the discomfort of dirtiness is chiefly suffered by other people. It is not really very uncomfortable to be dirty – not nearly so uncomfortable as having a cold bath on a winter morning.

further if you do not realise that snobbishness is bound up with a species of idealism. It derives from the early training in which a middle-class child is taught almost simultaneously to wash his neck, to be ready to die for his country, and to despise the 'lower classes'.

Here I shall be accused of being behind the times, for I was a child before and during the war and it may be claimed that children nowadays are brought up with more enlightened notions. It is probably true that class-feeling is for the moment a very little less bitter than it was. The working class are submissive where they used to be openly hostile, and the post-war manufacture of cheap clothes and the general softening of manners have toned down the surface differences between class and class. But undoubtedly the essential feeling is still there. Every middle-class person has a dormant class-prejudice which needs only a small thing to arouse it; and if he is over forty he probably has a firm conviction that his own class has been sacrificed to the class below. Suggest to the average unthinking person of gentle birth who is struggling to keep up appearances on four or five hundred a year that he is a member of an exploiting parasite class, and he will think you are mad. In perfect sincerity he will point out to you a dozen ways in which he is worse-off than a working man. In his eyes the workers are not a submerged race of slaves, they are a sinister flood creeping upwards to engulf himself and his friends and his family and to sweep all culture and all decency out of existence. Hence that queer watchful anxiety lest the working class shall grow too prosperous. In a number of *Punch* soon after the war, when coal was still fetching high prices, there is a picture of four or five miners with grim, sinister faces riding in a cheap motor-car. A friend they are passing calls out and asks them where they have borrowed it. They answer, 'We've bought the thing!' This, you see, is 'good enough for *Punch*'; for miners to buy a motor-car, even one car between four or five of them, is a monstrosity, a sort of crime against nature. That was the attitude of a dozen years ago, and I see no evidence of any fundamental change. The notion that the working class have been absurdly pampered, hopelessly demoralised by doles, old-age pensions, free education, etc., is still widely held; it has merely been a little shaken, perhaps, by the recent recognition that unemployment does exist. For quantities of middle-class people, probably for a large majority of those over fifty, the typical working man still rides to the Labour Exchange on a motor-bike and keeps coal in his bath-tub: 'And, if you'll believe it, my dear, they actually *get married* on the dole!'

The reason why class-hatred seems to be diminishing is that nowadays it tends not to get into print, partly owing to the mealy-mouthed habits of our time, partly because newspapers and even books now have to appeal to a working-class public. As a rule you can best study it in private conversations. But if you want some printed examples, it is worth having a look at the *obiter dicta* of the late Professor Saintsbury. Saintsbury was a very learned man and along certain lines a judicious literary critic, but when he talked of political or economic matters he only differed from the rest of his class by the fact that he was too thick-skinned and had been born too early to see any reason for pretending to common decency. According to Saintsbury, unemployment insurance was simply 'contributing . . . to the support of lazy ne'er-do-weels', and the whole trade union movement was no more than a kind of organised mendicancy:

> 'Pauper' is almost actionable now, is it not, when used as a word? though to *be* paupers, in the sense of being wholly or partly supported at the expense of other people, is the ardent, and to a considerable extent achieved, aspiration of a large proportion of our population, and of an entire political party.
>
> (*A Second Scrap Book.*)

It is to be noticed, however, that Saintsbury recognises that unemployment is bound to exist, and, in fact, thinks that it ought to exist, so long as the unemployed are made to suffer as much as possible:

> Is not 'casual' labour the very secret and safety-valve of a safe and sound labour-system generally?
>
> . . . In a complicated industrial and commercial state constant employment at regular wages is impossible; while dole-supported unemployment, at anything like the wages of employment, is demoralising to begin with and ruinous at its more or less quickly arriving end.
>
> (*A Last Scrap Book.*)

What exactly is to happen to the 'casual labourers' when no casual labour happens to be available is not made clear. Presumably (Saintsbury speaks approvingly of 'good Poor Laws') they are to go into the workhouse or sleep in the streets. As to the notion that every human being ought as a matter of course to have the chance of earning at least a tolerable livelihood, Saintsbury dismisses it with contempt:

> Even the 'right to live' . . . extends no further than the right of protection against murder. Charity certainly will, morality possibly may, and public utility perhaps ought to add to this protection supererogatory provision for continuance of life; but it is questionable whether strict justice demands it.
>
> As for the insane doctrine that being born in a country gives some right to the possession of the soil of that country, it hardly requires notice.
>
> (*A Last Scrap Book.*)

It is worth reflecting for a moment upon the beautiful implications of this last passage. The interest of passages like these (and they are scattered all through Saintsbury's work) lies in their having been printed at all. Most people are a little shy of putting that kind of thing on paper. But what Saintsbury is saying here is what any little worm with a fairly safe five hundred a year *thinks*, and therefore in a way one must admire him for saying it. It takes a lot of guts to be *openly* such a skunk as that.

This is the outlook of a confessed reactionary. But how about the middle-class person whose views are not reactionary but 'advanced'? Beneath his revolutionary mask, is he really so different from the other?

A middle-class person embraces Socialism and perhaps even joins the Communist Party. How much real difference does it make? Obviously, living within the framework of capitalist society, he has got to go on earning his living, and one cannot blame him if he clings to his bourgeois economic status. But is there any change in his tastes, his habits, his manners, his imaginative background – his 'ideology', in Communist jargon? Is there *any* change in him except that he now votes Labour, or, when possible, Communist at the elections? It is noticeable that he still habitually associates with his own class; he is vastly more at home with a member of his own class, who thinks him a dangerous Bolshie, than with a member of the working class who supposedly agrees with him; his tastes in food, wine, clothes, books, pictures, music, ballet, are still recognisably bourgeois tastes; most significant of all, he invariably marries into his own class. Look at any bourgeois Socialist. Look at Comrade X, member of the CPGB and author of *Marxism for Infants.* Comrade X, it so happens, is an old Etonian. He would be ready to die on the barricades, in theory anyway, but you notice that he still leaves his bottom waistcoat button undone. He idealises the proletariat, but it is remarkable how little his habits resemble theirs. Perhaps once, out of sheer bravado, he has smoked a cigar with the band on, but it would be almost physically impossible for him to put pieces of cheese into his mouth on the point of his knife, or to sit indoors with his cap on, or even to drink his tea out of the saucer. Perhaps table-manners are not a bad test of sincerity. I have known numbers of bourgeois Socialists, I have listened by the hour to their tirades against their own class, and yet never, not even once, have I met one who had picked up proletarian table-manners. Yet, after all, why not? Why should a man who thinks all virtue resides in the proletariat still take such pains to drink his soup silently? It can only be because in his heart he feels that proletarian manners are disgusting. So you see he is still responding to the training of his childhood, when he was taught to hate, fear, and despise the working class.

IX

When I was fourteen or fifteen I was an odious little snob, but no worse than other boys of my own age and class. I suppose there is no place in the world where snobbery is quite so ever-present or where it is cultivated in such refined and subtle forms as in an English public school. Here at least one cannot say that English 'education' fails to do its job. You forget your Latin and Greek within a few months of leaving school – I studied Greek for eight or ten years, and now, at thirty-three, I cannot even repeat the Greek alphabet – but your snobbishness, unless you persistently root it out like the bindweed it is, sticks by you till your grave.

At school I was in a difficult position, for I was among boys who, for the most part, were much richer than myself, and I only went to an expensive public school because I happened to win a scholarship. This is the common experience of boys of the lower-upper-middle class, the sons of clergymen, Anglo-Indian officials, etc., and the effects it had on me were probably the usual ones. On the one hand it made me cling tighter than ever to my gentility; on the other hand it filled me with resentment against the boys whose parents were richer than mine and who took care to let me know it. I despised anyone who was not describable as a 'gentleman', but also I hated the hoggishly rich, especially those who had grown rich too recently. The correct and elegant thing, I felt, was to be of gentle birth but to have no money. This is part of the *credo* of the lower-upper-middle class. It has a romantic, Jacobite-in-exile feeling about it which is very comforting.

But those years, during and just after the war, were a queer time to be at school, for England was nearer revolution than she has been since or had been for a century earlier. Throughout almost the whole nation there was running a wave of revolutionary feeling which has since been reversed and forgotten, but which has left various deposits of sediment behind. Essentially, though of course one could not then see it in perspective, it was a revolt of youth against age, resulting directly from the war. In the war the young had been sacrificed and the old had behaved in a way which, even at this distance of time, is horrible to contemplate; they had been sternly patriotic in safe places while their sons went down like swathes of hay before the German machine-guns. Moreover, the war had been conducted mainly by old men and had been conducted with supreme incompetence. By 1918 everyone under forty was in a bad temper with his elders, and the mood of anti-militarism which followed naturally upon the fighting was extended into a general revolt against orthodoxy and authority. At that time there was, among the young, a curious cult of hatred of 'old men'. The dominance of 'old men' was held to be responsible for every evil known to humanity, and every accepted institution from Scott's novels to the House of Lords was derided merely because 'old men' were in favour of it. For several years it was all the fashion to be a 'Bolshie', as people then called it. England was full of half-baked antinomian opinions. Pacifism, internationalism, humanitarianism of all kinds, feminism, free love, divorce-reform, atheism, birth-control – things like these were getting a better hearing than they would get in normal times. And of course the revolutionary mood extended to those who had been too young to fight, even to public-schoolboys. At that time we all thought of ourselves as enlightened creatures of a new age, casting off the orthodoxy that had been forced upon us by those detested 'old men'. We retained, basically, the snobbish outlook of our class, we took it for granted that we should continue to draw our dividends or tumble into soft jobs, but also it seemed natural to us to be 'agin the government'. We derided the OTC, the Christian religion, and perhaps even compulsory games and the Royal Family, and we did not realise that we were merely taking part in a world-wide gesture of distaste for war. Two incidents stick in my mind as examples of the queer revolutionary feeling of that time. One day the master who taught us English set us a kind of general knowledge paper of which one of the questions was, 'Whom do you consider the ten greatest men now living?' Of sixteen boys in the class (our average age was about seventeen) fifteen included Lenin in their list. This was at a snobbish expensive public school, and the date was 1920, when the horrors of the Russian Revolution were still fresh in everyone's mind. Also there were the so-called peace celebrations in 1919. Our elders had decided for us that we should celebrate peace in the traditional manner by whooping over the fallen foe. We were to march into the school-yard, carrying torches, and sing jingo songs of the type of 'Rule, Britannia'. The boys – to their honour, I think – guyed the whole proceeding and sang blasphemous and seditious words to the tunes provided. I doubt whether things would happen in quite that manner now. Certainly the public schoolboys I meet nowadays, even the intelligent ones, are much more right-wing in their opinions than I and my contemporaries were fifteen years ago.

Hence, at the age of seventeen or eighteen, I was both a snob and a revolutionary. I was against all authority. I had read and re-read the entire published works of Shaw, Wells, and Galsworthy (at that time still regarded as dangerously 'advanced' writers), and I loosely described myself as a Socialist. But I had not much grasp of what Socialism meant, and no notion that the working class were human beings. At a distance, and through the medium of books – Jack London's *The People of the Abyss*, for instance – I could agonise over their sufferings, but I still hated them and despised them when I came anywhere near them. I was still revolted by their accents and infuriated by their habitual rudeness. One must remember that just then, immediately after the war, the English working class were in a fighting mood. That was the period of the great coal strikes, when a miner was thought of as a fiend incarnate and old ladies looked under their beds every night lest Robert Smillie should be concealed there. All through the war and for a little time afterwards there had been high wages and abundant employment; things were now returning to something worse than normal, and naturally the working class resisted. The men who had fought had been lured into the army by gaudy promises, and now they were coming home to a world where there were no jobs and not even any houses. Moreover, they had been at war and were coming home with the soldier's attitude to life, which is fundamentally, in spite of discipline, a lawless attitude. There was a turbulent feeling in the air. To that time belongs the song with the memorable refrain:

There's nothing sure but
The rich get richer and the poor get children;
In the mean time,
In between time,
Ain't we got fun?

People had not yet settled down to a lifetime of unemployment mitigated by endless cups of tea. They still vaguely expected the Utopia for which they had fought, and even more than before they were openly hostile to the aitch-pronouncing class. So to the shock-absorbers of the bourgeoisie, such as myself, 'common people' still appeared brutal and repulsive. Looking back upon that period, I seem to have spent half the time in denouncing the capitalist system and the other half in raging over the insolence of bus-conductors.

When I was not yet twenty I went to Burma, in the Indian Imperial Police. In an 'outpost of Empire' like Burma the class-question appeared at first sight to have been shelved. There was no obvious class-friction here, because the all-important thing was not whether you had been to one of the right schools but whether your skin was technically white. As a matter of fact most of the white men in Burma were not of the type who in England would be called 'gentlemen', but except for the common soldiers and a few nondescripts they lived lives appropriate to 'gentlemen' – had servants, that is, and called their evening meal 'dinner' – and officially they were regarded as being all of the same class. They were 'white men', in contradistinction to the other and inferior class, the 'natives'. But one did not feel towards the 'natives' as one felt towards the 'lower classes' at home. The essential point was that the 'natives', at any rate the Burmese, were not felt to be physically repulsive. One looked down on them as 'natives', but one was quite ready to be physically intimate with them; and this, I noticed, was the case even with white men who had the most vicious colour-prejudice. When you have a lot of servants you soon get into lazy habits, and I habitually allowed myself, for instance, to be dressed and undressed by my Burmese boy. This was because he was a Burman and undisgusting; I could not have endured to let an English manservant handle me in that intimate manner. I felt towards a Burman almost as I felt towards a woman. Like most other races, the Burmese have a distinctive smell – I cannot describe it: it is a smell that makes one's teeth tingle – but this smell never disgusted me. (Incidentally, orientals say that *we* smell. The Chinese, I believe, say that a white man smells like a corpse. The Burmese say the same – though no Burman was ever rude enough to say so to me.) And in a way my attitude was defensible, for if one faces facts one must admit that most Mongolians have much nicer bodies than most white men. Compare the firm-knit silken skin of the Burman, which does not wrinkle at all till he is past forty, and then merely withers up like a piece of dry leather, with the coarse-grained, flabby, sagging skin of the white man. The white man has lank ugly hair growing down his legs and the backs of his arms and in an ugly patch on his chest. The Burman has only a tuft or two of stiff black hair at the appropriate places; for the rest he is quite hairless and is usually beardless as well. The white man almost always goes bald, the Burman seldom or never. The Burman's teeth are perfect, though generally discoloured by betel juice, the white man's teeth invariably decay. The white man is generally ill-shaped, and when he grows fat he bulges in improbable places; the Mongol has beautiful bones and in old age he is almost as shapely as in youth. Admittedly the white races throw up a few individuals who for a few years are supremely beautiful; but on the whole, say what you will, they are far less comely than orientals. But it was not of this that I was thinking when I found the English 'lower classes' so much more repellent than Burmese 'natives'. I was still thinking in terms of my early-acquired class-prejudice. When I was not much past twenty I was attached for a short time to a British regiment. Of course I admired and liked the private soldiers as any youth of twenty would admire and like hefty, cheery youths five years older than himself with the medals of the Great War on their chests. And yet, after all, they faintly repelled me; they were 'common people' and I did not care to be too close to them. In the hot mornings when the company marched down the road, myself in the rear with one of the junior subalterns, the steam of those hundred sweating bodies in front made my stomach turn. And this, you observe, was pure prejudice. For a soldier is probably as inoffensive, physically, as it is possible for a male white person to be. He is generally young, he is nearly always healthy from fresh air and exercise, and a rigorous discipline compels him to be clean. But I could not see it like that. All I knew was that it was *lower-class* sweat that I was smelling, and the thought of it made me sick.

When later on I got rid of my class-prejudice, or part of it, it was in a roundabout way and by a process that took several years. The thing that changed my attitude to the class-issue was something only indirectly connected with it – something almost irrelevant.

I was in the Indian Police five years, and by the end of that time I hated the imperialism I was serving with a bitterness which I probably cannot make clear. In the free air of England that kind of thing is not fully intelligible. In order to hate imperialism you have got to be part of it. Seen from the outside the British rule in India appears – indeed, it *is* – benevolent and even necessary; and so no doubt are the French rule in Morocco and the Dutch rule in Borneo, for people usually govern foreigners better than they govern themselves. But it is not possible to be part of such a system without recognising it as an unjustifiable tyranny. Even the thickest-skinned Anglo-Indian is aware of this. Every 'native' face he sees in the street brings home to him his monstrous intrusion. And the majority of Anglo-Indians, intermittently at least, are not nearly so complacent about their position as people in England believe. From the most unexpected people, from gin-pickled old scoundrels high up in the Government service, I have heard some such remark as: 'Of course we've no right in this blasted country at all. Only now we're here for God's sake let's stay here.' The truth is that no modern man, in his heart of hearts, believes that it is right to invade a foreign country and hold the population down by force. Foreign oppression is a much more obvious, understandable evil than economic oppression. Thus in England we tamely admit to being robbed in order to keep half a million worthless idlers in luxury, but we would fight to the last man sooner than be ruled by Chinamen; similarly, people who live on unearned dividends without a single qualm of conscience, see clearly enough that it is wrong to go and lord it in a foreign country where you are not wanted. The result is that every Anglo-Indian is haunted by a sense of guilt which he usually conceals as best he can, because there is no freedom of speech, and merely to be overheard making a seditious remark may damage his career. All over India there are Englishmen who secretly loathe the system of which they are part; and just occasionally, when they are quite certain of being in the right company, their hidden bitterness overflows. I remember a night I spent on the train with a man in the Educational Service, a stranger to myself whose name I never discovered. It was too hot to sleep and we spent the night in talking. Half an hour's cautious questioning decided each of us that the other was 'safe'; and then for hours, while the train jolted slowly through the pitch-black night, sitting up in our bunks with bottles of beer handy, we damned the British Empire – damned it from the inside, intelligently and intimately. It did us both good. But we had been speaking forbidden things, and in the haggard morning light when the train crawled into Mandalay, we parted as guiltily as any adulterous couple.

So far as my observation goes nearly all Anglo-Indian officials have moments when their conscience troubles them. The exceptions are men who are doing something which is demonstrably useful and would still have to be done whether the British were in India or not: forest officers, for instance, and doctors and engineers. But I was in the police, which is to say that I was part of the actual machinery of despotism. Moreover, in the police you see the dirty work of Empire at close quarters, and there is an appreciable difference between doing dirty work and merely profiting by it. Most people approve of capital punishment, but most people wouldn't do the hangman's job. Even the other Europeans in Burma slightly looked down on the police because of the brutal work they had to do. I remember once when I was inspecting a police station, an American missionary whom I knew fairly well came in for some purpose or other. Like most Nonconformist missionaries he was a complete ass but quite a good fellow. One of my native sub-inspectors was bullying a suspect (I described this scene in *Burmese Days*). The American watched it, and then turning to me said thoughtfully, 'I wouldn't care to have your job.' It made me horribly ashamed. So *that* was the kind of job I had! Even an ass of an American missionary, a teetotal cock-virgin from the Middle West, had the right to look down on me and pity me! But I should have felt the same shame even if there had been no one to bring it home to me. I had begun to have an indescribable loathing of the whole machinery of so-called justice. Say what you will, our criminal law (far more humane, by the way, in India than in England) is a horrible thing. It needs very insensitive people to administer it. The wretched prisoners squatting in the reeking cages of the lock-ups, the grey cowed faces of the long-term convicts, the scarred buttocks of the men who had been flogged with bamboos, the women and children howling when their menfolk were led away under arrest – things like these are beyond bearing when you are in any way directly responsible for them. I watched a man hanged once; it seemed to me worse than a thousand murders. I never went into a jail without feeling (most visitors to jails feel the same) that my place was on the other side of the bars. I thought then – I think now, for that matter – that the worst criminal who ever walked is morally superior to a hanging judge. But of course I had to keep those notions to myself, because of the almost utter silence that is imposed on every Englishman in the East. In the end I worked out an anarchistic theory that all government is evil, that the punishment always does more harm than the crime and that people can be trusted to behave decently if only you will let them alone. This of course was sentimental nonsense. I see now as I did not see then, that it is always necessary to protect peaceful people from violence. In any state of society where crime can be profitable you have got to have a harsh criminal law and administer it ruthlessly; the alternative is Al Capone. But the feeling that punishment is evil arises inescapably in those who have to administer it. I should expect to find that even in England many policemen, judges, prison warders, and the like are haunted by a secret horror of what they do. But in Burma it was a double oppression that we were committing. Not only were we hanging people and putting them in jail and so forth; we were doing it in the capacity of unwanted foreign invaders. The Burmese themselves never really recognised our jurisdiction. The thief whom we put in prison did not think of himself as a criminal justly punished, he thought of himself as the victim of a foreign conqueror. The thing that was done to him was merely a wanton meaningless cruelty. His face, behind the stout teak bars of the lock-up and the iron bars of the jail, said so clearly. And unfortunately I had not trained myself to be indifferent to the expression of the human face.

When I came home on leave in 1927 I was already half determined to throw up my job, and one sniff of English air decided me. I was not going back to be a part of that evil despotism. But I wanted much more than merely to escape from my job. For five years I had been part of an oppressive system, and it had left me with a bad conscience. Innumerable remembered faces – faces of prisoners in the dock, of men waiting in the condemned cells, of subordinates I had bullied and aged peasants I had snubbed, of servants and coolies I had hit with my fist in moments of rage (nearly everyone does these things in the East, at any rate occasionally: orientals can be very provoking) – haunted me intolerably. I was conscious of an immense weight of guilt that I had got to expiate. I suppose that sounds exaggerated; but if you do for five years a job that you thoroughly disapprove of, you will probably feel the same. I had reduced everything to the simple theory that the oppressed are always right and the oppressors are always wrong: a mistaken theory, but the natural result of being one of the oppressors yourself. I felt that I had got to escape not merely from imperialism but from every form of man's dominion over man. I wanted to submerge myself, to get right down among the oppressed, to be one of them and on their side against their tyrants. And, chiefly because I had had to think everything out in solitude, I had carried my hatred of oppression to extraordinary lengths. At that time failure seemed to me to be the only virtue. Every suspicion of self-advancement, even to 'succeed' in life to the extent of making a few hundreds a year, seemed to me spiritually ugly, a species of bullying.

It was in this way that my thoughts turned towards the English working class. It was the first time that I had ever been really aware of the working class, and to begin with it was only because they supplied an analogy. They were the symbolic victims of injustice, playing the same part in England as the Burmese played in Burma. In Burma the issue had been quite simple. The whites were up and the blacks were down, and therefore as a matter of course one's sympathy was with the blacks. I now realised that there was no need to go as far as Burma to find tyranny and exploitation. Here in England, down under one's feet, were the submerged working class, suffering miseries which in their different way were as bad as any an oriental ever knows. The word 'unemployment' was on everyone's lips. That was more or less new to me, after Burma, but the drivel which the middle classes were still talking ('These unemployed are all unemployables', etc. etc.) failed to deceive me. I often wonder whether that kind of stuff deceives even the fools who utter it. On the other hand I had at that time no interest in Socialism or any other economic theory. It seemed to me then – it sometimes seems to me now, for that matter – that economic injustice will stop the moment we want it to stop, and no sooner, and if we genuinely want it to stop the method adopted hardly matters.

But I knew nothing about working-class conditions. I had read the unemployment figures but I had no notion of what they implied; above all, I did not know the essential fact that 'respectable' poverty is always the worst. The frightful doom of a decent working man suddenly thrown on the streets after a lifetime of steady work, his agonised struggles against economic laws which he does not understand, the disintegration of families, the corroding sense of shame – all this was outside the range of my experience. When I thought of poverty I thought of it in terms of brute starvation. Therefore my mind turned immediately towards the extreme cases, the social outcasts: tramps, beggars, criminals, prostitutes. These were 'the lowest of the low', and these were the people with whom I wanted to get in contact. What I profoundly wanted, at that time, was to find some way of getting out of the respectable world altogether. I meditated upon it a great deal, I even planned parts of it in detail; how one could sell everything, give everything away, change one's name and start out with no money and nothing but the clothes one stood up in. But in real life nobody ever does that kind of thing; apart from the relatives and friends who have to be considered, it is doubtful whether an educated man *could* do it if there were any other course open to him. But at least I could go among these people, see what their lives were like and feel myself temporarily part of their world. Once I had been among them and accepted by them, I should have touched bottom, and – this is what I felt: I was aware even then that it was irrational – part of my guilt would drop from me.

I thought it over and decided what I would do. I would go suitably disguised to Limehouse and Whitechapel and such places and sleep in common lodging-houses and pal up with dock-labourers, street hawkers, derelict people, beggars, and, if possible, criminals. And I would find out about tramps and how you got in touch with them and what was the proper procedure for entering the casual ward; and then, when I felt that I knew the ropes well enough, I would go on the road myself.

At the start it was not easy. It meant masquerading and I have no talent for acting. I cannot, for instance, disguise my accent, at any rate not for more than a very few minutes. I imagined – notice the frightful class-consciousness of the Englishman – that I should be spotted as a 'gentleman' the moment I opened my mouth; so I had a hard luck story ready in case I should be questioned. I got hold of the right kind of clothes and dirtied them in appropriate places. I am a difficult person to disguise, being abnormally tall, but I did at least know what a tramp looks like. (How few people do know this, by the way! Look at any picture of a tramp in *Punch*. They are always twenty years out of date.) One evening, having made ready at a friend's house, I set out and wandered eastward till I landed up at a common lodging-house in Limehouse Causeway. It was a dark, dirty-looking place. I knew it was a common lodging-house by the sign 'Good Beds for Single Men' in the window. Heavens, how I had to screw up my courage before I went in! It seems ridiculous now. But you see I was still half afraid of the working class. I wanted to get in touch with them, I even wanted to become one of them, but I still thought of them as alien and dangerous; going into the dark doorway of that common lodging-house seemed to me like going down into some dreadful subterranean place – a sewer full of rats, for instance. I went in fully expecting a fight. The people would spot that I was not one of themselves and immediately infer that I had come to spy on them; and then they would set upon me and throw me out – that was what I expected. I felt that I had got to do it, but I did not enjoy the prospect.

Inside the door a man in shirt-sleeves appeared from somewhere or other. This was the 'deputy', and I told him that I wanted a bed for the night. My accent did not make him stare, I noticed; he merely demanded ninepence and then showed me the way to a frowzy firelit kitchen underground. There were stevedores and navvies and a few sailors sitting about and playing draughts and drinking tea. They barely glanced at me as I entered. But this was Saturday night and a hefty young stevedore was drunk and was reeling about the room. He turned, saw me and lurched towards me with broad red face thrust out and a dangerous-looking fishy gleam in his eyes. I stiffened myself. So the fight was coming already! The next moment the stevedore collapsed on my chest and flung his arms round my neck. ''Ave a cup of tea, chum!' he cried tearfully; ''ave a cup of tea!'

I had a cup of tea. It was a kind of baptism. After that my fears vanished. Nobody questioned me, nobody showed offensive curiosity; everybody was polite and gentle and took me utterly for granted. I stayed two or three days in that common lodging-house, and a few weeks later, having picked up a certain amount of information about the habits of destitute people, I went on the road for the first time.

I have described all this in *Down and Out in Paris and London* (nearly all the incidents described there actually happened, though they have been rearranged) and I do not want to repeat it. Later I went on the road for much longer periods, sometimes from choice, sometimes from necessity. I have lived in common lodging-houses for months together. But it is that first expedition that sticks most vividly in my mind, because of the strangeness of it – the strangeness of being at last down there among 'the lowest of the low', and on terms of utter equality with working-class people. A tramp, it is true, is not a typical working-class person; still, when you are among tramps you are at any rate merged in one section – one sub-caste – of the working class, a thing which so far as I know can happen to you in no other way. For several days I wandered through the northern outskirts of London with an Irish tramp. I was his mate, temporarily. We shared the same cell at night, and he told me the history of his life and I told him a fictitious history of mine, and we took it in turns to beg at likely-looking houses and divided up the proceeds. I was very happy. Here I was, among 'the lowest of the low', at the bedrock of the Western world! The class-bar was down, or seemed to be down. And down there in the squalid and, as a matter of fact, horribly boring sub-world of the tramp I had a feeling of release, of adventure, which seems absurd when I look back, but which was sufficiently vivid at the time.

X

But unfortunately you do not solve the class problem by making friends with tramps. At most you get rid of some of your own class-prejudice by doing so.

Tramps, beggars, criminals and social outcasts generally are very exceptional beings and no more typical of the working class as a whole than, say, the literary intelligentsia are typical of the bourgeoisie. It is quite easy to be on terms of intimacy with a foreign 'intellectual', but it is not at all easy to be on terms of intimacy with an ordinary respectable foreigner of the middle class. How many Englishmen have seen the inside of an ordinary French bourgeois family, for instance? Probably it would be quite impossible to do so, short of marrying into it. And it is rather similar with the English working class. Nothing is easier than to be bosom pals with a pickpocket, if you know where to look for him; but it is very difficult to be bosom pals with a bricklayer.

But why is it so easy to be on equal terms with social outcasts? People have often said to me, 'Surely when you are with the tramps they don't really accept you as one of themselves? Surely they notice that you are different – notice the difference of accent?' etc. etc. As a matter of fact, a fair proportion of tramps, well over a quarter I should say, notice nothing of the kind. To begin with, many people have no ear for accent and judge you entirely by your clothes. I was often struck by this fact when I was begging at back doors. Some people were obviously surprised by my 'educated' accent, others completely failed to notice it; I was dirty and ragged and that was all they saw. Again, tramps come from all parts of the British Isles and the variation in English accents is enormous. A tramp is used to hearing all kinds of accents among his mates, some of them so strange to him that he can hardly understand them, and a man from, say, Cardiff or Durham or Dublin does not necessarily know which of the south English accents is an 'educated' one. In any case men with 'educated' accents, though rare among tramps, are not unknown. But even when tramps are aware that you are of different origin from themselves, it does not necessarily alter their attitude. From their point of view all that matters is that you, like themselves, are 'on the bum'. And in that world it is not done to ask too many questions. You can tell people the history of your life if you choose, and most tramps do so on the smallest provocation, but you are under no compulsion to tell it and whatever story you tell will be accepted without question. Even a bishop could be at home among tramps if he wore the right clothes; and even if they knew he was a bishop it might not make any difference, provided that they also knew or believed that he was genuinely destitute. Once you are in that world and seemingly *of* it, it hardly matters what you have been in the past. It is a sort of world-within-a-world where everyone is equal, a small squalid democracy – perhaps the nearest thing to a democracy that exists in England.

But when you come to the normal working class the position is totally different. To begin with, there is no short cut into their midst. You can become a tramp simply by putting on the right clothes and going to the nearest casual ward, but you can't become a navvy or a coal-miner. You couldn't get a job as a navvy or a coal-miner even if you were equal to the work. Via Socialist politics you can get in touch with the working-class intelligentsia, but they are hardly more typical than tramps or burglars. For the rest you can only mingle with the working class by staying in their houses as a lodger, which always has a dangerous resemblance to 'slumming'. For some months I lived entirely in coal-miners' houses. I ate my meals with the family, I washed at the kitchen sink, I shared bedrooms with miners, drank beer with them, played darts with them, talked to them by the hour together. But though I was among them, and I hope and trust they did not find me a nuisance, I was not one of them, and they knew it even better than I did. However much you like them, however interesting you find their conversation, there is always that accursed itch of class-difference, like the pea under the princess's mattress. It is not a question of dislike or distaste, only of *difference*, but it is enough to make real intimacy impossible. Even with miners who described themselves as Communists I found that it needed tactful manoeuvrings to prevent them from calling me 'sir'; and all of them, except in moments of great animation, softened their northern accents for my benefit. I liked them and hoped they liked me; but I went among them as a foreigner, and both of us were aware of it. Whichever way you turn this curse of class-difference confronts you like a wall of stone. Or rather it is not so much like a stone wall as the plate-glass pane of an aquarium; it is so easy to pretend that it isn't there, and so impossible to get through it.

Unfortunately it is nowadays the fashion to pretend that the glass is penetrable. Of course everyone knows that class-prejudice exists, but at the same time everyone claims that *he*, in some mysterious way, is exempt from it. Snobbishness is one of those vices which we can discern in everyone else but never in ourselves. Not only the *croyant et pratiquant* Socialist, but every 'intellectual' takes it as a matter of course that *he* at least is outside the class-racket; *he*, unlike his neighbours, can see through the absurdity of wealth, ranks, titles, etc. etc. 'I'm not a snob' is nowadays a kind of universal *credo*. Who is there who has not jeered at the House of Lords, the military caste, the Royal Family, the public schools, the huntin' and shootin' people, the old ladies in Cheltenham boarding-houses, the horrors of 'county' society and the social hierarchy generally? To do so has become an automatic gesture. You notice this particularly in novels. Every novelist of serious pretensions adopts an ironic attitude towards his upper-class characters. Indeed when a novelist has to put a definitely upper-class person – a duke or a baronet or whatnot – into one of his stories he guys him more or less instinctively. There is an important subsidiary cause of this in the poverty of the modern upper-class dialect. The speech of 'educated' people is now so lifeless and characterless that a novelist can do nothing with it. By far the easiest way of making it amusing is to burlesque it, which means pretending that every upper-class person is an ineffectual ass. The trick is imitated from novelist to novelist, and in the end becomes almost a reflex action.

And yet all the while, at the bottom of his heart, everyone knows that this is humbug. We all rail against class-distinctions, but very few people seriously want to abolish them. Here you come upon the important fact that every revolutionary opinion draws part of its strength from a secret conviction that nothing can be changed.

If you want a good illustration of this, it is worth studying the novels and plays of John Galsworthy, keeping one eye on their chronology. Galsworthy is a very fine specimen of the thin-skinned, tear-in-the-eye, pre-war humanitarian. He starts out with a morbid pity-complex which extends even to thinking that every married woman is an angel chained to a satyr. He is in a perpetual quiver of indignation over the sufferings of overworked clerks, of underpaid farm hands, of fallen women, of criminals, of prostitutes, of animals. The world, as he sees it in his earlier books (*The*

Man of Property, *Justice*, etc.), is divided into oppressors and oppressed, with the oppressors sitting on top like some monstrous stone idol which all the dynamite in the world cannot overthrow. But is it so certain that he really wants it overthrown? On the contrary, in his fight against an immovable tyranny he is upheld by the consciousness that it *is* immovable. When things happen unexpectedly and the world-order which he has known begins to crumble, he feels somewhat differently about it. So, having set out to be the champion of the underdog against tyranny and injustice, he ends by advocating (*vide The Silver Spoon*) that the English working class, to cure their economic ills, shall be deported to the colonies like batches of cattle. If he had lived ten years longer he would quite probably have arrived at some genteel version of Fascism. This is the inevitable fate of the sentimentalist. All his opinions change into their opposites at the first brush of reality.

The same streak of soggy half-baked insincerity runs through all 'advanced' opinion. Take the question of imperialism, for instance. Every left-wing 'intellectual' is, as a matter of course, an anti-imperialist. He claims to be outside the empire-racket as automatically and self-righteously as he claims to be outside the class-racket. Even the right-wing 'intellectual', who is not definitely in revolt against British imperialism, pretends to regard it with a sort of amused detachment. It is so easy to be witty about the British Empire. The White Man's Burden and 'Rule, Britannia' and Kipling's novels and Anglo-Indian bores – who could even mention such things without a snigger? And is there any cultured person who has not at least once in his life made a joke about that old Indian havildar who said that if the British left India there would not be a rupee or a virgin left between Peshawar and Delhi (or wherever it was)? That is the attitude of the typical left-winger towards imperialism, and a thoroughly flabby, boneless attitude it is. For in the last resort, the only important question is, Do you want the British Empire to hold together or do you want it to disintegrate? And at the bottom of his heart no Englishman, least of all the kind of person who is witty about Anglo-Indian colonels, does want it to disintegrate. For, apart from any other consideration, the high standard of life we enjoy in England depends upon our keeping a tight hold on the Empire, particularly the tropical portions of it such as India and Africa. Under the capitalist system, in order that

England may live in comparative comfort, a hundred million Indians must live on the verge of starvation – an evil state of affairs, but you acquiesce in it every time you step into a taxi or eat a plate of strawberries and cream. The alternative is to throw the Empire overboard and reduce England to a cold and unimportant little island where we should all have to work very hard and live mainly on herrings and potatoes. That is the very last thing that any left-winger wants. Yet the left-winger continues to feel that he has no moral responsibility for imperialism. He is perfectly ready to accept the products of Empire and to save his soul by sneering at the people who hold the Empire together.

It is at this point that one begins to grasp the unreality of most people's attitude towards the class question. So long as it is merely a question of ameliorating the worker's lot, every decent person is agreed. Take a coal-miner, for example. Everyone, barring fools and scoundrels, would *like* to see the miner better off. If, for instance, the miner could ride to the coal face in a comfortable trolley instead of crawling on his hands and knees, if he could work a three-hour shift instead of seven and a half hours, if he could live in a decent house with five bedrooms and a bathroom and have ten pounds a week wages – splendid! Moreover, anyone who uses his brain knows perfectly well that this is within the range of possibility. The world, potentially at least, is immensely rich; develop it as it might be developed, and we could all live like princes, supposing that we wanted to. And to a very superficial glance the social side of the question looks equally simple. In a sense it is true that almost everyone would like to see class-distinctions abolished. Obviously this perpetual uneasiness between man and man, from which we suffer in modern England, is a curse and a nuisance. Hence the temptation to believe that it can be shouted out of existence with a few scoutmasterish bellows of good will. Stop calling me 'sir', you chaps! Surely we're all men? Let's pal up and get our shoulders to the wheel and remember that we're all equal, and what the devil does it matter if I know what kind of ties to wear and you don't, and I drink my soup comparatively quietly and you drink yours with the noise of water going down a waste-pipe – and so on and so on and so on; all of it the most pernicious rubbish, but quite alluring when it is suitably expressed.

But unfortunately you get no further by merely wishing class-distinctions away. More exactly, it *is* necessary to wish them away, but your wish has no efficacy unless you grasp what it involves. The fact that has got to be faced is that to abolish class-distinctions means abolishing a part of yourself. Here am I, a typical member of the middle class. It is easy for me to say that I want to get rid of class-distinctions, but nearly everything I think and do is a result of class-distinctions. All my notions – notions of good and evil, of pleasant and unpleasant, of funny and serious, of ugly and beautiful – are essentially *middle-class* notions; my taste in books and food and clothes, my sense of honour, my table manners, my turns of speech, my accent, even the characteristic movements of my body, are the products of a special kind of upbringing and a special niche about halfway up the social hierarchy. When I grasp this I grasp that it is no use clapping a proletarian on the back and telling him that he is as good a man as I am; if I want real contact with him, I have got to make an effort for which very likely I am unprepared. For to get outside the class-racket I have got to suppress not merely my private snobbishness, but most of my other tastes and prejudices as well. I have got to alter myself so completely that at the end I should hardly be recognisable as the same person. What is involved is not merely the amelioration of working-class conditions, nor an avoidance of the more stupid forms of snobbery, but a complete abandonment of the upper-class and middle-class attitude to life. And whether I say Yes or No probably depends upon the extent to which I grasp what is demanded of me.

Many people, however, imagine that they can abolish class-distinctions without making any uncomfortable change in their own habits and 'ideology'. Hence the eager class-breaking activities which one can see in progress on all sides. Everywhere there are people of good will who quite honestly believe that they are working for the overthrow of class-distinctions. The middle-class Socialist enthuses over the proletariat and runs 'summer schools' where the proletarian and the repentant bourgeois are supposed to fall upon one another's necks and be brothers for ever; and the bourgeois visitors come away saying how wonderful and inspiring it has all been (the proletarian ones come away saying something different). And then there is the outer-suburban creeping Jesus, a hangover from the William Morris period, but still surprisingly common, who goes about saying 'Why must we level *down*? Why not level *up*?' and proposes to level the working class 'up' (up to his own standard) by means of hygiene, fruit-juice, birth-control, poetry, etc. Even the Duke of York (now King George VI) runs a yearly camp where public-schoolboys and boys from the slums are supposed to mix on exactly equal terms, and *do* mix for the time being, rather like the animals in one of those 'Happy Family' cages where a dog, a cat, two ferrets, a rabbit and three canaries preserve an armed truce while the showman's eye is on them.

All such deliberate, conscious efforts at class-breaking are, I am convinced, a very serious mistake. Sometimes they are merely futile, but where they do show a definite result it is usually to *intensify* class-prejudice. This, if you come to think of it, is only what might be expected. You have forced the pace and set up an uneasy, unnatural equality between class and class; the resultant friction brings to the surface all kinds of feelings that might otherwise have remained buried, perhaps for ever. As I said apropos of Galsworthy, the opinions of the sentimentalist change into their opposites at the first touch of reality. Scratch the average pacifist and you find a jingo. The middle-class ILP'er and the bearded fruit-juice drinker are all for a classless society so long as they see the proletariat through the wrong end of the telescope; force them into any *real* contact with a proletarian – let them get into a fight with a drunken fish-porter on Saturday night, for instance – and they are capable of swinging back to the most ordinary middle-class snobbishness. Most middle-class Socialists, however, are very unlikely to get into fights with drunken fish-porters; when they do make a genuine contact with the working class, it is usually with the working-class intelligentsia. But the working-class intelligentsia is sharply divisible into two different types. There is the type who remains working-class – who goes on working as a mechanic or a dock-labourer or whatever it may be and does not bother to change his working-class accent and habits, but who 'improves his mind' in his spare time and works for the ILP or the Communist Party; and there is the type who does alter his way of life, at least externally, and who by means of State scholarships succeeds in climbing into the middle class. The first is one of the finest types of man we have. I can think of some I have met whom not even the most hidebound Tory could help liking and admiring. The other type, with exceptions – D. H. Lawrence, for example – is less admirable.

To begin with, it is a pity, though it is a natural result of the scholarship system, that the proletariat should tend to interpenetrate the middle class via the literary intelligentsia. For it is not easy to crash your way into the literary intelligentsia if you happen to be a decent human being. The modern English literary world, at any rate the highbrow section of it, is a sort of poisonous jungle where only weeds can flourish. It is just possible to be a literary gent and to keep your decency if you are a definitely *popular* writer – a writer of detective stories, for instance; but to be a highbrow, with a footing in the snootier magazines, means delivering yourself over to horrible campaigns of wire-pulling and backstairs-crawling. In the highbrow world you 'get on', if you 'get on' at all, not so much by your literary ability as by being the life and soul of cocktail parties and kissing the bums of verminous little lions. This, then, is the world that most readily opens its doors to the proletarian who is climbing out of his own class. The 'clever' boy of a working-class family, the sort of boy who wins scholarships and is obviously not fitted for a life of manual labour, may find other ways of rising into the class above – a slightly different type, for instance, rises via Labour Party politics – but the literary way is by far the most usual. Literary London now teems with young men who are of proletarian origin and have been educated by means of scholarships. Many of them are very disagreeable people, quite unrepresentative of their class, and it is most unfortunate that when a person of bourgeois origin does succeed in meeting a proletarian face to face on equal terms, this is the type he most commonly meets. For the result is to drive the bourgeois, who has idealised the proletariat so long as he knew nothing about them, back into frenzies of snobbishness. The process is sometimes very comic to watch, if you happen to be watching it from the outside. The poor well-meaning bourgeois, eager to embrace his proletarian brother, leaps forward with open arms; and only a little while later he is in retreat, minus a borrowed five pounds and exclaiming dolefully, 'But, dash it, the fellow's not a gentleman!'

The thing that disconcerts the bourgeois in a contact of this kind is to find certain of his own professions being taken seriously. I have pointed out that the left-wing opinions of the average 'intellectual' are mainly spurious. From pure imitativeness he jeers at things which in fact he believes in. As one example out of many, take the public-school code of honour, with its 'team spirit' and 'Don't hit a man when he's down', and all the rest of that familiar bunkum. Who has not laughed at it? Who, calling himself an 'intellectual', who dare *not* to laugh at it? But it is a bit different when you meet somebody who laughs at it *from the outside*; just as we spend our lives in abusing England but grow very angry when we hear a foreigner saying exactly the same things. No one has been more amusing about the public schools than 'Beachcomber' of the *Express*. He laughs, quite rightly, at the ridiculous code which makes cheating at cards the worst of all sins. But would 'Beachcomber' like it if one of his own friends was caught cheating at cards? I doubt it. It is only when you meet someone of a different culture from yourself that you begin to realise what your own beliefs really are. If you are a bourgeois 'intellectual' you too readily imagine that you have somehow become unbourgeois because you find it easy to laugh at patriotism and the C of E and the Old School Tie and Colonel Blimp and all the rest of it. But from the point of view of the proletarian 'intellectual', who at least by origin is genuinely outside the bourgeois culture, your resemblances to Colonel Blimp may be more important than your differences. Very likely he looks upon you and Colonel Blimp as practically equivalent persons; and in a way he is right, though neither you nor Colonel Blimp would admit it. So that the meeting of proletarian and bourgeois, when they do succeed in meeting, is not always the embrace of long-lost brothers; too often it is the clash of alien cultures which can only meet in war.

I have been looking at this from the point of view of the bourgeois who finds his secret beliefs challenged and is driven back to a frightened conservatism. But one has also got to consider the antagonism that is aroused in the proletarian 'intellectual'. By his own efforts and sometimes with frightful agonies he has struggled out of his own class into another where he expects to find a wider freedom and a greater intellectual refinement; and all he finds, very often, is a sort of hollowness, a deadness, a lack of any warm human feeling – of any real life whatever. Sometimes the bourgeoisie seem to him just dummies with money and water in their veins instead of blood. This at any rate is what he *says*, and almost any young highbrow of proletarian origin will spin you this line of talk. Hence the 'proletarian' cant from which we now suffer. Everyone knows, or ought to know by this time, how it runs: the bourgeoisie are 'dead' (a favourite word of abuse nowadays and very effective because meaningless), bourgeois culture is bankrupt, bourgeois 'values' are despicable, and so on and so forth; if you want examples, see any number of the *Left Review* or any of the younger Communist writers such as Alec Brown, Philip Henderson, etc. The sincerity of much of this is suspect, but D. H. Lawrence, who was sincere, whatever else he may not have been, expresses the same thought over and over again. It is curious how he harps upon that idea that the English bourgeoisie are all *dead*, or at least gelded. Mellors, the gamekeeper in *Lady Chatterley's Lover* (really Lawrence himself), has had the opportunity to get out of his own class and does not particularly want to return to it, because English working people have various 'disagreeable habits'; on the other hand the bourgeoisie, with whom he has also mixed to some extent, seem to him half dead, a race of eunuchs. Lady Chatterley's husband, symbolically, is impotent in the actual physical sense. And then there is the poem about the young man (once again Lawrence himself) who 'got up to the top of the tree' but came down saying:

Oh you've got to be like a monkey
if you climb up the tree!
You've no more use for the solid earth
and the lad you used to be.
You sit in the boughs and gibber
with superiority.

They all gibber and gibber and chatter,
and never a word they say
comes really out of their guts, lad,
they make it up half way . . .

I tell you something's been done to 'em,
to the pullets up above;
there's not a cock bird among 'em . . . etc. etc.

You could hardly have it in plainer terms than that. Possibly by the people at 'the top of the tree' Lawrence only means the real bourgeoisie, those in the £2,000 a year class and over, but I doubt it. More probably he means everyone who is more or less within the bourgeois culture –

everyone who was brought up with a mincing accent and in a house where there were one or two servants. And at this point you realise the danger of the 'proletarian' cant – realise, I mean, the terrible antagonism that it is capable of arousing. For when you come to such an accusation as this, you are up against a blank wall. Lawrence tells me that because I have been to a public school I am a eunuch. Well, what about it? I can produce medical evidence to the contrary, but what good will that do? Lawrence's condemnation remains. If you tell me I am a scoundrel I may mend my ways, but if you tell me I am a eunuch you are tempting me to hit back in any way that seems feasible. If you want to make an enemy of a man, tell him that his ills are incurable.

This then is the net result of most meetings between proletarian and bourgeois: they lay bare a real antagonism which is intensified by the 'proletarian' cant, itself the product of forced contacts between class and class. The only sensible procedure is to go slow and not force the pace. If you secretly think of yourself as a gentleman and as such the superior of the greengrocer's errand boy, it is far better to say so than to tell lies about it. Ultimately you have got to drop your snobbishness, but it is fatal to pretend to drop it before you are really ready to do so.

Meanwhile one can observe on every side that dreary phenomenon, the middle-class person who is an ardent Socialist at twenty-five and a sniffish Conservative at thirty-five. In a way his recoil is natural enough – at any rate, one can see how his thoughts run. Perhaps a classless society *doesn't* mean a beatific state of affairs in which we shall all go on behaving exactly as before except that there will be no class-hatred and no snobbishness; perhaps it means a bleak world in which all our ideals, our codes, our tastes – our 'ideology', in fact – will have no meaning. Perhaps this class-breaking business isn't so simple as it looked! On the contrary, it is a wild ride into the darkness, and it may be that at the end of it the smile will be on the face of the tiger. With loving though slightly patronising smiles we set out to greet our proletarian brothers, and behold! our proletarian brothers – in so far as we understand them – are not asking for our greetings, they are asking us to commit suicide. When the bourgeois sees it in *that* form he takes to flight, and if his flight is rapid enough it may carry him to Fascism.

XI

Meanwhile, what about Socialism?

It hardly needs pointing out that at this moment we are in a very serious mess, so serious that even the dullest-witted people find it difficult to remain unaware of it. We are living in a world in which nobody is free, in which hardly anybody is secure, in which it is almost impossible to be honest and to remain alive. For enormous blocks of the working class the conditions of life are such as I have described in the opening chapters of this book, and there is no chance of those conditions showing any fundamental improvement. The very best the English working class can hope for is an occasional temporary decrease in unemployment when this or that industry is artificially stimulated by, for instance, rearmament. Even the middle classes, for the first time in their history, are feeling the pinch. They have not known actual hunger yet, but more and more of them find themselves floundering in a sort of deadly net of frustration in which it is harder and harder to persuade yourself that you are either happy, active or useful. Even the lucky ones at the top, the real bourgeoisie, are haunted periodically by a consciousness of the miseries below, and still more by fears of the menacing future. And this is merely a preliminary stage, in a country still rich with the loot of a hundred years. Presently there may be coming God knows what horrors – horrors of which, in this sheltered island, we have not even a traditional knowledge.

And all the while everyone who uses his brain knows that Socialism, as a world-system and wholeheartedly applied, is a way out. It would at least ensure our getting enough to eat even if it deprived us of everything else. Indeed, from one point of view, Socialism is such elementary common sense that I am sometimes amazed that it has not established itself already. The world is a raft sailing through space with, potentially, plenty of provisions for everybody; the idea that we must all co-operate and see to it that everyone does his fair share of the work and gets his fair share of the provisions, seems so blatantly obvious that one would say that no one could possibly fail to accept it unless he had some corrupt motive for clinging to the present system. Yet the fact that we have got to face is that Socialism is *not* establishing itself. Instead of going forward, the cause of Socialism is visibly going back. At this moment Socialists almost everywhere are in retreat before the onslaught of Fascism, and events are moving at terrible speed. As I write this the Spanish Fascist forces are bombarding Madrid, and it is quite likely that before the book is printed we shall have another Fascist country to add to the list, not to mention a Fascist control of the Mediterranean which may have the effect of delivering British foreign policy into the hands of Mussolini. I do not, however, want here to discuss the wider political issues. What I am concerned with is the fact that Socialism is losing ground exactly where it ought to be gaining it. With so much in its favour – for every empty belly is an argument for Socialism – the *idea* of Socialism is less widely accepted than it was ten years ago. The average thinking person nowadays is not merely not a Socialist, he is actively hostile to Socialism. This must be due chiefly to mistaken methods of propaganda. It means that Socialism, in the form in which it is now presented to us, has about it something inherently distasteful – something that drives away the very people who ought to be flocking to its support.

A few years ago this might have seemed unimportant. It seems only yesterday that Socialists, especially orthodox Marxists, were telling me with superior smiles that Socialism was going to arrive of its own accord by some mysterious process called 'historic necessity'. Possibly that belief still lingers, but it has been shaken, to say the least of it. Hence the sudden attempts of Communists in various countries to ally themselves with democratic forces which they have been sabotaging for years past. At a moment like this it is desperately necessary to discover just *why* Socialism has failed in its appeal. And it is no use writing off the current distaste for Socialism as the product of stupidity or corrupt motives. If you want to remove that distaste you have got to understand it, which means getting inside the mind of the ordinary objector to Socialism, or at least regarding his viewpoint sympathetically. No case is really answered until it has had a fair hearing. Therefore, rather paradoxically, in order to defend Socialism it is necessary to start by attacking it.

In the last three chapters I tried to analyse the difficulties that are raised by our anachronistic class-system; I shall have to touch on that subject again, because I believe that the present intensely stupid handling of the class-issue may stampede quantities of potential Socialists into Fascism. In the chapter following this one I want to discuss certain underlying assumptions that alienate sensitive minds from Socialism. But in the present chapter I am merely dealing with the obvious, preliminary objections – the kind of thing that the person who is not a Socialist (I don't mean the 'Where's the money to come from?' type) always starts by saying when you tax him on the subject. Some of these objections may appear frivolous or self-contradictory, but that is beside the point; I am merely discussing symptoms. Anything is relevant which helps to make clear why Socialism is not accepted. And please notice that I am arguing *for* Socialism, not *against* it. But for the moment I am *advocatus diaboli*. I am making out a case for the sort of person who is in sympathy with the fundamental aims of Socialism, who has the brains to see that Socialism would 'work', but who in practice always takes to flight when Socialism is mentioned.

Question a person of this type, and you will often get the semi-frivolous answer: 'I don't object to Socialism, but I do object to Socialists.' Logically it is a poor argument, but it carries weight with many people. As with the Christian religion, the worst advertisement for Socialism is its adherents.

The first thing that must strike any outside observer is that Socialism in its developed form is a theory confined entirely to the middle class. The typical Socialist is not, as tremulous old ladies imagine, a ferocious-looking working man with greasy overalls and a raucous voice. He is either a youthful snob-Bolshevik who in five years' time will quite probably have made a wealthy marriage and been converted to Roman Catholicism; or, still more typically, a prim little man with a white-collar job, usually a secret teetotaller and often with vegetarian leanings, with a history of Nonconformity behind him, and, above all, with a social position which he has no intention of forfeiting. This last type is surprisingly common in Socialist parties of every shade; it has perhaps been taken over *en bloc* from the old Liberal Party. In addition to this there is the horrible – the really disquieting – prevalence of cranks wherever Socialists are gathered together. One sometimes gets the impression that the mere words 'Socialism' and 'Communism' draw towards them with magnetic force every fruit-juice drinker, nudist, sandal-wearer, sex-maniac, Quaker, 'Nature Cure' quack, pacifist and feminist in England. One day this summer I was riding through Letchworth when the bus stopped and two dreadful-looking old men got onto it. They were both about sixty, both very short, pink and chubby, and both hatless. One of them was obscenely bald, the other had long grey hair bobbed in the Lloyd George style. They were dressed in pistachio-coloured shirts and khaki shorts into which their huge bottoms were crammed so tightly that you could study every dimple. Their appearance created a mild stir of horror on top of the bus. The man next to me, a commercial traveller I should say, glanced at me, at them, and back again at me, and murmured, 'Socialists', as who should say, 'Red Indians'. He was probably right – the ILP were holding their summer school at Letchworth. But the point is that to him, as an ordinary man, a crank meant a Socialist and a Socialist meant a crank. Any Socialist, he probably felt, could be counted on to have *something* eccentric about him. And some such notion seems to exist even among Socialists themselves. For instance, I have here a prospectus from another summer school which states its terms per week and then asks me to say 'whether my diet is ordinary or vegetarian'. They take it for granted, you see, that it is necessary to ask this question. This kind of thing is by itself sufficient to alienate plenty of decent people. And their instinct is perfectly sound, for the food-crank is by definition a person willing to cut himself off from human society in hopes of adding five years onto the life of his carcase; that is, a person out of touch with common humanity.

To this you have got to add the ugly fact that most middle-class Socialists, while theoretically pining for a classless society, cling like glue to their miserable fragments of social prestige. I remember my sensations of horror on first attending an ILP branch meeting in London. (It might have been rather different in the North, where the bourgeoisie are less thickly scattered.) Are *these* mingy little beasts, I thought, the champions of the working class? For every person there, male and female, bore the worst stigmata of sniffish middle-class superiority. If a real working man, a miner dirty from the pit, for instance, had suddenly walked into their midst, they would have been embarrassed, angry, and disgusted; some, I should think, would have fled holding their noses. You can see the same tendency in Socialist literature, which, even when it is not openly written *de haut en bas*, is always completely removed from the working class in idiom and manner of thought. The Coles, Webbs, Stracheys, etc., are not *exactly* proletarian writers. It is doubtful whether anything describable as proletarian literature now exists – even the *Daily Worker* is written in standard South English – but a good music-hall comedian comes nearer to producing it than any Socialist writer I can think of. As for the technical jargon of the Communists, it is as far removed from the common speech as the language of a mathematical textbook. I remember hearing a professional Communist speaker address a working-class audience. His speech was the usual bookish stuff, full of long sentences and parentheses and 'Notwithstanding' and 'Be that as it may', besides the usual jargon of 'ideology' and 'class-consciousness' and 'proletarian solidarity' and all the rest of it. After him a Lancashire working man got up and spoke to the crowd in their own broad lingo. There was not much doubt which of the two was nearer to his audience, but I do not suppose for a moment that the Lancashire working man was an orthodox Communist.

For it must be remembered that a working man, so long as he remains a genuine working man, is seldom or never a Socialist in the complete, logically consistent sense. Very likely he votes Labour, or even Communist if he gets the chance, but his conception of Socialism is quite different from that of the book-trained Socialist higher up. To the ordinary working man, the sort you would meet in any pub on Saturday night, Socialism does not mean much more than better wages and shorter hours and nobody bossing you about. To the more revolutionary type, the type who is a hunger-marcher and is blacklisted by employers, the word is a sort of rallying-cry against the forces of oppression, a vague threat of future violence. But, so far as my experience goes, no genuine working man grasps the deeper implications of Socialism. Often, in my opinion, he is a truer Socialist than the orthodox Marxist, because he does remember, what the other so often forgets, that Socialism means justice and common decency. But what he does not grasp is that Socialism cannot be narrowed down to mere economic justice and that a reform of that magnitude is bound to work immense changes in our civilisation and his own way of life. His vision of the Socialist future is a vision of present society with the worst abuses left out, and with interest centring round the same things as at present – family life, the pub, football, and local politics. As for the philosophic side of Marxism, the pea-and-thimble trick with those three mysterious entities, thesis, antithesis, and synthesis, I have never met a working man who had the faintest interest in it. It is of course true that plenty of people of working-class *origin* are Socialists of the theoretical bookish type. But they are never people who have *remained* working men;

they don't work with their hands, that is. They belong either to the type I mentioned in the last chapter, the type who squirms into the middle class via the literary intelligentsia, or the type who becomes a Labour MP or a high-up trade-union official. This last type is one of the most desolating spectacles the world contains. He has been picked out to fight for his mates, and all it means to him is a soft job and the chance of 'bettering' himself. Not merely while but *by* fighting the bourgeoisie he becomes a bourgeois himself. And meanwhile it is quite possible that he has remained an orthodox Marxist. But I have yet to meet a *working* miner, steelworker, cotton-weaver, docker, navvy or whatnot who was 'ideologically' sound.

One of the analogies between Communism and Roman Catholicism is that only the 'educated' are completely orthodox. The most immediately striking thing about the English Roman Catholics – I don't mean the real Catholics, I mean the converts: Ronald Knox, Arnold Lunn *et hoc genus* – is their intense self-consciousness. Apparently they never think, certainly they never write, about anything but the fact that they *are* Roman Catholics; this single fact and the self-praise resulting from it form the entire stock-in-trade of the Catholic literary man. But the really interesting thing about these people is the way in which they have worked out the supposed implications of orthodoxy until the tiniest details of life are involved. Even the liquids you drink, apparently, can be orthodox or heretical; hence the campaigns of Chesterton, 'Beachcomber', etc., against tea and in favour of beer. According to Chesterton, tea-drinking is 'pagan', while beer-drinking is 'Christian', and coffee is 'the puritan's opium'. It is unfortunate for this theory that Catholics abound in the 'Temperance' movement and the greatest tea-boozers in the world are the Catholic Irish; but what I am interested in here is the attitude of mind that can make even food and drink an occasion for religious intolerance. A working-class Catholic would never be so absurdly consistent as that. He does not spend his time in brooding on the fact that he is a Roman Catholic, and he is not particularly conscious of being different from his non-Catholic neighbours. Tell an Irish dock-labourer in the slums of Liverpool that his cup of tea is 'pagan', and he will call you a fool. And even in more serious matters he does not always grasp the implications of his faith. In the Roman Catholic homes of Lancashire you see the crucifix on the wall and the *Daily Worker* on the table. It is only the 'educated' man, especially the literary man, who knows how to be a bigot. And, *mutatis mutandis*, it is the same with Communism. The creed is never found in its pure form in a genuine proletarian.

It may be said, however, that even if the theoretical book-trained Socialist is not a working man himself, at least he is actuated by a love of the working class. He is endeavouring to shed his bourgeois status and fight on the side of the proletariat – that, obviously, must be his motive.

But is it? Sometimes I look at a Socialist – the intellectual, tract-writing type of Socialist, with his pullover, his fuzzy hair, and his Marxian quotation – and wonder what the devil his motive really *is*. It is often difficult to believe that it is a love of anybody, especially of the working class, from whom he is of all people the furthest removed. The underlying motive of many Socialists, I believe, is simply a hypertrophied sense of order. The present state of affairs offends them not because it causes misery, still less because it makes freedom impossible, but because it is untidy; what they desire, basically, is to reduce the world to something resembling a chess-board. Take the plays of a lifelong Socialist like Shaw. How much understanding or even awareness of working-class life do they display? Shaw himself declares that you can only bring a working man on the stage 'as an object of compassion'; in practice he doesn't bring him on even as that, but merely as a sort of W. W. Jacobs figure of fun – the ready-made comic East Ender, like those in *Major Barbara* and *Captain Brassbound's Conversion*. At best his attitude to the working class is the sniggering *Punch* attitude, in more serious moments (consider, for instance, the young man who symbolises the dispossessed classes in *Misalliance*) he finds them merely contemptible and disgusting. Poverty and, what is more, the habits of mind created by poverty, are something to be abolished *from above*, by violence if necessary; perhaps even preferably by violence. Hence his worship of 'great' men and appetite for dictatorships, Fascist or Communist; for to him, apparently (*vide* his remarks apropos of the Italo-Abyssinian war and the Stalin-Wells conversations), Stalin and Mussolini are almost equivalent persons. You get the same thing in a more mealy-mouthed form in Mrs Sidney Webb's autobiography, which gives, unconsciously, a most revealing picture of the high-minded Socialist slum-visitor. The truth is that to many people, calling themselves Socialists, revolution does not mean a movement of the masses with which they hope to associate themselves; it means a set of reforms which 'we', the clever ones, are going to impose upon 'them', the Lower Orders. On the other hand, it would be a mistake to regard the book-trained Socialist as a bloodless creature entirely incapable of emotion. Though seldom giving much evidence of affection for the exploited, he is perfectly capable of displaying hatred – a sort of queer, theoretical, *in vacuo* hatred – against the exploiters. Hence the grand old Socialist sport of denouncing the bourgeoisie. It is strange how easily almost any Socialist writer can lash himself into frenzies of rage against the class to which, by birth or by adoption, he himself invariably belongs. Sometimes the hatred of bourgeois habits and 'ideology' is so far-reaching that it extends even to bourgeois characters in books. According to Henri Barbusse, the characters in the novels of Proust, Gide, etc., are 'characters whom one would dearly love to have at the other side of a barricade'. 'A barricade', you observe. Judging from *Le Feu*, I should have thought Barbusse's experience of barricades had left him with a distaste for them. But the imaginary bayoneting of 'bourgeois', who presumably don't hit back, is a bit different from the real article.

The best example of bourgeois-baiting literature that I have yet come across is Mirsky's *Intelligentsia of Great Britain.* This is a very interesting and ably-written book, and it should be read by everyone who wants to understand the rise of Fascism. Mirsky (formerly Prince Mirsky) was a White Russian *émigré* who came to England and was for some years a lecturer in Russian literature at London University. Later he was converted to Communism, returned to Russia, and produced this book as a sort of 'show-up' of the British intelligentsia from a Marxist standpoint. It is a viciously malignant book, with an unmistakable note of 'Now I'm out of your reach I can say what I like about you' running all through it, and apart from a general distortion it contains some quite definite and probably intentional misrepresentation: as, for instance, when Conrad is declared to be 'no less imperialist than Kipling', and D. H. Lawrence is described as writing 'bare-bodied pornography' and as having 'succeeded in erasing all clues to his proletarian origin' – as though Lawrence had been a pork-butcher climbing into the House of Lords! This kind of thing is very disquieting when one remembers that it is addressed to a Russian audience who have no means of checking its accuracy. But what I am thinking of at the moment is the effect of such a book on the English public. Here you have a literary man of aristocratic extraction, a man who had probably never in his life spoken to a working man on anything approaching equal terms, uttering venomous screams of libel against his 'bourgeois' colleagues. Why? So far as appearances go, from pure malignity. He is battling *against* the British intelligentsia, but what is he battling *for*? Within the book itself there is no indication. Hence the net effect of books like this is to give outsiders the impression that there is nothing in Communism except *hatred*. And here once again you come upon that queer resemblance between Communism and (convert) Roman Catholicism. If you want to find a book as evil-spirited as *The Intelligentsia of Great Britain*, the likeliest place to look is among the popular Roman Catholic apologists. You will find there the same venom and the same dishonesty, though, to do the Catholic justice, you will not usually find the same bad manners. Queer that Comrade Mirsky's spiritual brother should be Father —— ——! The Communist and the Catholic are not saying the same thing, in a sense they are even saying opposite things, and each would gladly boil the other in oil if circumstances permitted; but from the point of view of an outsider they are very much alike.

The fact is that Socialism, *in the form in which it is now presented*, appeals chiefly to unsatisfactory or even inhuman types. On the one hand you have the warm-hearted unthinking Socialist, the typical working-class Socialist, who only wants to abolish poverty and does not always grasp what this implies. On the other hand, you have the intellectual, book-trained Socialist, who understands that it is necessary to throw our present civilisation down the sink and is quite willing to do so. And this type is drawn, to begin with, entirely from the middle class, and from a rootless town-bred section of the middle class at that. Still more unfortunately, it includes – so much so that to an outsider it even appears to be composed of – the kind of people I have been discussing; the foaming denouncers of the bourgeoisie, and the more-water-in-your-beer reformers of whom Shaw is the prototype, and the astute young social-literary climbers who are Communists now, as they will be Fascists five years hence, because it is all the go, and all that dreary tribe of high-minded women and sandal-wearers and bearded fruit-juice drinkers who come flocking towards the smell of 'progress' like bluebottles to a dead cat. The ordinary decent person, who is in sympathy with the *essential* aims of Socialism, is given the impression that there is no room for his kind in any Socialist party that means business. Worse, he is driven to the cynical conclusion that Socialism is a kind of doom which is probably coming but must be staved off as long as possible. Of course, as I have suggested already, it is not strictly fair to judge a movement by its adherents; but the point is that people invariably do so, and that the popular conception of Socialism is coloured by the conception of a Socialist as a dull or disagreeable person. 'Socialism' is pictured as a state of affairs in which our more vocal Socialists would feel thoroughly at home. This does great harm to the cause. The ordinary man may not flinch from a dictatorship of the proletariat, if you offer it tactfully; offer him a dictatorship of the prigs, and he gets ready to fight.

There is a widespread feeling that any civilisation in which Socialism was a reality would bear the same relation to our own as a brand-new bottle of colonial burgundy bears to a few spoonfuls of first-class Beaujolais. We live, admittedly, amid the wreck of a civilisation, but it has been a great civilisation in its day, and in patches it still flourishes almost undisturbed. It still has its bouquet, so to speak; whereas the imagined Socialist future, like the colonial burgundy, tastes only of iron and water. Hence the fact, which is really a disastrous one, that artists of any consequence can never be persuaded into the Socialist fold. This is particularly the case with the writer whose political opinions are more directly and obviously connected with his work than those of, say, a painter. If one faces facts one must admit that nearly everything describable as Socialist literature is dull, tasteless, and bad. Consider the situation in England at the present moment. A whole generation has grown up more or less in familiarity with the idea of Socialism; and yet the high-water mark, so to speak, of Socialist literature is W. H. Auden, a sort of gutless Kipling,* and the even feebler poets who are associated with him. Every writer of consequence and every book worth reading is on the other side. I am willing to believe that it is otherwise in Russia – about which I know nothing,

* Orwell somewhat retracted this remark later. See 'Inside the Whale', *England Your England*, p. 120 (note added to Secker & Warburg Uniform Edition).

however – for presumably in post-revolutionary Russia the mere violence of events would tend to throw up a vigorous literature of sorts. But it is certain that in Western Europe Socialism has produced no literature worth having. A little while ago, when the issues were less clear, there were writers of some vitality who called themselves Socialists, but they were using the word as a vague label. Thus, if Ibsen and Zola described themselves as Socialists, it did not mean much more than that they were 'progressives', while in the case of Anatole France it meant merely that he was an anticlerical. The real Socialist writers, the propagandist writers, have always been dull, empty windbags – Shaw, Barbusse, Upton Sinclair, William Morris, Waldo Frank, etc. etc. I am not, of course, suggesting that Socialism is to be condemned because literary gents don't like it; I am not even suggesting that it ought necessarily to produce literature on its own account, though I do think it a bad sign that it has produced no songs worth singing. I am merely pointing to the fact that writers of genuine talent are usually indifferent to Socialism, and sometimes actively and mischievously hostile. And this is a disaster, not only for the writers themselves, but for the cause of Socialism, which has great need of them.

This, then, is the superficial aspect of the ordinary man's recoil from Socialism. I know the whole dreary argument very thoroughly, because I know it from both sides. Everything that I say here I have both said to ardent Socialists who were trying to convert me, and had said to me by bored non-Socialists whom I was trying to convert. The whole thing amounts to a kind of *malaise* produced by dislike of individual Socialists, especially of the cocksure Marx-quoting type. Is it childish to be influenced by that kind of thing? Is it silly? Is it even contemptible? It is all that, but the point is that *it happens,* and therefore it is important to keep it in mind.

XII

However, there is a much more serious difficulty than the local and temporary objections which I discussed in the last chapter.

Faced by the fact that intelligent people are so often on the other side, the Socialist is apt to set it down to corrupt motives (conscious or unconscious), or to an ignorant belief that Socialism would not 'work', or to a mere dread of the horrors and discomforts of the revolutionary period before Socialism is established. Undoubtedly all these are important, but there are plenty of people who are influenced by none of them and are nevertheless hostile to Socialism. Their reason for recoiling from Socialism is spiritual, or 'ideological'. They object to it not on the ground that it would not 'work', but precisely because it would 'work' too well. What they are afraid of is not the things that are going to happen in their own lifetime, but the things that are going to happen in the remote future when Socialism is a reality.

I have very seldom met a convinced Socialist who could grasp that thinking people may be repelled by the *objective* towards which Socialism appears to be moving. The Marxist, especially, dismisses this kind of thing as bourgeois sentimentality. Marxists as a rule are not very good at reading the minds of their adversaries; if they were, the situation in Europe might be less desperate than it is at present. Possessing a technique which seems to explain everything, they do not often bother to discover what is going on inside other people's heads. Here, for instance, is an illustration of the kind of thing I mean. Discussing the widely held theory – which in one sense is certainly true – that Fascism is a product of Communism, Mr N. A. Holdaway, one of the ablest Marxist writers we possess, writes as follows:

> The hoary legend of Communism leading to Fascism . . . The element of truth in it is this: that the appearance of Communist activity warns the ruling class that democratic Labour Parties are no longer capable of holding the working class in check, and that capitalist dictatorship must assume another form if it is to survive.

You see here the defects of the method. Because he has detected the underlying economic cause of Fascism, he tacitly assumes that the spiritual side of it is of no importance. Fascism is written off as a manoeuvre of the 'ruling class', which at bottom it is. But this in itself would only explain why Fascism appeals to capitalists. What about the millions who are not capitalists, who in a material sense have nothing to gain from Fascism and are often aware of it, and who, nevertheless, are Fascists? Obviously their approach has been purely along the ideological line. They could only be stampeded into Fascism because Communism attacked or seemed to attack certain things (patriotism, religion, etc.) which lay deeper than the economic motive; and in *that* sense it is perfectly true that Communism leads to Fascism. It is a pity that Marxists nearly always concentrate on letting economic cats out of ideological bags; it does in one sense reveal the truth, but with this penalty, that most of their propaganda misses its mark. It is the spiritual recoil from Socialism, especially as it manifests itself in sensitive people, that I want to discuss in this chapter. I shall have to analyse it at some length, because it is very widespread, very powerful and, among Socialists, almost completely ignored.

The first thing to notice is that the idea of Socialism is bound up, more or less inextricably, with the idea of machine-production. Socialism is essentially an *urban* creed. It grew up more or less concurrently with industrialism, it has always had its roots in the town proletariat and the town intellectual, and it is doubtful whether it could ever have arisen in any but an industrial society. Granted industrialism, the idea of Socialism presents itself naturally, because private ownership is only tolerable when every individual (or family or other unit) is at least moderately self-supporting; but the effect of industrialism is to make it impossible for anyone to be self-supporting even for a moment. Industrialism, once it rises above a fairly low level, *must* lead to some form of collectivism. Not necessarily to Socialism, of course; conceivably it might lead to the Slave-State of which Fascism is a kind of prophecy. And the converse is also true. Machine-production suggests Socialism, but Socialism as a world-system implies machine-production, because it demands certain things not compatible with a primitive way of life. It demands, for instance, constant intercommunication and exchange of goods between all parts of the earth; it demands some degree of centralised control; it demands an approximately equal standard of life for all human beings and probably a certain uniformity of education. We may take it, therefore, that any world in which Socialism was a reality would be at least as highly mechanised as the United States at this moment, probably much more so. In any case, no Socialist would think of denying this. The Socialist world is always pictured as a completely mechanised, immensely organised world, depending on the machine as the civilisations of antiquity depended on the slave.

So far so good, or so bad. Many, perhaps a majority, of thinking people are not in love with machine-civilisation, but everyone who is not a fool knows that it is nonsense to talk at this moment about scrapping the machine. But the unfortunate thing is that Socialism, as usually presented, is bound up with the idea of mechanical progress, not merely as a necessary development but as an end in itself, almost as a kind of religion. This idea is implicit in, for instance, most of the propagandist stuff that is written about the rapid mechanical advance in Soviet Russia (the Dnieper dam, tractors, etc. etc.). Karel Čapek hits it off well enough in the horrible ending of *RUR*, when the Robots, having slaughtered the last human being, announce their intention to 'build many houses' (just for the sake of building houses, you see). The kind of person who most readily accepts Socialism is also the kind of person who views mechanical progress, *as such*, with enthusiasm. And this is so much the case that Socialists are often unable to grasp that the opposite opinion exists. As a rule the most persuasive argument they can think of is to tell you that the present mechanisation of the world is as nothing to what we shall see when Socialism is established. Where there is one aeroplane now, in those days there will be fifty! All the work that is now done by hand will then be done by machinery: everything that is now made of leather, wood or stone will be made of rubber, glass or steel; there will be no disorder, no loose ends, no wildernesses, no wild animals, no weeds, no disease, no poverty, no pain – and so on and so forth. The Socialist world is to be above all things an *ordered* world, an *efficient* world. But it is precisely from that vision of the future as a sort of glittering Wells-world that sensitive minds recoil. Please notice that this essentially fat-bellied version of 'progress' is not an integral part of Socialist doctrine; but it has come to be thought of as one, with the result that the temperamental conservatism which is latent in all kinds of people is easily mobilised against Socialism.

Every sensitive person has moments when he is suspicious of machinery and to some extent of physical science. But it is important to sort out the various motives, which have differed greatly at different times, for hostility to science and machinery, and to disregard the jealousy of the modern literary gent who hates science because science has stolen literature's thunder. The earliest full-length attack on science and machinery that I am acquainted with is in the third part of *Gulliver's Travels*. But Swift's attack, though brilliant as a *tour de force*, is irrelevant and even silly, because it is written from the standpoint – perhaps this seems a queer thing to say of the author of *Gulliver's Travels* – of a man who lacked imagination. To Swift, science was merely a kind of futile muckraking and the machines were nonsensical contraptions that would never work. His standard was that of practical usefulness, and he lacked the vision to see that an experiment which is not demonstrably useful at the moment may yield results in the future. Elsewhere in the book he names it as the best of all achievements 'to make two blades of grass grow where one grew before'; not seeing, apparently, that this is just what the machine can do. A little later the despised machines began working, physical science increased its scope, and there came the celebrated conflict between religion and science which agitated our grandfathers. That conflict is over and both sides have retreated and claimed a victory, but an anti-scientific bias still lingers in the minds of most religious believers. All through the nineteenth century protesting voices were raised against science and machinery (see Dickens's *Hard Times*, for instance), but usually for the rather shallow reason that industrialism in its first stages was cruel and ugly. Samuel Butler's attack on the machine in the well-known chapter of *Erewhon* is a different matter. But Butler himself lived in a less desperate age than our own, an age in which it was still possible for a first-rate man to be a dilettante part of the time, and therefore the whole thing appeared to him as a kind of intellectual exercise. He saw clearly enough our abject dependence on the machine, but instead of bothering to work out its consequences he preferred to exaggerate it for the sake of what was not much more than a joke. It is only in our own age, when mechanisation has finally triumphed, that we can actually *feel* the tendency of the machine to make a fully human life impossible. There is probably no one capable of thinking and feeling who has not occasionally looked at a gas-pipe chair and reflected that the machine is the enemy of life. As a rule, however, this feeling is instinctive rather than reasoned. People know that in some way or another 'progress' is a swindle, but they reach this conclusion by a kind of mental shorthand; my job here is to supply the logical steps that are usually left out. But first one must ask, what is the function of the machine? Obviously its primary function is to save work, and the type of person to whom machine-civilisation is entirely acceptable seldom sees any reason for looking further. Here for instance is a person who claims, or rather screams, that he is thoroughly at home in the modern mechanised world. I am quoting from *World Without Faith*, by Mr John Beevers. This is what he says:

It is plain lunacy to say that the average £2 10*s.* to £4 a week man of today is a lower type than an eighteenth-century farm labourer. Or than the labourer or peasant of any exclusively agricultural community now or in the past. It just isn't true. It is so damn silly to cry out about the civilising effects of work in the fields and farmyards as against that done in a big locomotive works or an automobile factory. Work is a nuisance. We work because we have to and all work is done to provide us with leisure and the means of spending that leisure as enjoyably as possible.

And again:

Man is going to have time enough and power enough to hunt for his own heaven on earth without worrying about the supernatural one. The earth will be so pleasant a place that the priest and the parson won't be left with much of a tale to tell. Half the stuffing is knocked out of them by one neat blow. Etc. etc. etc.

There is a whole chapter to this effect (Chapter IV of Mr Beevers's book), and it is of some interest as an exhibition of machine-worship in its most completely vulgar, ignorant and half-baked form. It is the authentic voice of a large section of the modern world. Every aspirin-eater in the outer suburbs would echo it fervently. Notice the shrill wail of anger ('It just isn't troo-o-o!' etc.) with which Mr Beevers meets the suggestion that his grandfather may have been a better man than himself; and the still more horrible suggestion that if we returned to a simpler way of life he might have to toughen his muscles with a job of work. Work, you see, is done 'to provide us with leisure'. Leisure for what? Leisure to become more like Mr Beevers, presumably. Though as a matter of fact, from that line of talk about 'heaven on earth', you can make a fairly good guess at what he would like civilisation to be; a sort of Lyons Corner House lasting *in saecula saeculorum* and getting bigger and noisier all the time. And in any book by anyone who feels at home in the machine-world – in any book by H. G. Wells, for instance – you will find passages of the same kind. How often have we not heard it, that glutinously uplifting stuff about 'the machines, our new race of slaves, which will set humanity free', etc. etc. etc. To these people, apparently, the only danger of the machine is its possible use for destructive purposes; as, for instance, aeroplanes are used in war. Barring wars and unforeseen disasters, the future is envisaged as an ever more rapid march of mechanical progress; machines to save work, machines to save thought, machines to save pain, hygiene, efficiency, organisation, more hygiene, more efficiency, more organisation, more machines – until finally you land up in the by now familiar Wellsian Utopia, aptly caricatured by Huxley in *Brave New World*, the paradise of little fat men. Of course in their day-dreams of the future the little fat men are neither fat nor little; they are Men Like Gods. But why should they be? All mechanical progress is towards greater and greater efficiency; ultimately, therefore, towards a world in which *nothing goes wrong*. But in a world in which nothing went wrong, many of the qualities which Mr Wells regards as 'godlike' would be no more valuable than the animal faculty of moving the ears. The beings in *Men Like Gods* and *The Dream* are represented, for example, as brave, generous and physically strong. But in a world from which physical danger had been banished – and obviously mechanical progress tends to eliminate danger – would physical courage be likely to survive? *Could* it survive? And why should physical strength survive in a world where there was never the need for physical labour? As for such qualities as loyalty, generosity, etc., in a world where nothing went wrong, they would be not only irrelevant but probably unimaginable. The truth is that many of the qualities we admire in human beings can only function in opposition to some kind of disaster, pain or difficulty; but the tendency of mechanical progress is to eliminate disaster, pain and difficulty. In books like *The Dream* and *Men Like Gods* it is assumed that such qualities as strength, courage, generosity, etc., will be kept alive because they are comely qualities and necessary attributes of a full human being. Presumably, for instance, the inhabitants of Utopia would create artificial dangers in order to exercise their courage, and do dumb-bell exercises to harden muscles which they would never be obliged to use. And here you observe the huge contradiction which is usually present in the idea of progress. The tendency of mechanical progress is to make your environment safe and soft; and yet you are striving to keep yourself brave and hard. You are at the same moment furiously pressing forward and desperately holding back. It is as though a London stockbroker should go to his office in a suit of chain mail and insist on talking medieval Latin. So in the last analysis the champion of progress is also the champion of anachronisms.

Meanwhile I am assuming that the tendency of mechanical progress *is* to make life safe and soft. This may be disputed, because at any given moment the effect of some recent mechanical invention may appear to be the opposite. Take for instance the transition from horses to motor vehicles. At a first glance one might say, considering the enormous toll of road deaths, that the motor-car does not exactly tend to make life safer. Moreover it probably needs as much toughness to be a first-rate dirt-track rider as to be a broncho-buster or to ride in the Grand National. Nevertheless the *tendency* of all machinery is to become safer and easier to handle. The danger of accidents would disappear if we chose to tackle our road-planning problem seriously, as we shall do sooner or later; and meanwhile the motor-car has evolved to a point at which anyone who is not blind or paralytic can drive it after a few lessons. Even now it needs far less nerve and skill to drive a car ordinarily well than to ride a horse ordinarily well; in twenty years' time it may need no nerve or skill at all. Therefore, one must say that, taking society as a whole, the result of the transition from horses to cars has been an increase in human softness. Presently somebody comes along with another invention, the aeroplane for instance, which does not at first sight appear to make life safer. The first men who went up in aeroplanes were superlatively brave, and even today it must need an exceptionally good nerve to be a pilot. But the same tendency as before is at work. The aeroplane, like the motor-car, will be made foolproof; a million engineers are working, almost unconsciously, in that direction. Finally – this is the objective, though it may never quite be reached – you will get an aeroplane whose pilot needs no more skill or courage than a baby needs in its perambulator. And all mechanical progress is and must be in this direction. A machine evolves by becoming more efficient, that is, more foolproof; hence the objective of mechanical progress is a foolproof world – which may or may not mean a world inhabited by fools. Mr Wells would probably retort that the world can never become foolproof, because, however high a standard of efficiency you have reached, there is always some greater difficulty ahead. For example (this is Mr Wells's favourite idea – he has used it in goodness knows how many perorations), when you have got this planet of ours perfectly into trim, you start upon the enormous task of reaching and colonising another. But this is merely to push the objective further into the future; the objective itself remains the same. Colonise another planet, and the game of mechanical progress begins anew; for the foolproof world you have substituted the foolproof solar system – the foolproof universe. In tying yourself to the ideal of mechanical efficiency, you tie yourself to the ideal of softness. But softness is repulsive; and thus all progress is seen to be a frantic struggle towards an objective which you hope and pray will never be reached. Now and again, but not often, you meet somebody who grasps that what is usually called progress also entails what is usually called degeneracy, and who is nevertheless in favour of progress. Hence the fact that in Mr Shaw's Utopia a statue was erected to Falstaff, as the first man who ever made a speech in favour of cowardice.

But the trouble goes immensely deeper than this. Hitherto I have only pointed out the absurdity of aiming at mechanical progress and also at the preservation of qualities which mechanical progress makes unnecessary. The question one has got to consider is whether there is *any* human activity which would not be maimed by the dominance of the machine.

The function of the machine is to save work. In a fully mechanised world all the dull drudgery will be done by machinery, leaving us free for more interesting pursuits. So expressed, this sounds splendid. It makes one sick to see half a dozen men sweating their guts out to dig a trench for a water-pipe, when some easily devised machine would scoop the earth out in a couple of minutes. Why not let the machine do the work and the men go and do something else? But presently the question arises, what else are they to do? Supposedly they are set free from 'work' in order that they may do something which is not 'work'. But what is work and what is not work? Is it work to dig, to carpenter, to plant trees, to fell trees, to ride, to fish, to hunt, to feed chickens, to play the piano, to take photographs, to build a house, to cook, to sew, to trim hats, to mend motor-bicycles? All of these things are work to somebody, and all of them are play to somebody. There are in fact very few activities which cannot be classed either as work or play according as you choose to regard them. The labourer set free from digging may want to spend his leisure, or part of it, in playing the piano, while the professional pianist may be only too glad to get out and dig at the potato patch. Hence the antithesis between work, as something intolerably tedious, and not-work, as something desirable, is false. The truth is that when a human being is not eating, drinking, sleeping, making love, talking, playing games or merely lounging about – and these things will not fill up a lifetime – he needs work and usually looks for it, though he may not call it work. Above the level of a third- or fourth-grade moron, life has got to be lived largely in terms of effort. For man is not, as the vulgarer hedonists seem to suppose, a kind of walking stomach; he has also got a hand, an eye and a brain. Cease to use your hands, and you have lopped off a huge chunk of your consciousness. And now consider again those half-dozen men who were digging the trench for the water-pipe. A machine has set them free from digging, and they are going to amuse themselves with something else – carpentering, for instance. But whatever they want to do, they will find that another machine has set them free from *that.* For in a fully mechanised world there would be no more need to carpenter, to cook, to mend motor-bicycles, etc., than there would be to dig. There is scarcely anything, from catching a whale to carving a cherry stone, that could not conceivably be done by machinery. The machine would even encroach upon the activities we now class as 'art'; it is doing so already, via the camera and the radio. Mechanise the world as fully as it might be mechanised, and whichever way you turn there will be some machine cutting you off from the chance of working – that is, of living.

At a first glance this might not seem to matter. Why should you not get on with your 'creative work' and disregard the machines that would do it for you? But it is not so simple as it sounds. Here am I, working eight hours a day in an insurance office; in my spare time I want to do something 'creative', so I choose to do a bit of carpentering – to make myself a table, for instance. Notice that from the very start there is a touch of artificiality about the whole business, for the factories can turn me out a far better table than I can make for myself. But even when I get to work on my table, it is not possible for me to feel towards it as the cabinet-maker of a hundred years ago felt towards his table, still less as Robinson Crusoe felt towards his. For before I start, most of the work has already been done for me by machinery. The tools I use demand the minimum of skill. I can get, for instance, planes which will cut out any moulding; the cabinet-maker of a hundred years ago would have had to do the work with chisel and gouge, which demanded real skill of eye and hand. The boards I buy are ready planed and the legs are ready turned by the lathe. I can even go to the wood-shop and buy all the parts of the table ready-made and only needing to be fitted together, my work being reduced to driving in a few pegs and using a piece of sandpaper. And if this is so at present, in the mechanised future it will be enormously more so. With the tools and materials available *then*, there will be no possibility of mistake, hence no room for skill. Making a table will be easier and duller than peeling a potato. In such circumstances it is nonsense to talk of 'creative work'. In any case the arts of the hand (which have got to be transmitted by apprenticeship) would long since have disappeared. Some of them have disappeared already, under the competition of the machine. Look round any country churchyard and see whether you can find a decently-cut tombstone later than 1820. The art, or rather the craft, of stonework has died out so completely that it would take centuries to revive it.

But it may be said, why not retain the machine *and* retain 'creative work'? Why not cultivate anachronisms as a spare-time hobby? Many people have played with this idea; it seems to solve with such beautiful ease the problems set by the machine. The citizen of Utopia, we are told, coming home from his daily two hours of turning a handle in the tomato-canning factory, will deliberately revert to a more primitive way of life and solace his creative instincts with a bit of fretwork, pottery-glazing or handloom-weaving. And why is this picture an absurdity – as it is, of course? Because of a principle that is not always recognised, though always acted upon: that so long as the machine *is there*, one is under an obligation to use it. No one draws water from the well when he can turn on the tap. One sees a good illustration of this in the matter of travel. Everyone who has travelled by primitive methods in an undeveloped country knows that the difference between that kind of travel and modern travel in trains, cars, etc., is the difference between life and death. The nomad who walks or rides, with his baggage stowed on a camel or an ox-cart, may suffer every kind of discomfort, but at least he is living while he is travelling; whereas for the passenger in an express train or a luxury liner his journey is an interregnum, a kind of temporary death. And yet so long as the railways exist, one has got to travel by train – or by car or aeroplane. Here am I, forty miles from London. When I want to go up to London why do I not pack my luggage onto a mule and set out on foot, making a two days' march of it? Because, with the Green Line buses whizzing past me every ten minutes, such a journey would be intolerably irksome. In order that one may enjoy primitive methods of travel, it is necessary that no other method should be available. No human being ever wants to do anything in a more cumbrous way than is necessary. Hence the absurdity of that picture of Utopians saving their souls with fretwork. In a world where everything could be done by machinery, everything would be done by machinery. Deliberately to revert to primitive methods, to use archaic tools, to put silly little difficulties in your own way, would be a piece of dilettantism, of pretty-pretty arty and craftiness. It would be like solemnly sitting down to eat your dinner with stone implements. Revert to handwork in a machine age, and you are back in Ye Olde Tea Shoppe or the Tudor villa with the sham beams tacked to the wall.

The tendency of mechanical progress, then, is to frustrate the human need for effort and creation. It makes unnecessary and even impossible the activities of the eye and the hand. The apostle of 'progress' will sometimes declare that this does not matter, but you can usually drive him into a corner by pointing out the horrible lengths to which the process can be carried. Why, for instance, use your hands at all – why use them even for blowing your nose or sharpening a pencil? Surely you could fix some kind of steel and rubber contraption to your shoulders and let your arms wither into stumps of skin and bone? And so with every organ and every faculty. There is really no reason why a human being should do more than eat, drink, sleep, breathe and procreate; *everything* else could be done for him by machinery. Therefore the logical end of mechanical progress is to reduce the human being to something resembling a brain in a bottle. That is the goal towards which we are already moving, though, of course, we have no intention of getting there; just as a man who drinks a bottle of whisky a day does not actually intend to get cirrhosis of the liver. The implied objective of 'progress' is – not *exactly*, perhaps, the brain in the bottle, but at any rate some frightful sub-human depth of softness and helplessness. And the unfortunate thing is that at present the word 'progress' and the word 'Socialism' are linked inseparably in almost everyone's mind. The kind of person who hates machinery also takes it for granted to hate Socialism; the Socialist is always in favour of mechanisation, rationalisation, modernisation – or at least thinks that he ought to be in favour of them. Quite recently, for instance, a prominent ILP'er confessed to me with a sort of wistful shame – as though it were something faintly improper – that he was 'fond of horses'. Horses, you see, belong to the vanished agricultural past, and all sentiment for the past carries with it a vague smell of heresy. I do not believe that this need necessarily be so, but undoubtedly it is so. And in itself it is quite enough to explain the alienation of decent minds from Socialism.

A generation ago every intelligent person was in some sense a revolutionary; nowadays it would be nearer the mark to say that every intelligent person is a reactionary. In this connection it is worth comparing H. G. Wells's *When the Sleeper Wakes* with Aldous Huxley's *Brave New World*, written thirty years later. Each is a pessimistic Utopia, a vision of a sort of prig's paradise in which all the dreams of the 'progressive' person come true. Considered merely as a piece of imaginative construction *When the Sleeper Wakes* is, I think, much superior, but it suffers from vast contradictions because of the fact that Wells, as the arch-priest of 'progress', cannot write with any conviction *against* 'progress'. He draws a picture of a glittering, strangely sinister world in which the privileged classes live a life of shallow gutless hedonism, and the workers, reduced to a state of utter slavery and sub-human ignorance, toil like troglodytes in caverns underground. As soon as one examines this idea – it is further developed in a splendid short story in *Stories of Space and Time* – one sees its inconsistency. For in the immensely mechanised world that Wells is imagining, why should the workers have to work harder than at present? Obviously the tendency of the machine is to eliminate work, not to increase it. In the machine-world the workers might be enslaved, ill-treated and even underfed, but they certainly would not be condemned to ceaseless manual toil; because in that case what would be the function of the machine? You can have machines doing all the work or human beings doing all the work, but you can't have both. Those armies of underground workers, with their blue uniforms and their debased, half-human language, are only put in 'to make your flesh creep'. Wells wants to suggest that 'progress' might take a wrong turning; but the only evil he cares to imagine is inequality – one class grabbing all the wealth and power and oppressing the others, apparently out of pure spite. Give it quite a small twist, he seems to suggest, overthrow the privileged class – change over from world-capitalism to Socialism, in fact – and all will be well. The machine-civilisation is to continue, but its products are to be shared out equally. The thought he dare not face is that the machine itself may be the enemy. So in his more characteristic Utopias (*The Dream*, *Men like Gods*, etc.), he returns to optimism and to a vision of humanity, 'liberated' by the machine, as a race of enlightened sunbathers whose sole topic of conversation is their own superiority to their ancestors. *Brave New World* belongs to a later time and to a generation which has seen through the swindle of 'progress'. It contains its own contradictions (the most important of them is pointed out in Mr John Strachey's *The Coming Struggle for Power*), but it is at least a memorable assault on the more fat-bellied type of perfectionism. Allowing for the exaggerations of caricature, it probably expresses what a majority of thinking people feel about machine-civilisation.

The sensitive person's hostility to the machine is in one sense unrealistic, because of the obvious fact that the machine has come to stay. But as an attitude of mind there is a great deal to be said for it. The machine has got to be accepted, but it is probably better to accept it rather as one accepts a drug – that is, grudgingly and suspiciously. Like a drug, the machine is useful, dangerous and habit-forming. The oftener one surrenders to it the tighter its grip becomes. You have only to look about you at this moment to realise with what sinister speed the machine is getting us into its power.

To begin with, there is the frightful debauchery of taste that has already been effected by a century of mechanisation. This is almost too obvious and too generally admitted to need pointing out. But as a single instance, take taste in its narrowest sense – the taste for decent food. In the highly mechanised countries, thanks to tinned food, cold storage, synthetic flavouring matters, etc., the palate is almost a dead organ. As you can see by looking at any greengrocer's shop, what the majority of English people mean by an apple is a lump of highly-coloured cotton wool from America or Australia; they will devour these things, apparently with pleasure, and let the English apples rot under the trees. It is the shiny, standardised, machine-made look of the American apple that appeals to them; the superior taste of the English apple is something they simply do not notice. Or look at the factory-made, foil-wrapped cheeses and 'blended' butter in any grocer's; look at the hideous rows of tins which usurp more and more of the space in any food-shop, even a dairy; look at a sixpenny Swiss roll or a twopenny ice-cream; look at the filthy chemical by-product that people will pour down their throats under the name of beer. Wherever you look you will see some slick machine-made article triumphing over the old-fashioned article that still tastes of something other than sawdust. And what applies to food applies also to furniture, houses, clothes, books, amusements and everything else that makes up our environment. There are now millions of people, and they are increasing every year, to whom the blaring of a radio is not only a more acceptable but a more *normal* background to their thoughts than the lowing of cattle or the song of birds. The mechanisation of the world could never proceed very far while taste, even the taste-buds of the tongue, remained uncorrupted, because in that case most of the products of the machine would be simply unwanted. In a healthy world there would be no demand for tinned food, aspirins, gramophones, gas-pipe chairs, machine guns, daily newspapers, telephones, motor-cars, etc. etc.; and on the other hand there would be a constant demand for the things the machine cannot produce. But meanwhile the machine is here, and its corrupting effects are almost irresistible. One inveighs against it, but one goes on using it. Even a bare-arse savage, given the chance, will learn the vices of civilisation within a few months. Mechanisation leads to the decay of taste, the decay of taste leads to the demand for machine-made articles and hence to more mechanisation, and so a vicious circle is established.

But in addition to this there is a tendency for the mechanisation of the world to proceed as it were automatically, whether we want it or not. This is due to the fact that in modern Western man the faculty of mechanical invention has been fed and stimulated till it has reached almost the status of an instinct. People invent new machines and improve existing ones almost unconsciously, rather as a somnambulist will go on working in his sleep. In the past, when it was taken for granted that life on this planet is harsh or at any rate laborious, it seemed the natural fate to go on using the clumsy implements of your forefathers, and only a few eccentric persons, centuries apart, proposed innovations; hence throughout enormous ages such things as the ox-cart, the plough, the sickle, etc., remained radically unchanged. It is on record that screws have been in use since remote antiquity and yet that it was not till the middle of the nineteenth century that anyone thought of making screws with points on them; for several thousand years they remained flat-ended and holes had to be drilled for them before they could be inserted. In our own epoch such a thing would be unthinkable. For almost every modern Western man has his inventive faculty to some extent developed; the Western man invents machines as naturally as the Polynesian islander swims. Give a Western man a job of work and he immediately begins devising a machine that would do it for him; give him a machine and he thinks of ways of improving it. I understand this tendency well enough, for in an ineffectual sort of way I have that type of mind myself. I have not either the patience or the mechanical skill to devise any machine that would work, but I am perpetually seeing, as it were, the ghosts of possible machines that might save me the trouble of using my brain or muscles. A person with a more definite mechanical turn would probably construct some of them and put them into operation. But under our present economic system, whether he constructed them – or rather, whether anyone else had the benefit of them – would depend upon whether they were commercially valuable. The Socialists are right, therefore, when they claim that the rate of mechanical progress will be much more rapid once Socialism is established. Given a mechanical civilisation the process of invention and improvement will always continue, but the tendency of capitalism is to slow it down, because under capitalism any invention which does not promise fairly immediate profits is neglected; some, indeed, which threaten to reduce profits are suppressed almost as ruthlessly as the flexible glass mentioned by Petronius.[1] Establish Socialism – remove the profit principle – and the inventor will have a free hand. The mechanisation of the world, already rapid enough, would be or at any rate could be enormously accelerated.

And this prospect is a slightly sinister one, because it is obvious even now that the process of mechanisation is out of control. It is happening

[1] For example: Some years ago someone invented a gramophone needle that would last for decades. One of the big gramophone companies bought up the patent rights, and that was the last that was ever heard of it.

merely because humanity has got the habit. A chemist perfects a new method of synthesising rubber, or a mechanic devises a new pattern of gudgeon-pin. Why? Not for any clearly understood purpose, but simply from the impulse to invent and improve, which has now become instinctive. Put a pacifist to work in a bomb-factory and in two months he will be devising a new type of bomb. Hence the appearance of such diabolical things as poison gases, which are not expected even by their inventors to be beneficial to humanity. Our attitude towards such things as poison gases *ought* to be the attitude of the king of Brobdingnag towards gunpowder; but because we live in a mechanical and scientific age we are infected with the notion that, whatever else happens, 'progress' must continue and knowledge must never be suppressed. Verbally, no doubt, we would agree that machinery is made for man and not man for machinery; in practice any attempt to check the development of the machine appears to us as an attack on knowledge and therefore a kind of blasphemy. And even if the whole of humanity suddenly revolted against the machine and decided to escape to a simpler way of life, the escape would still be immensely difficult. It would not do, as in Butler's *Erewhon*, to smash every machine invented after a certain date; we should also have to smash the habit of mind that would, almost involuntarily, devise fresh machines as soon as the old ones were smashed. And in all of us there is at least a tinge of that habit of mind. In every country in the world the large army of scientists and technicians, with the rest of us panting at their heels, is marching along the road of 'progress' with the blind persistence of a column of ants. Comparatively few people want it to happen, plenty of people actively want it *not* to happen, and yet it is happening. The process of mechanisation has itself become a machine, a huge glittering vehicle whirling us we are not certain where, but probably towards the padded Wells-world and the brain in the bottle.

This, then, is the case against the machine. Whether it is a sound or unsound case hardly matters. The point is that these or very similar arguments would be echoed by every person who is hostile to machine-civilisation. And unfortunately, because of that nexus of thought, 'Socialism - progress - machinery - Russia - tractors - hygiene - machinery - progress', which exists in almost everyone's mind, it is usually the *same* person who is hostile to Socialism. The kind of person who hates central heating and gas-pipe chairs is also the kind of person who, when you mention Socialism, murmurs something about 'beehive state' and moves away with a pained expression. So far as my observation goes, very few Socialists grasp why this is so, or even that it *is* so. Get the more vocal type of Socialist into a corner, repeat to him the substance of what I have said in this chapter, and see what kind of answer you get. As a matter of fact you will get several answers; I am so familiar with them that I know them almost by heart.

In the first place he will tell you that it is impossible to 'go back' (or to 'put back the hand of progress' – as though the hand of progress hadn't been pretty violently put back several times in human history!), and will then accuse you of being a medievalist and begin to descant upon the horrors of the Middle Ages, leprosy, the Inquisition, etc. As a matter of fact, most attacks upon the Middle Ages and the past generally by apologists of modernity are beside the point, because their essential trick is to project a modern man, with his squeamishness and his high standards of comfort, into an age when such things were unheard of. But notice that in any case this is not an answer. For a dislike of the mechanised future does not imply the smallest reverence for any period of the past. D. H. Lawrence, wiser than the medievalist, chose to idealise the Etruscans about whom we know conveniently little. But there is no need to idealise even the Etruscans – or the Pelasgians, or the Aztecs, or the Sumerians, or any other vanished and romantic people. When one pictures a desirable civilisation, one pictures it merely as an objective; there is no need to pretend that it has ever existed in space and time. Press this point home, explain that you wish merely to aim at making life simpler and harder instead of softer and more complex, and the Socialist will usually assume that you want to revert to a 'state of nature' – meaning some stinking palaeolithic cave: as though there were nothing between a flint scraper and the steel mills of Sheffield, or between a skin coracle and the *Queen Mary*!

Finally, however, you will get an answer which is rather more to the point and which runs roughly as follows: 'Yes, what you are saying is all very well in its way. No doubt it would be very noble to harden ourselves and do without aspirins and central heating and so forth. But the point is, you see, that nobody seriously wants it. It would mean going back to an agricultural way of life, which means beastly hard work and isn't at all the same thing as playing at gardening. I don't want hard work, you don't want hard work – nobody wants it who knows what it means. You only talk as you do because you've never done a day's work in your life,' etc. etc.

Now this in a sense is true. It amounts to saying, 'We're soft – for God's sake let's stay soft!' which at least is realistic. As I have pointed out already, the machine has got us in its grip and to escape will be immensely difficult. Nevertheless this answer is really an evasion, because it fails to make clear what we mean when we say that we 'want' this or that. I am a degenerate modern semi-intellectual who would die if I did not get my early morning cup of tea and my *New Statesman* every Friday. Clearly I do not, in a sense, 'want' to return to a simpler, harder, probably agricultural way of life. In the same sense I don't 'want' to cut down my drinking, to pay my debts, to take enough exercise, to be faithful to my wife, etc. etc. But in another and more permanent sense I do want these things, and perhaps in the same sense I want a civilisation in which 'progress' is not definable as making the world safe for little fat men. These that I have outlined are practically the only arguments that I have been able to get from Socialists – thinking, book-trained Socialists – when I have tried to explain to them just *how* they are driving away possible adherents. Of course there is also the old argument that Socialism is going to arrive anyway, whether people like it or not, because of that trouble-saving thing, 'historic necessity'. But 'historic necessity', or rather the belief in it, has failed to survive Hitler.

Meanwhile the thinking person, by intellect usually left-wing, but by temperament often right-wing, hovers at the gate of the Socialist fold. He is no doubt aware that he *ought* to be a Socialist. But he observes first the dullness of individual Socialists, then the apparent flabbiness of Socialist ideals, and veers away. Till quite recently it was natural to veer towards indifferentism. Ten years ago, even five years ago, the typical literary gent wrote books on baroque architecture and had a soul above politics. But that attitude is becoming difficult and even unfashionable. The times are growing harsher, the issues are clearer, the belief that nothing will ever change (i.e. that your dividends will always be safe) is less prevalent. The fence on which the literary gent sits, once as comfortable as the plush cushion of a cathedral stall, is now pinching his bottom intolerably; more and more he shows a disposition to drop off on one side or the other. It is interesting to notice how many of our leading writers, who a dozen years ago were art for art's saking for all they were worth and would have considered it too vulgar for words even to vote at a general election, are now taking a definite political standpoint; while most of the younger writers, at least those of them who are not mere footlers, have been 'political' from the start. I believe that when the pinch comes there is a terrible danger that the main movement of the intelligentsia will be towards Fascism. Just how soon the pinch will come it is difficult to say; it depends, probably, upon events in Europe; but it may be that within two years or even a year we shall have reached the decisive moment. That will also be the moment when every person with any brains or any decency will know in his bones that he ought to be on the Socialist side. But he will not necessarily come there of his own accord; there are too many ancient prejudices standing in the way. He will have to be persuaded, and by methods that imply an understanding of his viewpoint. Socialists cannot afford to waste any more time in preaching to the converted. Their job now is to make Socialists as rapidly as possible; instead of which, all too often, they are making Fascists.

When I speak of Fascism in England, I am not necessarily thinking of Mosley and his pimpled followers. English Fascism, when it arrives, is likely to be of a sedate and subtle kind (presumably, at any rate at first, it won't be *called* Fascism), and it is doubtful whether a Gilbert and Sullivan heavy dragoon of Mosley's stamp would ever be much more than a joke to the majority of English people; though even Mosley will bear watching, for experience shows (*vide* the careers of Hitler, Napoleon III) that to a political climber it is sometimes an advantage not to be taken too seriously at the beginning of his career. But what I am thinking of at this moment is the Fascist attitude of mind, which beyond any doubt is gaining ground among people who ought to know better. Fascism as it appears in the intellectual is a sort of mirror-image – not actually of Socialism but of a plausible travesty of Socialism. It boils down to a determination to do the *opposite* of whatever the mythical Socialist does. If you present Socialism in a bad and misleading light – if you let people imagine that it does not mean much more than pouring European civilisation down the sink at the command of Marxist prigs – you risk driving the intellectual into Fascism.

You frighten him into a sort of angry defensive attitude in which he simply refuses to listen to the Socialist case. Some such attitude is already quite clearly discernible in writers like Pound, Wyndham Lewis, Roy Campbell, etc., in most of the Roman Catholic writers and many of the Douglas Credit group, in certain popular novelists and even, if one looks below the surface, in su-superior conservative highbrows like Eliot and his countless followers. If you want some unmistakable illustrations of the growth of Fascist feeling in England, have a look at some of the innumerable letters that were written to the Press during the Abyssinian war, approving the Italian action, and also the howl of glee that went up from both Catholic and Anglican pulpits (see the *Daily Mail* of August 17th, 1936) over the Fascist rising in Spain.

In order to combat Fascism it is necessary to understand it, which involves admitting that it contains some good as well as much evil. In practice, of course, it is merely an infamous tyranny, and its methods of attaining and holding power are such that even its most ardent apologists prefer to talk about something else. But the underlying feeling of Fascism, the feeling that first draws people into the Fascist camp, may be less contemptible. It is not *always*, as the *Saturday Review* would lead one to suppose, a squealing terror of the Bolshevik bogey-man. Everyone who has given the movement so much as a glance knows that the rank-and-file Fascist is often quite a well-meaning person – quite genuinely anxious, for instance, to better the lot of the unemployed. But more important than this is the fact that Fascism draws its strength from the good as well as the bad varieties of conservatism. To anyone with a feeling for tradition and for discipline it comes with its appeal ready-made. Probably it is very easy, when you have had a bellyful of the more tactless kind of Socialist propaganda, to see Fascism as the last line defence of all that is good in European civilisation. Even the Fascist bully at his symbolic worst, with rubber truncheon in one hand and castor-oil bottle in the other, does not necessarily feel himself a bully; more probably he feels like Roland in the pass at Roncevaux, defending Christendom against the barbarian. We have got to admit that if Fascism is everywhere advancing, this is largely the fault of Socialists themselves. Partly it is due to the mistaken Communist tactic of sabotaging democracy, i.e. sawing off the branch you are sitting on; but still more to the fact that Socialists have, so to speak, presented their case wrong side foremost. They have never made it sufficiently clear that the essential aims of Socialism are justice and liberty. With their eyes glued to economic facts, they have proceeded on the assumption that man has no soul, and explicitly or implicitly they have set up the goal of a materialistic Utopia. As a result Fascism has been able to play upon every instinct that revolts against hedonism and a cheap conception of 'progress'. It has been able to pose as the upholder of the European tradition, and to appeal to Christian belief, to patriotism and to the military virtues. It is far worse than useless to write Fascism off as 'mass sadism', or some easy phrase of that kind. If you pretend that it is merely an aberration which will presently pass off of its own accord, you are dreaming a dream from which you will awake when somebody coshes you with a rubber truncheon. The only possible course is to examine the Fascist case, grasp that there is something to be said for it, and then make it clear to the world that whatever good Fascism contains is also implicit in Socialism.

At present the situation is desperate. Even if nothing worse befalls us, there are the conditions which I described in the earlier part of this book and which are not going to improve under our present economic system. Still more urgent is the danger of Fascist domination in Europe. And unless Socialist doctrine, in an effective form, can be diffused widely and very quickly, there is no certainty that Fascism will ever be overthrown. For Socialism is the only real enemy that Fascism has to face. The capitalist-imperialist governments, even though they themselves are about to be plundered, will not fight with any conviction against Fascism as such. Our rulers, those of them who understand the issue, would probably prefer to hand over every square inch of the British Empire to Italy, Germany and Japan than to see Socialism triumphant. It was easy to laugh at Fascism when we imagined that it was based on hysterical nationalism, because it seemed obvious that the Fascist states, each regarding itself as the chosen people and patriotic *contra mundum*, would clash with one another. But nothing of the kind is happening. Fascism is now an international movement, which means not only that the Fascist nations can combine for purposes of loot, but that they are groping, perhaps only half consciously as yet, towards a world-system. For the vision of the totalitarian state there is being substituted the vision of the totalitarian world. As I pointed out earlier, the advance of machine-technique must lead ultimately to some form of collectivism, but that form need not necessarily be equalitarian; that is, it need not be Socialism. *Pace* the economists, it is quite easy to imagine a world-society, economically collectivist – that is, with the profit principle eliminated – but with all political, military and educational power in the hands of a small caste of rulers and their bravos. That or something like it is the objective of Fascism. And that, of course, is the slave-state, or rather the slave-world; it would probably be a stable form of society, and the chances are, considering the enormous wealth of the world if scientifically exploited, that the slaves would be well-fed and contented. It is usual to speak of the Fascist objective as the 'beehive state', which does a grave injustice to bees. A world of rabbits ruled by stoats would be nearer the mark. It is against this beastly possibility that we have got to combine.

The only thing *for* which we can combine is the underlying ideal of Socialism; justice and liberty. But it is hardly strong enough to call this ideal 'underlying'. It is almost completely forgotten. It has been buried beneath layer after layer of doctrinaire priggishness, partly squabbles and half-baked 'progressivism' until it is like a diamond hidden under a mountain of dung. The job of the Socialist is to get it out again. Justice and liberty! *Those* are the words that have got to ring like a bugle across the world. For a long time past, certainly for the last ten years, the devil has had all the best tunes. We have reached a stage when the very word 'Socialism' calls up, on the one hand, a picture of aeroplanes, tractors and huge glittering factories of glass and concrete; on the other, a picture of vegetarians with wilting beards, of Bolshevik commissars (half gangster, half gramophone), of earnest ladies in sandals, shock-headed Marxists chewing polysyllables, escaped Quakers, birth-control fanatics and Labour Party backstairs-crawlers. Socialism, at least in this island, does not smell any longer of revolution and the overthrow of tyrants; it smells of crankishness, machine-worship and the stupid cult of Russia. Unless you can remove that smell, and very rapidly, Fascism may win.

XIII

And finally, is there anything one can do about it?

In the first part of this book I illustrated, by a few brief sidelights, the kind of mess we are in; in this second part I have been trying to explain why, in my opinion, so many normal decent people are repelled by the only remedy, namely by Socialism. Obviously the most urgent need of the next few years is to capture those normal decent ones before Fascism plays its trump card. I do not want to raise here the question of parties and political expedients. More important than any party label (though doubtless the mere menace of Fascism will presently bring some kind of Popular Front into existence) is the diffusion of Socialist doctrine in an effective form. People have got to be made ready to *act* as Socialists. There are, I believe, countless people who, without being aware of it, are in sympathy with the essential aims of Socialism, and who could be won over almost without a struggle if only one could find the word that would move them. Everyone who knows the meaning of poverty, everyone who has a genuine hatred of tyranny and war, is on the Socialist side, potentially. My job here, therefore, is to suggest – necessarily in very general terms – how a reconciliation might be effected between Socialism and its more intelligent enemies.

First, as to the enemies themselves – I mean all those people who grasp that capitalism is evil but who are conscious of a sort of queasy, shuddering sensation when Socialism is mentioned. As I have pointed out, this is traceable to two main causes. One is the personal inferiority of many individual Socialists; the other is the fact that Socialism is too often coupled with a fat-bellied, godless conception of 'progress' which revolts anyone with a feeling for tradition or the rudiments of an aesthetic sense. Let me take the second point first.

The distaste for 'progress' and machine-civilisation which is so common among sensitive people is only defensible as an attitude of mind. It is not valid as a reason for rejecting Socialism, because it presupposes an alternative which does not exist. When you say, 'I object to mechanisation and standardisation – therefore I object to Socialism', you are saying in effect, 'I am free to do without the machine if I choose', which is nonsense. We are all dependent upon the machine, and if the machines stopped working most of us would die. You may hate the machine-civilisation, probably you are right to hate it, but for the present there can be no question of accepting or rejecting it. The machine-civilisation *is here*, and it can only be criticised from the inside, because all of us are inside it. It is only romantic fools who flatter themselves that they have escaped, like the literary gent in his Tudor cottage with bathroom h and c, and the he-man who goes off to live a 'primitive' life in the jungle with a Mannlicher rifle and four wagon-loads of tinned food. And almost certainly the machine-civilisation will continue to triumph. There is no reason to think that it will destroy itself or stop functioning of its own accord. For some time past it has been fashionable to say that war is presently going to 'wreck civilisation' altogether; but, though the next full-sized war will certainly be horrible enough to make all previous ones seem a joke, it is immensely unlikely that it will put a stop to mechanical progress. It is true that a very vulnerable country like England, and perhaps the whole of western Europe, could be reduced to chaos by a few thousand well-placed bombs, but no war is at present thinkable which could wipe out industrialism in all countries simultaneously. We may take it that the return to a simpler, freer, less mechanised way of life, however desirable it may be, is not going to happen. This is not fatalism, it is merely acceptance of facts. It is meaningless to oppose Socialism on the ground that you object to the beehive state, for the beehive state *is here*. The choice is not, as yet, between a human and an inhuman world. It is simply between Socialism and Fascism, which at its very best is Socialism with the virtues left out.

The job of the thinking person, therefore, is not to reject Socialism but to make up his mind to humanise it. Once Socialism is in a way to being established, those who can see through the swindle of 'progress' will probably find themselves resisting. In fact, it is their special function to do so. In the machine-world they have got to be a sort of permanent opposition, which is not the same thing as being an obstructionist or a traitor. But in this I am speaking of the future. For the moment the only possible course for any decent person, however much of a Tory or an anarchist by temperament, is to work for the establishment of Socialism. Nothing else can save us from the misery of the present or the nightmare of the future. To oppose Socialism *now*, when twenty million Englishmen are underfed and Fascism has conquered half Europe, is suicidal. It is like starting a civil war when the Goths are crossing the frontier.

Therefore it is all the more important to get rid of that mere nervous prejudice against Socialism which is not founded on any serious objection. As I have pointed out already, many people who are not repelled by Socialism are repelled by Socialists. Socialism, as now presented, is unattractive largely because it appears, at any rate from the outside, to be the plaything of cranks, doctrinaires, parlour Bolsheviks and so forth. But it is worth remembering that this is only so because the cranks, doctrinaires, etc., have been allowed to get there first; if the movement were invaded by better brains and more common decency, the objectionable types would cease to dominate it. For the present one must just set one's teeth and ignore them; they will loom much smaller when the movement has been humanised. Besides, they are irrelevant. We have got to fight for justice and liberty, and Socialism does mean justice and liberty when the nonsense is stripped off it. It is only the essentials that are worth remembering. To recoil from Socialism because so many individual Socialists are inferior people is as absurd as refusing to travel by train because you dislike the ticket-collector's face.

And secondly, as to the Socialist himself – more especially the vocal, tract-writing type of Socialist.

We are at a moment when it is desperately necessary for left-wingers of all complexions to drop their differences and hang together. Indeed this is already happening to a small extent. Obviously, then, the more intransigent kind of Socialist has now got to ally himself with people who are not in perfect agreement with him. As a rule he is rightly unwilling to do so, because he sees the very real danger of watering the whole Socialist movement down to some kind of pale-pink humbug even more ineffectual than the parliamentary Labour Party. At the moment, for instance, there is great danger that the Popular Front which Fascism will presumably bring into existence will not be genuinely Socialist in character, but will simply be a manoeuvre against German and Italian (not English) Fascism. Thus the need to unite against Fascism might draw the Socialist into alliance with his very worse enemies. But the principle to go upon is this: that you are never in danger of allying yourself with the wrong people provided that you keep the essentials of your movement in the foreground.

And what are the essentials of Socialism? What is the mark of a real Socialist? I suggest that the real Socialist is one who wishes – not merely conceives it as desirable, but actively wishes – to see tyranny overthrown. But I fancy that the majority of orthodox Marxists would not accept that definition, or would only accept it very grudgingly. Sometimes, when I listen to these people talking, and still more then I read their books, I get the impression that, to them, the whole Socialist movement is no more than a kind of exciting heresy-hunt – a leaping to and fro of frenzied witch-doctors to the beat of tom-toms and the tune of 'Fee fi, fo, fum, I smell the blood of a right-wing deviationist!'. It is because of this kind of thing that it is so much easier to feel yourself a Socialist when you are among working-class people. The working-class Socialist, like the working-class Catholic, is weak on doctrine and can hardly open his mouth without uttering a heresy, but he has the heart of the matter in him. He does grasp the central fact that Socialism means the overthrow of tyranny, and the 'Marseillaise', if it were translated for his benefit, would appeal to him more deeply than any learned treatise on dialectical materialism. At this moment it is a waste of time to insist that acceptance of Socialism means acceptance of the philosophic side of Marxism, plus adulation of Russia. The Socialist movement has not time to be a league of dialectical materialists; it has got to be a league of the oppressed against the oppressors. You have got to attract the man who means business, and you have got to drive away the mealy-mouthed Liberal who wants foreign Fascism destroyed in order that he may go on drawing his dividends peacefully – the type of humbug who passes resolutions 'against Fascism and Communism', i.e. against rats and rat-poison. Socialism means the overthrow of tyranny, at home as well as abroad. So long as you keep *that* fact well to the front, you will never be in much doubt as to who are your real supporters. As for minor differences – and the profoundest philosophical difference is unimportant compared with saving the twenty million Englishmen whose bones are rotting from malnutrition – the time to argue about them is afterwards.

I do not think the Socialist need make any sacrifice of essentials, but certainly he will have to make a great sacrifice of externals. It would help enormously, for instance, if the smell of crankishness which still clings to the Socialist movement could be dispelled. If only the sandals and the pistachio-coloured shirts could be put in a pile and burnt, and every vegetarian, teetotaller and creeping Jesus sent home to Welwyn Garden City to do his yoga exercises quietly! But that, I am afraid, is not going to happen. What *is* possible, however, is for the more intelligent kind of Socialist to stop alienating possible supporters in silly and quite irrelevant ways. There are so many minor priggishnesses which could so easily be dropped. Take for instance the dreary attitude of the typical Marxist towards literature. Out of the many that come into my mind, I will give just one example. It sounds trivial, but it isn't. In the old *Worker's Weekly* (one of the forerunners of the *Daily Worker*) there used to be a column of literary chat of the 'Books on the Editor's Table' type. For several weeks running there had been a certain amount of talk about Shakespeare; whereupon an incensed reader wrote to say, 'Dear Comrade, we don't want to hear about these bourgeois writers like Shakespeare. Can't you give us something a bit more proletarian?' etc. etc. The editor's reply was simple. 'If you will turn to the index of Marx's *Capital*,' he wrote, 'you will find that Shakespeare is mentioned several times.' And please notice that this was enough to silence the objector. Once Shakespeare had received the benediction of Marx, he became respectable. *That* is the mentality that drives ordinary sensible people away from the Socialist movement. You do not need to care about Shakespeare to be repelled by that kind of thing. Again, there is the horrible jargon that nearly all Socialists think it necessary to employ. When the ordinary person hears phrases like 'bourgeois ideology' and 'proletarian solidarity' and 'expropriation of the expropriators', he is not inspired by them, he is merely disgusted. Even the single word 'Comrade' has done its dirty little bit towards discrediting the Socialist movement. How many a waverer has halted on the brink, gone perhaps to some public meeting and watched self-conscious Socialists dutifully addressing one another as 'Comrade', and then slid away, disillusioned, into the nearest four-ale bar! And his instinct is sound; for where is the sense of sticking onto yourself a ridiculous label which even after long practice can hardly be mentioned without a gulp of shame? It is fatal to let the ordinary enquirer get away with the idea that being a Socialist means wearing sandals and burbling about dialectical materialism. You have got to make it clear that there is room in the Socialist movement for human beings, or the game is up.

And this raises a great difficulty. It means that the issue of class, as distinct from mere economic status, has got to be faced more realistically than it is being faced at present.

I devoted three chapters to discussing the class-difficulty. The principal fact that will have emerged, I think, is that though the English class-system has outlived its usefulness, it *has* outlived it and shows no signs of dying. It greatly confuses the issue to assume, as the orthodox Marxist so often does (see for instance Mr Alec Brown's in some ways interesting book, *The Fate of the Middle Classes*), that social status is determined solely by income. Economically, no doubt, there are only two classes, the rich and the poor, but socially there is a whole hierarchy of classes, and the manners and traditions learned by each class in childhood are not only very different but – this is the essential point – generally persist from birth to death. Hence the anomalous individuals that you find in every class of society. You find writers like Wells and Bennett who have grown immensely rich and have yet preserved intact their lower-middle-class Nonconformist prejudices; you find millionaires who cannot pronounce their aitches; you find petty shopkeepers whose income is far lower than that of the bricklayer and who, nevertheless, consider themselves (and are considered) the bricklayer's social superiors; you find board-school boys ruling Indian provinces and public-school men touting vacuum cleaners. If social stratification corresponded precisely to economic stratification, the public-school man would assume a Cockney accent the day his income dropped below £200 a year. But does he? On the contrary, he immediately becomes twenty times more Public School than before. He clings to the Old School Tie as to a life-line. And even the aitchless millionaire, though sometimes he goes to an elocutionist and learns a BBC accent, seldom succeeds in disguising himself as completely as he would like to. It is in fact very difficult to escape, culturally, from the class into which you have been born.

As prosperity declines, social anomalies grow commoner. You don't get more aitchless millionaires, but you do get more and more public-school men touting vacuum cleaners and more and more small shopkeepers driven into the workhouse. Large sections of the middle class are being gradually proletarianised; but the important point is that they do not, at any rate in the first generation, adopt a proletarian outlook. Here am I, for instance, with a bourgeois upbringing and a working-class income. Which class do I belong to? Economically I belong to the working class, but it is almost impossible for me to think of myself as anything but a member of the bourgeoisie. And supposing I had to take sides, whom should I side with, the upper class which is trying to squeeze me out of existence, or the working class whose manners are not my manners? It is probable that I personally, in any important issue, would side with the working class. But what about the tens or hundreds of thousands of others who are in approximately the same position? And what about that far larger class, running into millions this time – the office-workers and black-coated employees of all kinds – whose traditions are less definitely middle class but who would certainly not thank you if you called them proletarians? All of these people have the same interests and the same enemies as the working class. All are being robbed and bullied by the same system. Yet how many of them realise it? When the pinch came nearly all of them would side with their oppressors and against those who ought to be their allies. It is quite easy to imagine a middle class crushed down to the worst depths of poverty and still remaining bitterly anti-working class in sentiment; this being, of course, a ready-made Fascist Party.

Obviously the Socialist movement has got to capture the exploited middle class before it is too late; above all it must capture the office-workers, who are so numerous and, if they knew how to combine, so powerful. Equally obviously it has so far failed to do so. The very last person in whom you can hope to find revolutionary opinions is a clerk or a commercial traveller. Why? Very largely, I think, because of the 'proletarian' cant with which Socialist propaganda is mixed up. In order to symbolise the class war, there has been set up the more or less mythical figure of a 'proletarian', a muscular but downtrodden man in greasy overalls, in contradistinction to a 'capitalist', a fat, wicked man in a top hat and fur coat. It is tacitly assumed that there is no one in between; the truth being, of course, that in a country like England about a quarter of the population is in between. If you are going to harp on the 'dictatorship of the proletariat', it is an elementary precaution to start by explaining who the proletariat *are.* But because of the Socialist tendency to idealise the manual worker as such, this has never been made sufficiently clear.

How many of the wretched shivering army of clerks and shopwalkers, who in some ways are actually worse off than a miner or a dock-hand, think of themselves as proletarians? A proletarian – so they have been taught to think – means a man without a collar. So that when you try to move them by talking about 'class war', you only succeed in scaring them; they forget their incomes and remember their accents, and fly to the defence of the class that is exploiting them.

Socialists have a big job ahead of them here. They have got to demonstrate, beyond possibility of doubt, just where the line of cleavage between exploiter and exploited comes. Once again it is a question of sticking to essentials; and the essential point here is that all people with small, insecure incomes are in the same boat and ought to be fighting on the same side. Probably we could do with a little less talk about 'capitalist' and 'proletarian' and a little more about the robbers and the robbed. But at any rate we must drop that misleading habit of pretending that the only proletarians are manual labourers. It has got to be brought home to the clerk, the engineer, the commercial traveller, the middle-class man who has 'come down in the world', the village grocer, the lower-grade civil servant and all other doubtful cases that they *are* the proletariat, and that Socialism means a fair deal for them as well as for the navvy and the factory-hand. They must not be allowed to think that the battle is between those who pronounce their aitches and those who don't; for if they think that, they will join in on the side of the aitches.

I am implying that different classes must be persuaded to act together without, for the moment, being asked to drop their class-differences. And that sounds dangerous. It sounds rather too like the Duke of York's summer camp and that dismal line of talk about class co-operation and putting our shoulders to the wheel, which is eyewash or Fascism, or both. There can be no co-operation between classes whose real interests are opposed. The capitalist cannot co-operate with the proletarian. The cat cannot co-operate with the mouse; and if the cat does suggest co-operation and the mouse is fool enough to agree, in a very little while the mouse will be disappearing down the cat's throat. But it is always possible to co-operate so long as it is upon a basis of common interests. The people who have got to act together are all those who cringe to the boss and all those who shudder when they think of the rent. This means that the small-holder has got to ally himself with the factory-hand, the typist with the coal-miner, the schoolmaster with the garage mechanic. There is some hope of getting them to do so if they can be made to understand where their interest lies. But this will not happen if their social prejudices, which in some of them are at least as strong as any economic consideration, are needlessly irritated. There is, after all, a real difference of manners and traditions between a bank clerk and a dock labourer, and the bank clerk's feeling of superiority is very deeply rooted. Later on he will have to get rid of it, but this is not a good moment for asking him to do so. Therefore it would be a very great advantage if that rather meaningless and mechanical bourgeois-baiting, which is a part of nearly all Socialist propaganda, could be dropped for the time being. Throughout left-wing thought and writing – and the whole way through it, from the leading articles in the *Daily Worker* to the comic columns in the *News Chronicle* – there runs an anti-genteel tradition, a persistent and often very stupid gibing at genteel mannerisms and genteel loyalties (or, in Communist jargon, 'bourgeois values'). It is largely humbug, coming as it does from bourgeois-baiters who are bourgeois themselves, but it does great harm, because it allows a minor issue to block a major one. It directs attention away from the central fact that poverty is poverty, whether the tool you work with is a pick-axe or a fountain pen.

Once again, here am I, with my middle-class origins and my income of about three pounds a week from all sources. From what I am worth it would be better to get me in on the Socialist side than to turn me into a Fascist. But if you are constantly bullying me about my 'bourgeois ideology', if you give me to understand that in some subtle way I am an inferior person because I have never worked with my hands, you will only succeed in antagonising me. For you are telling me either that I am inherently useless or that I ought to alter myself in some way that is beyond my power. I cannot proletarianise my accent or certain of my tastes and beliefs, and I would not if I could. Why should I? I don't ask anybody else to speak my dialect; why should anybody else ask me to speak his? It would be far better to take these miserable class-stigmata for granted and emphasise them as little as possible. They are comparable to a race-difference, and experience shows that one *can* co-operate with foreigners, even with foreigners whom one dislikes, when it is really necessary. Economically, I am in the same boat with the miner, the navvy and the farm-hand; remind me of that and I will fight at their side. But culturally I am different from the miner, the navvy and the farm-hand; lay the emphasis on that and you may arm me against them. If I were a solitary anomaly I should not matter, but what is true of myself is true of countless others. Every bank clerk dreaming of the sack, every shopkeeper teetering on the brink of bankruptcy, is in essentially the same position. These are the sinking middle class, and most of them are clinging to their gentility under the impression that it keeps them afloat. It is not good policy to *start* by telling them to throw away the life-belt. There is a quite obvious danger that in the next few years large sections of the middle class will make a sudden and violent swing to the Right. In doing so they may become formidable. The weakness of the middle class hitherto has lain in the fact that they have never learned to combine; but if you frighten them into combining *against* you, you may find that you have raised up a devil. We had a brief glimpse of this possibility in the General Strike.

To sum up: There is no chance of righting the conditions I described in the earlier chapters of this book, or of saving England from Fascism, unless we can bring an effective Socialist party into existence. It will have to be a party with genuinely revolutionary intentions, and it will have to be numerically strong enough to act. We can only get it if we offer an objective which fairly ordinary people will recognise as desirable. Beyond all else, therefore, we need intelligent propaganda. Less about 'class consciousness', 'expropriation of the expropriators', 'bourgeois ideology', and 'proletarian solidarity', not to mention the sacred sisters, thesis, antithesis and synthesis; and more about justice, liberty and the plight of the unemployed. And less about mechanical progress, tractors, the Dnieper dam and the latest salmon-canning factory in Moscow; that kind of thing is not an integral part of Socialist doctrine, and it drives away many people whom the Socialist cause needs, including most of those who can hold a pen. All that is needed is to hammer two facts home into the public consciousness. One, that the interests of all exploited people are the same; the other, that Socialism is compatible with common decency.

As for the terribly difficult issue of class-distinctions, the only possible policy for the moment is to go easy and not frighten more people than can be helped. And above all, no more of those muscular-curate efforts at class-breaking. If you belong to the bourgeoisie, don't be too eager to bound forward and embrace your proletarian brothers; they may not like it, and if they show that they don't like it you will probably find that your class-prejudices are not so dead as you imagined. And if you belong to the proletariat, by birth or in the sight of God, don't sneer too automatically at the Old School Tie; it covers loyalties which can be useful to you if you know how to handle them.

Yet I believe there is some hope that when Socialism is a living issue, a thing that large numbers of Englishmen genuinely care about, the class-difficulty may solve itself more rapidly than now seems thinkable. In the next few years we shall either get that effective Socialist party that we need, or we shall not get it. If we do not get it, then Fascism is coming; probably a slimy Anglicised form of Fascism, with cultured policemen instead of Nazi gorillas and the lion and the unicorn instead of the swastika. But if we do get it there will be a struggle, conceivably a physical one, for our plutocracy will not sit quiet under a genuinely revolutionary government. And when the widely separate classes who, necessarily, would form any real Socialist party have fought side by side, they may feel differently about one another. And then perhaps this misery of class-prejudice will fade away, and we of the sinking middle class – the private schoolmaster, the half-starved free-lance journalist, the colonel's spinster daughter with £75 a year, the jobless Cambridge graduate, the ship's officer without a ship, the clerks, the civil servants, the commercial travellers and the thrice-bankrupt drapers in the country towns – may sink without further struggles into the working class where we belong, and probably when we get there it will not be so dreadful as we feared, for, after all, we have nothing to lose but our aitches.

THE END

Coal-searchers

South Wales: Miners of the Fernhill Colliery come to the surface after a stay-in strike of nearly two weeks underground

Cilfynydd, Pontypridd, South Wales: Unemployed miners watching the buckets tipping slag in the hope that some coal may fall

Nine Mile Point Colliery, Newport: Relatives and friends waiting at the pit-head for news of the miners, who are conducting a stay-in strike below

A row of undermined houses in Blaenavon, Monmouthshire

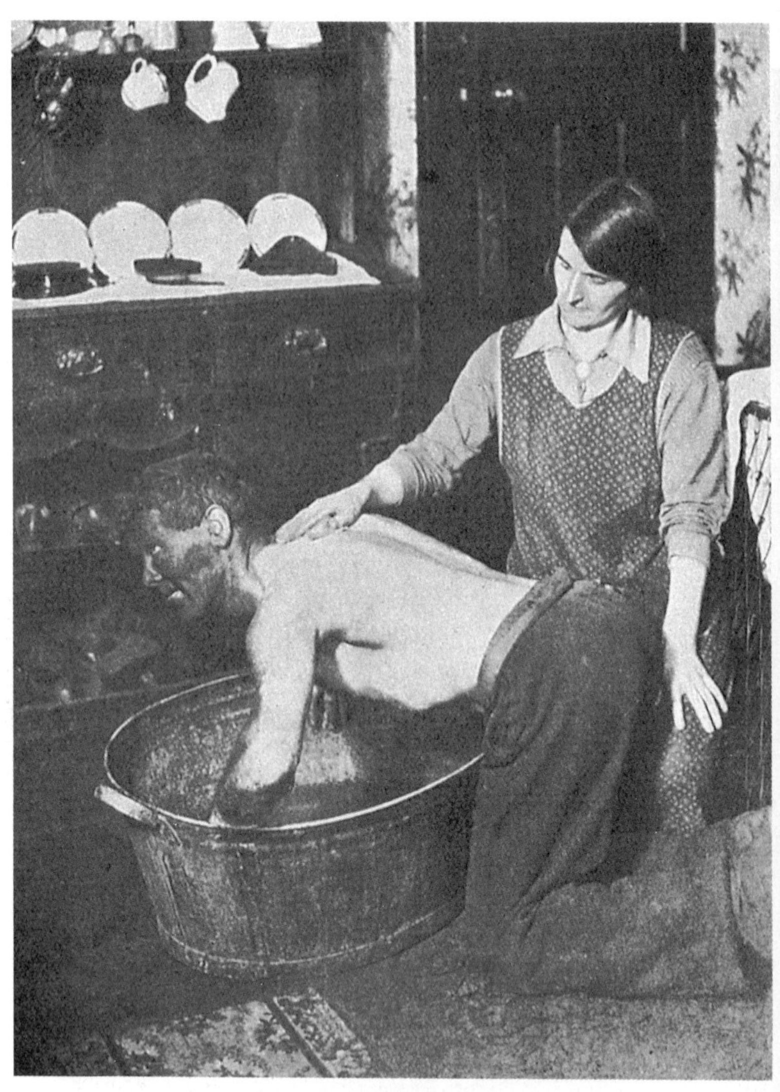

A South Wales miner takes his bath

Miners' cottages

Outside Newcastle: Whole families of miners live in these tiny and insanitary dwellings, for which a rent of seven shillings is charged

Miners' cottages at Coatbridge

Miners' cottages at Blantyre

Blaina, Wales: Rotting interior of a slum dwelling

House near Swansea threatened by slag-heap

Blaina, Wales

Gap by a window of a school in Wales

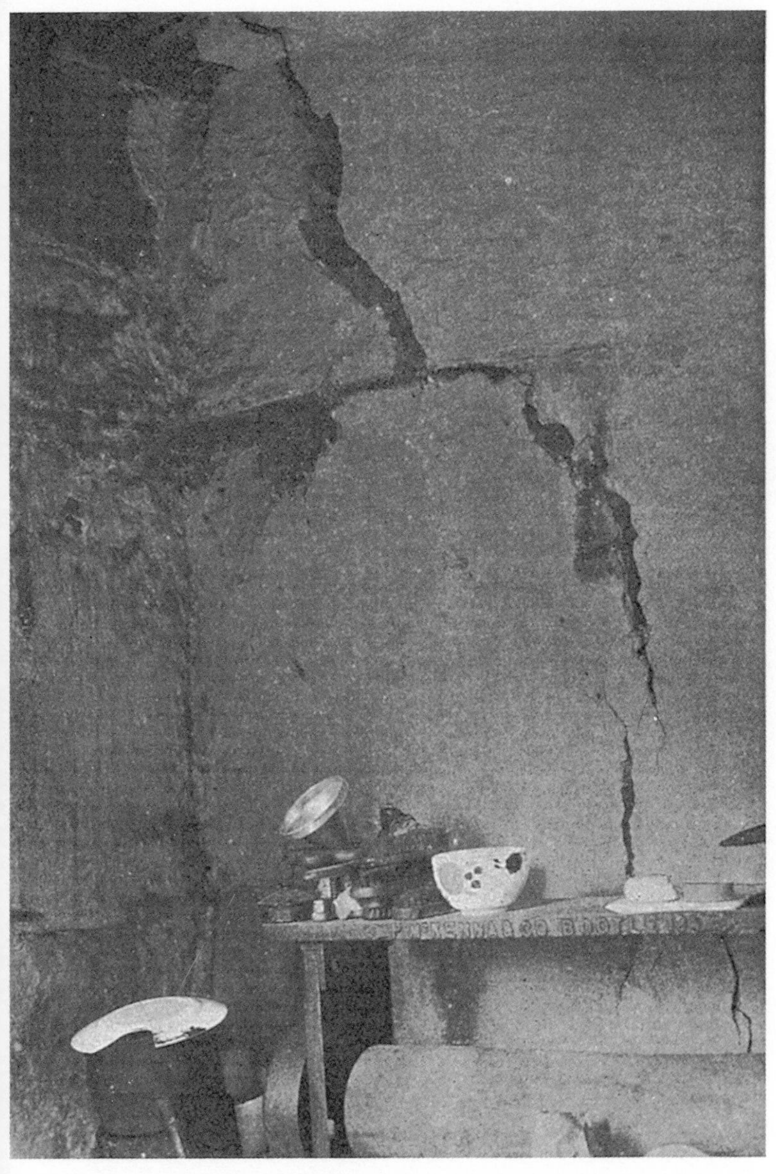

Scullery in an 'offshoot' coming away from the main building (now reconditioned)

A basement in Limehouse: One of a whole street (note the parrot in a cage)

Limehouse

Limehouse

Scullery in Limehouse

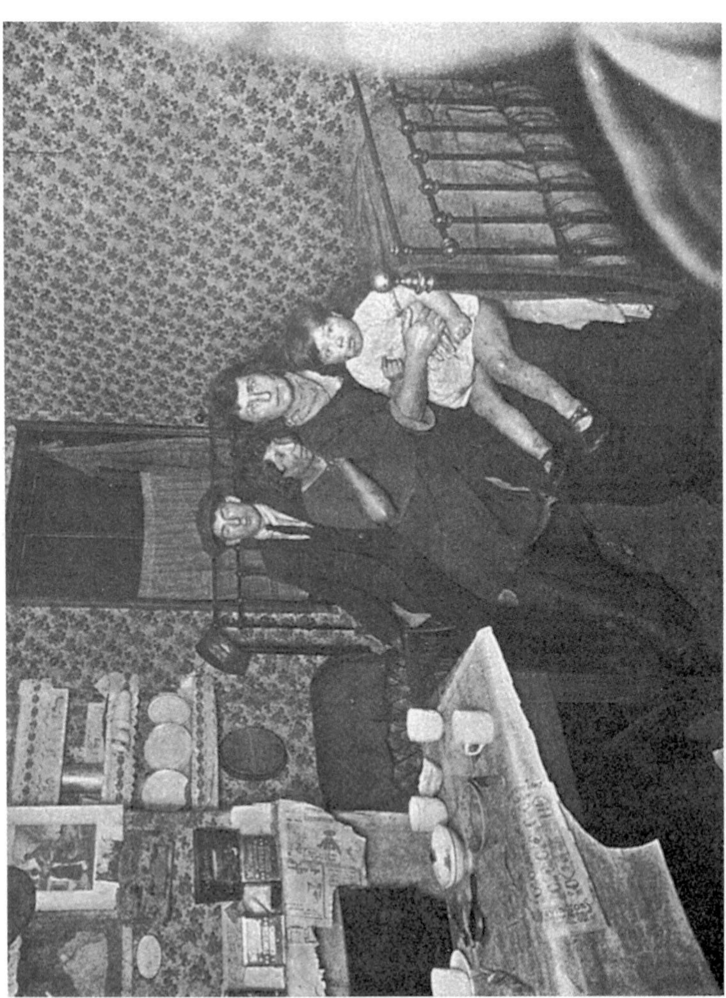

Bethnal Green

Bethnal Green

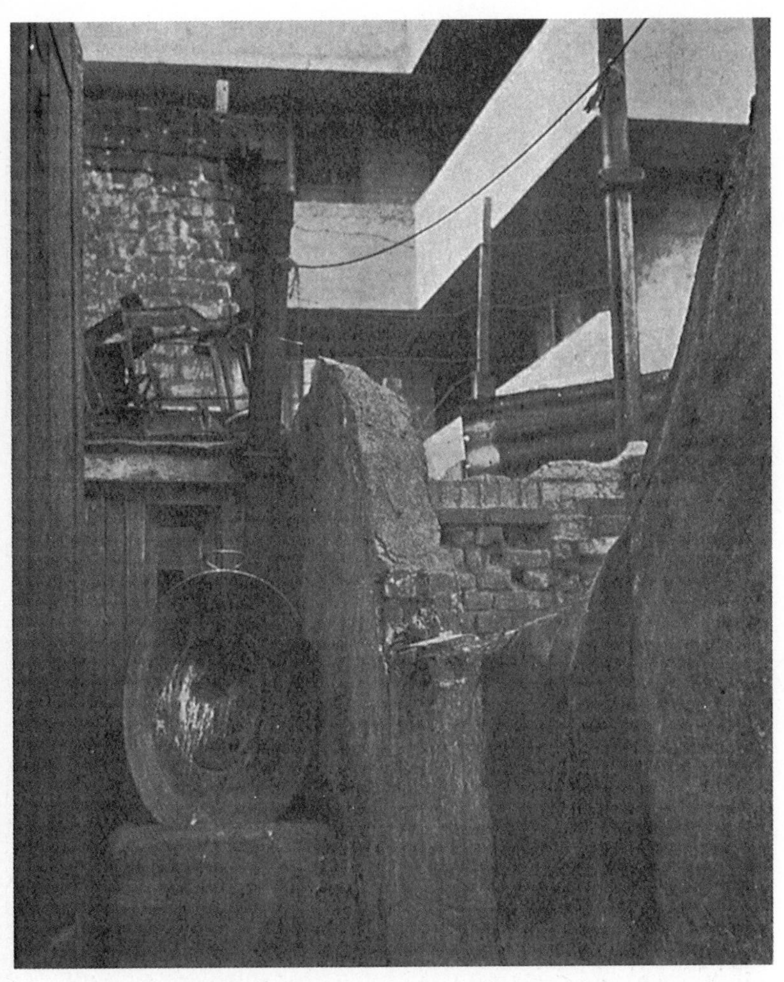

Stepney: Compare the new housing in the background

Stepney: Shadwell district

Stepney: Shadwell district

Dinner on the table in Poplar

By courtesy of the St. Pancras House Improvement Society

St Pancras: Before the slum clearance

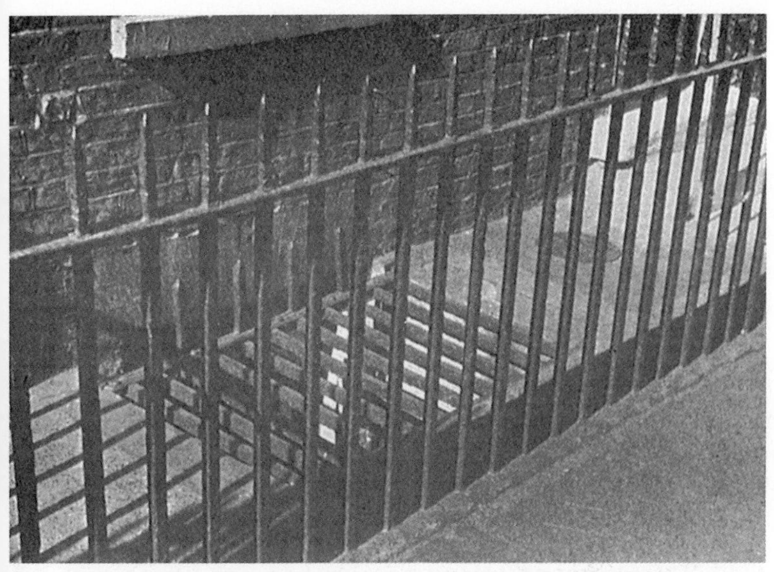

Poplar: The basement is lived in

Caravan-dwellers near a Durham quarry

[2384]

Extract from 'Your Questions Answered': Wigan Pier[1]

BBC Broadcast, 2 December 1943

WILLS: And now we've got time for just one more question, asked by Sergeant Salt and Signalman McGrath serving in India. They say: 'How long is the Wigan Pier and what is the Wigan Pier?' Well, if anybody ought to know, it should be George Orwell who wrote a book called *The Road to Wigan Pier*. And here's what he's got to say on the subject.

ORWELL: Well, I am afraid I must tell you that Wigan Pier doesn't exist. I made a journey specially to see it in 1936, and I couldn't find it. It did exist once, however, and to judge from the photographs it must have been about twenty feet long.[2]

Wigan is in the middle of the mining areas, and though it's a very pleasant place in some ways its scenery is not its strong point. The landscape is mostly slag-heaps, looking like the mountains of the moon, and mud and soot and so forth. For some reason, though it's not worse than fifty other places, Wigan has always been picked on as a symbol of the ugliness of the industrial areas. At one time, on one of the little muddy canals that run round the town, there used to be a tumble-down wooden jetty; and by way of a joke someone nicknamed this Wigan Pier. The joke caught on locally, and then the music-hall comedians got hold of it, and they are the ones who have succeeded in keeping Wigan Pier alive as a by-word, long after the place itself had been demolished.

WILLS: And so Signalman Salt and Sergeant McGrath, if you meant to floor the experts with a question about Wigan Pier, you'll have to try again with something else! Now our time's up for this week but we'll be back again on the air at the same time next week to answer some more of your questions.

1. Broadcast in the General Overseas Service of the BBC; repeated on 3 December 1943. Colin Wills was an Australian war commentator. He broadcast with Orwell in 'Answering You', 18 October 1942. See *Orwell and the Second Nation* in this series and XIV/*1584*.
2. See the illustration in *George Orwell: The Road to 1984*, by Peter Lewis, 51, and the English Tourist Board leaflet on Wigan (1988), which advertises a local exhibition, 'The Way We Were' (*c.* 1900), in the 'Wigan Pier Heritage Centre', Wallgate.

---

[409]

Review of The Problem of the Distressed Areas *by Wal Hannington;*[1] Grey Children *by James Hanley;* The Fight for the Charter *by Neil Stewart*

Time and Tide, *27 November 1937*

As everyone knows – or ought to know – Mr. Hannington has worked harder and more effectively for the unemployed than anyone else in England. He knows the derelict areas inside out, he has been prominent in every demonstration and hunger march, his activities have got him into prison at least five times, and above all he is largely responsible for the existence of the N.U.W.M.,[2] an organization which has not only helped the unemployed to fight back against victimization but has also done a great deal to prevent them from being converted, as they so easily might have been, into a huge army of blacklegs.

His book is partly a survey of the present condition of the distressed areas, partly an enquiry as to what has been done by successive governments to solve the unemployment problem – the answer, of course, being 'Nothing'. Periodically there is talk of 'land settlement' – smallholdings for the unemployed – which, as Mr. Hannington perceives, is plain eyewash. The only positive move has been the establishment of the so-called social service centres, which at best are a charitable sop and at worst are dangerously like a device for providing the local authorities with free labour. Meanwhile unemployment continues almost unabated, the Means Test breaks up families and brings into existence an army of spies and informers, and it is estimated that twenty million people in Great Britain are undernourished.

There are one or two points on which I do not agree with Mr. Hannington. He sees clearly enough the danger of large-scale unemployment leading to Fascism, but he is too ready to think of Fascism in terms of Hitler and Mosley. English Fascism, if it ever comes, is likely to be a lot subtler than that; Sir Oswald is, in fact, merely a red herring in a black shirt. Also Mr. Hannington's 'immediate programme' for dealing with the distressed areas, which he sets out in detail, is too optimistic. On paper it is a workable scheme and it would no doubt go a long way towards solving the problem, but it involves taxing the rich out of existence, which is simply not thinkable under our present system of government. But perhaps Mr. Hannington is aware of that and hopes that the moral will point itself.

Mr. Hanley's book deals only with South Wales, but it dovetails neatly into Mr. Hannington's, the one supplying what the other lacks. Mr. Hannington gives you the facts and figures; Mr. Hanley tells you, by recording a series of conversations with unemployed people, what it *feels* like to be on the Means Test. By its cumulative effect this is a terribly moving book. Mr. Hanley's writing is certainly improving by leaps and bounds. In some ways, although his range is smaller, he sees more deeply into the problem than Mr. Hannington – is more interested in what the people in the distressed areas actually feel and think. Also he grasps the tragic failure of theoretical Socialism to make any contact with the normal working class, especially at present, when the whole movement is losing itself in internecine struggles. As he says, it is a terrible thing that in the midst of squalor and degradation the Socialist parties should be flying at one another's throats upon the question of whether Trotsky is guilty. This book leaves behind it an even deeper feeling of hopelessness than Mr. Hannington's. And perhaps that is all to the good, for, as Mr. Hanley says, 'the thing *is* terrible, and the only way of forcing it home on people is to keep on saying so'.

The Fight for the Charter is a good short history of the Chartist movement. As Marx pointed out, if the essential point of the People's Charter[3] (manhood suffrage) had been won at the time when it was demanded, it would in effect have meant revolution, because in the 'hungry forties' the bulk of the population was a definitely revolutionary working class. Later, when universal suffrage became law, it made no difference, because by that time England was prosperous and large sections of the working class had 'turned respectable'. In spite of renewed misery their respectability remains with them, and the job-swapping game of English politics continues almost unchanged. Incidentally, the behaviour of the middle-class leaders of the Chartist movement is worth study by those who believe in the Popular Front.[4]

1. *The Problem of the Distressed Areas*, a Left Book Club volume, had, like *The Road to Wigan Pier*, a thirty-two-page insert of plates. Hannington also wrote an account of the 1930s, *Ten Lean Years* (1940). Orwell, in his Diary for 11 February 1936, described hearing him speak at Wigan Co-op Hall. Hannington was, he wrote, 'A poor speaker, using all the padding and clichés of the Socialist orator, and with the wrong kind of cockney accent (once again, though a Communist entirely a bourgeois), but he got the people well worked up' (X/424). In his London Letter to *Partisan Review*, 23 May 1943 (XV/*2096*), Orwell included him with Harry Pollitt among those who, 'After all the years they have had on the job', cannot imagine 'any occupation except boosting Soviet Russia'.
2. National Unemployed Workers' Movement.
3. Chartism was mainly a working-class reform movement. Its People's Charter was published in 1839. In addition to manhood suffrage it asked for the abandonment of property rights for MPs, equal-size constituencies, a secret ballot, payment of MPs and annual elections. Parliament rejected the Petition in 1839 and 1842. The Charter is a significant feature of Disraeli's *Sybil, or The Two Nations* (1845); Sybil is the daughter of the militant Chartist leader, Walter Gerard.
4. The Popular Front was a (sometimes loose) alliance of Communists, Socialists and other left-inclined parties and individuals. It was fostered by the Communist International in 1935 and was seen by many (including Orwell) as a Communist-front organization. In France, a Popular Front government under Léon Blum took power in 1936–7 and briefly in 1938. The Front made less headway in England and the Nazi-Soviet Pact of 23 August 1939 virtually destroyed its fortunes, though they revived somewhat after the Germans invaded the Soviet Union on 22 June 1941.

---

[468]

Eileen Blair to Jack Common

20 July 1938 *Handwritten*

Chapel Ridding,[1] Windermere, Westmorland

Dear Jack Common,

I suppose you have or soon will have my wild telegram. I hope I'll have one from you long before you get this letter but we'll just have to play a peculiarly complicated cat's-cradle for a few days because posts leave here practically never & then at strange hours like 3.30. I haven't yet heard about my letters being delivered anywhere else. Perhaps they aren't. Using the telephone, we can't hear the local exchange, so don't try that.

If you do want the cottage, it's a pity I didn't know last week because you could perfectly well have had it – I really hoped to pack it up one way or the other before coming away. But the difference between packing it up for store & for lending is considerable – e.g. one fills the drawers to store them & empties them to lend – so I couldn't do anything constructive or much destructive. I suppose you, & more importantly your wife, know what the cottage is like – that it hasn't got a bathroom or any hot water, that it frequently absorbs water like a sponge (perhaps very frequently; in some mysterious way the wind seems responsible), that it's 3½ miles from a shop, that the sitting-room chimney is not manageable by me though it may be by someone efficient. That's all I can think of at the moment, except that we never bought any furniture for it. But you saw yourself what it looked like. On the other hand it is habitable & it won't cost money. The goat still has her kid because I like goats & don't like goat's milk, but if you don't like killing kids a man will do it & you'll then have about 2½–3 pints of milk for about 1½d. a day. I didn't stock the garden for the winter because I thought noone would be there, but we can still put in some greens & there are potatoes, parsnips & onions, & a few french & runner beans; also a good crop of cooking apples on one tree & quite a few plums. If you can transport them you could bring things like tools & wheelbarrows – very usefully, because Eric made a wheelbarrow which is permanently in the field as its wheel developed a split personality & I can't persuade it all to go home together. I don't know what Eric has told you about the place. It has the sitting-room you'll remember, a kind of passage-room with a fireplace that we used to have as a sitting-room when we kept the shop, an ill-designed kitchen with a sink & cold water, a Calor-gas oven (this is very convenient for quick heating but the cylinders are expensive & I've always been meaning to combine it with an oil cooker – there is an old Rippingill & a couple of Beatrices[2] that are good for slow boiling); upstairs a square landing we use as a dining-room, which is actually very warm & can be heated enough in any weather by one of the Beatrices, & two bedrooms opening off it, one with a double bed & one with a single bed. The place isn't over-furnished & you could probably bring anything special, such as an easy chair or/and a chest of drawers etc. I did mean to buy it a number of things but again thinking it would be empty I haven't done so. Heaven knows I don't want to put you off – from my point of view your coming has every advantage. If you wire that you want the place & I hear nothing more I'll be in the cottage on Monday to hand it over. If you could arrive in the afternoon or early evening I could demonstrate the creatures. Goats are not difficult to manage but there are some growing chickens who need special food for a few more weeks. You could send a postcard to Wallington with any last minute alterations – I'll actually arrive some time on Saturday or Sunday morning. A letter posted to me here after Thursday will miss me.

I must say I hope you are strong-minded enough to take Wallington on.

Yours sincerely
Eileen Blair.

1. Why Eileen went to Chapel Ridding is not known. The house is now St Anne's School. Through a previous headmaster, Michael P. Hawkins, a former owner's niece, Mrs Mary Varcoe, provided the earlier history of the house. From 1931 it was a guest house run by her aunt, Esther Moss, for semi-permanent and passing visitors and for public-school boys needing a home during vacations. Percy W. Molony, a guest, married Esther Moss, and they ran the guest house jointly until about 1947. No link has been traced between Eileen and either Esther Moss or Percy Molony, although Esther, a nurse during World War I, was also then one of the first women motorcyclists, as was Marjorie Blair, Orwell's sister. Chapel Ridding is a very fine house in beautiful grounds, a sharp contrast with The Stores in 1936, wondering where the next meal was coming from and subsisting on potatoes (see XI/*496*).

2. Trade names for two types of domestic oil-stove.

---

[476]

To Jack Common

25 August 1938 *Handwritten*

New Hostel, Preston Hall, Aylesford, Kent[1]

Dear Jack,

Thanks for yours. Bad job about the cock. I expect he picked up a bit of poison or something. We won't get another till about next Feb when we start breeding again, as it is no use feeding an idle bird during the winter.

He wasn't a bad cock. We called him Henry Ford because he had such a brisk businesslike way of going about his job, in fact he trod his first hen literally within 5 seconds of being put into the run. Muriel[2] should stay in milk for easily a year, ie. till next July, but I expect we'll get her mated again when we come back from Africa. As to the milking you'll probably find it easier by degrees. I did tell you to grease your fingers, didn't I? It makes it easier. She ought to give 2–3 pints a day, & you can generally send the yield up or down a bit according to the amount of fat-producing food (especially flaked maize), but of course they have to have a fair amount of oats etc. to keep up their strength as well. She comes on heat once in 3 weeks & is usually a bit of a nuisance then, stamping round & bleating instead of grazing quietly.

We're going to leave England by Sept. 2nd. We've booked as far as Gibraltar, then we take another boat to Casa Blanca° & then I'm not sure, but I think we head for the Atlas mountains, wherever they may be. Our geography was so poor that both E. & I thought French Morocco gave on the Mediterranean, whereas it's really the Atlantic. As soon as we've a permanent adress° we'll let you know. We've just been down for two days to Southwold to see my father who is very old & has been ill but I am glad to say is rather better.

Love to all.

Yours
Eric

P.S. I don't know whether these milking hints may be of use. Give the goat her food, then get her up against the wall (if she gives trouble you can steady her with your shoulder), & having greased your fingers massage the udder a little & then grip the nearest teat pretty firmly at the root, ie. where it joins the udder. If you are gripping it at the right place you will feel it fill with milk & thicken in your hand. Then, still gripping pretty hard (if you are hurting her she will soon let you know) draw the hand down the teat, being careful not to relax the pressure till you reach the end. When no more milk comes out of this teat, go on to the other. When that is exhausted return to the first & milk each teat a second time. Between the first & second operations it is better to massage the udder again & give a slight upward knocking with your hand, the same as the kid does with its head. The whole operation should take about 5 minutes. It's better to do it at regular times of the day. I used to do it at about 8 am & 7 pm in the winter, but somewhat later in the evenings in the summer as she can go on grazing as long as it is light.

1. Orwell suffered a tubercular lesion in one lung on 8 March 1938. He was a patient at Preston Hall Sanatorium at Aylesford, Kent, from 15 March to 1 September 1938. It was thought, erroneously as it proved, that Orwell's health might improve if he spent the winter in a hot, dry climate and Morocco was chosen. An anonymous gift of £300 from the novelist L. H. Myers (1881–1944), a Communist, enabled Orwell and his wife, Eileen, to travel to Marrakesh and spent seven months there (2 September 1938 to 26 March 1939). Orwell never knew Myers provided the money; he always regarded it as a loan and later repaid it. While in Marrakesh he wrote the novel *Coming Up for Air* (1939). See Crick, 368–70, 419–20; Shelden, 316–19, 324–5; and *A Literary Life*, 111–12, 129.
2. Muriel was Orwell's favourite goat. She is illustrated in Crick, plate 19, and Muriel was immortalized by Orwell in *Animal Farm*.

Extracts from Orwell's Domestic Diaries, 1938–9, and War-time Diaries, 1940–42

Orwell compiled many diaries; some he illustrated. Not all have survived. The following brief extracts are from one of four Domestic Diaries (though numbered five – see X/xxiv and XIV/1573, n. 3), and his two War-time Diaries. The extracts are grouped together here rather than in their chronological positions. In their different ways each suggests his love of England. The extant diaries are given in full in the Complete Works. *The ellipses in the War-time Diary represent cuts made by Orwell when the original manuscript (now lost) was typed.*

[518]

August 9, 1938 [Preston Hall Sanatorium, Aylesford, Kent]: Caught a large snake in the herbaceous border beside the drive. About 2′6″ long, grey colour, black markings on belly but none on back except, on back of neck, a mark resembling an arrow-head (⌂). Not certain whether an adder, as these I think usually have a sort of broad arrow mark (⩓) all down the back. Did not care to handle it too recklessly, so only picked it up by extreme tip of tail. Held thus it could nearly turn far enough to bite my hand, but not quite. Marx[1] interested at first, but after smelling it was frightened & ran away. The people here normally kill all snakes. As usual, the tongue referred to as the 'fangs'.[2]

August 10: Drizzly. Dense mist in evening. Yellow moon.

August 11: This morning all surfaces, even indoors, damp as result of mist. A curious deposit all over my snuff-box, evidently result of moisture acting on lacquer.

Very hot, but rain in afternoon.

Am told the men caught another snake this morning – definitely a grass snake this time. The man who saw them said they had tied a string round its neck & were trying to cut out its tongue with a knife, the idea being that after this it could not 'sting'.

The first Beauty of Bath apples today.

August 12: Very hot in the morning. In the afternoon sudden thunder-storm & very heavy rain. About 50 yards from the gate the road & pavement flooded a foot deep after only 1½ hours rain.

Blackberries beginning to redden.

August 16: Several days past uncertain weather, rainy & sometimes hot.

Most of the wheat & barley now cut & stacked. Children picking more or less ripe blackberries two days ago.

Saw a white owl two nights ago – the first in about two years. Also in the distance another bird probably a little owl.

Horse-chestnuts full-size but not ripe yet. Hops about the size of hazel-nuts.

Yesterday went to the Zoo* again. Another litter of lion-cubs, which are a bit bigger than a domestic cat & spotted all over. Those born just a year ago are about the size of a St Bernard dog. The ration of meat for a lion – I suppose its only meal in the day – seems to be about 6 or 7 lbs.

The Sardinian mouflon sheep[3] has a large udder like a goat & would probably yield a pint or more. I notice that the zebra's hooves, at least the front ones, are quite perpendicular, but those of the ass-zebra hybrid are like those of a horse. The hybrid has very slightly larger ears, otherwise so far as shape goes almost exactly like the zebra.

August 17: Warm & fine, rather windy.

* ie. near Maidstone [Orwell's note].

The barley from the 22-acre field is not stacked yet, but the wheat is stacked & makes two stacks measuring so far as I can judge it 30′ by 18′ × 24′(high) & 18′ × 15′ × 20′(high). If these estimates are correct, this works out at 14,040 cubic feet of stack for about 14 acres of ground. Allowing 1 tone per acre, it seems 1000 cubic feet of stack represent a ton of grain. NB. to check when the whole field is stacked.
Catmint, peppermint & tansies full out. Ragwort & willow-herb going to seed. A few ripe blackberries. Elder-berries beginning to turn purple.
Oak planks etc. made from the boughs instead of the trunk is known as bastard oak & is somewhat cheaper.
Disused railway sleepers here sold off at £1=1=0 10 cwt. This probably works out at about 1/– each, ie. 2d a foot.
August 22: Warmish day, with showers. Nights are getting colder & more like autumn. A few oaks beginning to yellow very slightly. After the rain enormous slugs crawling about, one measuring about 3″long. Large holes, presumably ear-holes, some distance behind head. They were of two distinct colours, some light fawn & others white, but both have a band of bright orange round the edge of the belly, which makes one think they are of the same species & vary individually in colour. On the tip of their tails they had blobs of gelatinous stuff like the casing of water-snails' eggs.
A large beetle, about the size of a female stag-beetle but not the same, extruding from her hindquarters a yellow tube about the length of herself. Possibly some sort of tube through which eggs are laid?
August 22.[4] *Southwold:* Cool this morning & raining most of the day.
Most of the crops in & stacked. Blackberries in Suffolk much less forward than Kent, otherwise little difference in the vegetation.
When clipping fowls' wings, clip only one wing, preferably the right (left wing keeps the ovaries warm).
Cold tea is good fertiliser for geraniums.
August 25. Preston Hall: Everything in Suffolk is much more dried-up than in Kent. Until the day we arrived there had been no rain for many weeks & various crops had failed. Near S'wold saw several fields of oats & barley being harvested which had grown only 1′or 18″high. Ears nevertheless seemed normal. Wheat crop all over the world said to be heavy.
A bedstraw hawk-moth found in our back garden & mounted by Dr

Collings.[5] Evidently a straggler from the continent. Said to be the first seen in that locality for 50 years.
Little owl very common round here. Brown owl does not seem to exist.
Dr C. says the snake I caught was the 'smooth snake', non-poisonous & not very common.
Today hot again.
Gipsies beginning to arrive for the hop-picking. As soon as they have pitched their caravans the chickens are let loose & apparently can be depended on not to stray. The strips of tin for clothes-pegs are cut out of biscuit boxes. Three people were on the job, one shaping the sticks, one cutting out the tin & another nailing it on. I should say one person doing all these jobs (also splitting the pegs after nailing) could make 10–15 pegs an hour.
Another white owl this evening.

[582]
10.4.39. Southwold: Have been here since 1.4.39, but spent most of the last week in bed.
A week ago, on arrival, weather mostly coldish, very still & rather misty. Thick sea mist on 2.4.39. Blackthorn flowering in places. Primroses abundant. Wild daffodils also plentiful, but for the most part not completely open. Fruit trees budding fairly strongly. Saw one of I do not know what kind (purplish flower) in blossom in a sheltered place two days ago. Roses, herbaceous plants etc. sprouting strongly. Starlings still in flocks on 2.4.39. Larks singing hard. Some asparagus heads a few inches above ground.
12.4.39. Wallington: Yesterday exceedingly warm & fine, said to have been the warmest day for that date for 70 years. Today even more so.
We have now 26 hens, the youngest about 11 months. Yesterday 7 eggs (the hens have only recently started laying again). Everything greatly neglected, full of weeds etc., ground very hard & dry, attributed to heavy falls of rain, then no rain at all for some weeks.
Although the hedges etc. are more forward when one gets away from the sea, the spring on the whole seems backward.
Flowers now in bloom in the garden: polyanthus, aubretia, scilla, grape

hyacinth, oxalis, a few narcissi. Many daffodils in the field. These are very° double & evidently not real wild daffodil but bulbs dropped there by accident. Bullaces & plums coming into blossom. Apple trees budding but no blossom yet. Pears in full blossom. Roses sprouting fairly strongly. I note that one of the standards which died is sprouting from the root, so evidently the stock can live when the scion is dead. Peonies sprouting strongly. Crocuses are just over. A few tulips in bud. A few leeks & parsnips in the garden (the latter have survived the winter without covering up & tops are still green), otherwise no vegetables. It appears that owing to severe frosts there are no winter greens locally.
Bats out everywhere. Have not found any birds' nests yet.
Wildflowers out: violets, primroses, celandine, anemones.
A little rhubarb showing. Blackcurrant bushes etc. for the most part have grown very weedy, probably for lack of hoeing round etc. Strawberries have all run & are covered with weeds but look fairly strong.
Sowed cos lettuce.
Leaf mould (beech) put down at end of 1937 is now well rotted down.
Found two thrush's eggs under the hedge – no nest, somewhat mysterious, but perhaps left there by a child.
Today a stack being thrashed – oats, & seemingly no rats & few mice. Tried Marx with a live baby mouse. He smelt & licked it but made no move to eat it.
Pigeons making their mating flight fly steeply up into the air then volplane down.
Four eggs.
13.4.39: Not so warm. A very light shower in the evening. Very dark night. A few pansies & wallflowers starting to bloom. Pansies spread by self-sowing almost as much as marigolds. Red saxifrage coming into flower. Ten eggs.
14.4.39: Cloudy, & a few small showers. Cold after dark.
Saw two swallows (not martins). This is rather early for this locality & a latish year. No one else has seen any.
All day cleaning out strawberries, which have not been touched since last year. It seems one plant will put out anything up to 12 or 15 runners. These seem to develop the best roots when they have rooted in very hard soil. Used some of them to fill up gaps & make another row. Doubtful

whether they will take, but Titley[6] says it is not too late. Wallflowers in sheltered positions are full out. No apple blossom anywhere yet.

The 12 pullets which the Hollingsworths got from 24 of our eggs (White Leghorn × Buff Orpington – Sussex) have laid 1500 eggs since last autumn, or about 20 eggs per bird per month. They have been fed throughout on pig meal instead of ordinary laying mash. In the same period our own pullets of the same mating have not laid (ie. are only beginning now) owing to underfeeding.

Eight eggs.

For the first time M.[7] gave a quart today.

1. The Orwells' dog, a large poodle, described by Humphrey Dakin as 'a very nice dog'. He and his wife, Orwell's sister, Marjorie, looked after Marx when the Orwells were in North Africa.

2. It was an ancient belief that a poisonous snake injects its poison by means of its forked tongue and not, as is the case, through two fangs. So Shakespeare, in *Richard II* (III.ii): 'Guard it, I pray thee, with a lurking adder / Whose double tongue may with a mortal touch / Throw death upon thy sovereign's enemies.'

3. A wild sheep found in the mountains of Sardinia and Corsica but, by extension, any large, wild, big-horned sheep.

4. Because the previous diary entry was dated 22 August, it is likely that this was 23 August. Orwell had gone to Southwold to see his parents before leaving for North Africa.

5. The Blairs' family doctor at Southwold from 1921. His son, Dennis, was a friend of Orwell.

6. Titley was one of Orwell's neighbours at Wallington.

7. Muriel, Orwell's goat (see n. 2 to letter to Jack Common, above).

---

[637]

8.6.40 [London]: In the middle of a fearful battle in which, I suppose, thousands of men are being killed every day, one has the impression that there is no news. The evening papers are the same as the morning ones, the morning ones are the same as those of the night before, and the radio repeats what is in the papers. As to truthfulness of news, however, there is probably more suppression than downright lying. Borkenau[1] considers that the effect of the radio has been to make war comparatively truthful, and that the only large-scale lying hitherto has been the German claims of British ships sunk. These have certainly been fantastic. Recently one of the evening papers which had made a note of the German announcements pointed out that in about 10 days the Germans claimed to have sunk 25 capital ships, ie. 10 more than we ever possessed.

Stephen Spender[2] said to me recently, 'Don't you feel that any time during the past ten years you have been able to foretell events better than, say, the Cabinet?' I had to agree to this. Partly it is a question of not being blinded by class interests etc., eg. anyone not financially interested could see at a glance the strategic danger to England of letting Germany and Italy dominate Spain, whereas many rightwingers, even professional soldiers, simply could not grasp this most obvious fact. But where I feel that people like us understand the situation better than so-called experts is not in any power to foretell specific events, but in the power to grasp what *kind* of world we are living in. At any rate I have known since about 1931 (Spender says he has known since 1929) that the future must be catastrophic. I could not say exactly what wars and revolutions would happen, but they never surprised me when they came. Since 1934 I have known war between England and Germany was coming, and since 1936 I have known it with complete certainty. I could feel it in my belly, and the chatter of the pacifists on the one hand, and the Popular Front people who pretended to fear that Britain was preparing for war against Russia on the other, never deceived me. Similarly such horrors as the Russian purges never surprised me, because I had always felt that – not *exactly* that, but something *like* that – was implicit in Bolshevik rule. I could feel it in their literature.

. . . . Who would have believed seven years ago that Winston Churchill had any kind of political future before him? A year ago Cripps[3] was the naughty boy of the Labour Party, who expelled him and refused even to hear his defence. On the other hand, from the Conservative point of view he was a dangerous Red. Now he is ambassador in Moscow, the Beaverbrook press[4] having led the cry for his appointment. Impossible to say yet whether he is the right man. If the Russians are disposed to come round to our side, he probably is, but if they are still hostile, it would have been better to send a man who does not admire the Russian régime.

10.6.40: Have just heard, though it is not in the papers, that Italy has declared war. . . . The allied troops are withdrawing from Norway, the reason given being that they can be used elsewhere and Narvik after its capture was rendered useless to the Germans. But in fact Narvik will not be necessary to them till the winter, it wouldn't have been much use anyway when Norway had ceased to be neutral, and I shouldn't have thought the allies had enough troops in Norway to make much difference. The real reason is probably so as not to have to waste warships.

This afternoon I remembered very vividly that incident with the taxi-driver in Paris in 1936, and was going to have written something about it in this diary.[5] But now I feel so saddened that I can't write it. Everything is disintegrating. It makes me writhe to be writing book-reviews etc. at such a time, and even angers me that such time-wasting should still be permitted. The interview at the War Office on Saturday *may* come to something,[6] if I am clever at faking my way past the doctor. If once in the army, I know by the analogy of the Spanish war that I shall cease to care about public events. At present I feel as I felt in 1936 when the Fascists were closing in on Madrid, only far worse. But I will write about the taxi-driver some time.

12.6.40: E[ileen] and I last night walked through Soho to see whether the damage to Italian shops etc. was as reported. It seemed to have been exaggerated in the newspapers, but we did see, I think, 3 shops which had had their windows smashed. The majority had hurriedly labelled themselves 'British'. Gennari's, the Italian grocer's, was plastered all over with printed placards saying 'This establishment is entirely British'. The Spaghetti House, a shop specialising in Italian foodstuffs, had renamed itself 'British Food Shop'. Another shop proclaimed itself Swiss, and even a French restaurant had labelled itself British. The interesting thing is that all these placards must evidently have been printed beforehand and kept in readiness.

. . . . Disgusting though these attacks on harmless Italian shopkeepers are, they are an interesting phenomenon, because English people, ie. people of a kind who would be likely to loot shops, don't as a rule take a spontaneous interest in foreign politics. I don't think there was anything of this kind during the Abyssinian war, and the Spanish war simply did not touch the mass of the people. Nor was there any popular move against the Germans resident in England until the last month or two. The low-down cold-blooded meanness of Mussolini's declaration of war at that moment must have made an impression even on people who as [a] rule barely read the newspapers.

13.6.40: Yesterday to a group conference of the L.D.V.,[7] held in the

Committee Room at Lord's. . . . Last time I was at Lord's must have been at the Eton-Harrow match in 1921. At that time I should have felt that to go into the Pavilion, not being a member of the M.C.C.,[8] was on a par with pissing on the altar, and years later would have had some vague idea that it was a legal offence for which you could be prosecuted.

I notice that one of the posters recruiting for the Pioneers, of a foot treading on a swastika with the legend 'Step on it', is cribbed from a Government poster of the Spanish war, ie. cribbed as to the idea. Of course it is vulgarised and made comic, but its appearance at any rate shows that the Government are beginning to be willing to learn.

The Communist candidate in the Bow[9] by-election got about 500 votes. This is a new depth-record, though the Blackshirts[10] have often got less (in one case about 150). The more remarkable because Bow was Lansbury's seat[11] and might be expected to contain a lot of pacifists. The whole poll was very low, however.

14.6.40: The Germans are definitely in Paris, one day ahead of schedule. It can be taken as a certainty that Hitler will go to Versailles. Why don't they mine it and blow it up while he is there? Spanish troops have occupied Tangier, obviously with a view to letting the Italians use it as a base. To conquer Spanish Morocco from French Morocco would probably be easy at this date, and to do so, ditto the other Spanish colonies, and set up Negrín[12] or someone of his kind as an alternative government, would be a severe blow at Franco. But even the present British government would never think of doing such a thing. One has almost lost the power of imagining that the Allied governments can ever take the initiative.

Always, as I walk through the Underground stations, sickened by the advertisements, the silly staring faces and strident colours,[13] the general frantic struggle to induce people to waste labour and material by consuming useless luxuries or harmful drugs. How much rubbish this war will sweep away, if only we can hang on throughout the summer. War is simply a reversal of civilised life, its motto is 'Evil be thou my good',[14] and so much of the good of modern life is actually evil that it is questionable whether on balance war does harm.

1. Dr Franz Borkenau (1900–1957), Austrian sociologist and political writer. From 1921 to 1929 he was a member of the German Communist Party. His *Zur Soziologie des Faschismus* was published in 1929, the year he emigrated because of the rise of the Nazis. Orwell

admired him and his work. He reviewed his *The Spanish Cockpit* (reproduced in *Orwell in Spain* in this series; X/*379*), *The Communist International* (reproduced in *Orwell and Politics* in this series; XI/*485*) and *The Totalitarian Enemy* (XII/*620*). Orwell recommended Borkenau as a writer to the Information Research Department of the Foreign Office on 6 April 1949 (XX/*3590B*).

2. Stephen Spender (1909–95; Kt., 1983), prolific poet, novelist, critic and translator. He edited *Horizon* with Cyril Connolly, 1940–41, and was co-editor of *Encounter*, 1953–65, serving on the editorial board until 1967, when it was discovered the journal was being financed in part by the CIA. Before meeting Spender, Orwell included him among the 'parlour Bolsheviks' but after they met they became friends.

3. Sir Stafford Cripps (1899–1952), a lawyer who, in 1927, became the youngest King's Counsel. Entered Parliament for Labour in 1931 but was expelled from the Labour Party, 1939–45. Ambassador to the Soviet Union, 1940–42, Minister of Aircraft Production, 1942–5, Chancellor of the Exchequer in the Labour Government, 1947–50. He was a man of stern integrity.

4. Right-wing papers owned by Lord Beaverbrook (1879–1964). These included the *Daily Express, Sunday Express* and *Evening Standard.* A bold but untimely headline in the *Daily Express* for 7 August 1939 proclaimed, 'No War this Year'. Beaverbrook (formerly Max Aitken) was Canadian and preceded Sir Stafford Cripps as Minister of Aircraft Production, in which he was effective but controversial. At the end of World War I he had served as Minister of Information.

5. Orwell wrote about this incident in 'As I Please', 42, 15 September 1942 (XVI/*2549*); it is reprinted in this series in *Orwell in Spain.*

6. Orwell hoped to serve in the Army. He was rejected on medical grounds.

7. Local Defence Volunteers, later the Home Guard. Orwell joined on 12 June what became C Company, 5th County of London Battalion, and he was soon promoted to sergeant, with ten men to instruct. He took his duties very seriously. See Crick, 396–401 and XX/*3590B*, n. 15.

8. Marylebone Cricket Club, the body that then controlled national and international cricket.

9. A working-class constituency in the East End of London.

10. The Blackshirts in the UK were the uniformed members of Mosley's British Union of Fascists.

11. George Lansbury (1859–1940), leader of the Labour Party, 1931–5; he was a pacifist and resigned on that issue.

12. Dr Juan Negrín (1889–1956), Socialist Prime Minister of the Republic of Spain, September 1936–March 1938. He fled to France, where he died in exile.

13. For Orwell's hatred of such ad-posters featuring idiotic, grinning, yard-wide, ham-pink faces, see *Keep the Aspidistra Flying,* published four years earlier; for example, *CW*, IV/14, 16, 257.

14. Milton, *Paradise Lost,* IV.110.

---

[639]

16.6.40: This morning's papers make it reasonably clear that at any rate until after the presidential election, the U.S.A. will not do anything, ie.

will not declare war, which in fact is what matters. For if the U.S.A. is not actually in the war there will never be sufficient control of either business or labour to speed up production of armaments. In the last war this was the case even when the U.S.A. was a belligerent.

It is impossible even yet to decide what to do in the case of German conquest of England. The one thing I will not do is to clear out, at any rate not further than Ireland, supposing that to be feasible. If the fleet is intact and it appears that the war is to be continued from America and the Dominions, then one must remain alive if possible, if necessary in the concentration camp. If the U.S.A. is going to submit to conquest as well, there is nothing for it but to die fighting, but one must above all die *fighting* and have the satisfaction of killing somebody else first.

Talking yesterday to M.,[1] one of the Jewish members of my L.D.V. section, I said that if and when the present crisis passed there would be a revolt in the Conservative party against Churchill and an attempt to force wages down again, etc. He said that in that case there would be revolution, 'or at least he hoped so'. M. is a manufacturer and I imagine fairly well off.

17.6.40: The French have surrendered. This could be foreseen from last night's broadcast and in fact should have been foreseeable when they failed to defend Paris, the one place where it might have been possible to stop the German tanks. Strategically all turns on the French fleet, of which there is no news yet. . . .

Considerable excitement today over the French surrender, and people everywhere to be heard discussing it. Usual line, 'Thank God we've got a navy'. A Scottish private, with medals of the last war, partly drunk, making a patriotic speech in a carriage in the Underground, which the other passengers seemed rather to like. Such a rush on evening papers that I had to make four attempts before getting one.

Nowadays, when I write a review, I sit down at the typewriter and type it straight out. Till recently, indeed till six months ago, I never did this and would have said that I could not do it. Virtually all that I wrote was written at least twice, and my books as a whole three times – individual passages as many as five or ten times. It is not really that I have gained in facility, merely that I have ceased to care, so long as the work will pass inspection and bring in a little money. It is a deterioration directly due to the war.

Considerable throng at Canada House, where I went to make enquiries, as G.[2] contemplates sending her child to Canada. Apart from mothers, they are not allowing anyone between 16 and 60 to leave, evidently fearing a panic rush.

20.6.40: Went to the office of the [*New Statesman*][3] to see what line they are taking about home defence. C.,[4] who is now in reality the big noise there, was rather against the 'arm the people' line and said that its dangers outweighed its possible advantages. If a German invading force finds civilians armed it may commit such barbarities as will cow the people altogether and make everyone anxious to surrender. He said it was dangerous to count on ordinary people being courageous and instanced the case of some riot in Glasgow when a tank was driven round the town and everyone fled in the most cowardly way. The circumstances were different, however, because the people in that case were unarmed and, as always in internal strife, conscious of fighting with ropes round their necks. . . . C. said that he thought Churchill, though a good man up to a point, was incapable of doing the necessary thing and turning this into a revolutionary war, and for that reason shielded Chamberlain and Co. and hesitated to bring the whole nation into the struggle. I don't of course think Churchill sees it in quite the same colours as we do, but I don't think he would jib at any step (eg. equalisation of incomes, independence for India) which he thought necessary for winning the war. Of course it's possible that today's secret session *may* achieve enough to get Chamberlain and Co. out for good. I asked C. what hope he thought there was of this, and he said none at all. But I remember that the day the British began to evacuate Namsos[5] I asked Bevan and Strauss,[6] who had just come from the House, what hope there was of this business unseating Chamberlain, and they also said none at all. Yet a week or so later the new government was formed.[7]

The belief in direct treachery in the higher command is now widespread, enough so to be dangerous. . . . Personally I believe that such conscious treachery as exists is only in the pro-Fascist element of the aristocracy and perhaps in the Army command. Of course the unconscious sabotage and stupidity which have got us into this situation, eg. the idiotic handling of Italy and Spain, is a different matter. R.H.[8] says that private soldiers back from Dunkirk whom he has spoken to all complain of the conduct of their officers, saying that the latter cleared off in cars and left them in the soup, etc., etc. This sort of thing is always said after a defeat and may or may not be true. One could verify it by studying the lists of casualties, if and when they are published in full. But it is not altogether bad that that sort of thing should be said, provided it doesn't lead to sudden panic, because of the absolute need for getting the whole thing onto a new class basis. In the new armies middle-class people are bound to predominate as officers, they did so even, for instance, in the Spanish militias, but it is a question of umblimping.[9] Ditto with the L.D.V. Under the stress of emergency we shall umblimp if we have time, but time is all.

A thought that occurred to me yesterday: how is it that England, with one of the smallest armies in the world, has so many retired colonels?

I notice that all the 'left' intellectuals I meet believe that Hitler if he gets here will take the trouble to shoot people like ourselves and will have very extensive lists of undesirables. C.[10] says there is a move on foot to get our police records (no doubt we all have them) at Scotland Yard destroyed. Some hope! The police are the very people who would go over to Hitler once they were certain he had won. Well, if only we can hold out for a few months, in a year's time we shall see red militia billeted in the Ritz, and it would not particularly surprise me to see Churchill or Lloyd George at the head of them.

Thinking always of my island in the Hebrides,[11] which I suppose I shall never possess nor even see. Compton Mackenzie says even now most of the islands are uninhabited (there are 500 of them, only 10 per cent inhabited at normal times), and most have water and a little cultivable land, and goats will live on them. According to R.H., a woman who rented an island in the Hebrides in order to avoid air raids was the first air raid casualty of the war, the R.A.F. dropping a bomb there by mistake. Good if true.

The first air raid of any consequence on Great Britain the night before last. Fourteen killed, seven German aeroplanes claimed shot down. The papers have photos of three wrecked German planes, so possibly the claim is true.

1. Possibly Michael, the owner of the small clothing factory mentioned in Orwell's diary entry of 3.9.40.

2. Gwen O'Shaughnessy, Eileen's sister-in-law. In the early stages of the war, there was a government-sponsored scheme to evacuate children to Canada and the US. Gwen's son,

Laurence, nineteen months old in June 1940, went to Canada on one of the last ships to take evacuees before the evacuee-ship *City of Benares* was sunk in the Atlantic.

3. *New Statesman* seems probable here, though the diary has five hyphens.

4. Probably Richard Crossman (1907–74), scholar, intellectual, journalist and left-wing politician, who was assistant editor of the *New Statesman*, 1938–55, and editor, 1970–72. He was also a Labour MP, 1945–70; Minister of Housing and Local Government, 1964–6, and Minister of Health and Social Security, 1964–70.

5. The British 146th Infantry Brigade landed at Namsos, Norway, on the coast some 300 miles north of Oslo, on 16–17 April 1940. They withdrew 2–3 May. The last Allied forces left Norway on 9 June.

6. Aneurin (Nye) Bevan (1897–1960), a collier from Tredegar who represented Ebbw Vale as Labour MP from 1927 until his death. He was an impassioned orator, beloved of those on the left, disliked, even feared, by those on the right. As Minister of Health, 1945–50, he was responsible for the creation of the National Health Service. He resigned from the second Labour government in 1951 over disarmament and was defeated when he stood for Leader of the party in 1955. As a director of *Tribune* he allowed Orwell complete freedom, even to opposing the policies of the Labour Party. G. R. Strauss (1901–93; Life Peer, 1979), Labour MP and director of *Tribune*. Expelled from the Labour Party, 1939–40, for supporting the Popular Front (see above, p. 220, n. 4).

7. Neville Chamberlain's government fell on 10 May 1940, and a coalition government under Winston Churchill was formed. Magnanimously, Churchill included Chamberlain in his Cabinet.

8. Rayner Heppenstall (1911–81), novelist, critic, broadcaster, and crime historian. He and Orwell shared a flat in 1935 and, despite coming to blows, they remained lifelong friends. He produced Orwell's adaptation of *Animal Farm* for radio in 1947 and his own version in 1957. His *Four Absentees* (1960) has reminiscences of Orwell; the relevant portions are reprinted in *Orwell Remembered*, 106–15.

9. A blimp was originally a World War I observation balloon and came to be adopted for an old-fashioned, portly, peppery, retired army officer, especially in cartoons – Colonel Blimp. 'Unblimping' was a frequent concern of Orwell. See, for example, 'Don't Let Colonel Blimp Ruin the Home Guard' (1941; XII/*743*).

10. Not certainly identified. Possibly Richard Crossman again (see n. 4 above) or Cyril Connolly. Inez Holden suggested either Christopher Hollis or a mysterious man known as Carter, whom Orwell's friends never met.

11. This is the first reference to Orwell's dream of living in the Hebrides, to be realized in 1945 when he rented Barnhill, on Jura. Compare Winston Smith's vision of 'the Golden Country' in *Nineteen Eighty-Four*, IX/129–130; see also Orwell's review of *Priest Island*, XII/*640*.

---

[677]

23.8.40: This morning an air-raid warning about 3 a.m. Got up, looked at the time, then felt unable to do anything and promptly went to sleep again. They are talking of rearranging the alarm system, and they will have to do so if they are to prevent every alarm from costing thousands of pounds in wasted time, lost sleep, etc. The fact that at present the alarm sounds all over a wide area when the German planes are only operating in one part of it, means not only that people are unnecessarily woken up or taken away from work, but that an impression is spread that an air-raid alarm will *always* be false, which is obviously dangerous.

Have got my Home Guard uniform, after 2½ months.

Last night to a lecture by General —,[1] who is in command of about a quarter of a million men. He said he had been 41 years in the army. Was through the Flanders campaign, and no doubt limogé[2] for incompetence. Dilating on the Home Guard being a static defensive force, he said contemptuously and in a rather marked way that he saw no use in our practising taking cover, 'crawling about on our stomachs', etc., etc., evidently as a hit at the Osterley Park training school.[3] Our job, he said, was to die at our posts. Was also great on bayonet practice, and hinted that regular army ranks, saluting, etc., were to be introduced shortly. . . . . These wretched old blimps, so obviously silly and senile, and so degenerate in everything except physical courage, are merely pathetic in themselves, and one would feel rather sorry for them if they were not hanging round our necks like millstones. The attitude of the rank and file at these would-be pep-talks – so anxious to be enthusiastic, so ready to cheer and laugh at the jokes, and yet all the time half feeling that there is something wrong – always strikes me as pathetic. The time has almost arrived when one will only have to jump up on the platform and tell them how they are being wasted and how the war is being lost, and by whom, for them to rise up and shovel the blimps into the dustbin. When I watch them listening to one of these asinine talks, I always remember that passage in Samuel Butler's Notebook about a young calf he once saw eating dung.[4] It could not quite make up its mind whether it liked the stuff or not, and all it needed was some experienced cow to give it a prod with her horn, after which it would have remembered for life that dung is not good to eat.

It occurred to me yesterday, how will the Russian state get on without Trotsky? Or the Communists elsewhere? Probably they will be forced to invent a substitute.

1. Unidentified. Tom Hopkinson, one of the founders of the unofficial Home Guard Training School at Osterley Park, tells how a Brigadier Whitehead attempted to have the school stopped in the autumn of 1940 because it did not have a licence; see *Of This Our Time* (1982), 180. Orwell cannot be referring to Lieutenant-General Sir T. R. Eastwood, who took command of the Home Guard in the autumn of 1940; he was under fifty.
2. Passed over for promotion.
3. This was run by Tom Wintringham (see XII/*721*, n. 1) and Hugh (Humphrey) Slater (see XII/*731*, n. 1). They taught guerrilla tactics and street-fighting based on experience with the International Brigade during the Spanish Civil War.
4. 'Art of Knowing What Gives One Pleasure', *Further Extracts from the Note-Books of Samuel Butler*, chosen and edited by A. T. Bartholomew (1934), 165–6. This book was reviewed by Orwell in 1934; see X/*197*.

---

[689]

14.9.40: On the first night of the barrage,[1] which was the heaviest, they are said to have fired 500,000 shells, i.e. at an average cost of £5 per shell, £2½ millions worth. But well worth it, for the effect on morale.

15.9.40: This morning, for the first time, saw an aeroplane shot down. It fell slowly out of the clouds, nose foremost, just like a snipe that has been shot high overhead. Terrific jubilation among the people watching, punctuated every now and then by the question, 'Are you sure it's a German?' So puzzling are the directions given, and so many the types of aeroplane, that no one even knows which are German planes and which are our own. My only test is that if a bomber is seen over London it must be a German, whereas a fighter is likelier to be ours.

17.9.40: Heavy bombing in this area last night till about 11 p.m. . . . I was talking in the hallway of this house to two young men and a girl who was with them. Psychological attitude of all 3 was interesting. They were quite openly and unashamedly frightened, talking about how their knees were knocking together, etc., and yet at the same time excited and interested, dodging out of doors between bombs to see what was happening and pick up shrapnel splinters. Afterwards in Mrs. C.'s little reinforced room downstairs, with Mrs. C. and her daughter, the maid, and three young girls who are also lodgers here. All the women, except the maid, screaming in unison, clasping each other and hiding their faces, every time a bomb went past, but betweenwhiles quite happy and normal, with animated conversation proceeding. The dog subdued and obviously frightened, knowing something to be wrong. Marx[2] is also like this during raids, i.e. subdued and uneasy. Some dogs, however, go wild and savage during a raid and have had to be shot. They allege here, and E. says the same thing about Greenwich,[3] that all the dogs in the park now bolt for home when they hear the siren.

Yesterday when having my hair cut in the City, asked the barber if he carried on during raids. He said he did. And even if he was shaving someone? I said. Oh, yes, he carried on just the same. And one day a bomb will drop near enough to make him jump, and he will slice half somebody's face off.

Later, accosted by a man, I should think some kind of commercial traveller, with a bad type of face, while I was waiting for a bus. He began a rambling talk about how he was getting himself and his wife out of London, how his nerves were giving way and he suffered from stomach trouble, etc., etc. I don't know how much of this kind of thing there is. . . . There has of course been a big exodus from the East End, and every night what amount to mass migrations to places where there is sufficient shelter accommodation. The practice of taking a 2d ticket and spending the night in one of the deep Tube stations, e.g. Piccadilly, is growing. . . . Everyone I have talked to agrees that the empty furnished houses in the West End should be used for the homeless; but I suppose the rich swine still have enough pull to prevent this from happening. The other day 50 people from the East End, headed by some of the Borough Councillors, marched into the Savoy and demanded to use the air-raid shelter. The management didn't succeed in ejecting them till the raid was over, when they went voluntarily. When you see how the wealthy are *still* behaving, in what is manifestly developing into a revolutionary war, you think of St. Petersburg in 1916.

(Evening). Almost impossible to write in this infernal racket. (Electric lights have just gone off. Luckily I have some candles.) So many streets in (lights on again) the quarter roped off because of unexploded bombs, that to get home from Baker Street, say 300 yards, is like trying to find your way to the heart of a maze.

1. When the Germans first bombed London, there appeared to be no anti-aircraft defence. Sometimes a single plane would be cruising above and people could only wait anxiously, often for seemingly long periods, for a bomb to be dropped. At other times there would be

a concentrated attack of incendiary bombs, high explosives, or both. After all the anti-aircraft guns available had been regrouped around London, quite unexpectedly they all opened up on the night of 10 September. Orwell is absolutely correct about the effect on morale.

2. Marx was the Orwells' dog.

3. E. = Eileen, Orwell's wife. Her family lived in Greenwich.

[*1261*]

4.7.42 [Callow End, Worcs.]:[1] Pubs in this village shut quite a lot of the time for lack of beer. Possibly only due to the recent spell of hot weather. This is a hop area and I find the farmers have been asked not to cut down their acreage of hops, indeed some have increased it. All these hops go for beer, at least all the high-grade ones.

10.7.42: A day or two ago a couple of lorries belonging to the Navy arrived with a party of Wrens[2] and sailors who put in several hours work weeding out the turnips in Mr. Phillips's[3] field. All the village women delighted by the appearance of the sailors in their blue trousers and white singlets. 'Don't they look clean, like! I like sailors. They always look so clean'. The sailors and Wrens also seemed to enjoy their outing and drinks in the pub afterwards. It appeared that they belonged to some volunteer organisation which sends workers out as they are needed. Mrs Phillips explains it: 'It's the voluntary organisation from Malvern.[4] Sometimes it's A.T.s[5] they send and sometimes sailors. Of course we like having them. Well, it makes you a bit independent of your own work-people, you see. The work-people, they're awful nowadays. Just do so much and no more. They know you can't do without them, you see. And you can't get a woman to do a bit indoors nowadays. The girls won't stay here, with no picture-house in the village. I do have a woman who comes in, but I can't get any work out of her. It helps a bit when you get a few voluntary workers. Makes you more independent, like.'

How right and proper it all is when you consider how necessary it is that agricultural work should not be neglected, and how right and proper also that town people should get a bit of contact with the soil. Yet these voluntary organisations, plus the work done by soldiers in the hay-making etc., and the Italian prisoners, are simply blackleg labour.

The Government wins at Salisbury. Hipwell,[6] the editor of *Reveille*, was the Independent candidate. Wherever this mountebank stands the

Government wins automatically. How grateful they must be to him, if indeed they aren't actually paying him to do it.

The 'Blue Bell' again shut for lack of beer. Quite serious boozing for 4 or 5 days of the week, then drought. Sometimes, however, when they are shut the local officers are to be seen drinking in a private room, the common soldiers as well as the labourers being shut out. The 'Red Lion' in the next village, goes on a different system which the proprietor explains to me: 'I don't hold with giving it all to the summer visitors. If beer's short, let the locals come first, I say. A lot of days I keep the pub door shut, and then only the locals know the way in at the back. A man that's working in the fields needs his beer, 'specially with the food they got to eat nowadays. But I rations 'em. I says to 'em, "Now look here, you want your beer regular, don't you? Wouldn't you rather have a pint with your dinner every day than four pints one day and three the next?" Same with the soldiers. I don't like to refuse beer to a soldier, but I only lets 'em have a pint their first drink. After that it's "Half pints only, boys". Like that it gets shared out a bit.'

1. Orwell was on a fortnight's leave from the BBC. He stayed on a farm at Callow End, Worcestershire, and was able to enjoy his favourite sport, fishing, though with little luck. In two weeks he only caught eighteen dace, one perch, and two eels (XIII/*1262*). See n. 5 to review of *The Way of a Countryman*, below.
2. Women's Royal Naval Service.
3. Presumably the farmer on whose farm Orwell was staying. There is no indication as to whether Eileen was able to get leave at the same time as her husband.
4. Malvern, far inland, might seem an unlikely setting for a naval establishment, but a radar research base and an initial training unit were sited there.
5. Auxiliary Territorial Service, the women's army service, now the WRAC, Women's Royal Army Corps.
6. W. R. Hipwell.

---

[694]

'My Country Right or Left'[1]

Folios of New Writing, *No. 2, Autumn 1940*

Contrary to popular belief, the past was not more eventful than the present. If it seems so it is because when you look backward things that happened years apart are telescoped together, and because very few of your memories come to you genuinely virgin. It is largely because of the books, films and reminiscences that have come between that the war of 1914–18 is now supposed to have had some tremendous, epic quality that the present one lacks.

But if you were alive during that war, and if you disentangle your real memories from their later accretions, you find that it was not usually the big events that stirred you at the time. I don't believe that the battle of the Marne, for instance, had for the general public the melodramatic quality that it was afterwards given. I do not even remember hearing the phrase 'battle of the Marne' till years later. It was merely that the Germans were 22 miles from Paris – and certainly that was terrifying enough, after the Belgian atrocity stories – and then for some reason they had turned back. I was eleven when the war started. If I honestly sort out my memories and disregard what I have learned since, I must admit that nothing in the whole war moved me so deeply as the loss of the *Titanic* had done a few years earlier.[2] This comparatively petty disaster shocked the whole world, and the shock has not quite died away even yet. I remember the terrible, detailed accounts read out at the breakfast table (in those days it was a common habit to read the newspaper aloud), and I remember that in all the long list of horrors the one that most impressed me was that at the last the *Titanic* suddenly up-ended and sank bow-foremost, so that the people clinging to the stern were lifted no less than three hundred feet into the air before they plunged into the abyss. It gave me a sinking sensation in the belly which I can still all but feel. Nothing in the war ever gave me quite that sensation.

Of the outbreak of war I have three vivid memories which, being petty and irrelevant, are uninfluenced by anything that has come later. One is of the cartoon of the 'German Emperor' (I believe the hated name 'Kaiser' was not popularized till a little later) that appeared in the last days of July. People were mildly shocked by this guying of royalty ('But he's such a handsome man, really!'), although we were on the edge of war. Another is of the time when the Army commandeered all the horses in our little country town,[3] and a cabman burst into tears in the market-place when his horse, which had worked for him for years, was taken away from him. And another is of a mob of young men at the railway station, scrambling for the evening papers that had just arrived on the London train. And I remember the pile of pea-green papers (some of them were still green in those days), the high collars, the tightish trousers and the bowler hats, far better than I can remember the names of the terrific battles that were already raging on the French frontier.

Of the middle years of the war, I remember chiefly the square shoulders, bulging calves and jingling spurs of the artillerymen, whose uniform I much preferred to that of the infantry. As for the final period, if you ask me to say truthfully what is my chief memory, I must answer simply – margarine. It is an instance of the horrible selfishness of children that by 1917 the war had almost ceased to affect us, except through our stomachs. In the school library a huge map of the western front was pinned on an easel, with a red silk thread running across on a zig-zag of drawing-pins. Occasionally the thread moved half an inch this way or that, each movement meaning a pyramid of corpses. I paid no attention. I was at school among boys who were above the average level of intelligence, and yet I do not remember that a single major event of the time appeared to us in its true significance.[4] The Russian Revolution, for instance, made no impression, except on the few whose parents happened to have money invested in Russia. Among the very young the pacifist reaction had set in long before the war ended. To be as slack as you dared on O.T.C.[5] parades, and to take no interest in the war, was considered a mark of enlightenment. The young officers who had come back, hardened by their terrible experience and disgusted by the attitude of the younger generation to whom this experience meant just nothing, used to lecture us for our softness. Of course they could produce no argument that we were capable of understanding. They could only bark at you that war was 'a good thing', it 'made you tough', 'kept you fit', etc., etc. We merely sniggered at them. Ours was the one-eyed pacifism that is peculiar to sheltered countries with strong navies. For years after the war, to have any knowledge of or interest in military matters, even to know which end of a gun the bullet comes out of, was suspect in 'enlightened' circles. 1914–18 was written off as a meaningless slaughter, and even the men who had been slaughtered were held to be in some way to blame. I have often laughed to think of that recruiting poster, 'What did you do in the Great War, daddy?' (a child is asking this question of its shame-stricken father), and of all the men who must have been lured into the army by just that poster and afterwards despised by their children for not being Conscientious Objectors.

But the dead men had their revenge after all. As the war fell back into the past, my particular generation, those who had been 'just too young', became conscious of the vastness of the experience they had missed. You felt yourself a little less than a man, because you had missed it. I spent the years 1922–7 mostly among men a little older than myself who had been through the war.[6] They talked about it unceasingly, with horror, of course, but also with a steadily-growing nostalgia. You can see this nostalgia perfectly clearly in the English war-books. Besides, the pacifist reaction was only a phase, and even the 'just too young' had all been trained for war. Most of the English middle class are trained for war from the cradle onwards, not technically but morally. The earliest political slogan I can remember is 'We want eight (eight dreadnoughts) and we won't wait'.[7] At seven years old I was a member of the Navy League[8] and wore a sailor suit with 'H.M.S. *Invincible*' on my cap. Even before my public-school O.T.C. I had been in a private-school cadet corps. On and off, I have been toting a rifle ever since I was ten, in preparation not only for war but for a particular kind of war, a war in which the guns rise to a frantic orgasm of sound, and at the appointed moment you clamber out of the trench, breaking your nails on the sandbags, and stumble across mud and wire into the machine-gun barrage. I am convinced that part of the reason for the fascination that the Spanish civil war had for people of about my age was that it was so like the Great War. At certain moments Franco was able to scrape together enough aeroplanes to raise the war to a modern level, and these were the turning-points. But for the rest it was a bad copy of 1914–18, a positional war of trenches, artillery, raids, snipers, mud, barbed wire, lice and stagnation. In early 1937 the bit of the Aragón front that I was on must have been very like a quiet sector in France in 1915. It was only the artillery that was lacking. Even on the rare occasions when all the guns in Huesca and outside it were firing simultaneously, there were only enough of them to make a fitful unimpressive noise like the ending of a thunderstorm. The shells from Franco's six-inch guns crashed loudly enough, but there were never more than a dozen of them at a time. I know that what I felt when I first heard artillery fired 'in anger', as they say, was at least partly disappointment. It was so different from the tremendous, unbroken roar that my senses had been waiting for for twenty years.

I don't quite know in what year I first knew for certain that the present war was coming. After 1936, of course, the thing was obvious to anyone except an idiot. For several years the coming war was a nightmare to me, and at times I even made speeches and wrote pamphlets against it. But the night before the Russo-German pact was announced I dreamed that the war had started. It was one of those dreams which, whatever Freudian inner meaning they may have, do sometimes reveal to you the real state of your feelings. It taught me two things, first, that I should be simply relieved when the long-dreaded war started, secondly, that I was patriotic at heart, would not sabotage or act against my own side, would support the war, would fight in it if possible. I came downstairs to find the newspaper announcing Ribbentrop's flight to Moscow.[9] So war was coming, and the Government, even the Chamberlain Government, was assured of my loyalty. Needless to say this loyalty was and remains merely a gesture. As with almost everyone I know, the Government has flatly refused to employ me in any capacity whatever, even as a clerk or a private soldier. But that does not alter one's feelings. Besides, they will be forced to make use of us sooner or later.

If I had to defend my reasons for supporting the war, I believe I could do so. There is no real alternative between resisting Hitler and surrendering to him, and from a Socialist point of view I should say that it is better to resist; in any case I can see no argument for surrender that does not make nonsense of the Republican resistance in Spain, the Chinese resistance to Japan, etc., etc. But I don't pretend that that is the emotional basis of my actions. What I knew in my dream that night was that the long drilling in patriotism which the middle classes go through had done its work, and that once England was in a serious jam it would be impossible for me to sabotage. But let no one mistake the meaning of this, Patriotism has nothing to do with conservatism. It is devotion to something that is changing but is felt to be mystically the same, like the devotion of the ex-White Bolshevik to Russia. To be loyal both to Chamberlain's England and to the England of tomorrow might seem an impossibility, if one did not know it to be an everyday phenomenon. Only revolution can save England, that has been obvious for years, but now the revolution has started, and it may proceed quite quickly if only we can keep Hitler out. Within two years, maybe a year, if only we can hang on, we shall see changes that will surprise the idiots who have no foresight. I dare say the London gutters will have to run with blood. All right, let them, if it is necessary. But when the red militias are billeted in the Ritz I shall still feel that the England I was taught to love so long ago and for such different reasons is somehow persisting.

I grew up in an atmosphere tinged with militarism, and afterwards I spent five boring years within the sound of bugles. To this day it gives me a faint feeling of sacrilege not to stand to attention during 'God save the King'. That is childish, of course, but I would sooner have had that kind of upbringing than be like the left-wing intellectuals who are so 'enlightened' that they cannot understand the most ordinary emotions. It is exactly the people whose hearts have *never* leapt at the sight of a Union Jack who will flinch from revolution when the moment comes. Let anyone compare the poem John Cornford[10] wrote not long before he was killed ('Before the Storming of Huesca') with Sir Henry Newbolt's 'There's a breathless hush in the Close tonight'.[11] Put aside the technical differences, which are merely a matter of period, and it will be seen that the emotional content of the two poems is almost exactly the same. The young Communist who died heroically in the International Brigade was public school to the core. He had changed his allegiance but not his emotions. What does that prove? Merely the possibility of building a Socialist on the bones of a Blimp, the power of one kind of loyalty to transmute itself into another, the spiritual need for patriotism and the military virtues, for which, however little the boiled rabbits of the Left may like them, no substitute has yet been found.

1. The title adapts Stephen Decatur's 'Toast Given at Norfolk [Virginia]' (1816), 'My country right or wrong'. Decatur (1779–1820) was a successful naval officer, especially in the 1812 war with the United Kingdom. He was killed in a duel with a fellow officer.

2. The *Titanic* sank, after colliding with an iceberg, on 15 April 1912, with the loss of more than 1,500 of 2,340 passengers and crew.

3. Orwell then lived at Shiplake. He presumably refers to Twyford or Henley-on-Thames.

4. Orwell could be referring to either his preparatory school at Eastbourne, St Cyprian's, where he was from September 1911 to December 1916 (see 'Such, Such Were the Joys', below), or to Eton, where he studied from March 1917 to December 1921. (He was at Wellington for the intervening term.) The reference to the Russian Revolution, 1917, suggests that Eton is more likely.

5. Officers' Training Corps, set up in Public Schools for the training of army officers. Cadet

corps were established a little earlier; they were associated with relevant regiments (e.g., Rifle Regiments).

6. See 'From Burma to Paris', above.

7. The slogan dates from 1909, when Orwell was six.

8. The Navy League was founded in 1895 to foster interest in the Royal Navy.

9. On 23 August 1939, Germany and the Soviet Union signed, in the persons of Ribbentrop and Molotov, a non-aggression pact in Moscow, completely reversing the balance of relationships in Europe. A secret protocol provided for the partition of Poland between the signatories. Hitler was informed of the signing of an Anglo-Polish agreement at 4.30 p.m. on 25 August and three hours later cancelled an order given at 3.00 p.m. for his troops to invade Poland. The invasion was postponed until 1 September 1939.

10. Rupert John Cornford (1915–36), son of the poet, Frances Cornford. He was named Rupert after Rupert Brooke. He studied at LSE and Cambridge, fought at Madrid, and was killed at Cordoba. His poems, with extracts from his letters and political writings, were published in *John Cornford: a Memoir*, ed. P. Sloan (1938), and there is a selection in *Spanish Civil War Verse*, ed. Valentine Cunningham (Penguin, 1980). One poem (not included in the Penguin selection) is 'Keep Culture out of Cambridge'.

11. Sir Henry Newbolt (1862–1937) is now out of fashion but in Orwell's youth he was a popular poet and many schoolboys learned such poems as 'Drake's Drum' and 'Vitaï Lampada', perhaps better known even today from its first line, 'There's a breathless hush in the Close tonight' and its refrain at the end of each of its three stanzas, 'Play up! play up! and play the game!', though the setting has shifted from a public school cricket field to one in which 'The sand of the desert is sodden red' – with the blood of British soldiers. The cruel irony, not intended by Newbolt, is that war is seen as some kind of game. The refrain was once engraved at a corner of Lord's Cricket Ground in London. The Close is that at Clifton College, Newbolt's school.

---

[762]

Film review of Eyes of the Navy; The Heart of Britain; Unholy War

15 February 1941

Between 5 October 1940 and 16 August 1941 Orwell wrote twenty-six film reviews of forty-three films; he was also writing play and theatre reviews. His review of these three documentary films was the second part of a review that also discussed Dulcy. *Orwell described* Dulcy, *a Hollywood film, as a 'fairly amusing piece of rubbish' with a 'complete lack of any sense of character or probability to match up with [its] brilliant technique and snappy dialogue' (*XII/389*). Dulcy was played by Ann Sothern.*

The supporting programme is made up of three short propaganda films, one American and two British. Although above I have pointed out one of the faults of the American film, one sees in this short piece (*Eyes of the Navy* – it deals with the U.S.A. naval air arm) the immense technical superiority of the Americans, their understanding of what is and is not impressive, their intolerance of amateurishness generally. The British films (*The Heart of Britain*, produced by the G.P.O.,[1] and *Unholy War*, produced by the Ministry of Information[2]) are terrible. What is the use, in the middle of a desperate war, in which propaganda is a major weapon, of wasting time and money on producing this kind of stuff? *Unholy War* takes as its theme the 'anti-Christian' nature of Nazism, and illustrates this with a series of photographs of wrecked churches, with much blah about the architectural glories that have perished. Hitler wants to destroy the Christian religion, and therefore his airmen drop bombs on churches – that is the argument. Cannot our leaders realize (a) that to ninety-nine people out of a hundred the destruction of a church seems much less important than the destruction of a dwelling house, (b) that even very ignorant people know that a bomb does not necessarily hit the object that it is aimed at, and (c) that anyone who understands the anti-Christian nature of Nazism knows that the Christian religion, or any other, does not stand or fall with the stones of its churches? If we have got to rouse resentment against the enemy, which is an inevitable part of war, surely we can find something more effective to say than that the Germans have a spite against Gothic architecture? And, since films of this kind need a spoken commentary, why cannot the M.O.I.[3] choose someone who speaks the English language as it is spoken in the street? Some day perhaps it will be realized that that dreadful B.B.C. voice, with its blurred vowels, antagonizes the whole English-speaking world except for a small area in southern England, and is more valuable to Hitler than a dozen new submarines.[4] In a war in which words are at least as important as guns, these two films are a wretched achievement to set beside Wavell's victories.

1. General Post Office, but here standing for the GPO Film Unit, developed from the Empire Film Marketing Board under John Grierson, 'father' of British documentary films. The unit, later the Crown Film Unit, was closed down by Churchill in January 1952. *The Heart of Britain*, directed by Humphrey Jennings, edited by Stewart McAllister, was the first of a

group of films described by Elizabeth Sussex, in her less-than-sycophantic study, *The Rise and Fall of British Documentary* (1975), as bringing 'a new inspiration to British documentary'.
2. The Ministry of Information, which supervised Britain's wartime propaganda, was responsible for many documentary films. It was based at Senate House, University of London, the origin of the Ministry of Truth in *Nineteen-Eighty-Four* (see XI/45–6).
3. The Ministry of Information became the setting for Minitrue in *Nineteen Eighty-Four.*
4. A letter signed 'Southerner' was published in *Time and Tide* on 1 March 1941 and made this comment on Orwell's remarks about 'that dreadful B.B.C. voice': 'This pronouncement causes one to wonder whom Mr Orwell would choose as an exponent of English as it should be spoken. Is there such a thing as "the King's English", and would Mr Orwell consider that either the King, the Prime Minister or Mr John Gielgud speaks it? If so, to what degree does this speech differ from that of Messrs Alvar Liddell or Bruce Belfrage? Criticism of the voices of B.B.C. speakers obviously delights a great many people, but it puzzles others. Perhaps Mr Orwell would elaborate his criticism a little: as it stands it seems rather like inverted snobbery.' (Liddell and Belfrage were well-known and well-respected BBC newsreaders.)

---

[763]

The Lion and the Unicorn: Socialism and the English Genius

19 February 1941

Searchlight Books, of which this was the first, were planned by Fredric Warburg, Tosco Fyvel and Orwell during the summer of 1940 'in the lush garden of Scarlett's Farm', the home of the Warburgs near Twyford, Berkshire, where the Fyvels also were living, 'while German bombs . . . began to fall on London; and while above our heads . . . the Spitfires and Hurricanes of the RAF accomplished their decisive air victory of the war, we talked about the future' (Tosco Fyvel, George Orwell: A Personal Memoir, *1982, 106; ch. 10 gives a good account of the genesis of the series). Orwell was persuaded, rather against his will, to write the first book – in effect, a sixty-four-page pamphlet. Having agreed, he wrote at speed, delivering the manuscript in November 1940, the month that also saw the publication of Fyvel's 'war aims book,* The Malady and the Vision*' (Fyvel, 111). Seventeen Searchlight Books were planned; nine were published in 1941 and two in 1942; the remainder did not appear.*

The Lion and the Unicorn *was published by Secker & Warburg on 19 February 1941 at 2s 0d (10p). Initially, 5,000 copies were printed, but in response to the book's quick sale, the run was increased to 7,500; a second impression of 5,000 copies was ordered in March 1941, the first thousand being delivered in June. However, when Plymouth was bombed, the type, with that of* Homage to Catalonia, *was destroyed when the Mayflower Press was hit. The book is in three parts: 'England Your England' (reprinted here); 'Shopkeepers at War' and 'The English Revolution' (reprinted in* Orwell and Politics *in this series). In the second half of 1949, Orwell listed four books that were not to be reprinted (*XX/*3728): this book,* The English People, A Clergyman's Daughter *and* Keep the Aspidistra Flying. *However, in his 'Notes for My Literary Executor' in 1945 (*XVII/*2648), he wrote that after he was dead he did 'not object to cheap editions of any book which may bring in a few pounds for my heirs'. Orwell may have taken against the two novels because of the way that they had been garbled (to use his own word), and the same might be said of* The English People. *In his lifetime, a Polish version of 'England Your England' was published in* Kultura, *4 (Paris, April 1948).*

PART I: ENGLAND YOUR ENGLAND

I

As I write, highly civilized human beings are flying overhead, trying to kill me.

They do not feel any enmity against me as [an] individual, nor I against them. They are 'only doing their duty', as the saying goes. Most of them, I have no doubt, are kind-hearted law-abiding men who would never dream of committing murder in private life. On the other hand, if one of them succeeds in blowing me to pieces with a well-placed bomb, he will never sleep any the worse for it. He is serving his country, which has the power to absolve him from evil.

One cannot see the modern world as it is unless one recognizes the overwhelming strength of patriotism, national loyalty. In certain circumstances it can break down, at certain levels of civilization it does not exist, but as a *positive* force there is nothing to set beside it. Christianity and international Socialism are as weak as straw in comparison with it. Hitler and Mussolini rose to power in their own countries very largely because they could grasp this fact and their opponents could not.

Also, one must admit that the divisions between nation and nation are founded on real differences of outlook. Till recently it was thought proper to pretend that all human beings are very much alike, but in fact anyone able to use his eyes knows that the average of human behaviour differs enormously from country to country. Things that could happen in one country could not happen in another. Hitler's June Purge,[1] for instance, could not have happened in England. And, as western peoples go, the English are very highly differentiated. There is a sort of backhanded admission of this in the dislike which nearly all foreigners feel for our national way of life. Few Europeans can endure living in England, and even Americans often feel more at home in Europe.

When you come back to England from any foreign country, you have immediately the sensation of breathing a different air. Even in the first few minutes dozens of small things conspire to give you this feeling. The beer is bitterer, the coins are heavier, the grass is greener, the advertisements are more blatant. The crowds in the big towns, with their mild knobby faces, their bad teeth and gentle manners, are different from a European crowd. Then the vastness of England swallows you up, and you lose for a while your feeling that the whole nation has a single identifiable character. Are there really such things as nations? Are we not 46 million individuals, all different?[2] And the diversity of it, the chaos! The clatter of clogs in the Lancashire mill towns, the to-and-fro of the lorries on the Great North Road, the queues outside the Labour Exchanges, the rattle of pin-tables in the Soho pubs, the old maids biking to Holy Communion through the mists of the autumn mornings – all these are not only fragments, but *characteristic* fragments, of the English scene. How can one make a pattern out of this muddle?

But talk to foreigners, read foreign books or newspapers, and you are brought back to the same thought. Yes, there *is* something distinctive and recognizable in English civilization. It is a culture as individual as that of Spain. It is somehow bound up with solid breakfasts and gloomy Sundays, smoky towns and winding roads, green fields and red pillar-boxes. It has a flavour of its own. Moreover it is continuous, it stretches into the future and the past, there is something in it that persists, as in a living creature. What can the England of 1940 have in common with the England of 1840? But then, what have you in common with the child of five whose photograph your mother keeps on the mantelpiece? Nothing, except that you happen to be the same person.

And above all, it is *your* civilization, it is *you*. However much you hate it or laugh at it, you will never be happy away from it for any length of time. The suet puddings and the red pillar-boxes have entered into your soul. Good or evil, it is yours, you belong to it, and this side the grave you will never get away from the marks that it has given you.

Meanwhile England, together with the rest of the world, is changing. And like everything else it can change only in certain directions, which up to a point can be foreseen. That is not to say that the future is fixed, merely that certain alternatives are possible and others not. A seed may grow or not grow, but at any rate a turnip seed never grows into a parsnip. It is therefore of the deepest importance to try and determine what England *is*, before guessing what part England *can play* in the huge events that are happening.

II

National characteristics are not easy to pin down, and when pinned down they often turn out to be trivialities or seem to have no connection with one another. Spaniards are cruel to animals, Italians can do nothing without making a deafening noise, the Chinese are addicted to gambling. Obviously such things don't matter in themselves. Nevertheless, nothing is causeless, and even the fact that Englishmen have bad teeth can tell one something about the realities of English life.

Here are a couple of generalizations about England that would be accepted by almost all observers. One is that the English are not gifted artistically. They are not as musical as the Germans or Italians, painting and sculpture have never flourished in England as they have in France. Another is that, as Europeans go, the English are not intellectual. They have a horror of abstract thought, they feel no need for any philosophy or systematic 'world-view'. Nor is this because they are 'practical', as they are so fond of claiming for themselves. One has only to look at their methods of town-planning and water-supply, their obstinate clinging to everything that is out of date and a nuisance, a spelling system that defies analysis and a system of weights and measures that is intelligible only to the compilers of arithmetic books, to see how little they care about mere efficiency. But they have a certain power of acting without taking thought. Their world-famed hypocrisy – their double-faced attitude towards the Empire, for instance – is bound up with this. Also, in moments of supreme crisis the whole nation can suddenly draw together and act upon a species of instinct, really a code of conduct which is understood by almost everyone, though never formulated. The phrase that Hitler coined for the Germans, 'a sleep-walking people',[3] would have been better applied to the English. Not that there is anything to be proud of in being a sleep-walker.

But here it is worth noticing a minor English trait which is extremely well marked though not often commented on, and that is a love of flowers. This is one of the first things that one notices when one reaches England from abroad, especially if one is coming from southern Europe. Does it not contradict the English indifference to the arts? Not really, because it is found in people who have no aesthetic feelings whatever. What it does link up with, however, is another English characteristic which is so much a part of us that we barely notice it, and that is the addiction to hobbies and spare-time occupations, the *privateness* of English life. We are a nation of flower-lovers, but also a nation of stamp-collectors, pigeon-fanciers, amateur carpenters, coupon-snippers, darts-players, crossword-puzzle fans. All the culture that is most truly native centres round things which even when they are communal are not official – the pub, the football match, the back garden, the fireside and the 'nice cup of tea'. The liberty of the individual is still believed in, almost as in the nineteenth century. But this has nothing to do with economic liberty, the right to exploit others for profit. It is the liberty to have a home of your own, to do what you like in your spare time, to choose your own amusements instead of having them chosen for you from above. The most hateful of all names in an English ear is Nosey Parker. It is obvious, of course, that even this purely private liberty is a lost cause. Like all other modern peoples, the English are in process of being numbered, labelled, conscripted, 'co-ordinated'. But the pull of their impulses is in the other direction, and the kind of regimentation that can be imposed on them will be modified in consequence. No party rallies, no Youth Movements, no coloured shirts, no Jew-baiting or 'spontaneous' demonstrations. No Gestapo either, in all probability.

But in all societies the common people must live to some extent *against* the existing order. The genuinely popular culture of England is something that goes on beneath the surface, unofficially and more or less frowned on by the authorities. One thing one notices if one looks directly at the common people, especially in the big towns, is that they are not puritanical. They are inveterate gamblers, drink as much beer as their wages will permit, are devoted to bawdy jokes, and use probably the foulest language in the world. They have to satisfy these tastes in the face of astonishing, hypocritical laws (licensing laws, lottery acts, etc., etc.) which are designed to interfere with everybody but in practice allow everything to happen. Also, the common people are without definite religious belief, and have been so for centuries. The Anglican Church never had a real hold on them, it was simply a preserve of the landed gentry, and the Nonconformist sects only influenced minorities. And yet they have retained a deep tinge of Christian feeling, while almost forgetting the name of Christ. The power-worship which is the new religion of Europe, and which has infected the English intelligentsia, has never touched the common people. They have never caught up with power politics. The 'realism' which is preached in Japanese and Italian newspapers would horrify them. One can learn a good deal about the spirit of England from the comic coloured postcards that you see in the windows of cheap stationers' shops. These things are a sort of diary upon which the English people have unconsciously recorded themselves. Their old-fashioned outlook, their graded snobberies, their mixture of bawdiness and hypocrisy, their extreme gentleness, their deeply moral attitude to life, are all mirrored there.

The gentleness of the English civilization is perhaps its most marked characteristic. You notice it the instant you set foot on English soil. It is a land where the bus conductors are good-tempered and the policemen carry no revolvers. In no country inhabited by white men is it easier to shove people off the pavement. And with this goes something that is always written off by European observers as 'decadence' or hypocrisy, the English hatred of war and militarism. It is rooted deep in history, and it is strong in the lower-middle class as well as the working class. Successive wars have shaken it but not destroyed it. Well within living memory it was common for 'the redcoats' to be booed at in the street and for the landlords of respectable public-houses to refuse to allow soldiers on the premises. In peace-time, even when there are two million unemployed, it is difficult to fill the ranks of the tiny standing army, which is officered by the county gentry and a specialized stratum of the middle class, and manned by farm labourers and slum proletarians. The mass of the people are without military knowledge or tradition, and their attitude towards war is invariably defensive. No politician could rise to power by promising them conquests or military 'glory', no Hymn of Hate has ever made any appeal to them. In the last war the songs which the soldiers made up and sang of their own accord were not vengeful but humorous and mock-defeatist.* The only enemy they ever named was the sergeant-major.

In England all the boasting and flag-wagging, the 'Rule Britannia' stuff, is done by small minorities. The patriotism of the common people is not vocal or even conscious. They do not retain among their historical memories the name of a single military victory. English literature, like other literatures, is full of battle-poems, but it is worth noticing that the ones that have won for themselves a kind of popularity are always a tale of disasters and retreats. There is no popular poem about Trafalgar or Waterloo, for instance.[5] Sir John Moore's army at Corunna, fighting a desperate rear-guard action before escaping overseas (just like Dunkirk!) has more appeal than a brilliant victory.[6] The most stirring battle-poem in English is about a brigade of cavalry which charged in the wrong direction.[7] And of the last war, the four names which have really engraved themselves on the popular memory are Mons, Ypres, Gallipoli and Passchendaele, every time a disaster. The names of the great battles that finally broke the German armies are simply unknown to the general public.

The reason why the English anti-militarism disgusts foreign observers is that it ignores the existence of the British Empire. It looks like sheer hypocrisy. After all, the English have absorbed a quarter of the earth and held on to it by means of a huge navy. How dare they then turn round and say that war is wicked?

It is quite true that the English are hypocritical about their Empire. In

* For example: 'I don't want to join the bloody Army, / I don't want to go unto the war; / I want no more to roam, / I'd rather stay at home / Living on the earnings of a whore.' But it was not in that spirit that they fought [Orwell's footnote].

the working class this hypocrisy takes the form of not knowing that the Empire exists. But their dislike of standing armies is a perfectly sound instinct. A navy employs comparatively few people, and it is an external weapon which cannot affect home politics directly. Military dictatorships exist everywhere, but there is no such thing as a naval dictatorship. What English people of nearly all classes loathe from the bottom of their hearts is the swaggering officer type, the jingle of spurs and the crash of boots. Decades before Hitler was ever heard of, the word 'Prussian' had much the same significance in England as 'Nazi' has today. So deep does this feeling go that for a hundred years past the officers of the British Army, in peace-time, have always worn civilian clothes when off duty.

One rapid but fairly sure guide to the social atmosphere of a country is the parade-step of its army. A military parade is really a kind of ritual dance, something like a ballet, expressing a certain philosophy of life. The goose-step, for instance, is one of the most horrible sights in the world, far more terrifying than a dive-bomber. It is simply an affirmation of naked power; contained in it, quite consciously and intentionally, is the vision of a boot crashing down on a face. Its ugliness is part of its essence, for what it is saying is 'Yes, I *am* ugly, and you daren't laugh at me', like the bully who makes faces at his victim. Why is the goose-step not used in England? There are, heaven knows, plenty of army officers who would be only too glad to introduce some such thing. It is not used because the people in the street would laugh. Beyond a certain point, military display is only possible in countries where the common people dare not laugh at the army. The Italians adopted the goose-step at about the time when Italy passed definitely under German control, and, as one would expect, they do it less well than the Germans. The Vichy government,[8] if it survives, is bound to introduce a stiffer parade-ground discipline into what is left of the French army. In the British army the drill is rigid and complicated, full of memories of the eighteenth century, but without definite swagger; the march is merely a formalized walk. It belongs to a society which is ruled by the sword, no doubt, but a sword which must never be taken out of the scabbard.

And yet the gentleness of English civilization is mixed up with barbarities and anachronisms. Our criminal law is as out of date as the muskets in the Tower. Over against the Nazi Storm Trooper you have got to set that typically English figure, the hanging judge, some gouty old bully with his mind rooted in the nineteenth century, handing out savage sentences. In England people are still hanged by the neck and flogged with the cat o' nine tails. Both of these punishments are obscene as well as cruel, but there has never been any genuinely popular outcry against them. People accept them (and Dartmoor and Borstal) almost as they accept the weather. They are part of 'the law', which is assumed to be unalterable.

Here one comes upon an all-important English trait: the respect for constitutionalism and legality, the belief in 'the law' as something above the State and above the individual, something which is cruel and stupid, of course, but at any rate *incorruptible*.

It is not that anyone imagines the law to be just. Everyone knows that there is one law for the rich and another for the poor. But no one accepts the implications of this, everyone takes it for granted that the law, such as it is, will be respected, and feels a sense of outrage when it is not. Remarks like 'They can't run me in; I haven't done anything wrong', or 'They can't do that; it's against the law', are part of the atmosphere of England. The professed enemies of society have this feeling as strongly as anyone else. One sees it in prison-books like Wilfred Macartney's *Walls Have Mouths* or Jim Phelan's *Jail Journey*,[9] in the solemn idiocies that take place at the trials of Conscientious Objectors, in letters to the papers from eminent Marxist professors, pointing out that this or that is a 'miscarriage of British justice'. Everyone believes in his heart that the law can be, ought to be, and, on the whole, will be impartially administered. The totalitarian idea that there is no such thing as law, there is only power, has never taken root. Even the intelligentsia have only accepted it in theory.

An illusion can become a half-truth, a mask can alter the expression of a face. The familiar arguments to the effect that democracy is 'just the same as' or 'just as bad as' totalitarianism never take account of this fact. All such arguments boil down to saying that half a loaf is the same as no bread. In England such concepts as justice, liberty and objective truth are still believed in. They may be illusions, but they are very powerful illusions. The belief in them influences conduct, national life is different because of them. In proof of which, look about you. Where are the rubber truncheons, where is the castor oil? The sword is still in the scabbard, and while it stays there corruption cannot go beyond a certain point. The English electoral system, for instance, is an all-but open fraud. In a dozen obvious ways it is gerrymandered in the interest of the moneyed class. But until some deep change has occurred in the public mind, it cannot become *completely* corrupt. You do not arrive at the polling booth to find men with revolvers telling you which way to vote, nor are the votes miscounted, nor is there any direct bribery. Even hypocrisy is a powerful safeguard. The hanging judge, that evil old man in scarlet robe and horsehair wig, whom nothing short of dynamite will ever teach what century he is living in, but who will at any rate interpret the law according to the books and will in no circumstances take a money bribe, is one of the symbolic figures of England. He is a symbol of the strange mixture of reality and illusion, democracy and privilege, humbug and decency, the subtle network of compromises, by which the nation keeps itself in its familiar shape.

III

I have spoken all the while of 'the nation', 'England', 'Britain', as though 45 million souls could somehow be treated as a unit. But is not England notoriously two nations, the rich and the poor?[10] Dare one pretend that there is anything in common between people with £100,000 a year and people with £1 a week? And even Welsh and Scottish readers are likely to have been offended because I have used the word 'England' oftener than 'Britain', as though the whole population dwelt in London and the Home Counties and neither north nor west possessed a culture of its own.

One gets a better view of this question if one considers the minor point first. It is quite true that the so-called races of Britain feel themselves to be very different from one another. A Scotsman, for instance, does not thank you if you call him an Englishman. You can see the hesitation we feel on this point by the fact that we call our islands by no less than six different names, England, Britain, Great Britain, the British Isles, the United Kingdom and, in very exalted moments, Albion. Even the differences between north and south England loom large in our own eyes. But somehow these differences fade away the moment that any two Britons are confronted by a European. It is very rare to meet a foreigner, other than an American, who can distinguish between English and Scots or even English and Irish. To a Frenchman, the Breton and the Auvergnat seem very different beings, and the accent of Marseilles is a stock joke in Paris. Yet we speak of 'France' and 'the French', recognizing France as an entity, a single civilization, which in fact it is. So also with ourselves. Looked at from the outside, even the cockney and the Yorkshireman have a strong family resemblance.

And even the distinction between rich and poor dwindles somewhat when one regards the nation from the outside. There is no question about the inequality of wealth in England. It is grosser than in any European country, and you have only to look down the nearest street to see it. Economically, England is certainly two nations, if not three or four. But at the same time the vast majority of the people *feel* themselves to be a single nation and are conscious of resembling one another more than they resemble foreigners. Patriotism is usually stronger than class-hatred, and always stronger than any kind of internationalism. Except for a brief moment in 1920 (the 'Hands off Russia' movement)[11] the British working class have never thought or acted internationally. For two and a half years they watched their comrades in Spain slowly strangled, and never aided them by even a single strike.* But when their own country (the country of Lord Nuffield[12] and Mr. Montagu Norman[13]) was in danger, their attitude was very different. At the moment when it seemed likely that England might be invaded, Anthony Eden appealed over the radio for Local Defence Volunteers.[14] He got a quarter of a million men in the first twenty-four hours, and another million in the subsequent month. One has only to compare these figures with, for instance, the number of Conscientious Objectors to see how vast is the strength of traditional loyalties compared with new ones.

In England patriotism takes different forms in different classes, but it runs like a connecting thread through nearly all of them. Only the Europeanized intelligentsia are really immune to it. As a positive emotion it is stronger in the middle class than in the upper class – the cheap public schools, for instance, are more given to patriotic demonstrations than the expensive ones – but the number of definitely treacherous rich men, the

* It is true that they aided them to a certain extent with money. Still, the sums raised for the various aid-Spain funds would not equal five per cent of the turnover of the Football Pools during the same period [Orwell's footnote].

Laval-Quisling type[15] type, is probably very small. In the working class patriotism is profound, but it is unconscious. The working man's heart does not leap when he sees a Union Jack. But the famous 'insularity' and 'xenophobia' of the English is far stronger in the working class than in the bourgeoisie. In all countries the poor are more national than the rich, but the English working class are outstanding in their abhorrence of foreign habits. Even when they are obliged to live abroad for years they refuse either to accustom themselves to foreign food or to learn foreign languages. Nearly every Englishman of working-class origin considers it effeminate to pronounce a foreign word correctly. During the war of 1914–18 the English working class were in contact with foreigners to an extent that is rarely possible. The sole result was that they brought back a hatred of all Europeans, except the Germans, whose courage they admired. In four years on French soil they did not even acquire a liking for wine. The insularity of the English, their refusal to take foreigners seriously, is a folly that has to be paid for very heavily from time to time. But it plays its part in the English *mystique*, and the intellectuals who have tried to break it down have generally done more harm than good. At bottom it is the same quality in the English character that repels the tourist and keeps out the invader.

Here one comes back to two English characteristics that I pointed out, seemingly rather at random, at the beginning of the last chapter. One is the lack of artistic ability. This is perhaps another way of saying that the English are outside the European culture. For there is one art in which they have shown plenty of talent, namely literature. But this is also the only art that cannot cross frontiers. Literature, especially poetry, and lyric poetry most of all, is a kind of family joke, with little or no value outside its own language-group. Except for Shakespeare, the best English poets are barely known in Europe, even as names. The only poets who are widely read are Byron, who is admired for the wrong reasons, and Oscar Wilde, who is pitied as a victim of English hypocrisy. And linked up with this, though not very obviously, is the lack of philosophical faculty, the absence in nearly all Englishmen of any need for an ordered system of thought or even for the use of logic.

Up to a point, the sense of national unity is a substitute for a 'world-view'. Just because patriotism is all but universal and not even the rich are uninfluenced by it, there can come moments when the whole nation suddenly swings together and does the same thing, like a herd of cattle facing a wolf. There was such a moment, unmistakably, at the time of the disaster in France. After eight months of vaguely wondering what the war was about, the people suddenly knew what they had got to do: first, to get the army away from Dunkirk, and secondly to prevent invasion. It was like the awakening of a giant. Quick! Danger! The Philistines be upon thee, Samson![16] And then the swift unanimous action – and then, alas, the prompt relapse into sleep. In a divided nation that would have been exactly the moment for a big peace movement to arise. But does this mean that the instinct of the English will always tell them to do the right thing? Not at all, merely that it will tell them to do the same thing. In the 1931 General Election, for instance, we all did the wrong thing in perfect unison.[17] We were as single-minded as the Gadarene swine.[18] But I honestly doubt whether we can say that we were shoved down the slope against our will.

It follows that British democracy is less of a fraud than it sometimes appears. A foreign observer sees only the huge inequality of wealth, the unfair electoral system, the governing-class control over the Press, the radio and education, and concludes that democracy is simply a polite name for dictatorship. But this ignores the considerable agreement that does unfortunately exist between the leaders and the led. However much one may hate to admit it, it is almost certain that between 1931 and 1940 the National Government represented the will of the mass of the people. It tolerated slums, unemployment and a cowardly foreign policy. Yes, but so did public opinion. It was a stagnant period, and its natural leaders were mediocrities.

In spite of the campaigns of a few thousand left-wingers, it is fairly certain that the bulk of the English people were behind Chamberlain's foreign policy.[19] More, it is fairly certain that the same struggle was going on in Chamberlain's mind as in the minds of ordinary people. His opponents professed to see in him a dark and wily schemer, plotting to sell England to Hitler, but it is far likelier that he was merely a stupid old man doing his best according to his very dim lights. It is difficult otherwise to explain the contradictions of his policy, his failure to grasp any of the courses that were open to him. Like the mass of the people, he did not want to pay the price either of peace or of war. And public opinion was behind him all the while, in policies that were completely incompatible with one another. It was behind him when he went to Munich,[20] when he tried to come to an understanding with Russia, when he gave the guarantee to Poland, when he honoured it, and when he prosecuted the war half-heartedly. Only when the results of his policy became apparent did it turn against him; which is to say that it turned against its own lethargy of the past seven years. Thereupon the people picked a leader nearer to their mood, Churchill, who was at any rate able to grasp that wars are not won without fighting. Later, perhaps, they will pick another leader who can grasp that only Socialist nations can fight effectively.

Do I mean by all this that England is a genuine democracy? No, not even a reader of the *Daily Telegraph*[21] could quite swallow that.

England is the most class-ridden country under the sun. It is a land of snobbery and privilege, ruled largely by the old and silly. But in any calculation about it one has got to take into account its emotional unity, the tendency of nearly all its inhabitants to feel alike and act together in moments of supreme crisis. It is the only great country in Europe that is not obliged to drive hundreds of thousands of its nationals into exile or the concentration camp. At this moment, after a year of war, newspapers and pamphlets abusing the Government, praising the enemy and clamouring for surrender are being sold on the streets, almost without interference. And this is less from a respect for freedom of speech than from a simple perception that these things don't matter. It is safe to let a paper like *Peace News* be sold, because it is certain that ninety-five per cent of the population will never want to read it. The nation is bound together by an invisible chain. At any normal time the ruling class will rob, mismanage, sabotage, lead us into the muck; but let popular opinion really make itself heard, let them get a tug from below that they cannot avoid feeling, and it is difficult for them not to respond. The left-wing writers who denounce the whole of the ruling class as 'pro-Fascist' are grossly over-simplifying. Even among the inner clique of politicians who brought us to our present pass, it is doubtful whether there were any *conscious* traitors. The corruption that happens in England is seldom of that kind. Nearly always it is more in the nature of self-deception, of the right hand not knowing what the left hand doeth. And being unconscious, it is limited. One sees this at its most obvious in the English Press. Is the

English press honest or dishonest? At normal times it is deeply dishonest. All the papers that matter live off their advertisements, and the advertisers exercise an indirect censorship over news. Yet I do not suppose there is one paper in England that can be straightforwardly bribed with hard cash. In the France of the Third Republic all but a very few of the newspapers could notoriously be bought over the counter like so many pounds of cheese. Public life in England has never been *openly* scandalous. It has not reached the pitch of disintegration at which humbug can be dropped.

England is not the jewelled isle of Shakespeare's much-quoted passage,[22] nor is it the inferno depicted by Dr. Goebbels. More than either it resembles a family, a rather stuffy Victorian family, with not many black sheep in it but with all its cupboards bursting with skeletons. It has rich relations who have to be kow-towed to and poor relations who are horribly sat upon, and there is a deep conspiracy of silence about the source of the family income. It is a family in which the young are generally thwarted and most of the power is in the hands of irresponsible uncles and bedridden aunts. Still, it is a family. It has its private language and its common memories, and at the approach of an enemy it closes its ranks. A family with the wrong members in control – that, perhaps, is as near as one can come to describing England in a phrase.

IV

Probably the battle of Waterloo *was* won on the playing-fields of Eton, but the opening battles of all subsequent wars have been lost there. One of the dominant facts in English life during the past three-quarters of a century has been the decay of ability in the ruling class.

In the years between 1920 and 1940 it was happening with the speed of a chemical reaction. Yet at the moment of writing it is still possible to speak of a ruling class. Like the knife which has had two new blades and three new handles, the upper fringe of English society is still almost what it was in the mid-nineteenth century. After 1832[23] the old landowning aristocracy steadily lost power, but instead of disappearing or becoming a fossil they simply intermarried with the merchants, manufacturers and financiers who had replaced them, and soon turned them into accurate copies of themselves. The wealthy ship-owner or cotton-miller set up for himself an alibi as a country gentleman, while his sons learned the right mannerisms at public schools which had been designed for just that purpose. England was ruled by an aristocracy constantly recruited from parvenus. And considering what energy the self-made men possessed, and considering that they were buying their way into a class which at any rate had a tradition of public service, one might have expected that able rulers could be produced in some such way.

And yet somehow the ruling class decayed, lost its ability, its daring, finally even its ruthlessness, until a time came when stuffed shirts like Eden or Halifax[24] could stand out as men of exceptional talent. As for Baldwin,[25] one could not even dignify him with the name of stuffed shirt. He was simply a hole in the air. The mishandling of England's domestic problems during the nineteen-twenties had been bad enough, but British foreign policy between 1931 and 1939 is one of the wonders of the world. Why? What had happened? What was it that at every decisive moment made every British statesman do the wrong thing with so unerring an instinct?

The underlying fact was that the whole position of the monied class had long ceased to be justifiable. There they sat, at the centre of a vast empire and a world-wide financial network, drawing interest and profits and spending them – on what? It was fair to say that life within the British Empire was in many ways better than life outside it. Still, the Empire was undeveloped, India slept in the Middle Ages, the Dominions lay empty, with foreigners jealously barred out, and even England was full of slums and unemployment. Only half a million people, the people in the country houses, definitely benefited from the existing system. Moreover, the tendency of small businesses to merge together into large ones robbed more and more of the monied class of their function and turned them into mere *owners*, their work being done for them by salaried managers and technicians. For long past there had been in England an entirely functionless class, living on money that was invested they hardly knew where, the 'idle rich', the people whose photographs you can look at in the *Tatler* and the *Bystander*,[26] always supposing that you want to. The existence of these people was by any standard unjustifiable. They were simply parasites, less useful to society than his fleas are to a dog.

By 1920 there were many people who were aware of all this. By 1930 millions were aware of it. But the British ruling class obviously could not admit to themselves that their usefulness was at an end. Had they done that they would have had to abdicate. For it was not possible for them to turn themselves into mere bandits, like the American millionaires, consciously clinging to unjust privileges and beating down opposition by bribery and tear-gas bombs. After all, they belonged to a class with a certain tradition, they had been to public schools where the duty of dying for your country, if necessary, is laid down as the first and greatest of the Commandments. They had to *feel* themselves true patriots, even while they plundered their countrymen. Clearly there was only one escape for them – into stupidity. They could keep society in its existing shape only by being *unable* to grasp that any improvement was possible. Difficult though this was, they achieved it, largely by fixing their eyes on the past and refusing to notice the changes that were going on round them.

There is much in England that this explains. It explains the decay of country life, due to the keeping-up of a sham feudalism which drives the more spirited workers off the land. It explains the immobility of the public schools, which have barely altered since the 'eighties of the last century. It explains the military incompetence which has again and again startled the world. Since the 'fifties [1850s] every war in which England has engaged has started off with a series of disasters, after which the situation has been saved by people comparatively low in the social scale. The higher commanders, drawn from the aristocracy, could never prepare for modern war, because in order to do so they would have had to admit to themselves that the world was changing. They have always clung to obsolete methods and weapons, because they inevitably saw each war as a repetition of the last. Before the Boer War they prepared for the Zulu War, before 1914 for the Boer War, and before the present war for 1914. Even at this moment hundreds of thousands of men in England are being trained with the bayonet, a weapon entirely useless except for opening tins. It is worth noticing that the navy and, latterly, the Air Force, have always been more efficient than the regular army. But the navy is only partially, and the Air Force hardly at all, within the ruling-class orbit.

It must be admitted that so long as things were peaceful the methods of the British ruling class served them well enough. Their own people manifestly tolerated them. However unjustly England might be organized, it was at any rate not torn by class warfare or haunted by secret police. The Empire was peaceful as no area of comparable size has ever been. Throughout its vast extent, nearly a quarter of the earth, there were fewer armed men than would be found necessary by a minor Balkan state. As people to live under, and looking at them merely from a liberal, *negative* standpoint, the British ruling class had their points. They were preferable to the truly modern men, the Nazis and Fascists. But it had long been obvious that they would be helpless against any serious attack from the outside.

They could not struggle against Nazism or Fascism, because they could not understand them. Neither could they have struggled against Communism, if Communism had been a serious force in western Europe. To understand Fascism they would have had to study the theory of Socialism, which would have forced them to realize that the economic system by which they lived was unjust, inefficient and out of date. But it was exactly this fact that they had trained themselves never to face. They dealt with Fascism as the cavalry generals of 1914 dealt with the machine gun – by ignoring it. After years of aggression and massacres, they had grasped only one fact, that Hitler and Mussolini were hostile to Communism. Therefore, it was argued, they *must* be friendly to the British dividend-drawer. Hence the truly frightening spectacle of Conservative M.P.s wildly cheering the news that British ships, bringing food to the Spanish Republican government, had been bombed by Italian aeroplanes. Even when they had begun to grasp that Fascism was dangerous, its essentially revolutionary nature, the huge military effort it was capable of making, the sort of tactics it would use, were quite beyond their comprehension. At the time of the Spanish civil war, anyone with as much political knowledge as can be acquired from a sixpenny pamphlet on Socialism knew that if Franco won, the result would be strategically disastrous for England; and yet generals and admirals who had given their lives to the study of war were unable to grasp this fact. This vein of political ignorance runs right through English official life, through Cabinet ministers, ambassadors, consuls, judges, magistrates, policemen. The policeman who arrests the 'Red' does not understand the theories the 'Red' is preaching; if he did, his own position as bodyguard of the monied class might seem less pleasant to him. There is reason to think that even military espionage is hopelessly hampered by ignorance of the new economic doctrines and the ramifications of the underground parties.

The British ruling class were not altogether wrong in thinking that Fascism was on their side. It is a fact that any rich man, unless he is a Jew, has less to fear from Fascism than from either Communism or democratic Socialism. One ought never to forget this, for nearly the whole of German and Italian propaganda is designed to cover it up. The natural instinct of men like Simon, Hoare,[27] Chamberlain, etc., was to come to an agreement with Hitler. But – and here the peculiar feature of English life that I have spoken of, the deep sense of national solidarity, comes in – they could only do so by breaking up the Empire and selling their own people into semi-slavery. A truly corrupt class would have done this without hesitation, as in France. But things had not gone that distance in England. Politicians who would make cringing speeches about 'the duty of loyalty to our conquerors' are hardly to be found in English public life. Tossed to and fro between their incomes and their principles, it was impossible that men like Chamberlain should do anything but make the worst of both worlds.

One thing that has always shown that the English ruling class are *morally* fairly sound, is that in time of war they are ready enough to get themselves killed. Several dukes, earls and what-not were killed in the recent campaign in Flanders. That could not happen if these people were the cynical scoundrels that they are sometimes declared to be. It is important not to misunderstand their motives, or one cannot predict their actions. What is to be expected of them is not treachery or physical cowardice, but stupidity, unconscious sabotage, an infallible instinct for doing the wrong thing. They are not wicked, or not altogether wicked; they are merely unteachable. Only when their money and power are gone will the younger among them begin to grasp what century they are living in.

V

The stagnation of the Empire in the between-war years affected everyone in England, but it had an especially direct effect upon two important sub-sections of the middle class. One was the military and imperialist middle class, generally nicknamed the Blimps, and the other the left-wing intelligentsia. These two seemingly hostile types, symbolic opposites –

the halfpay colonel with his bull neck and diminutive brain, like a dinosaur, the highbrow with his domed forehead and stalk-like neck – are mentally linked together and constantly interact upon one another; in any case they are born to a considerable extent into the same families.

Thirty years ago the Blimp class was already losing its vitality. The middle-class families celebrated by Kipling, the prolific lowbrow families whose sons officered the army and navy and swarmed over all the waste places of the earth from the Yukon to the Irrawaddy, were dwindling before 1914. The thing that had killed them was the telegraph. In a narrowing world, more and more governed from Whitehall, there was every year less room for individual initiative. Men like Clive, Nelson, Nicholson, Gordon[28] would find no place for themselves in the modern British Empire. By 1920 nearly every inch of the colonial empire was in the grip of Whitehall. Well-meaning, over-civilized men, in dark suits and black felt hats, with neatly-rolled umbrellas crooked over the left forearm, were imposing their constipated view of life on Malaya and Nigeria, Mombasa and Mandalay. The one-time empire-builders were reduced to the status of clerks, buried deeper and deeper under mounds of paper and red tape. In the early 'twenties one could see, all over the Empire, the older officials, who had known more spacious days, writhing impotently under the changes that were happening. From that time onwards it has been next door to impossible to induce young men of spirit to take any part in imperial administration. And what was true of the official world was true also of the commercial. The great monopoly companies swallowed up hosts of petty traders. Instead of going out to trade adventurously in the Indies one went to an office stool in Bombay or Singapore. And life in Bombay or Singapore was actually duller and safer than life in London. Imperialist sentiment remained strong in the middle class, chiefly owing to family tradition, but the job of administering the Empire had ceased to appeal. Few able men went east of Suez if there was any way of avoiding it.

But the general weakening of imperialism, and to some extent of the whole British morale, that took place during the nineteen-thirties, was partly the work of the left-wing intelligentsia, itself a kind of growth that had sprouted from the stagnation of the Empire.

It should be noted that there is now no intelligentsia that is not in some sense 'Left'. Perhaps the last right-wing intellectual was T. E. Lawrence.[29] Since about 1930 everyone describable as an 'intellectual' has lived in a state of chronic discontent with the existing order. Necessarily so, because society as it was constituted had no room for him. In an Empire that was simply stagnant, neither being developed nor falling to pieces, and in an England ruled by people whose chief asset was their stupidity, to be 'clever' was to be suspect. If you had the kind of brain that could understand the poems of T. S. Eliot or the theories of Karl Marx, the higher-ups would see to it that you were kept out of any important job. The intellectuals could find a function for themselves only in the literary reviews and the left-wing political parties.

The mentality of the English left-wing intelligentsia can be studied in half a dozen weekly and monthly papers. The immediately striking thing about all these papers is their generally negative, querulous attitude, their complete lack at all times of any constructive suggestion. There is little in them except the irresponsible carping of people who have never been and never expect to be in a position of power. Another marked characteristic is the emotional shallowness of people who live in a world of ideas and have little contact with physical reality. Many intellectuals of the Left were flabbily pacifist up to 1935, shrieked for war against Germany in the years 1935–9, and then promptly cooled off when the war started. It is broadly though not precisely true that the people who were most 'anti-Fascist' during the Spanish civil war are most defeatist now. And underlying this is the really important fact about so many of the English intelligentsia – their severance from the common culture of the country.

In intention, at any rate, the English intelligentsia are Europeanized. They take their cookery from Paris and their opinions from Moscow. In the general patriotism of the country they form a sort of island of dissident thought. England is perhaps the only great country whose intellectuals are ashamed of their own nationality. In left-wing circles it is always felt that there is something slightly disgraceful in being an Englishman and that it is a duty to snigger at every English institution, from horse-racing to suet puddings. It is a strange fact, but it is unquestionably true, that almost any English intellectual would feel more ashamed of standing to attention during 'God save the King' than of stealing from a poor box. All through the critical years many left-wingers were chipping away at

English morale, trying to spread an outlook that was sometimes squashily pacifist, sometimes violently pro-Russian, but always anti-British. It is questionable how much effect this had, but it certainly had some. If the English people suffered for several years a real weakening of morale, so that the Fascist nations judged that they were 'decadent' and that it was safe to plunge into war, the intellectual sabotage from the Left was partly responsible. Both the *New Statesman* and the *News Chronicle* cried out against the Munich settlement, but even they had done something to make it possible. Ten years of systematic Blimp-baiting affected even the Blimps themselves and made it harder than it had been before to get intelligent young men to enter the armed forces. Given the stagnation of the Empire the military middle class must have decayed in any case, but the spread of a shallow Leftism hastened the process.

It is clear that the special position of the English intellectuals during the past ten years, as purely *negative* creatures, mere anti-Blimps, was a by-product of ruling-class stupidity. Society could not use them, and they had not got it in them to see that devotion to one's country implies 'for better, for worse'. Both Blimps and highbrows took for granted, as though it were a law of nature, the divorce between patriotism and intelligence. If you were a patriot you read *Blackwood's Magazine*[30] and publicly thanked God that you were 'not brainy'. If you were an intellectual you sniggered at the Union Jack and regarded physical courage as barbarous. It is obvious that this preposterous convention cannot continue. The Bloomsbury highbrow, with his mechanical snigger, is as out of date as the cavalry colonel. A modern nation cannot afford either of them. Patriotism and intelligence will have to come together again. It is the fact that we are fighting a war, and a very peculiar kind of war, that may make this possible.

VI

One of the most important developments in England during the past twenty years has been the upward and downward extension of the middle class. It has happened on such a scale as to make the old classification of society into capitalists, proletarians and petit-bourgeois (small property-owners) almost obsolete.

England is a country in which property and financial power are concentrated in very few hands. Few people in modern England *own* anything at all, except clothes, furniture and possibly a house. The peasantry have long since disappeared, the independent shopkeeper is being destroyed, the small business-man is diminishing in numbers. But at the same time modern industry is so complicated that it cannot get along without great numbers of managers, salesmen, engineers, chemists and technicians of all kinds, drawing fairly large salaries. And these in turn call into being a professional class of doctors, lawyers, teachers, artists, etc., etc. The tendency of advanced capitalism has therefore been to enlarge the middle class and not to wipe it out as it once seemed likely to do.

But much more important than this is the spread of middle-class ideas and habits among the working class. The British working class are now better off in almost all ways than they were thirty years ago. This is partly due to the efforts of the Trade Unions, but partly to the mere advance of physical science. It is not always realized that within rather narrow limits the standard of life of a country can rise without a corresponding rise in real-wages. Up to a point, civilization can lift itself up by its boot-tags. However unjustly society is organized, certain technical advances are bound to benefit the whole community, because certain kinds of goods are necessarily held in common. A millionaire cannot, for example, light the streets for himself while darkening them for other people. Nearly all citizens of civilized countries now enjoy the use of good roads, germ-free water, police protection, free libraries and probably free education of a kind. Public education in England has been meanly starved of money, but it has nevertheless improved, largely owing to the devoted efforts of the teachers, and the habit of reading has become enormously more widespread. To an increasing extent the rich and the poor read the same books, and they also see the same films and listen to the same radio programmes. And the differences in their way of life have been diminished by the mass-production of cheap clothes and improvements in housing. So far as outward appearance goes, the clothes of rich and poor, especially in the case of women, differ far less than they did thirty or even fifteen years ago. As to housing, England still has slums which are a blot on civilization, but much building has been done during the past ten years, largely by the local authorities. The modern Council house, with its bathroom and electric light, is smaller than the stockbroker's villa, but it is recognizably the same kind of house, which the farm labourer's cottage is not. A person who has grown up in a Council housing estate is likely to be – indeed, visibly *is* – more middle class in outlook than a person who has grown up in a slum.

The effect of all this is a general softening of manners. It is enhanced by the fact that modern industrial methods tend always to demand less muscular effort and therefore to leave people with more energy when their day's work is done. Many workers in the light industries are less truly manual labourers than is a doctor or a grocer. In tastes, habits, manners and outlook the working class and the middle class are drawing together. The unjust distinctions remain, but the real differences diminish. The old-style 'proletarian' – collarless, unshaven and with muscles warped by heavy labour – still exists, but he is constantly decreasing in numbers; he only predominates in the heavy-industry areas of the north of England.

After 1918 there began to appear something that had never existed in England before: people of indeterminate social class. In 1910 every human being in these islands could be 'placed' in an instant by his clothes, manners and accent. That is no longer the case. Above all, it is not the case in the new townships that have developed as a result of cheap motor cars and the southward shift of industry. The place to look for the germs of the future England is in the light-industry areas and along the arterial roads. In Slough, Dagenham, Barnet, Letchworth, Hayes – everywhere, indeed, on the out-skirts of great towns – the old pattern is gradually changing into something new. In those vast new wildernesses of glass and brick the sharp distinctions of the older kind of town, with its slums and mansions, or of the country, with its manor-houses and squalid cottages, no longer exist. There are wide gradations of income, but it is the same kind of life that is being lived at different levels, in labour-saving flats or Council houses, along the concrete roads and in the naked democracy of the swimming-pools. It is a rather restless, cultureless life, centring round tinned food, *Picture Post*,[31] the radio and the internal combustion engine. It is a civilization in which children grow up with an intimate knowledge of magnetoes and in complete ignorance of the Bible. To that civilization belong the people who are most at home in and most definitely *of* the modern world, the technicians and the higher-paid skilled workers, the airmen and their mechanics, the radio experts, film producers, popular journalists and industrial chemists. They are the indeterminate stratum at which the older class distinctions are beginning to break down.

This war, unless we are defeated, will wipe out most of the existing class privileges. There are every day fewer people who wish them to continue. Nor need we fear that as the pattern changes life in England will lose its peculiar flavour. The new red cities of Greater London[32] are crude enough, but these things are only the rash that accompanies a change. In whatever shape England emerges from the war, it will be deeply tinged with the characteristics that I have spoken of earlier. The intellectuals who hope to see it Russianized or Germanized will be disappointed. The gentleness, the hypocrisy, the thoughtlessness, the reverence for law and the hatred of uniforms will remain, along with the suet puddings and the misty skies. It needs some very great disaster, such as prolonged subjugation by a foreign enemy, to destroy a national culture. The Stock Exchange will be pulled down, the horse plough will give way to the tractor, the country houses will be turned into children's holiday camps, the Eton and Harrow match[33] will be forgotten, but England will still be England, an everlasting animal stretching into the future and the past, and, like all living things, having the power to change out of recognition and yet remain the same.

1. The June Purge, or Night of the Long Knives, led to the execution, without trial, of Hitler's close friend Ernst Röhm, head of the SA (Sturmabteilung; the Brownshirts), and seventy-three leading Nazis, plus many others, prompted initially by Göring and Himmler, later by Hitler, in June 1934. The intention was to cut the power of the SA and win the support of the army.

2. Orwell's title specifies England. Here he seems to be confusing the population of England with that of the United Kingdom. The 1931 Census showed the population of England *and Wales* to be 39,950,000; that of Scotland, 4,843,000; and Northern Ireland's was estimated at 1,243,000: a total of 46,038,000. The population of England and Wales only reached 46,000,000 at the 1961 Census. But see Section III, paragraphs 1 and 2.

3. Hitler said of himself, 'I go the way that Providence dictates with the assurance of a sleepwalker' (speech at Munich, 15 March 1936, after Germany reoccupied the Rhineland; Alan Bullock, *Hitler: a Study in Tyranny* (Penguin, 1962), ch. 7, section 1, 375).

4. Soldiers (in the days before they wore khaki).

5. Orwell is not quite correct. He overlooks, for example, 'A Ballad of Waterloo' by Thomas Hood (1799–1845), a poem sardonic in words and illustration. Byron wrote a notable, and anthologized, poem, 'The Eve of Waterloo'.

6. Orwell is indirectly referring to the poem by Charles Wolfe (1791–1823), 'The Burial of Sir John Moore after Corunna', much anthologized and often set, in the first decades of the

twentieth century, for schoolboys to learn. Its sixth line was beloved by schoolboys of generations past: 'The sods with their bayonets turning'.

7. 'The Charge of the Light Brigade' (1855) by Alfred, Lord Tennyson (1809–92). At the Battle of Balaclava (26 September 1854), in the Crimean War, this misdirected charge led to the deaths of 247 of the 673 who took part.

8. After the fall of France to the Germans in 1940, a French government under Marshal Pétain was established at Vichy. It worked on the principle (as Orwell puts it later on) of having 'the duty of loyalty to our conquerors'. Henri Philippe Pétain (1856–1951) had successfully defended Verdun in 1916; he became a national hero and, in 1918, was created Marshal of France. He led the Vichy government until the end of the war and was then tried for collaboration with the Nazis and sentenced to death. President de Gaulle commuted his sentence to solitary confinement for life.

9. For Orwell's review of *Walls Have Mouths*, see above. He reviewed *Jail Journey* in June 1940; see XII/*629*.

10. A familiar theme, especially after the publication of Benjamin Disraeli's novel, *Sybil, or The Two Nations* (1845). See the first item in *Orwell and the Dispossessed* in this series.

11. Orwell refers to reaction to British (and Allied) intervention in Russia following the October 1917 Revolution. Attempts were made to support anti-Bolshevik forces (the 'Whites') but were badly managed. A British force sent to Vladivostock, led by Colonel Ward, Labour MP for Stoke, was so unsuited to its task that it was ridiculed as 'The Hernia Battalion' (Orlando Figes, *A People's Tragedy* (1996), 573–5, 651). An indication of the unpopularity of this intervention was the very serious dissent – even mutiny – in the Royal Navy on several occasions affecting operations in the Black Sea, the Baltic and Northern Russia. For example, the 6th Battalion, the Royal Marines, refused to advance and threw down its weapons; 87 men were court-martialled; 13 were sentenced to death (commuted to five years' penal servitude) and 71 to penal servitude of two to five years (commuted to six months). Ratings at Sheerness and Devonport refused to sail, in part for their not being paid war allowances (as were soldiers), despite the deaths of 127 men, and in part because of unpopularity of war with the Bolsheviks. British troops at Reval, French sailors at Odessa and American soldiers and sailors at Archangel also refused duty. For fuller details and sources, see Anthony Carew, *The Lower Deck of the Royal Navy, 1900–39* (1981), 110–13 and 238.

12. William Richard Morris (1877–1953; Viscount Nuffield) was largely responsible for the establishment of an automobile-manufacturing industry in Cowley, Oxford, following the success of his Morris-Oxford car in 1913. He devoted much of his wealth to philanthropic purposes.

13. Baron Montagu Norman (1871–1950) was Governor of the Bank of England, 1920–44. He was decorated for service in the Boer War. For Orwell's grouping of him with those who supported Fascism, see 'Looking Back on the Spanish War', *Orwell and Spain* in this series and XIII/*1421*.

14. Anthony Eden (1897–1977; Earl of Avon, 1961), Conservative politician. Foreign Secretary, 1935–8; he resigned in protest at Chamberlain's policy of appeasement. In 1940 he became Secretary of State for War and then Foreign Secretary until 1945, Prime Minister, 1955–7, but resigned following Britain's disastrous involvement in the Suez Canal Zone, 1956. The Local Defence Volunteers were later renamed the Home Guard.

15. Pierre Laval (1883–1945) served variously as French Minister of Public Works, Justice,

Labour, Colonies and Foreign Affairs, and as Prime Minister, 1931–2, 1935–6. He left the Socialist Party in 1920 and moved to the extreme right. On 7 January 1935, as Foreign Minister, he signed an agreement with Mussolini backing Italian claims to Abyssinia (Ethiopia). After the fall of France he became a prominent member of the Vichy government and provided French labour for work in German war production. His name became synonymous with treacherous collaboration. After the war, he attempted suicide but was tried and executed. Vidkun Quisling (1887–1945), Norwegian Fascist who led the puppet government of Norway under the Germans, was executed for treason. His name has been applied generally to collaborators.

16. Judges 16:9.

17. On 6 October 1931, following the devaluation of the pound and the mutiny of the Atlantic Fleet at Invergordon in September, the Labour Government called a General Election for 27 October. Labour was decisively defeated, its number of MPs being cut from 288 to 52. A National Government took office, with the Labour leader, Ramsay MacDonald (1866–1937), as Prime Minister, but with most of his party in opposition.

18. The story of the Gadarene swine is told in three Gospels: Matthew, Mark and Luke. Jesus cast out an unclean spirit who said his name was Legion, 'for we are many', from a man possessed who 'met him out of the tombs'. The spirits 'entered into the swine' which 'ran violently down a steep place into the sea' (of Galilee), where they drowned (Mark 5:2, 9, 13).

19. Neville Chamberlain (1869–1940) served several times as a Conservative Minister and was Chancellor of the Exchequer. He became Prime Minister in 1937; he was associated with the appeasement of Hitler and has been frequently castigated for that. Nevertheless, Eileen Blair's reaction at the time is worth noting: 'It's very odd to feel that Chamberlain is our only hope . . . certainly the man has courage' (XI/206). Chamberlain did initiate Britain's rearmament after the Munich Agreement (see next note). Following the failure of the Norwegian Campaign in April 1940, he resigned but then served under the new Prime Minister, Winston Churchill.

20. In September 1938, Sudeten Germans in the areas of Czechoslovakia bordering on Germany demanded reunification with Germany. The Czechs resisted but the French and British governments urged the Czechs to accede. Hitler called a conference at Munich attended by Czech, French and British representatives, Neville Chamberlain being one. As a result of the Munich Agreement, the Czechs were forced to give in and war was temporarily averted.

21. Half of the extracts abstracted by Orwell for his Diary of Events Leading Up to the War were taken from the *Daily Telegraph*.

22. Orwell refers to John of Gaunt's speech in *Richard II* in which he eulogizes England; England he describes as a 'precious stone set in the silver sea' (II.i.46).

23. The Reform Act of 1832 abolished 'rotten' boroughs and allowed for increased and more-fairly distributed representation. In the main, it benefited the middle class, but was the start of more thoroughgoing reforms. However, a secret ballot was not to come about for another forty years.

24. Lord Halifax (1881–1959), Edward Frederick Lindley Wood (Lord Irwin, 1925; 3rd Viscount Halifax, 1934; Earl of Halifax, 1944) was a Conservative politician; Viceroy of India, 1926–31; Foreign Secretary, 1938–40. The Labour Party representatives told R. A.

Butler that Halifax would be preferred as Chamberlain's successor as Prime Minister but the Party would accept Churchill (see n. 19). On Churchill's appointment he served as Ambassador to the United States, 1941–6.

25. Stanley Baldwin (1867–1947; Earl Baldwin, 1937) was Conservative Prime Minister three times, 1923–4, 1924–9 and 1935–7. He successfully negotiated the crisis occasioned by the abdication of King Edward VIII, but is generally blamed for Britain's failure to prepare adequately for the Second World War.

26. Fashionable 'society' magazines: the *Tatler* was founded in 1901 and amalgamated with the *Bystander* (founded 1903) in November 1940.

27. Sir John Simon (1873–1954; Viscount Simon, 1940) entered Parliament as a Liberal in 1906 and was instrumental in forming the National Liberal Party in 1931; Foreign Secretary 1931–5; Home Office, 1935–7; Chancellor of the Exchequer, 1937–40; Lord Chancellor, 1940–45. He sought to avoid entanglements on the Continent. Sir Samuel Hoare (1880–1959; Viscount Templewood, 1944), Conservative; Foreign Secretary June to December 1935, resigning because of opposition to his plans for settling the Abyssinian crisis. In June 1936 he became First Lord of the Admiralty and later Home Secretary. He supported the Munich Agreement and fell with Chamberlain in May 1940. He then became British Ambassador to Spain, negotiating the release of some 30,000 Allied prisoners and refugees from Spanish gaols.

28. John Nicholson (1821–1857), soldier and administrator, played an important role in the Indian Mutiny, 1857; he effected the Relief of Delhi but was mortally wounded after leading an assault on the Kashmir Gate. Robert Clive (1725–74) first worked as a clerk for the East India Company in Madras but later served in its army. He destroyed French power in India. His culminating victory was at Plassey (1757), which he took as the title of the barony conferred on him. He was twice Governor of Bengal and brought Calcutta, Behar and Orissa under British control. Although he fought corruption he was himself charged with corruption when he returned to England in 1767. He was acquitted but committed suicide. Charles George Gordon (1833–85) fought with distinction in the Crimean War (1854–6) and the Chinese Wars of 1859–60 and 1863–4 becoming known as 'Chinese Gordon'. He was Governor of Egyptian Sudan, 1874–6 and 1877–80, where he tried to abolish the slave trade. He was killed at Khartoum when the city was besieged by the Mahdi. Although a relief column was despatched, it arrived too late, held back by government procrastination, leading to fierce protests in England.

29. 'Lawrence of Arabia' (1888–1935) led the Arab Revolt against the Turks, 1916–18; see his *Seven Pillars of Wisdom* (1922; eight copies [*sic*]); abridged as *Revolt in the Desert* (1927).

30. *Blackwood's Magazine* (1817–1980) was a monthly founded in Edinburgh. It was affectionately known as 'the Maga'.

31. Founded by Edward Hulton, 1 October 1938, *Picture Post* ran until 1 June 1957. Its marriage of illustrations, captions and text, coupled with its social and political concerns, especially in its early days, showed how effectively popular interests could be aroused in serious issues.

32. Presumably new towns, such as Welwyn Garden City, founded in 1919.

33. An annual cricket match held at Lord's Cricket Ground – a 'society' event.

[2099]

Review of The English People *by D. W. Brogan*

The Listener, *27 May 1943*

This is a book written about England but at America, and in consequence slightly defiant in tone. Professor Brogan[1] was evidently travelling in the United States during the bad period of the summer and autumn of 1942,[2] and quite obviously he is perturbed by the fact that many Americans neither like us nor know anything about us. He is anxious to explain things and perhaps, in some cases, to explain them away. And apart from the Americans, he is also to some extent writing against the English literary intelligentsia, whose sneers have to be braved by anyone speaking a good word for England, and even against certain other minority groups, as his title implies: for it is almost a political act nowadays to use the word England instead of bowing to the noisy minority who want it called Britain.

How does Professor Brogan present us? The general build-up is of an unthinking but very gentle and civilised people, obstinate in adversity, snobbish but fairly neighbourly, inefficient but with sound instincts and therefore capable of avoiding really destructive mistakes. There is no doubt that his picture is broadly true, and in places (especially in the voluminous footnotes) extremely acute. The chapter entitled 'English Religion' does a particularly difficult job with distinction. Naturally, with his eye on the American reader, Professor Brogan spends most of his time in defending the things usually regarded as indefensible – the class system, the convolutions of English democracy, the public schools, India, and such minor matters as Sabbatarianism and the dreary ugliness of English towns. Some of what he says needed saying, though from time to time, with American susceptibilities in mind, he probably says things that he does not really believe – for example, that Britain's rule in India is likely to have come to an end 'long before the second centenary of Plassey'.[3] His defence of the monarchy as an institution is well worth reading, though perhaps he does not emphasise sufficiently the part played by hereditary monarchs in canalising and neutralising emotions which would otherwise attach themselves to real rulers with genuine powers for evil.

Witty and even exciting as this book is, it is a little spoiled by the ghostly American reader who seems to haunt every page and who forces Professor Brogan to drag in an American analogy wherever one can be plausibly said to exist. Inevitably one finds oneself appraising the book for its propaganda as well as its literary value, and this raises the question: does propaganda of this type ever make any real difference? As far as one can judge from the American press, pro-British and anti-British sentiment in the United States are constants, or at any rate are little affected by what is said and done in this country. The most one can do in the way of propaganda is to supply the pro-British faction with ammunition, and for that purpose statistics and hard facts generally are of more use than ingenious explanations of why the public-school system is not such a bad thing after all. Or on the other hand, if one is going to hit back at Britain's enemies in the United States – and Professor Brogan appears to be doing this in a few passages – any attempt to defend British institutions is useless; it would be far better to counter on *tu-quoque*[4] lines with remarks about the American negroes, etc. To say this is not to belittle Professor Brogan's book as a book. It is most stimulating reading, the kind of book with which one can violently agree or violently disagree at almost every page. But its value is chiefly for Englishmen or for Americans who have a general knowledge of its subject matter already. In propaganda, even more than in chess and war, it is a good rule that attack is the best defence, and a book so essentially defensive as this will not make many converts among the disciples of Colonel Lindbergh[5] or Father Coughlin.[6]

1. Dennis William Brogan (1900–1974; Kt., 1963), Scottish-born historian; he became Professor of Political Science, University of Cambridge, in 1963. He was best known for his books on America, including *The American Political System* (1933), *The American Problem* (1944, which Orwell reviewed, XVI/*2551*) and *The American Character* (1956).

2. The war went very badly for the United Kingdom in 1942. Reverses included the fall of Singapore in February, the Eighth Army driven back to El Alamein, all but four of thirty-three ships of convoy PQ-17 lost en route for Archangel owing to confusion in orders, and a disastrous raid on Dieppe entailing heavy losses in August. Elsewhere, Jews suffered terribly in the 'clearance' of the Warsaw Ghetto by the SS. However, at the very end of the year, General Montgomery's troops won a great victory at El Alamein, US troops landed in North Africa, and, in January 1943, the Germans surrendered at Stalingrad.

3. Brogan was right; Robert Clive was victorious at Plassey, Bengal, in 1757; British rule in India ended in 1948.

4. So are you!

5. Charles A. Lindbergh (1902–74), became a hero following his making the first solo

non-stop flight across the Atlantic in 1927. He was very active in opposing US involvement in World War II. However, after the Japanese attack on Pearl Harbor on 7 December 1941, his attitude changed and he saw active duty in the Pacific.

6. Father Charles E. Coughlin (1891–1979), born and educated in Canada, became a Roman Catholic priest, and achieved prominence through his radio broadcasts in the 1930s. As early as 1934, when he founded the National Union for Social Justice, he argued that the US was being manipulated by Britain into involvement in a European war. In his War-time Diary for 18 April 1942, Orwell refers to his magazine, *Social Justice*, which expressed near-Fascist views. Its circulation by mail was forbidden in the US because it contravened the Espionage Act. It ceased publication in 1942, the year Coughlin was silenced by his ecclesiastical superiors.

[2422]

Extract from 'As I Please', 12 ['A home of their own']

Tribune, *18 February 1944*

Orwell contributed to Tribune *on a couple of dozen occasions from 8 March 1940, but from 29 November 1943 to 4 April 1947 he was a regular contributor (with some breaks in order to concentrate on other activities). Initially Orwell served as literary editor. One of his principal contributions was a series of personal columns, 'As I Please', of which he wrote eighty. The title had been used briefly by Raymond Postgate (1896–1971; editor of* Tribune, *1940–41, an economist and a writer on food and wine) for a short series in the journal* Controversy *in 1939. The use of this title was suggested to Orwell by his friend Jon Kimche (1909–94). Kimche and Orwell worked together at Booklovers' Corner in Hampstead (see* X/*212); he went to Spain to meet Orwell, and he became acting editor and editor of* Tribune, *1942–6. See* Remembering Orwell, *54–6, 88–9, 94–5, 139–41, 215.*

After the war there is going to be a severe housing shortage in this country, and we shall not overcome it unless we resort to prefabrication. If we stick to our traditional building methods the necessary houses will take decades to produce, and the discomfort and misery that this will lead to, the patching-up of blitzed premises and filthy slums, the rent rackets and overcrowding, are easy to foresee. So are the effects of a housing shortage on our already perilous birthrate. Meanwhile not only prefabrication, but any large, concerted effort at rehousing, has powerful vested interests working against it. The building societies, and the brick and cement trades, are directly involved, and the whole principle of private ownership in land is threatened. How could you rebuild London, for instance, on a sane plan without disregarding private property rights? But the people who traffic in bugs and basements are not going to come out into the open and say clearly what they are fighting for. By far their best card is the Englishman's sentimental but partly justified yearning for a 'home of his own'. They will play this card over and over again, and it is up to us to counter it before it takes effect.

To begin with, prefabrication does not mean – as people are already beginning to fear that it means – that we shall all be forced to live in ugly, cramped, flimsy and unhomelike chicken houses. The thing that ought to be pointed out in this connection is that existing English houses are for the most part very badly built. They are not built to withstand either heat or cold, they are lacking in cupboards, their water pipes are so placed as to ensure that they will burst every time there is a hard frost, and they have no convenient means of rubbish-disposal. All these problems, which a speculative builder will tell you are insoluble, are easily solved in various other countries. If we tackled our rehousing problem boldly we could get rid of discomforts which have come to be accepted like the weather, but are in fact quite unnecessary. We could get rid of 'blind back' houses,[1] basements, geysers,[2] filth-collecting gas stoves, offices where the light of day never penetrates, outdoor w.c.s, uncleanable stone sinks, and other miseries. We could put a bath in every house and install bells that actually ring, plugs that pull at the first attempt, waste-pipes that don't get blocked by a spoonful of tea-leaves. We could even, if we chose, make our rooms relatively easy to clean by streamlining them and making the corners curved instead of rectangular. But all this depends on our being able to build houses rapidly, by mass-production. Failing that, the housing shortage will be so desperate that we shall have to 'make do' with every mouse-ridden ruin that remains, and encourage the speculative builder to do his worst as well.

Secondly, the dislike of flats will somehow have to be exorcised. If people are going to live in big towns they must either live in flats or put up with overcrowding: there is no way out of that. A big block of flats, covering only an acre or two of ground, will contain as many people as live in a small country town, and give them as much room-space as they would have in houses. Rebuild London in big blocks of flats, and there could be light and air for everybody, and room for green spaces, allotments, playgrounds. People could live out of the noise of the traffic, children would not grow up in a world of bricks and dustbins, and historic buildings like St. Paul's would be visible again instead of being swamped by seas of yellow brick.

Yet it is notorious that people, especially working-class people, don't like flats. They want a 'home of their own'. In a sense they are right, for it is true that in most blocks of working-class flats there isn't the privacy and freedom that you can get in a private house. They are not built to be noise-proof, the people who dwell in them are often burdened by nagging restrictions, and they are often quite unnecessarily uncomfortable. The first blocks built definitely as working-class flats did not even have baths. Even now they seldom have lifts, and they usually have stone stairs, which means that one lives in an endless clattering of boots. Much of this arises from the half-conscious conviction, so powerful in this country, that working-class people must not be made too comfortable. Deafening noise and irritating restrictions are not inherent in the nature of flats, and we ought to insist on that. For the feeling that four rooms are 'your own' if they are on the ground, and not 'your own' if they are in mid-air – and it is especially strong in women with children – is going to be a big obstacle in the way of replanning, even in areas where the Germans have already done the necessary clearance work.

1. See Orwell's description of 'blind back' houses, *The Road to Wigan Pier*, p. 92 [*CW*, V/51].

2. A metal cylinder containing cold water which was then heated by gas jets lighted below it. Early versions, especially when aged, were likely to explode on occasion.

[2439]

Review of The Way of a Countryman *by Sir William Beach Thomas*

Manchester Evening News, *23 March 1944*

It is uncertain whether the general public would think of Sir William Beach Thomas primarily as a war correspondent or as a naturalist,[1] but he is in no doubt about the matter himself. The world, as he sees it, really centres round the English village, and round the trees and hedges of that village rather than the houses and the people.

In a long life he has travelled to every corner of the earth and met everyone from George Meredith to Marshal Pétain, and from Frank Harris to Theodore Roosevelt, but a glimpse of a bittern in the East Anglian marches, a grizzly in the Canadian rockies, a twelve-pound trout in New Zealand, means more to him than any merely human celebrity.

Even the Battle of the Somme is chiefly memorable to him because, amid the tremendous roar of the opening bombardment, he saw a grey shrike for the first time.

This book is, in some sort, an autobiography, but it is only fair to give prospective readers the warning, 'If you don't like "nature books" keep away.'

Sir William's memories begin some time in the early seventies in a little village in the Shires, where his father was rector, and 'four species of animal provided the bulk of our amusements . . . ponies, dogs, rabbits and foxes'.

Later, he was to break records for the quarter-mile at Shrewsbury and Oxford, spend busy week-ends with Lord Northcliffe,[2] and 'cover' the Ruhr during the lamentable days of the French occupation, but none of it is so vivid to him as the memory of that village childhood.

'What a number of "necessities of life" we did without. We had no bicycles, of course, no motor-cars, no telephones, no wireless, no gramophone, no preserved fruit – except some repulsive dried apples – no tomatoes, no bananas, no keyless watches,[3] and few games . . . We journeyed to the nearest town, nine miles away, by pony, whose feet churned up inches of white dust.'

And, needless to say, Sir William preferred it like that, including the absence of games, for though a born athlete he rightly objects to the 'tyranny' of games, which was just beginning to become operative in his boyhood.

Sir William describes himself throughout as a 'countryman', but for his purposes 'the country' means sport, bird-watching and botanising rather than agriculture, and his book raises certain doubts about the whole of this class of literature.

There is no question that a love of what is loosely called 'nature' – a kingfisher flashing down a stream, a bullfinch's mossy nest, the caddis-flies in the ditch – is very widespread in England, cutting across age-groups and even class-distinctions, and attaining in some people an almost mystical intensity.

Whether it is a healthy symptom is another matter. It arises partly from the small size, equable climate and varied scenery of England, but it is also probably bound up with the decay of English agriculture. Real rustics are not conscious of being picturesque, they do not construct bird sanctuaries, they are uninterested in any plant or animal that does not affect them directly.

In many languages all the smaller birds are called by the same name. Even in England a genuine farm labourer usually thinks that a frog and a toad are the same thing, and nearly always believes that all snakes are poisonous and that they sting with their tongues.[4]

The fact is that those who really have to deal with nature have no cause to be in love with it. On the East Anglian coast the older cottages for the fishermen are built with their backs to the sea. The sea is simply an enemy from the fisherman's point of view.

Sir William's comparatively sentimental attitude towards the land is shown by the fact that he regrets the war-time destruction of the rabbit. Probably he would also regret the extermination of that even deadlier enemy of agriculture, the pheasant.

'Nature' books are a growth of the past two hundred years. The first and probably still the best of them is Gilbert White's *Natural History of Selborne.*[5]

Sir William couples with this Izaak Walton's *Compleat Angler*, written a century earlier,[6] but Walton's more limited and utilitarian book does not seem quite to belong in this category.

The most characteristic 'nature writers' of all are W. H. Hudson,[7] and

Richard Jefferies.[8] One may guess that it is on Jefferies that Sir William Beach Thomas has modelled himself. But Jefferies, for all his charm and his detailed observation, is curiously inhuman. His daydream expressed in a whole book was of an England from which the human beings had vanished and only the wild creatures remained.

The same outlook is implied in W. H. Hudson, whose only successful novel, *Green Mansions*, has a heroine who is half human and half bird. Hudson also wrote a whole rapturous essay on the spectacle of a field ruined by dandelions.

Nature-worship carried to this length is inherently anti-social. The more normal attitude is expressed by Crabbe, a true countryman, who wrote at least one diatribe against wild-flowers, which in his eyes were simply weeds.[9] Needless to say, Sir William does not much approve of Crabbe.

Sir William started his journalist career at about the same time as Shaw, Barrie, Max Beerbohm and J. L. Garvin.[10] That was in the bustling days when Northcliffe had just started the *Daily Mail*, and the journalistic reminiscences are probably the best thing in this book.

The war of 1914–18 is hardly mentioned, though it is interesting to learn that for the first year or two the whole British Press was only allowed to send five correspondents to the front, and these were as far as possible prevented from seeing anything.

The book ends with a plea for the preservation and revival of rural England, with which everyone can agree even while suspecting that Sir William's ideal picture of rural England might contain too many rabbits and not enough tractors.

1. William Beach Thomas (1868–1957; Kt., 1920), journalist and author, wrote on country matters from about 1898 until shortly before he died. He was a prolific author, and *The Way of a Countryman* was his second volume of autobiography, *Traveller in News* (1925) being the first. He proved an outstanding war correspondent in France for the *Daily Mail* (for which he had written a column on country life) and published *With the British on the Somme* in 1917. In 1918 he was sent to the US and met, among others, President Woodrow Wilson, Theodore Roosevelt and Henry Ford.

2. Lord Northcliffe (Alfred Harmsworth; 1865–1922) introduced popular journalism to the United Kingdom with the *Daily Mail* in 1896. He acquired *The Times* in 1908. His brother, Harold (1868–1940; Viscount Rothermere), himself a newspaper proprietor, took control of the *Daily Mail* when Northcliffe died.

3. A self-winding wrist watch, such as the Rotary, was wound up by movements of the wrist and arm.
4. R. V. Walton accused Orwell of lacking a knowledge of nature in a letter to the *Manchester Evening News*, 29 March 1944. To state that farm labourers confused frogs and toads and thought all snakes poisonous and that they stung with their tongues 'proves beyond doubt that Mr Orwell's natural history field is very limited'. He also disagreed that the pheasant was a deadlier enemy to agriculture than the rabbit and pointed out that the pheasant more than made up for the small amount of seed it ate by the large number of insects it consumed.
5. Gilbert White (1720–93), curate of Selborne, Hampshire, and naturalist. His *Natural History and Antiquities of Selborne* was published in 1789. The Selborne Society was founded in his memory in 1885.
6. Izaak Walton (1593–1683) was an ironmonger by trade but a keen fisherman by inclination. He published a number of biographies, including one of his friend John Donne (1640), and his discourse on fishing, *The Compleat Angler, or The Contemplative Man's Recreation*, in 1653. Fishing was Orwell's favourite pastime. See *Coming Up for Air*, VII/70–87 and especially 76: 'There's a kind of peacefulness even in the names of English coarse fish. Roach, rudd, dace, bleak, barbel, bream, gudgeon, pike, chub, carp, tench. They're solid kind of names. The people who made them up hadn't heard of machine-guns, they didn't live in terror of the sack or spend their time eating aspirins, going to the pictures and wondering how to keep out of the concentration camp.' All these names do go back to the Middle Ages except 'rudd', which enters the written language in 1606. Most of these fish appear in *Mrs Beeton's Book of Household Management* (1861).
7. William Henry Hudson (1841–1922) was born of American parents in South America but came to England in 1869. Most of his writings depict English life, notably *A Shepherd's Life* (1910), which describes Wiltshire country life. *Green Mansions* (1904) is set in the South American forests.
8. Richard Jefferies (1848–87), novelist and nature writer, who drew much of his inspiration from his home county, Wiltshire.
9. Orwell may have had in mind George Crabbe's condemnation of thistles, poppies, blue bugloss, slimy mallow and 'clasping tares', 'Rank weeds, that every art and care defy, / Reign o'er the land, and rob the blighted rye.' Crabbe asks of the impoverished peasant, 'Can poets soothe you' with 'tinsel trappings of poetic pride . . . when you pine for bread?', *The Village* (1783), from I, 48–76.
10. George Bernard Shaw (1856–1950), dramatist and polemicist; he worked as a journalist, music critic (as 'Corno de Bassetto') and theatre critic from 1885. Sir James Barrie (1860–1937), a dramatist (e.g. *Quality Street* (1901), *The Admirable Crichton* (1902) and *Peter Pan* (1904)) who began his working life as a journalist (see *When a Man's Single*, 1888). Sir Max Beerbohm (1872–1956) published his first book when he was twenty-four, under the ironic title *The Works of Max Beerbohm.* He succeeded Shaw as dramatic critic of the *Saturday Review* in 1898. Perhaps his best-remembered book is *Zuleika Dobson* (1911). J. L. Garvin (1868–1947) was a right-wing editor of the *Observer*, 1908–42.

[2455]

Review of Cricket Country *by Edmund Blunden*[1]

Manchester Evening News, *20 April 1944*

Cricket arouses strong feelings, both 'for' and 'against', and during recent years it is the anti-cricket school that has been in the ascendant. Cricket has been labelled the Sport of Blimps. It has been vaguely associated with top hats, school prize days, fox-hunting, and the poems of Sir Henry Newbolt.[2] It has been denounced by Left-wing writers, who imagine erroneously that it is played chiefly by the rich.

On the other hand, its two bitterest enemies of all are 'Beachcomber' and 'Timothy Shy',[3] who see in it an English institution which they feel it their duty to belittle, along with Wordsworth, William Blake and Parliamentary government. But there are other reasons besides spite and ignorance for the partial decline in the popularity of cricket, and some of them can be read between the lines of Mr. Blunden's apologia, eloquent though it is.

Mr Blunden is a true cricketer. The test of a true cricketer is that he shall prefer village cricket to 'good' cricket. Mr. Blunden's own form, one guesses, is somewhere midway between the village green and the county ground, and he has due reverence for the famous figures of the cricketing world, whose names pepper his pages. He is old enough to have seen Ranjitsinhji play his famous leg glide,[4] and since then he has watched first-class matches regularly enough to have seen every well-known player, English or Australian. But it is obvious that all his friendliest memories are of village cricket: and not even cricket at the country-house level, where white trousers are almost universal and a pad on each leg is *de rigueur*, but the informal village game, where everyone plays in braces, where the blacksmith is liable to be called away in mid-innings on an urgent job, and sometimes, about the time when the light begins to fail, a ball driven for four kills a rabbit on the boundary.

In his love of cricket Mr. Blunden is in good literary company. He could, he says, almost make up an eleven of poets and writers. It would include Byron (who played for Harrow), Keats, Cowper, Trollope, Francis Thompson, Gerard Manley Hopkins, Robert Bridges and Siegfried Sassoon. Mr. Blunden might have included Blake, one of whose fragments mentions an incident all too common in village cricket, but he is perhaps wrong to number Dickens among the lovers of cricket, for Dickens's only reference to the game (in *Pickwick Papers*) shows that he was ignorant of its rules. But the essential thing in this book, as in nearly everything that Mr. Blunden writes, is his nostalgia for the golden age before 1914, when the world was peaceful as it has never since been.

The well-known lines from one of his poems:

> I have been young and now am not too old,
> And I have seen the righteous man forsaken,
> His wealth, his honour, and his quality taken:
> This is not what we were formerly told[5]

sound as though they had been written after the dictators had swallowed Europe. Actually, however, they refer to the war of 1914–18, the great turning-point of Mr. Blunden's life. The war shattered the leisurely world he had known, and, as he sadly perceives, cricket has never been quite the same since.

Several things have combined to make it less popular. To begin with, the increasing hurry and urbanisation of life are against a game which needs green fields and abundant spare time. Then there is the generally-admitted dullness of first-class cricket. Like nearly everyone else, Mr. Blunden abhors the kind of game in which 20 successive maiden overs are nothing unusual and a batsman may be in for an hour before he scores his first run. But they are the natural result of too-perfect grass and a too-solemn attitude towards batting averages. Then again cricket has been partly supplanted, at any rate among grown-up people, by golf and lawn tennis. There can be no doubt that this is a disaster for these games are not only far inferior aesthetically to cricket but they do not have the socially binding quality that cricket, at any rate, used to have.

Contrary to what its detractors say, cricket is not an inherently snobbish game, as Mr. Blunden is careful to point out. Since it needs about 25 people to make up a game it necessarily leads to a good deal of social mixing. The inherently snobbish game is golf, which causes whole stretches of country-side to be turned into carefully-guarded class preserves.

But there is another good reason for the decline in the popularity of cricket – a reason Mr. Blunden does not point out, the extent to which it has been thrust down everybody's throat. For a long period cricket was treated as though that were a kind of religious ritual incumbent on every Englishman. Interminable Test matches with their astronomical scores were given large headlines in most newspapers, and every summer tens of thousands of unwilling boys were – and still are – drilled in a game which merely bored them. For cricket has the peculiarity that either you like it or you don't, and either you have a gift for it, or you have not. Unlike most games, it cannot be learned if you have no talent to start with. In the circumstances there was bound to be a large-scale revolt against cricket.

Even by children it is now less played than it was. It was most truly rooted in the national life when it was voluntary and informal – as in the Rugby of Tom Brown's schooldays, or in the village matches on lumpy wickets, which are Mr. Blunden's most cherished memory.

Will cricket survive? Mr. Blunden believes so, in spite of the competition from other interests that it has to face, and we may hope that he is right. It is pleasant to find him, towards the end of his book, still finding time for a game or two during the war, against R.A.F. teams. This book touches on much else besides cricket, for at the bottom of his heart it is perhaps less the game itself than the physical surroundings that appeals to Mr. Blunden. He is the kind of cricketer who when his side is batting is liable to stroll away from the pavilion to have a look at the village church, and perhaps come across a quaint epitaph.

In places this book is a little over-written, because Mr. Blunden is no more able to resist a quotation than some people are to refuse a drink. But it is pleasant reading, and a useful reminder that peace means something more than a temporary stoppage of the guns.

1. Edmund Charles Blunden (1896–1974), poet and scholar. He was awarded the Hawthornden Prize in 1922 for his volume of poems *The Shepherd*, and the Benson Medal of the Royal Society of Literature in 1931. From 1924 to 1927 he was Professor of English Literature at Tokyo University. For some years after 1931 he was Fellow and Tutor in English Literature at Merton College, Oxford. Blunden served in World War I and was awarded the Military Cross. His experiences are memorably recalled in *Undertones of War* (1928). He made several broadcasts to India for Orwell. After World War II he became Professor of English, University of Hong Kong, and then Professor of Poetry, University of Oxford, 1966–8; he resigned owing to ill health. In addition to publishing much poetry, he edited the work of

others, including John Clare, Bret Harte, Christopher Smart, Leigh Hunt, William Collins and Wilfred Owen, and wrote biographies of Leigh Hunt, Lamb, Shelley and Keats. *Cricket Country* (1944) was published in the same series as Orwell's *The English People*, see below.
2. For Newbolt, see n. 11 to 'My Country Right or Left', above.
3. The 'Beachcomber' column in the *Daily Express* was started by D. B. Wyndham Lewis (1891–1969) and continued from 1924 by J. B. Morton (1893–1979), a fellow Roman Catholic. Wyndham Lewis then contributed a column as 'Timothy Shy' to the *News Chronicle*. Both authors produced a fair amount of comic and nonsense writing, but both also wrote biographies and Morton wrote fiction. Orwell made a number of pejorative references to them. In his Wigan Pier Diary for 27 February 1936 (X/*287*), he refers to 'the [G. K.] Chesterton-Beachcomber type of writer' who is 'always in favour of private ownership and against Socialist legislation and "progress" generally'. This he typified as 'The Roman Catholic ideal'. See also p. 170, above.
4. Maharaja Shri Ranjitsinhji Vibhaji, Maharaja Jam Saheb of Nawanagar (1872–1933), Indian prince and equally distinguished cricketer. He was a particularly elegant batsman, famed, as Orwell says, for his leg glide.
5. The first stanza of 'Report on Experience'.

[2475]

The English People

The English People, *published in 1947, was commissioned in September 1943 by W. J. Turner (1869–1946), Collins's General Editor for the series 'Britain in Pictures' and also at that time literary editor of* The Spectator. *Orwell evidently completed his text by 22 May 1944, because he entered it in his Payments Book against that date with the note, 'Payment to be made later'.*

*In a letter to Leonard Moore of 23 June 1945 (*XVII / *2682) asking him to chase Collins for payment, Orwell describes the book as 'a piece of propaganda for the British Council' – the idea for the series actually emanated from the Ministry of Information – and states that Collins had wanted him to make changes to his text but he had refused to do so. Orwell recorded in his Payments Book that he received an advance of £20 on 14 July 1945. He wrote to Moore, also on 14 July 1947, outlining the hesitant progress of the book's production – he had corrected the proofs a year ago – and asking him to find out what was happening (*XIX / *3248).* The English People *was published the following month, with some references updated, because publication had been so long delayed, and with twenty-five illustrations,* eight of which were full-page colour plates. These were selected by the publisher; W. J. Turner may have vetted the final selection. All were modern, two-thirds of them having been drawn or painted between 1940 and 1946 by artists including Edward Ardizzone, Dame Laura Knight, L. S. Lowry, Henry Moore and Feliks Topolski. Although Orwell probably played no part in the selection, John Minton's 'Hop Picking near Maidstone, Kent', 1945, might have been chosen with him in mind.

The long delay in publication, the association with propaganda, and the alterations made to update the text (almost certainly without Orwell's knowledge or consent – Collins did not even bother to tell Orwell the book was about to be published, hence his letter to his agent on 14 July 1947 asking what was happening), may have led to Orwell stating in his Notes for his Literary Executors that he did not wish the book to be reprinted (see p. 251, above). However, it is an attractive book and has become increasingly in demand. Collins printed 23,118 copies: 18,275 were sold, 316 remaindered, the rest were unsold. The series, 'Britain in Pictures' published 126 volumes and, in its day, The English People was the sixty-first most popular (James Fisher's The Birds of Britain was the most popular, selling 84,218 copies). By the end of the century it had become the most costly volume secondhand. (See Michael Carney, Britain in Pictures: A History and Bibliography (1995), 37, 65, 107, 121–3.) In Orwell's lifetime there were Danish and German translations.

No typescript has survived, nor can amendments introduced by Collins be always identified precisely. Some are doubtless innocuous (e.g., the reference to the 1945 election, p. 305, below), but letters have come to light since the Complete Works was published – from Lord David Cecil (1902–86; CH, 1949; Professor of English Literature, Oxford, 1948–69), who was on the advisory committee for the series, to W. J. Turner protesting strongly that the book should be rejected. He thought Orwell was using the series as 'a platform for political debate' and that this 'factious and inaccurate pamphlet only blackens England's reputation'. He said he spent much time participating in the then popular BBC radio series 'The Brains Trust', 'refuting precisely the attack, he, Orwell, makes' (undated letter, CW, 2nd edn, XV / 2278A). It is not known whether Cecil's objections led to changes being covertly made. Orwell's attitude, rather than Cecil's, seems to have worn better.

ENGLAND AT FIRST GLANCE

In peacetime, it is unusual for foreign visitors to this country to notice the existence of the English people. Even the accent referred to by Americans as 'the English accent' is not in fact common to more than a quarter of the population. In cartoons in Continental papers England is personified by an aristocrat with a monocle, a sinister capitalist in a top hat, or a spinster in a Burberry. Hostile or friendly, nearly all the generalisations that are made about England base themselves on the property-owning class and ignore the other forty-five million.

But the chances of war brought to England, either as soldiers or as refugees, hundreds of thousands of foreigners who would not normally have come here, and forced them into intimate contact with ordinary people. Czechs, Poles, Germans and Frenchmen to whom 'England' meant Piccadilly and the Derby found themselves quartered in sleepy East Anglian villages, in northern mining towns, or in the vast working-class areas of London whose names the world had never heard until they were blitzed. Those of them who had the gift of observation will have seen for themselves that the real England is not the England of the guide-books. Blackpool is more typical than Ascot, the top hat is a moth-eaten rarity, the language of the B.B.C. is barely intelligible to the masses. Even the prevailing physical type does not agree with the caricatures, for the tall, lanky physique which is traditionally English is almost confined to the upper classes: the working classes, as a rule, are rather small, with short limbs and brisk movements, and with a tendency among the women to grow dumpy in early middle life.

It is worth trying for a moment to put oneself in the position of a foreign observer, new to England, but unprejudiced, and able because of his work to keep in touch with ordinary, useful, unspectacular people. Some of his generalisations would be wrong, because he would not make enough allowance for the temporary dislocations resulting from war. Never having seen England in normal times, he might underrate the power of class distinctions, or think English agriculture healthier than it is, or be too much impressed by the dinginess of the London streets or the prevalence of drunkenness. But with his fresh eyes he would see a great deal that a native observer misses, and his probable impressions are worth tabulating. Almost certainly he would find the salient characteristics of the English common people to be artistic insensibility, gentleness, respect for legality, suspicion of foreigners, sentimentality about animals, hypocrisy, exaggerated class distinctions, and an obsession with sport.

As for our artistic insensibility, ever-growing stretches of beautiful countryside are ruined by planless building, the heavy industries are allowed to convert whole counties into blackened deserts, ancient monuments are wantonly pulled down or swamped by seas of yellow brick, attractive vistas are blocked by hideous statues to nonentities – and all this without any *popular* protest whatever. When England's housing problem is discussed, its aesthetic aspect simply does not enter the mind of the average man. Nor is there any widespread interest in any of the arts, except perhaps music. Poetry, the art in which above all others England has excelled, has for more than a century had no appeal whatever for the common people. It is only acceptable when – as in some popular songs and mnemonic rhymes – it is masquerading as something else. Indeed the very word 'poetry' arouses either derision or embarrassment in ninety-eight people out of a hundred.

Our imaginary foreign observer would certainly be struck by our gentleness: by the orderly behaviour of English crowds, the lack of pushing and quarrelling, the willingness to form queues, the good temper of harassed, overworked people like bus conductors. The manners of the English working class are not always very graceful, but they are extremely considerate. Great care is taken in showing a stranger the way, blind people can travel across London with the certainty that they will be helped on and off every bus and across every street. In wartime a few of the policemen carried revolvers, but England has nothing corresponding to the *gendarmerie*, the semi-military police living in barracks and armed with rifles (sometimes even with tanks and aeroplanes) who are the guardians of society all the way from Calais to Tokyo. And except for certain well-defined areas in half a dozen big towns there is very little crime or violence. The average of honesty is lower in the big towns than in the country, but even in London the newsvendor can safely leave his pile of pennies on the pavement while he goes for a drink. The prevailing gentleness of manners is a recent thing, however. Well within living memory it was impossible for a smartly dressed person to walk down

Ratcliff Highway[1] without being assaulted, and an eminent jurist, asked to name a typically English crime, could answer: 'Kicking your wife to death'.

There is no revolutionary tradition in England, and even in extremist political parties, it is only the middle-class membership that thinks in revolutionary terms. The masses still more or less assume that 'against the law' is a synonym for 'wrong'. It is known that the criminal law is harsh and full of anomalies and that litigation is so expensive as always to favour the rich against the poor: but there is a general feeling that the law, such as it is, will be scrupulously administered, that a judge or magistrate cannot be bribed, that no one will be punished without trial. An Englishman does not believe in his bones, as a Spanish or Italian peasant does, that the law is simply a racket. It is precisely this general confidence in the law that has allowed a good deal of recent tampering with Habeas Corpus to escape public notice. But it also causes some ugly situations to end peacefully. During the worst of the London blitz the authorities tried to prevent the public from using the Tube stations as shelters. The people did not reply by storming the gates, they simply bought themselves penny-halfpenny tickets: they thus had legal status as passengers, and there was no thought of turning them out again.

The traditional English xenophobia is stronger among the working class than the middle class. It was partly the resistance of the Trade Unions that prevented a really large influx of refugees from the fascist countries before the war, and when the German refugees were interned in 1940, it was not the working class that protested. The difference in habits, and especially in food and language, makes it very hard for English working people to get on with foreigners. Their diet differs a great deal from that of any European nation, and they are extremely conservative about it. As a rule they will refuse even to sample a foreign dish, they regard such things as garlic and olive oil with disgust, life is unlivable to them unless they have tea and puddings. And the peculiarities of the English language make it almost impossible for anyone who has left school at fourteen to learn a foreign language after he has grown up. In the French Foreign Legion, for instance, the British and American legionaries seldom rise out of the ranks, because they cannot learn French, whereas a German learns French in a few months. English working people, as a rule, think it effeminate even to pronounce a foreign word correctly. This is bound up with the fact that the upper classes learn foreign languages as a regular part of their education. Travelling abroad, speaking foreign tongues, enjoying foreign food, are vaguely felt to be upper-class habits, a species of snobbery, so that xenophobia is reinforced by class jealousy.

Perhaps the most horrible spectacles in England are the Dogs' Cemeteries in Kensington Gardens, at Stoke Poges (it actually adjoins the churchyard where Gray wrote his famous *Elegy*) and at various other places. But there were also the Animals' A.R.P.[2] Centres, with miniature stretchers for cats, and in the first year of the war there was the spectacle of Animal Day being celebrated with all its usual pomp in the middle of the Dunkirk evacuation. Although its worst follies are committed by the upper-class women, the animal cult runs right through the nation and is probably bound up with the decay of agriculture and the dwindled birthrate. Several years of stringent rationing have failed to reduce the dog and cat population, and even in poor quarters of big towns the bird fanciers' shops display canary seed at prices ranging up to twenty-five shillings a pint.

Hypocrisy is so generally accepted as part of the English character that a foreign observer would be prepared to meet with it at every turn, but he would find especially ripe examples in the laws dealing with gambling, drinking, prostitution and profanity. He would find it difficult to reconcile the anti-imperialistic sentiments which are commonly expressed in England with the size of the British Empire. If he were a continental European he would notice with ironical amusement that the English think it wicked to have a big army but see nothing wrong in having a big navy. This too he would set down as hypocrisy – not altogether fairly, for it is the fact of being an island, and therefore not needing a big army, that has allowed British democratic institutions to grow up, and the mass of the people are fairly well aware of this.

Exaggerated class distinctions have been diminishing over a period of about thirty years, and the war has probably speeded up the process, but newcomers to England are still astonished and sometimes horrified by the blatant differences between class and class. The great majority of the people can still be 'placed' in an instant by their manners, clothes and general appearance. Even the physical type differs considerably, the upper classes being on an average several inches taller than the working class. But the most striking difference of all is in language and accent. The English working class, as Mr. Wyndham Lewis has put it, are 'branded on the tongue'. And though class distinctions do not exactly coincide with economic distinctions, the contrast between wealth and poverty is very much more glaring, and more taken for granted, than in most countries.

The English were the inventors of several of the world's most popular games, and have spread them more widely than any other product of their culture. The word 'football' is mispronounced by scores of millions who have never heard of Shakespeare or Magna Carta. The English themselves are not outstandingly good at all games, but they enjoy playing them, and to an extent that strikes foreigners as childish they enjoy reading about them and betting on them. During the between-war years the football pools did more than any other one thing to make life bearable for the unemployed. Professional footballers, boxers, jockeys and even cricketers enjoy a popularity that no scientist or artist could hope to rival. Nevertheless sport-worship is not carried to quite such imbecile lengths as one would imagine from reading the popular press. When the brilliant lightweight boxer, Kid Lewis,[3] stood for Parliament in his native borough, he only scored a hundred and twenty-five votes.

These traits that we have enumerated are probably the ones that would strike an intelligent foreign observer first. Out of them he might feel that he could construct a reliable picture of the English character. But then probably a thought would strike him: is there such a thing as 'the English character'? Can one talk about nations as though they were individuals? And supposing that one can, is there any genuine continuity between the England of today and the England of the past?

As he wandered through the London streets, he would notice the old prints in the bookshop windows, and it would occur to him that if these things are representative, then England must have changed a great deal. It is not much more than a hundred years since the distinguishing mark of English life was its brutality. The common people, to judge by the prints, spent their time in an almost unending round of fighting, whoring, drunkenness and bull-baiting. Moreover, even the physical type appears to have changed. Where are they gone, the hulking draymen and low-browed prize-fighters, the brawny sailors with their buttocks bursting out of their white trousers, and the great overblown beauties with their swelling bosoms, like the figure-heads of Nelson's ships? What had these people in common with the gentle-mannered, undemonstrative, law-abiding English of today? Do such things as 'national cultures' really exist?

This is one of those questions, like the freedom of the will or the identity of the individual, in which all the arguments are on one side and instinctive knowledge is on the other. It is not easy to discover the connecting thread that runs through English life from the sixteenth century onwards, but all English people who bother about such subjects feel that it exists. They feel that they understand the institutions that have come to them out of the past – Parliament, for instance, or sabbatarianism, or the subtle grading of the class system – with an inherited knowledge impossible to a foreigner. Individuals, too, are felt to conform to a national pattern. D. H. Lawrence is felt to be 'very English', but so is Blake; Dr. Johnson and G. K. Chesterton are somehow the same kind of person. The belief that we resemble our ancestors – that Shakespeare, say, is more like a modern Englishman than a modern Frenchman or German – may be unreasonable, but by existing it influences conduct. Myths which are believed in tend to become true, because they set up a type, or 'persona', which the average person will do his best to resemble.

During the bad period of 1940 it became clear that in Britain national solidarity is stronger than class antagonism. If it were really true that 'the proletarian has no country', 1940 was the time for him to show it. It was exactly then, however, that class feeling slipped into the background, only reappearing when the immediate danger had passed. Moreover, it is probable that the stolid behaviour of the British town populations under the bombing was partly due to the existence of the national 'persona' – that is, to their preconceived idea of themselves. Traditionally the Englishman is phlegmatic, unimaginative, not easily rattled: and since that is what he thinks he ought to be, that is what he tends to become. Dislike of hysteria and 'fuss', admiration for stubbornness, are all but universal in England, being shared by everyone except the intelligentsia. Millions of English people willingly accept as their national emblem the bulldog, an animal noted for its obstinacy, ugliness and impenetrable stupidity. They have a remarkable readiness to admit that foreigners are more 'clever' than themselves, and yet they feel that it would be an outrage against the laws of God and Nature for England to be ruled by foreigners. Our imaginary observer would notice, perhaps, that Wordsworth's sonnets during the Napoleonic war might almost have been written during this one. He would know already that England has produced poets and scientists rather than philosophers, theologians or pure theorists of any description. And he might end by deciding that a profound, almost unconscious patriotism and an inability to think logically are the abiding features of the English character, traceable in English literature from Shakespeare onwards.

THE MORAL OUTLOOK OF THE ENGLISH PEOPLE

For perhaps a hundred and fifty years, organised religion, or conscious religious belief of any kind, have had very little hold on the mass of the English people. Only about ten per cent of them ever go near a place of worship except to be married and buried. A vague theism and an intermittent belief in life after death are probably fairly widespread, but the main Christian doctrines have been largely forgotten. Asked what he meant by 'Christianity', the average man would define it wholly in ethical terms ('unselfishness', or 'loving your neighbour', would be the kind of definition he would give). This was probably much the same in the early days of the Industrial Revolution, when the old village life had been suddenly broken up and the Established Church had lost touch with its followers. But in recent times the Nonconformist sects have also lost much of their vigour, and within the last generation the Bible-reading which used to be traditional in England has lapsed. It is quite common now to meet with young people who do not know the Bible stories even as *stories.*

But there is one sense in which the English common people have remained more Christian than the upper classes, and probably than any other European nation. This is in their non-acceptance of the modern cult of power-worship. While almost ignoring the spoken doctrines of the Church, they have held on to the one that the Church never formulated, because taking it for granted: namely, that might is not right. It is here that the gulf between the intelligentsia and the common people is widest. From Carlyle onwards, but especially in the last generation, the British intelligentsia have tended to take their ideas from Europe and have been infected by habits of thought that derive ultimately from Machiavelli. All the cults that have been fashionable in the last dozen years, communism, fascism and pacifism, are in the last analysis forms of power-worship. It is significant that in this country, unlike most others, the Marxist version of Socialism has found its warmest adherents in the middle class. Its methods, if not its theories, obviously conflict with what is called '*bourgeois* morality' (i.e., common decency), and in moral matters it is the proletarians who are '*bourgeois*'.

One of the basic folk-tales of the English-speaking peoples is Jack the Giant-killer – the little man against the big man. Mickey Mouse, Popeye the Sailor and Charlie Chaplin are all essentially the same figure. (Chaplin's films, it is worth noticing, were banned in Germany as soon as Hitler came to power, and Chaplin has been viciously attacked by English fascist writers.) Not merely a hatred of bullying, but a tendency to support the weaker side merely because it is weaker, are almost general in England. Hence the admiration for a 'good loser' and the easy forgiveness of failures, either in sport, politics or war. Even in very serious matters the English people do not feel that an unsuccessful action is necessarily futile. An example in the 1939–45 war was the campaign in Greece.[4] No one expected it to succeed, but nearly everyone thought that it should be undertaken. And the popular attitude to foreign politics is nearly always coloured by the instinct to side with the under-dog.

An obvious recent instance was pro-Finnish sentiment in the Russo-Finnish war of 1940.[5] This was genuine enough, as several by-elections fought mainly on this issue showed. Popular feeling towards the U.S.S.R. had been increasingly friendly for some time past, but Finland was a small country attacked by a big one, and that settled the issue for most people. In the American Civil War the British working classes sided with the North – the side that stood for the abolition of slavery – in spite of the fact that the Northern blockade of the cotton ports was causing great hardship in Britain. In the Franco-Prussian war,[6] such pro-French sentiment as there was in England was among the working class. The small nationalities oppressed by the Turks found their sympathisers in the Liberal Party, at that time the party of the working class and the lower middle class. And in so far as it bothered with such issues at all, British mass sentiment was for the Abyssinians against the Italians, for the Chinese against the Japanese, and for the Spanish Republicans against Franco. It was also friendly to Germany during the period when Germany was weak and disarmed, and it is not surprising to see a similar swing of sentiment after the war.

The feeling that one ought always to side with the weaker party probably derives from the balance-of-power policy which Britain has followed from the eighteenth century onwards. A European critic would add that it is humbug, pointing in proof to the fact that Britain herself holds down subject populations in India and elsewhere. We don't, in fact, know what settlement the English common people would make with India if the decision were theirs. All political parties and all newspapers of whatever colour have conspired to prevent them from seeing the issue clearly. We do know, however, that they have sometimes championed the weak against the strong when it was obviously not to their own advantage. The best example is the Irish Civil War. The real weapon of the Irish rebels was British public opinion, which was substantially on their side and prevented the British Government from crushing the rebellion in the only way possible. Even in the Boer War there was a considerable volume of pro-Boer sentiment, though it was not strong enough to influence events. One must conclude that in this matter the English common people have lagged behind their century. They have failed to catch up with power politics, 'realism', *sacro egoismo*[7] and the doctrine that the end justifies the means.

The general English hatred of bullying and terrorism means that any kind of violent criminal gets very little sympathy. Gangsterism on American lines could not flourish in England, and it is significant that the American gangsters have never tried to transfer their activities to this country. At need, the whole nation would combine against people who kidnap babies and fire machine-guns in the street: but even the efficiency of the English police force really depends on the fact that the police have public opinion behind them. The bad side of this is the almost universal toleration of cruel and out-of-date punishments. It is not a thing to be proud of that England should still tolerate such punishments as flogging. It continues partly because of the widespread psychological ignorance, partly because men are only flogged for crimes that forfeit nearly everyone's sympathy. There would be an outcry if it were applied to non-violent crimes, or re-instituted for military offences. Military punishments are not taken for granted in England as they are in most countries. Public opinion is almost certainly opposed to the death penalty for cowardice and desertion, though there is no strong feeling against hanging murderers. In general the English attitude to crime is ignorant and old-fashioned, and humane treatment even of child offenders is a recent thing. Still, if Al Capone[8] were in an English jail, it would not be for evasion of income tax.

A more complex question than the English attitude to crime and violence is the survival of puritanism and the world-famed English hypocrisy.

The English people proper, the working masses who make up seventy-five per cent of the population, are not puritanical. The dismal theology of Calvinism never popularised itself in England as it did for a while in Wales and Scotland. But puritanism in the looser sense in which the word is generally used (that is, prudishness, asceticism, the 'kill-joy' spirit) is something that has been unsuccessfully forced upon the working class by the class of small traders and manufacturers immediately above them. In its origin it had a clear though unconscious economic motive behind it. If you could persuade the working man that every kind of recreation was sinful, you could get more work out of him for less money. In the early nineteenth century there was even a school of thought which maintained that the working man ought not to marry. But it would be unfair to suggest that the puritan moral code was mere humbug. Its exaggerated fear of sexual immorality, which extended to a disapproval of stage plays, dancing, and even bright-coloured clothes, was partly a protest against the real corruption of the later Middle Ages: there was also the new factor of syphilis, which appeared in England about the sixteenth century and worked frightful havoc for the next century or two. A little later there was another new factor in the introduction of distilled liquors – gin, brandy, and so forth – which were very much more intoxicating than the beer and mead which the English had been accustomed to. The 'temperance' movement was a well-meant reaction against the frightful drunkenness of the nineteenth century, product of slum conditions and cheap gin. But it was necessarily led by fanatics who regarded not merely drunkenness but even the moderate drinking of alcohol as sinful. During the past fifty years or so there has even been a similar drive against tobacco. A hundred years ago, or two hundred years ago, tobacco-smoking was much disapproved of, but only on the ground that it was dirty, vulgar and injurious to health: the idea that it is a wicked self-indulgence is modern.

This line of thought has never really appealed to the English masses. At most they have been sufficiently intimidated by middle-class puritanism to take some of their pleasures rather furtively. It is universally agreed that the working classes are far more moral than the upper classes, but the idea that sexuality is wicked in itself has no popular basis. Music-hall jokes, Blackpool postcards and the songs the soldiers make up are anything but puritanical. On the other hand, almost no one in England approves of prostitution. There are several big towns where prostitution is extremely blatant, but it is completely unattractive and has never been really tolerated. It could not be regulated and humanised as it has been in some countries, because every English person feels in his bones that it is wrong. As for the general weakening of sex morals that has happened during the past twenty or thirty years, it is probably a temporary thing, resulting from the excess of women over men in the population.

In the matter of drink, the only result of a century of 'temperance' agitation has been a slight increase in hypocrisy. The practical disappearance of drunkenness as an English vice has not been due to the anti-drink fanatics, but to competing amusements, education, the improvement in industrial conditions and the expensiveness of drink itself. The fanatics have been able to see to it that the Englishman drinks his glass of beer under difficulties and with a faint feeling of wrong-doing, but have not actually been able to prevent him from drinking it. The pub, one of the basic institutions of English life, carries on in spite of the harassing tactics of Nonconformist local authorities. So also with gambling. Most forms of gambling are illegal according to the letter of the law, but they all happen on an enormous scale. The motto of the English people might be the chorus of Marie Lloyd's song, 'A little of what you fancy does you good'.[9] They are not vicious, not even lazy, but they will have their bit of fun, whatever the higher-ups may say. And they seem to be gradually winning their battle against the kill-joy minorities. Even the horrors of the English Sunday have been much mitigated during the past dozen years. Some of the laws regulating pubs – designed in every case to discourage the publican and make drinking unattractive – were relaxed during the war. And it is a very good sign that the stupid rule forbidding children to enter pubs, which tended to dehumanise the pub and turn it into a mere drinking-shop, is beginning to be disregarded in some parts of the country.

Traditionally, the Englishman's home is his castle. In an age of conscription and identity cards this cannot really be true. But the hatred of regimentation, the feeling that your spare time is your own and that a man must not be persecuted for his opinions, is deeply ingrained, and the centralising processes inevitable in wartime, and still enforced, have not destroyed it.

It is a fact that the much-boasted freedom of the British press is theoretical rather than actual. To begin with, the centralised ownership of the press means in practice that unpopular opinions can only be printed in books or in newspapers with small circulations. Moreover, the English people as a whole are not sufficiently interested in the printed word to be very vigilant about this aspect of their liberties, and during the last twenty years there has been much tampering with the freedom of the press, with no real popular protest. Even the demonstrations against the suppression of the *Daily Worker*[10] were probably stage-managed by a small minority. On the other hand, freedom of speech is a reality, and respect for it is almost general. Extremely few English people are afraid to utter their political opinions in public, and there are not even very many who want to silence the opinions of others. In peacetime, when unemployment can be used as a weapon, there is a certain amount of petty persecution of 'reds', but the real totalitarian atmosphere, in which the State endeavours to control people's thoughts as well as their words, is hardly imaginable.

The safeguard against it is partly the respect for integrity of conscience, and the willingness to hear both sides, which can be observed at any public meeting. But it is also partly the prevailing lack of intellectuality. The English are not sufficiently interested in intellectual matters to be intolerant about them. 'Deviations' and 'dangerous thoughts' do not seem very important to them. An ordinary Englishman, Conservative, Socialist, Catholic, Communist, or what not, almost never grasps the full logical implications of the creed he professes: almost always he utters heresies without noticing it. Orthodoxies, whether of the Right or the Left, flourish chiefly among the literary intelligentsia, the people who ought in theory to be the guardians of freedom of thought.

The English people are not good haters, their memory is very short, their patriotism is largely unconscious, they have no love of military glory and not much admiration for great men. They have the virtues and the vices of an old-fashioned people. To twentieth-century political theories they oppose not another theory of their own, but a moral quality which must be vaguely described as decency. On the day in 1936 when the Germans re-occupied the Rhineland I was in a northern mining town. I happened to go into a pub just after this piece of news, which quite obviously meant war, had come over the wireless, and I remarked to the others at the bar, 'The German army has crossed the Rhine.' With a vague air of capping a quotation someone answered, 'Parley-voo.' No more response than that! Nothing will ever wake these people up, I thought. But later in the evening, at the same pub, someone sang a song which had recently come out, with the chorus –

> For you can't do that there 'ere,
> No, you can't do that there 'ere;
> Anywhere else you can do that there,
> But you can't do that there 'ere!

And it struck me that perhaps this was the English answer to fascism. At any rate it is true that it has not happened here, in spite of fairly favourable circumstances. The amount of liberty, intellectual or other, that we enjoy in England ought not to be exaggerated, but the fact that it did not markedly diminish in nearly six years of desperate war is a hopeful symptom.

THE POLITICAL OUTLOOK OF THE ENGLISH PEOPLE

The English people are not only indifferent to fine points of doctrine, but are remarkably ignorant politically. They are only now beginning to use the political terminology which has been current for years in Continental countries. If you asked a random group of people from any stratum of the population to define capitalism, socialism, communism, anarchism, Trotskyism, fascism, you would get mostly vague answers, and some of them would be surprisingly stupid ones.

But they are also distinctly ignorant about their own political system. During recent years, for various reasons, there has been a revival of political activity, but over a longer period the interest in party politics has been dwindling. Great numbers of adult English people have never in their lives bothered to vote in an election. In big towns it is quite common for people not to know the name of their M.P. or what constituency they live in. During the war years, owing to the failure to renew the registers, the young had no votes (at one time no one under twenty-nine had a vote), and did not seem much troubled by the fact. Nor does the anomalous electoral system, which usually favours the Conservative Party, though it happened to favour the Labour Party in 1945, arouse much protest. Attention focuses on policies and individuals (Chamberlain, Churchill, Cripps, Beveridge,[11] Bevin[12]) rather than on parties. The feeling that Parliament really controls events, and that sensational changes are to be expected when a new government comes in, has been gradually fading ever since the first Labour government in 1923.

In spite of many subdivisions, Britain has in effect only two political parties, the Conservative Party and the Labour Party, which between them broadly represent the main interests of the nation. But during the last twenty years the tendency of these two parties has been to resemble one another more and more. Everyone knows in advance that any government, whatever its political principles may be, can be relied upon not to do certain things. Thus, no Conservative government will ever revert to what would have been called Conservatism in the nineteenth century. No Socialist government will massacre the propertied class, nor even expropriate them without compensation. A good recent example of the changing temper of politics was the reception given to the Beveridge Report. Thirty years ago any Conservative would have denounced this as State charity, while most Socialists would have rejected it as a capitalist bribe. In 1944 the only discussion that arose was as to whether it would be adopted in whole or in part. This blurring of party distinctions is happening in almost all countries, partly because everywhere, except, perhaps, in the U.S.A., the drift is towards a planned economy, partly because in an age of power politics national survival is felt to be more important than class warfare. But Britain has certain peculiarities resulting from its being both a small island and the centre of an Empire. To begin with, given the present economic system, Britain's prosperity depends partly on the Empire, while all Left parties are theoretically anti-imperialist. Politicians of the Left are therefore aware – or have recently become aware – that once in power they choose between abandoning some of their principles or lowering the English standard of living. Secondly, it is impossible for Britain to go through the kind of revolutionary process that the U.S.S.R. went through. It is too small, too highly organised, too dependent on imported food. Civil war in England would mean starvation or conquest by some foreign power, or both. Thirdly and most important of all, civil war is not *morally* possible in England. In any circumstances that we can foresee, the proletariat of Hammersmith will not arise and massacre the *bourgeoisie* of Kensington: they are not different enough. Even the most drastic changes will have to happen peacefully and with a show of legality, and everyone except the 'lunatic fringes' of the various political parties is aware of this.

These facts make up the background of the English political outlook. The great mass of the people want profound changes, but they do not want violence. They want to preserve their own standard of living, and at the same time they want to feel that they are not exploiting less fortunate peoples. If you issued a questionnaire to the whole nation, asking, 'What do you want from politics?', the answer would be much the same in the overwhelming majority of cases. Substantially it would be: 'Economic security, a foreign policy which will ensure peace, more social equality and a settlement with India.' Of these, the first is by far the most important, unemployment being an even greater nightmare than war. But few people would think it necessary to mention either capitalism or socialism. Neither word has much emotional appeal. No one's heart beats faster at the thought of nationalising the Bank of England: on the other hand, the old line of talk about sturdy individualism and the sacred rights of property is no longer swallowed by the masses. They know it is not true that 'there's plenty of room at the top', and in any case most of them don't want to get to the top: they want steady jobs and a fair deal for their children.

During the last few years, owing to the social frictions arising out of the war, discontent with the obvious inefficiency of old-style capitalism, and admiration for Soviet Russia, public opinion has moved considerably to the Left, but without growing more doctrinaire or markedly bitterer.

None of the political parties which call themselves revolutionary have seriously increased their following. There are about half a dozen of these parties, but their combined membership, even if one counts the remnants of Mosley's Blackshirts, would probably not amount to 150,000. The most important of them is the Communist Party, but even the Communist Party, after twenty-five years of existence, must be held to have failed. Although it has had considerable influence at moments when circumstances favoured it, it has never shown signs of growing into a mass party of the kind that exists in France or used to exist in pre-Hitler Germany.

Over a long period of years, Communist Party membership has gone up or down in response to the changes in Russian foreign policy. When the U.S.S.R. is on good terms with Britain, the British Communists follow a 'moderate' line hardly distinguishable from that of the Labour Party, and their membership swells to some scores of thousands. When British and Russian policy diverge, the Communists revert to a 'revolutionary' line and membership slumps again. They can, in fact, only get themselves a worthwhile following by abandoning their essential objectives. The various other Marxist parties, all of them claiming to be the true and uncorrupted successors of Lenin, are in an even more hopeless position. The average Englishman is unable to grasp their doctrines and uninterested in their grievances. And in England the conspiratorial mentality which has been developed in police-ridden European countries is a great handicap. English people in large numbers will not accept any creed whose dominant notes are hatred and illegality. The ruthless ideologies of the Continent – not merely communism and fascism, but anarchism, Trotskyism, and even ultra-montane Catholicism – are accepted in their pure form only by the intelligentsia, who constitute a sort of island of bigotry amid the general vagueness. It is significant that English revolutionary writers are obliged to use a bastard vocabulary whose key phrases are mostly translations. There are no native English words for most of the concepts they are dealing with. Even the word 'proletarian', for instance, is not English and the great majority of English people do not know what it means. It is generally used, if at all, to mean simply 'poor'. But even so it is given a social rather than an economic slant and most people would tell you that a blacksmith or a cobbler is a proletarian and that a bank clerk is not. As for the word '*bourgeois*', it is used almost exclusively by people who are of *bourgeois* origin themselves. The only genuinely popular use of the word is as a printer's term.[13] It is then, as one might expect, anglicised and pronounced 'boorjoyce'.

But there is one abstract political term which is fairly widely used and has a loose but well-understood meaning attached to it. This is the word 'democracy'. In a way, the English people do feel that they live in a democratic country. Not that anyone is so stupid as to take this in a literal sense. If democracy means either popular rule or social equality, it is clear that Britain is not democratic. It is, however, democratic in the secondary sense which has attached itself to that word since the rise of Hitler. To begin with, minorities have some power of making themselves heard. But more than this, public opinion cannot be disregarded when it chooses to express itself. It may have to work in indirect ways, by strikes, demonstrations and letters to the newspapers, but it can and visibly does affect government policy. A British government may be unjust, but it cannot be quite arbitrary. It cannot do the kind of thing that a totalitarian government does as a matter of course. One example out of the thousands that might be chosen is the German attack on the U.S.S.R. The significant thing is not that this was made without a declaration of war – that was natural enough – but that it was made without any propaganda build-up beforehand. The German people woke up to find themselves at war with a country that they had been ostensibly on friendly terms with on the previous evening. Our own government would not dare to do such a thing, and the English people are fairly well aware of this. English political thinking is much governed by the word 'They'. 'They' are the higher-ups, the mysterious powers who do things to you against your will. But there is a widespread feeling that 'They', though tyrannical, are not omnipotent. 'They' will respond to pressure if you take the trouble to apply it: 'They' are even removable. And with all their political ignorance the English people will often show surprising sensitiveness when some small incident seems to show that 'They' are overstepping the mark. Hence, in the midst of seeming apathy, the sudden fuss every now and then over a rigged by-election or a too-Cromwellian handling of Parliament.

One thing that is extremely difficult to be certain about is the persistence in England of monarchist sentiment. There cannot be much doubt that at any rate in the south of England it was strong and genuine until the death of King George V. The popular response to the Silver Jubilee in 1935 took the authorities by surprise, and the celebrations had to be prolonged for an extra week. At normal times it is only the richer classes who are overtly royalist: in the West End of London, for instance, people stand to attention for 'God Save the King' at the end of a picture show, whereas in the poorer quarters they walk out. But the affection shown for George V at the Silver Jubilee was obviously genuine, and it was even possible to see in it the survival, or recrudescence, of an idea almost as old as history, the idea of the King and the common people being in a sort of alliance against the upper classes; for example, some of the London slum streets bore during the Jubilee the rather servile slogan 'Poor but Loyal'. Other slogans, however, coupled loyalty to the King with hostility to the landlord, such as 'Long Live the King. Down With the Landlord', or more often, 'No Landlords Wanted' or 'Landlords Keep Away'. It is too early to say whether royalist sentiment was killed outright by the Abdication, but unquestionably the Abdication dealt it a serious blow. Over the past four hundred years it has waxed or waned according to circumstances. Queen Victoria, for instance, was decidedly unpopular during part of her reign, and in the first quarter of the nineteenth century public interest in the Royal Family was not nearly as strong as it was a hundred years later. At this moment the mass of the English people are probably mildly republican. But it may well be that another long reign, similar to that of George V, would revive royalist feeling and make it – as it was between roughly 1880 and 1936 – an appreciable factor in politics.

THE ENGLISH CLASS SYSTEM

In time of war the English class system is the enemy propagandist's best argument. To Dr. Goebbels's charge that England is still 'two nations', the only truthful answer would have been that she is in fact three nations.[14] But the peculiarity of English class distinctions is not that they are unjust – for after all, wealth and poverty exist side by side in almost all countries – but that they are anachronistic. They do not exactly correspond to economic distinctions, and what is essentially an industrial and capitalist country is haunted by the ghost of a caste system.

It is usual to classify modern society under three headings: the upper class, or *bourgeoisie*, the middle class, or *petite bourgeoisie*, and the working class, or proletariat. This roughly fits the facts, but one can draw no useful inference from it unless one takes account of the subdivisions within the various classes and realises how deeply the whole English outlook is coloured by romanticism and sheer snobbishness.

England is one of the last remaining countries to cling to the outward forms of feudalism. Titles are maintained and new ones are constantly created, and the House of Lords, consisting mainly of hereditary peers, has real powers. At the same time England has no real aristocracy. The race difference on which aristocratic rule is usually founded was disappearing by the end of the Middle Ages, and the famous medieval families have almost completely vanished. The so-called old families are those that grew rich in the sixteenth, seventeenth and eighteenth centuries. Moreover, the notion that nobility exists in its own right, that you can be a nobleman even if you are poor, was already dying out in the age of Elizabeth, a fact commented on by Shakespeare. And yet, curiously enough, the English ruling class has never developed into a *bourgeoisie* plain and simple. It has never become purely urban or frankly commercial. The ambition to be a country gentleman, to own and administer land and draw at least a part of your income from rent, has survived every change. So it comes that each new wave of parvenus, instead of simply replacing the existing ruling class, has adopted its habits, intermarried with it, and, after a generation or two, become indistinguishable from it.

The basic reason for this may perhaps be that England is very small and has an equable climate and pleasantly varied scenery. It is almost impossible in England, and not easy even in Scotland, to be more than twenty miles from a town. Rural life is less inherently boorish than it is in bigger countries with colder winters. And the comparative integrity of the British ruling class – for when all is said and done they have not behaved so contemptibly as their European opposite numbers – is probably bound up with their idea of themselves as feudal landowners. This outlook is shared by considerable sections of the middle class. Nearly everyone who can afford to do so sets up as a country gentleman, or at least makes some effort in that direction. The manor-house with its park and its walled gardens reappears in reduced form in the stockbroker's week-end cottage, in the suburban villa with its lawn and herbaceous border, perhaps even in the potted nasturtiums on the window-sill of the

Bayswater flat. This widespread day-dream is undoubtedly snobbish, it has tended to stabilise class distinctions and has helped to prevent the modernisation of English agriculture: but it is mixed up with a kind of idealism, a feeling that style and tradition are more important than money.

Within the middle class there is a sharp division, cultural and not financial, between those who aim at gentility and those who do not. According to the usual classification, everyone between the capitalist and the weekly wage-earner can be lumped together as '*petite bourgeoisie*'. This means that the Harley Street physician, the army officer, the grocer, the farmer, the senior civil servant, the solicitor, the clergyman, the schoolmaster, the bank manager, the speculative builder, and the fisherman who owns his own boat, are all in the same class. But no one in England feels them to belong to the same class, and the distinction between them is not a distinction of income but of accent, manners and, to some extent, outlook. Anyone who pays any attention to class differences at all would regard an army officer with £1,000 a year as socially superior to a shopkeeper with £2,000 a year. Even within the upper class a similar distinction holds good, the titled person being almost always more deferred to than an untitled person of larger income. Middle-class people are really graded according to their degree of resemblance to the aristocracy: professional men, senior officials, officers in the fighting services, university lecturers, clergymen, even the literary and scientific intelligentsia, rank higher than business men, though on the whole they earn less. It is a peculiarity of this class that their largest item of expenditure is education. Whereas a successful tradesman will send his son to the local grammar school, a clergyman with half his income will underfeed himself for years in order to send his son to a public school, although he knows that he will get no direct return for the money he spends.

There is, however, another noticeable division in the middle class. The old distinction was between the man who is 'a gentleman' and the man who is 'not a gentleman'. In the last thirty years, however, the demands of modern industry, and the technical schools and provincial universities, have brought into being a new kind of man, middle class in income and to some extent in habits, but not much interested in his own social status. People like radio engineers and industrial chemists, whose education has not been of a kind to give them any reverence for the past, and who tend to live in blocks of flats or housing-estates where the old social pattern has broken down, are the most nearly classless beings that England possesses. They are an important section of society, because their numbers are constantly growing. The war, for instance, made necessary the formation of an enormous air force, and so you got thousands of young men of working-class origin graduating into the technical middle class by way of the R.A.F. Any serious reorganisation of industry now will have similar effects. And the characteristic outlook of the technicians is already spreading among the older strata of the middle class. One symptom of this is that intermarriage within the middle class is freer than it used to be. Another is the increasing unwillingness of people below the £2,000 a year level to bankrupt themselves in the name of education.

Another series of changes, probably dating from the Education Bill of 1871,[15] is occurring in the working class. One cannot altogether acquit the English working class either of snobbishness or of servility. To begin with there is a fairly sharp distinction between the better-paid working class and the very poor. Even in socialist literature it is common to find contemptuous references to slum-dwellers (the German word *lumpenproletariat* is much used), and imported labourers with low standards of living, such as the Irish, are greatly looked down on. There is also, probably, more disposition to accept class distinctions as permanent, and even to accept the upper classes as natural leaders, than survives in most countries. It is significant that in the moment of disaster the man best able to unite the nation was Churchill, a Conservative of aristocratic origins. The word 'Sir' is much used in England, and the man of obviously upper-class appearance can usually get more than his fair share of deference from commissionaires, ticket-collectors, policemen, and the like. It is this aspect of English life that seems most shocking to visitors from America and the Dominions. And the tendency towards servility probably did not decrease in the twenty years between the two wars: it may even have increased, owing chiefly to unemployment.

But snobbishness is never quite separable from idealism. The tendency to give the upper classes more than their due is mixed up with a respect for good manners and something vaguely describable as culture. In the South of England, at any rate, it is unquestionable that most working-class people want to resemble the upper classes in manners and habits. The traditional attitude of looking down on the upper classes as effeminate and 'la-di-dah' survives best in the heavy-industry areas. Hostile nicknames like 'toff' and 'swell' have almost disappeared, and even the *Daily Worker* displays advertisements for 'High-class Gentleman's Tailor'. Above all, throughout southern England there is almost general uneasiness about the Cockney accent. In Scotland and northern England snobbishness about the local accents does exist, but it is not nearly so strong or widespread. Many a Yorkshireman definitely prides himself on his broad U's and narrow A's, and will defend them on linguistic grounds. In London there are still people who say 'fice' instead of 'face', but there is probably no one who regards 'fice' as superior. Even a person who claims to despise the *bourgeoisie* and all its ways will still take care that his children grow up pronouncing their aitches.

But side by side with this there has gone a considerable growth of political consciousness and an increasing impatience with class privilege. Over a period of twenty or thirty years the working class has grown politically more hostile to the upper class, culturally less hostile. There is nothing incongruous in this: both tendencies are symptoms of the levelling of manners which results from machine civilisation and which makes the English class system more and more of an anachronism.

The obvious class differences still surviving in England astonish foreign observers, but they are far less marked, and far less real, than they were thirty years ago. People of different social origins, thrown together during the war in the armed forces, or in factories or offices, or as firewatchers and Home Guards, were able to mingle more easily than they did in the 1914–18 war. It is worth listing the various influences which – mechanically, as it were – tend to make Englishmen of all classes less and less different from one another.

First of all, the improvement in industrial technique. Every year less and less people are engaged in heavy manual labour which keeps them constantly tired and, by hypertrophying certain muscles, gives them a distinctive carriage. Secondly, improvements in housing. Between the two wars rehousing was done mostly by the local authorities, who have produced a type of house (the council house, with its bathroom, garden, separate kitchen, and indoor w.c.) which is nearer to the stockbroker's villa than it is to the labourer's cottage. Thirdly, the mass production of furniture which in ordinary times can be bought on the hire-purchase system. The effect of this is that the interior of a working-class house resembles that of a middle-class house very much more than it did a generation ago. Fourthly, and perhaps most important of all, the mass production of cheap clothes. Thirty years ago the social status of nearly everyone in England could be determined from his appearance, even at two hundred yards' distance. The working classes all wore ready-made clothes, and the ready-made clothes were not only ill-fitting but usually followed the upper-class fashions of ten or fifteen years earlier. The cloth cap was practically a badge of status. It was universal among the working class, while the upper classes only wore it for golf and shooting. This state of affairs is rapidly changing. Ready-made clothes now follow the fashions closely, they are made in many different fittings to suit every kind of figure, and even when they are of very cheap cloth they are superficially not very different from expensive clothes. The result is that it grows harder every year, especially in the case of women, to determine social status at a glance.

Mass-produced literature and amusements have the same effect. Radio programmes, for instance, are necessarily the same for everybody. Films, though often extremely reactionary in their implied outlook, have to appeal to a public of millions and therefore have to avoid stirring up class antagonisms. So also with some of the big-circulation newspapers. The *Daily Express*, for instance, draws its readers from all strata of the population. So also with some of the periodicals that have appeared in the past dozen years. *Punch* is obviously a middle- and upper-class paper, but *Picture Post* is not aimed at any particular class. And lending libraries and very cheap books, such as the Penguins,[16] popularise the habit of reading and probably have a levelling effect on literary taste. Even taste in food tends to grow more uniform owing to the multiplication of cheap but fairly smart restaurants such as those of Messrs. Lyons.[17]

We are not justified in assuming that class distinctions are actually disappearing. The essential structure of England is still almost what it was in the nineteenth century. But real differences between man and man are obviously diminishing, and this fact is grasped and even welcomed by people who only a few years ago were clinging desperately to their social prestige.

Whatever may be the ultimate fate of the very rich, the tendency of the working class and the middle class is evidently to merge. It may happen quickly or slowly, according to circumstances. It was accelerated by the war, and another ten years of all-round rationing, utility clothes, high income tax and compulsory national service may finish the process once and for all. The final effects of this we cannot foresee. There are observers, both native and foreign, who believe that the fairly large amount of individual freedom that is enjoyed in England depends on having a well-defined class system. Liberty, according to some, is incompatible with equality. But at least it is certain that the present drift *is* towards greater social equality, and that that is what the great mass of the English people desire.

THE ENGLISH LANGUAGE

The English language has two outstanding characteristics to which most of its minor oddities can be finally traced. These characteristics are a very large vocabulary and simplicity of grammar.

If it is not the largest in the world, the English vocabulary is certainly among the largest. English is really two languages, Anglo-Saxon and Norman-French, and during the last three centuries it has been reinforced on an enormous scale by new words deliberately created from Latin and Greek roots. But in addition the vocabulary is made much larger than it appears by the practice of turning one part of speech into another. For example, almost any noun can be used as a verb: this in effect gives an extra range of verbs, so that you have *knife* as well as *stab*, *school* as well as *teach*, *fire* as well as *burn*, and so on. Then again, certain verbs can be given as many as twenty different meanings simply by adding prepositions to them. (Examples are *get out of*, *get up*, *give out*, *take over*.) Verbs can also change into nouns with considerable freedom, and by the use of affixes such as *-y*, *-ful*, *-like*, any noun can be turned into an adjective. More freely than in most languages, verbs and adjectives can be turned into their opposites by means of the prefix *un-*. And adjectives can be made more emphatic or given a new twist by tying a noun to them: for example, *lily-white*, *sky-blue*, *coal-black*, *iron-hard*, etc.

But English is also, and to an unnecessary extent, a borrowing language. It readily takes over any foreign word that seems to fill a need, often altering the meaning in doing so. A recent example is the word *blitz*. As a verb this word did not appear in print till late in 1940, but it has already become part of the language. Other examples from the vast armoury of borrowed words are *garage, charabanc, alias, alibi, steppe, thug, role, menu, lasso, rendezvous, chemise.* It will be noticed that in most cases an English equivalent exists already, so that borrowing adds to the already large stock of synonyms.

English grammar is simple. The language is almost completely uninflected, a peculiarity which marks it off from almost all languages west of China. Any regular English verb has only three inflections, the third person singular, the present participle and the past participle. Thus, for instance, the verb to *kill* consists of *kill, kills, killing, killed*, and that is all. There is, of course, a great wealth of tenses, very much subtilised in meaning, but these are made by the use of auxiliaries which themselves barely inflect. *May, might, shall, will, should, would* do not inflect at all, except in the obsolete second person singular. The upshot is that every person in every tense of such a verb as *to kill* can be expressed in only about thirty words including the pronouns, or about forty if one includes the second person singular. The corresponding number in, for instance, French would be somewhere near two hundred. And in English there is the added advantage that the auxiliaries which are used to make the tenses are the same in every case.

There is no such thing in English as declension of nouns, and there is no gender. Nor are there many irregular plurals or comparatives. Moreover, the tendency is always towards greater simplicity, both in grammar and syntax. Long sentences with dependent clauses grow more and more unpopular, irregular but time-saving formations such as the 'American subjunctive' (*it is necessary that you go* instead of *it is necessary that you should go*) gain ground, and difficult rules, such as the difference between *shall* and *will*, or *that* and *which*, are more and more ignored. If it continues to develop along its present lines English will ultimately have more in common with the uninflected languages of East Asia than with the languages of Europe.

The greatest quality of English is its enormous range not only of meaning but of *tone*. It is capable of endless subtleties, and of everything from the most high-flown rhetoric to the most brutal coarseness. On the other hand, its lack of grammar makes it easily compressible. It is the language of lyric poetry, and also of headlines. On its lower levels it is very easy to learn, in spite of its irrational spelling. It can also for international purposes be reduced to very simple pidgin dialects, ranging from Basic to the 'Bêche-de-mer' English used in the South Pacific.[18] It is therefore well suited to be a world lingua franca, and it has in fact spread more widely than any other language.

But there are also great disadvantages, or at least great dangers, in speaking English as one's native tongue. To begin with, as was pointed out earlier in this book, the English are very poor linguists. Their own language is grammatically so simple that unless they have gone through the discipline of learning a foreign language in childhood, they are often quite unable to grasp what is meant by gender, person and case. A completely illiterate Indian will pick up English far faster than a British soldier will pick up Hindustani. Nearly five million Indians are literate in English and millions more speak it in a debased form. There are some tens of thousands of Indians who speak English as nearly as possible perfectly; yet the number of Englishmen speaking any Indian language perfectly would not amount to more than a few scores. But the great weakness of English is its capacity for debasement. Just because it is so easy to use, it is easy to use *badly*.

To write or even to speak English is not a science but an art. There are no reliable rules: there is only the general principle that concrete words are better than abstract ones, and that the shortest way of saying anything is always the best. Mere correctness is no guarantee whatever of good writing. A sentence like 'an enjoyable time was had by all present' is perfectly correct English, and so is the unintelligible mess of words on an income-tax return. Whoever writes English is involved in a struggle that never lets up even for a sentence. He is struggling against vagueness, against obscurity, against the lure of the decorative adjective, against the encroachment of Latin and Greek, and, above all, against the worn-out phrases and dead metaphors with which the language is cluttered up. In speaking, these dangers are more easily avoided, but spoken English differs from written English more sharply than is the case in most languages. In the spoken tongue every word that can be omitted is omitted, every possible abbreviation is used. Meaning is conveyed quite largely by emphasis, though curiously enough the English do not gesticulate, as one might reasonably expect them to do. A sentence like *No, I don't mean that one, I mean that one* is perfectly intelligible when spoken aloud, even without a gesture. But spoken English, when it tries to be dignified and logical, usually takes on the vices of written English, as you can see by spending half an hour either in the House of Commons or at the Marble Arch.

English is peculiarly subject to jargons. Doctors, scientists, business men, officials, sportsmen, economists and political theorists all have their characteristic perversion of the language, which can be studied in the appropriate magazines from the *Lancet* to the *Labour Monthly*. But probably the deadliest enemy of good English is what is called 'standard English'. This dreary dialect, the language of leading articles, White Papers, political speeches and B.B.C. news bulletins, is undoubtedly spreading: it is spreading downwards in the social scale, and outwards into the spoken language. Its characteristic is its reliance on ready-made phrases – *in due course, take the earliest opportunity, warm appreciation, deepest regret, explore every avenue, ring the changes, take up the cudgels, legitimate assumption, the answer is in the affirmative*, etc. etc. – which may once have been fresh and vivid, but have now become mere thought-saving devices, having the same relation to living English as a crutch has to a leg. Anyone preparing a broadcast or writing a letter to *The Times* adopts this kind of language almost instinctively, and it infects the spoken tongue as well. So much has our language been weakened that the imbecile chatter in Swift's essay on *Polite Conversation* (a satire on the upper-class talk of Swift's own day)[19] would actually be rather a good conversation by modern standards.

This temporary decadence of the English language is due, like so much else, to our anachronistic class system.[20] 'Educated' English has grown anaemic because for long past it has not been reinvigorated from below. The people likeliest to use simple concrete language, and to think of metaphors that really call up a visual image, are those who are in contact with physical reality. A useful word like *bottleneck*, for instance, would be most likely to occur to someone used to dealing with conveyor belts: or again, the expressive military phrase *to winkle out* implies acquaintance both with winkles and with machine-gun nests. And the vitality of English depends on a steady supply of images of this kind. It follows that language, at any rate the English language, suffers when the educated classes lose touch with the manual workers. As things are at present, nearly every Englishman, whatever his origins, feels the working-class manner of speech, and even working-class idioms, to be inferior. Cockney, the most widespread dialect, is the most despised of all. Any word or usage that is supposedly Cockney is looked on as vulgar, even when, as is sometimes the case, it is merely an archaism. An example is *ain't*, which is now abandoned in favour of the much weaker form *aren't*. But *ain't* was good enough English eighty years ago, and Queen Victoria would have said *ain't*.

During the past forty years, and especially the past dozen years, English has borrowed largely from American, while America has shown no tendency to borrow from English. The reason for this is partly political. Anti-British feeling in the United States is far stronger than anti-American feeling in England, and most Americans dislike using a word or phrase which they know to be British. But American has gained a footing in England partly because of the vivid, almost poetic quality of its slang, partly because certain American usages (for instance, the formation of verbs by adding *-ise* to a noun) save time, and most of all because one can adopt an American word without crossing a class barrier. From the English point of view American words have no class label. This applies even to thieves' slang. Words like *stooge* and *stool-pigeon* are considered much less vulgar than words like *nark* and *split*. Even a very snobbish English person would probably not mind calling a policeman a *cop*, which is American, but he would object to calling him a *copper*, which is working-class English. To the working classes, on the other hand, the use of Americanisms is a way of escaping from Cockney without adopting the B.B.C. dialect, which they instinctively dislike and cannot easily master. Hence, especially in the big towns, working-class children now use American slang from the moment that they learn to talk. And there is a noticeable tendency to use American words even when they are not slang and when an English equivalent already exists: for instance, *car* for *tram*, *escalator* for *moving staircase*, *automobile* for *motor-car*.

This process will probably continue for some time. One cannot check it simply by protesting against it, and in any case many American words and expressions are well worth adopting. Some are necessary neologisms, others (for instance, *fall* for *autumn*) are old words which we ought never to have dropped. But it ought to be realised that on the whole American is a bad influence and has already had a debasing effect.

To begin with, American has some of the vices of English in an exaggerated form. The interchangeability of different parts of speech has been carried further, the distinction between transitive and intransitive verbs tends to break down, and many words are used which have no meaning whatever. For example, whereas English alters the meaning of a verb by tacking a preposition on to it, the American tendency is to burden every verb with a preposition that adds nothing to its meaning (*win out, lose out, face up to,* etc.). On the other hand, American has broken more completely than English with the past and with literary traditions. It not only produces words like *beautician, moronic* and *sexualise,* but often replaces strong primary words by feeble euphemisms. For instance, many Americans seem to regard the word *death* and various words that go with it (*corpse, coffin, shroud*) as almost unmentionable. But above all, to adopt the American language wholeheartedly would probably mean a huge loss of vocabulary. For though American produces vivid and witty turns of speech, it is terribly poor in names for natural objects and localities. Even the streets in American cities are usually known by numbers instead of names. If we really intended to model our language upon American we should have, for instance, to lump the lady-bird, the daddy-long-legs, the sawfly, the water-boatman, the cockchafer, the cricket, the death-watch beetle and scores of other insects all together under the inexpressive name of *bug.* We should lose the poetic names of our wild flowers, and also, probably our habit of giving individual names to every street, pub, field, lane, and hillock. In so far as American is adopted, that is the tendency. Those who take their language from the films, or from papers such as *Life* and *Time,* always prefer the slick time-saving word to the one with a history behind it. As to accent, it is doubtful whether the American accent has the superiority which it is now fashionable to claim for it. The 'educated' English accent, a product of the last thirty years, is undoubtedly very bad and is likely to be abandoned, but the average English person probably speaks as clearly as the average American. Most English people blur their vowel sounds, but most Americans swallow their consonants. Many Americans pronounce, for instance, *water* as though it had no T in it, or even as though it had no consonant in it at all, except the w. On the whole we are justified in regarding the American language with suspicion. We ought to be ready to borrow its best words, but we ought not to let it modify the actual structure of our language.

However, there is no chance of resisting the American influence unless we can put new life into English itself. And it is difficult to do this while words and idioms are prevented from circulating freely among all sections of the population. English people of all classes now find it natural to express incredulity by the American slang phrase *sez you.* Many would even tell you in good faith that *sez you* has no English equivalent. Actually it has a whole string of them – for instance, *not half, I don't think, come off it, less of it, and then you wake up,* or simply *garn.* But most of these would be considered vulgar: you would never find an expression like *not half* in a *Times* leader, for instance. And on the other hand, many necessary abstract words, especially words of Latin origin, are rejected by the working class because they sound public-schoolish, 'tony' and effeminate. Language ought to be the joint creation of poets and manual workers, and in modern England it is difficult for these two classes to meet. When they can do so again – as, in a different way, they could in the feudal past – English may show more clearly than at present its kinship with the language of Shakespeare and Defoe.

THE FUTURE OF THE ENGLISH PEOPLE

This is not a book about foreign politics, but if one is to speak of the future of the English people, one must start by considering what kind of world they will probably be living in and what special part they can play in it.

Nations do not often die out, and the English people will still be in existence a hundred years hence, whatever has happened in the meantime. But if Britain is to survive as what is called a 'great' nation, playing an important and useful part in the world's affairs, one must take certain things as assured. One must assume that Britain will remain on good terms with Russia and Europe, will keep its special links with America and the Dominions, and will solve the problem of India in some amicable way. That is perhaps a great deal to assume, but without it there is not much hope for civilisation as a whole, and still less for Britain itself. If the savage international struggle of the last twenty years continues, there will only be room in the world for two or three great powers, and in the long run Britain will not be one of them. It has not either the population or the resources. In a world of power politics the English would ultimately dwindle to a satellite people, and the special thing that it is in their power to contribute might be lost.

But what is the special thing that they could contribute? The outstanding and – by contemporary standards – highly original quality of the English is their habit of *not killing one another*. Putting aside the 'model' small states, which are in an exceptional position, England is the only European country where internal politics are conducted in a more or less humane and decent manner. It is – and this was true long before the rise of fascism – the only country where armed men do not prowl the streets and no one is frightened of the secret police. And the whole British Empire, with all its crying abuses, its stagnation in one place and exploitation in another, at least has the merit of being internally peaceful. It has always been able to get along with a very small number of armed men, although it contains a quarter of the population of the earth. Between the wars its total armed forces amounted to about 600,000 men, of whom a third were Indians. At the outbreak of war the entire Empire was able to mobilise about a million trained men. Almost as many could have been mobilised by, say, Rumania. The English are probably more capable than most peoples of making revolutionary changes without bloodshed. In England, if anywhere, it would be possible to abolish poverty without destroying liberty. If the English took the trouble to make their own democracy work, they would become the political leaders of western Europe, and probably of some other parts of the world as well. They would provide the much-needed alternative to Russian authoritarianism on the one hand and American materialism on the other.

But to play a leading part the English have got to know what they are doing, and they have got to retain their vitality. For this, certain developments are needed within the next decade. These are a rising birthrate, more social equality, less centralisation and more respect for the intellect.

There was a small rise in the birthrate during the war years, but that is probably of no significance, and the general curve is downwards. The position is not quite so desperate as it is sometimes said to be, but it can only be put right if the curve not only rises sharply, but does so within ten or at most twenty years. Otherwise the population will not only fall, but, what is worse, will consist predominantly of middle-aged people. If that point is reached, the decline may never be retrievable.[21]

At bottom, the causes of the dwindled birthrate are economic. It is nonsense to say that it has happened because English people do not care for children. In the early nineteenth century they had an extremely high birthrate, and they also had an attitude towards children which now seems to us unbelievably callous. With very little public disapproval, children as young as six were sold into the mines and factories, and the death of a child, the most shocking event that modern people are able to imagine, was looked on as a very minor tragedy. In a sense it is true that modern English people have small families because they are too fond of children. They feel that it is wrong to bring a child into the world unless you are completely certain of being able to provide for him, and at a level not lower than your own. For the last fifty years, to have a big family has meant that your children must wear poorer clothes than others in the same group, must have less food and less attention, and probably must go to work earlier. This held good for all classes except the very rich and the unemployed. No doubt the dearth of babies is partly due to the competing attraction of cars and radios, but its main cause is a typically English mixture of snobbishness and altruism.

The philoprogenitive instinct will probably return when fairly large families are already the rule, but the first steps towards this must be economic ones. Half-hearted family allowances will not do the trick, especially when there is a severe housing shortage, as there is now. People should be better off for having children, just as they are in a peasant community, instead of being financially crippled, as they are in ours. Any government, by a few strokes of the pen, could make childlessness as unbearable an economic burden as a big family is now: but no government has chosen to do so, because of the ignorant idea that a bigger population means more unemployed. Far more drastically than anyone has proposed hitherto, taxation will have to be graded so as to encourage child-bearing and to save women with young children from being obliged to work outside the home. And this involves readjustment of rents, better public service in the matter of nursery schools and playing grounds, and the building of bigger and more convenient houses. It also probably involves the extension and improvement of free education, so that the middle-class family shall not, as at present, be crushed out of existence by impossibly high school fees.

The economic adjustments must come first, but a change of outlook is also needed. In the England of the last thirty years it has seemed all too natural that blocks of flats should refuse tenants with children, that parks and squares should be railed off to keep the children out of them, that abortion, theoretically illegal, should be looked on as a peccadillo, and that the main aim of commercial advertising should be to popularise the idea of 'having a good time' and staying young as long as possible. Even the cult of animals, fostered by the newspapers, has probably done its bit towards reducing the birthrate. Nor have the public authorities seriously interested themselves in this question till very recently. Britain today has a million and a half less children than in 1914, and a million and a half more dogs. Yet even now, when the government designs a prefabricated house, it produces a house with only two bedrooms – with room, that is to say, for two children at the most. When one considers the history of the years between the wars, it is perhaps surprising that the birthrate has not dropped more catastrophically than it has. But it is not likely to rise to the replacement level until those in power, as well as the ordinary people in the street, come to feel that children matter more than money.

The English are probably less irked by class distinctions, more tolerant of privilege and of absurdities like titles, than most peoples. There is nevertheless, as I have pointed out earlier, a growing wish for greater equality and a tendency, below the £2,000 a year level, for surface differences between class and class to disappear. At present this is happening only mechanically and quite largely as a result of the war. The question is how it can be speeded up. For even the change-over to a centralised economy, which, except, possibly, in the United States, is happening in all countries under one name or another, does of itself guarantee greater equality between man and man. Once civilisation has reached a fairly high technical level, class distinctions are an obvious evil. They not only lead great numbers of people to waste their lives in the pursuit of social prestige, but they also cause an immense wastage of talent. In England it is not merely the ownership of property that is concentrated in a few hands. It is also the case that all power, administrative as well as financial, belongs to a single class. Except for a handful of 'self-made men' and Labour politicians, those who control our destinies are the product of about a dozen public schools and two universities. A nation is using its capacities to the full when any man can get any job that he is fit for. One has only to think of some of the people who have held vitally important jobs during the past twenty years, and to wonder what would have happened to them if they had been born into the working class, to see that this is not the case in England.

Moreover, class distinctions are a constant drain on morale, in peace as well as in war. And the more conscious, the better educated, the mass of the people become, the more this is so. The word 'They', the universal feeling that 'They' hold all the power and make all the decisions, and that 'They' can only be influenced in indirect and uncertain ways, is a great handicap in England. In 1940 'They' showed a marked tendency to give place to 'We', and it is time that it did so permanently. Three measures are obviously necessary, and they would begin to produce their effect within a few years.

The first is a scaling-up and scaling-down of incomes. The glaring inequality of wealth that existed in England before the war must not be allowed to recur. Above a certain point – which should bear a fixed relation to the lowest current wage – all incomes should be taxed out of existence. In theory, at any rate, this has happened already, with beneficial results. The second necessary measure is greater democracy in education. A completely unified system of education is probably not desirable. Some adolescents benefit by higher education, others do not, there is need to differentiate between literary and technical education, and it is better that a few independent experimental schools should remain in existence. But it should be the rule, as it is in some countries already, for all children to attend the same schools up to the age of twelve or at least ten. After that age it becomes necessary to separate the more gifted children from the less gifted, but a uniform educational system for the early years would cut away one of the deepest roots of snobbery.

The third thing that is needed is to remove the class labels from the English language. It is not desirable that all the local accents should disappear, but there should be a manner of speaking that is definitely national and is not merely (like the accent of the B.B.C. announcers) a copy of the mannerisms of the upper classes. This national accent – a modification of Cockney, perhaps, or of one of the northern accents – should be taught as a matter of course to all children alike. After that they could, and in some parts of the country they probably would, revert to the local accent, but they should be able to speak standard English if they wished to. No one should be 'branded on the tongue'. It should be impossible, as it is in the United States and some European countries, to determine anyone's status from his accent.

We need, too, to be less centralised. English agriculture revived during the war, and the revival may continue, but the English people are still excessively urban in outlook. Culturally, moreover, the country is very much over-centralised. Not only is the whole of Britain in effect governed from London, but the sense of locality – of being, say, an East Anglian or a West Countryman as well as an Englishman – has been much weakened during the past century. The ambition of the farm labourer is usually to get to a town, the provincial intellectual always wants to get to London. In both Scotland and Wales there are nationalist movements, but they are founded on an economic grievance against England rather than on genuine local pride. Nor is there any important literary or artistic movement that is truly independent of London and the university towns.

It is uncertain whether this centralising tendency is completely reversible, but a good deal could be done to check it. Both Scotland and Wales could and should be a great deal more autonomous than they are at present. The provincial universities should be more generously equipped and the provincial press subsidised. (At present nearly the whole of England is 'covered' by eight London newspapers. No newspaper with a large circulation, and no first-class magazine, is published outside London.) The problem of getting people, and especially young, spirited people, to stay on the land would be partly solved if farm labourers had better cottages and if country towns were more civilised and cross-country bus services more efficient. Above all, local pride should be stimulated by teaching in the elementary schools. Every child ought as a matter of course to learn something of the history and topography of its own county. People ought to be proud of their own locality, they ought to feel that its scenery, its architecture and even its cookery are the best in the world. And such feelings, which do exist in some areas of the North but have lapsed throughout the greater part of England, would strengthen national unity rather than weaken it.

It has been suggested earlier that the survival of free speech in England is partly the result of stupidity. The people are not intellectual enough to be heresy-hunters. One does not wish them to grow less tolerant, nor, having seen the results, would one want them to develop the political sophistication that prevailed in pre-Hitler Germany or pre-Pétain France. But the instincts and traditions on which the English rely served them best when they were an exceptionally fortunate people, protected by geography from major disaster. In the twentieth century the narrow interests of the average man, the rather low level of English education, the contempt for 'highbrows' and the almost general deadness to aesthetic issues, are serious liabilities.

What the upper classes think about 'highbrows' can be judged from the Honours Lists. The upper classes feel titles to be important: yet almost never is any major honour bestowed on anyone describable as an intellectual. With very few exceptions, scientists do not get beyond baronetcies, or literary men beyond knighthoods. But the attitude of the man in the street is no better. He is not troubled by the reflection that England spends hundreds of millions every year on beer and the football pools while scientific research languishes for lack of funds; or that we can afford greyhound tracks innumerable but not even one National Theatre. Between the wars England tolerated newspapers, films, and radio programmes of unheard-of silliness, and these produced further stupefaction in the public, blinding their eyes to vitally important problems. This silliness of the English press is partly artificial, since it arises from the fact that newspapers live off advertisements for consumption goods. During the war the papers grew very much more intelligent without losing their public, and millions of people read papers which they would have rejected as impossibly 'highbrow' some years ago. There is, however, not only a low general level of taste, but a widespread unawareness that aesthetic considerations can possibly have any importance. Rehousing and town-planning, for instance, are normally discussed without even a mention of beauty or ugliness. The English are great lovers of flowers, gardening and 'nature', but this is merely a part of their vague aspiration towards an agricultural life. In the main they see no objection to 'ribbon development' or to the filth and chaos of the industrial towns. They see nothing wrong in scattering the woods with paper bags and filling every pool and stream with tin cans and bicycle frames. And they are all too ready to listen to any journalist who tells them to trust their instincts and despise the 'highbrow'..

One result of this has been to increase the isolation of the British intelligentsia. English intellectuals, especially the younger ones, are markedly hostile to their own country. Exceptions can, of course, be found, but it is broadly true that anyone who would prefer T. S. Eliot to Alfred Noyes[22] despises England, or thinks that he ought to do so. In 'enlightened' circles, to express pro-British sentiments needs considerable moral courage. On the other hand, during the past dozen years there has been a strong tendency to develop a violent nationalistic loyalty to some foreign country, usually Soviet Russia. This must probably have happened in any case, because capitalism in its later phases pushes the literary and even the scientific intellectual into a position where he has security without much responsibility. But the philistinism of the English public alienates the intelligentsia still further. The loss to society is very great. It means that the people whose vision is acutest – the people, for instance, who grasped that Hitler was dangerous ten years before this was discovered by our public men – are hardly able to make contact with the masses and grow less and less interested in English problems.

The English will never develop into a nation of philosophers. They will always prefer instinct to logic, and character to intelligence. But they must get rid of their downright contempt for 'cleverness'. They cannot afford it any longer. They must grow less tolerant of ugliness, and mentally more adventurous. And they must stop despising foreigners. They are Europeans and ought to be aware of it. On the other hand they have special links with the other English-speakers overseas, and special imperial responsibilities, in which they ought to take more interest than they have done during these past twenty years. The intellectual atmosphere of England is already very much livelier than it was. The war scotched if it did not kill certain kinds of folly. But there is still need for a conscious effort at national re-education. The first step towards this is an improvement in elementary education, which involves not only raising the school-leaving age but spending enough money to ensure that elementary schools are adequately staffed and equipped. And there are immense educational possibilities in the radio, the film, and – if it could be freed once and for all from commercial interests – the press.

These, then, appear to be the immediate necessities of the English people. They must breed faster, work harder, and probably live more simply, think more deeply, get rid of their snobbishness and their anachronistic class distinctions, and pay more attention to the world and less to their own backyards. Nearly all of them already love their country, but they must learn to love it intelligently. They must have a clear notion of their own destiny and not listen either to those who tell them that England is finished or to those who tell them that the England of the past can return.

If they can do that they can keep their feet in the post-war world, and if they can keep their feet they can give the example that millions of human beings are waiting for. The world is sick of chaos and it is sick of dictatorship. Of all peoples the English are likeliest to find a way of avoiding both. Except for a small minority they are fully ready for the drastic economic changes that are needed, and at the same time they have no desire either for violent revolution or for foreign conquests. They have known for forty years, perhaps, something that the Germans and the Japanese have only recently learned, and that the Russians and the Americans have yet to learn: they know that it is not possible for any one nation to rule the earth. They want above all things to live at peace, internally and externally. And the great mass of them are probably prepared for the sacrifices that peace entails.

But they will have to take their destiny into their own hands. England can only fulfil its special mission if the ordinary English in the street can somehow get their hands on power. We were told very frequently during the war years that this time, when the danger was over, there should be no lost opportunities, no recurrence of the past. No more stagnation punctuated by wars, no more Rolls-Royces gliding past dole queues, no return to the England of the Distressed Area, the endlessly stewing teapot, the empty pram and the Giant Panda.[23] We cannot be sure that this promise will be kept. Only we ourselves can make certain that it will come true, and if we do not, no further chance may be given to us. The past thirty years have been a long series of cheques drawn upon the accumulated good will of the English people. That reserve may not be inexhaustible. By the end of another decade it will be finally clear whether England is to survive as a great nation or not. And if the answer is to be 'Yes', it is the common people who must make it so.

1. There is a splendid description of Ratcliff Highway, adjacent to the Thames in the East End of London, in *Dickens's Dictionary of London, 1879: An Unconventional Handbook.* It was the scene at the St George's Church and of 'the famous riots of 1858–9' and, although until the last few years (of 1879) 'almost unique in Europe as a scene of coarse riot and debauchery, is now chiefly noteworthy as an example of what may be done by effective police supervision thoroughly carried out'. Dickens goes on: 'The dancing-rooms and foreign cafés of the Highway – now rechristened St George's Street – are still well worthy a visit from the student of human nature, and are each, for the most part, devoted almost exclusively to the accommodation of a single nationality'. Nancy of *Oliver Twist* lived there before moving to Field Lane, Holborn.
2. Air Raid Precautions.
3. Kid Lewis fought world title fights with Jack Britton (USA) in 1921 and Georges Carpentier (France) in 1922; both were at light heavyweight, though in the fight against Carpentier the latter's heavyweight title was also at stake. Carpentier knocked out Lewis. Lewis supported Sir Oswald Mosley's New Party for Whitechapel, his native borough, in 1931. See Orwell's letter to Julian Symons, 25 October 1947, in which he discussed Lewis (XIX/*3295*).
4. Allied forces attempted, without success, to assist the Greek army to stem the Italian and German invasion of Greece. At the end of April 1941, 50,732 Allied troops were evacuated by the Royal Navy. British and Commonwealth forces lost some 900 men killed, 1,200 wounded and 9,000 taken prisoner. The navy lost two troop transports and two destroyers in the course of the evacuation.
5. On 30 November 1939, Soviet Russia attacked Finland by land and air (bombing Helsinki). Despite early and remarkable successes against heavy odds, Finland, led by Field-Marshal Mannerheim (1867–1951), had to surrender in March 1940. Nearly half a million Finns had to evacuate land ceded to the Soviets. There was strong support for the Finns in the United Kingdom and Sibelius's 'Finlandia' became almost instantly familiar. When Germany invaded Russia, Finland allied itself to Germany. Churchill wrote a personal note to Mannerheim warning him that if the Finns went beyond their 1939 boundaries, 'out of loyalty to our ally Russia' Britain would be forced to declare war on Finland (29 November 1941). Mannerheim thanked Churchill for his courtesy but declined to halt his troops. Britain (and other countries) then declared war on Finland (and Romania and Hungary). See Winston Churchill, *The Second World War*, vol. 3 (1950), 474–5 (where the letters are printed).
6. The Franco-Prussian War, 1870–71, resulted in a crushing defeat for France at Sedan and Metz, with Paris besieged. Orwell was well-informed about this war. He refers to Zola's

book on this disaster, *La Débâcle* (1892), several times, recommending it as a 'best book' to Brenda Salkeld (X/*166*); his reference to it in 'How the Poor Die' (XVIII/*3104*) shows he had read it. In 'As I Please', 24 (12 May 1944; XVI/*2467*), he quotes the German Chancellor Bismarck's response when asked for better terms for the French troops who had surrendered at Sedan on the grounds that that would earn the gratitude of the French: we, the Germans, 'might build on the gratitude of a prince, but certainly not on the gratitude of a people – least of all the gratitude of the French'.

7. 'Sacred self-interest'; used of Italian foreign policy implying it was being pursued as if it had divine warrant.

8. Al(phonse) Capone (1899–1947), US gangster. He was a powerful mobster in Chicago during the prohibition era. It proved impossible to present sufficient evidence to convict him for racketeering but he was sentenced in 1931 to ten years' imprisonment for tax evasion.

9. Marie Lloyd (Matilda Alice Victoria Wood; 1870–1922) was one of, if not the, most popular stars of the music hall. Some of her songs are still performed but what characterized her act was first her rapport with her audiences, and second what was, before World War I, euphemistically termed 'ceruleanism' – 'blueness'. On that ground she was excluded from the first Royal Command Performance in 1912 and the second, to celebrate the end of World War I, in 1919. Nevertheless, she remained at the top of the bill until the end of her life. Her personal life was disastrously unhappy. After singing 'One of the Ruins that Cromwell knocked about a bit' – but, in truth, she seemed a ruin knocked about by life – at Edmonton on 4 October 1922, she collapsed in the wings and died three days later.

10. The *Daily Worker* presented Communist Party policies. It ran from 1 January 1930 to 23 April 1966 and was then incorporated in the *Morning Star*. It was suppressed by government order from 22 January 1941 to 6 September 1942.

11. Sir William Beveridge (1879–1963; Kt., 1919; Baron, 1946), economist and social reformer; Director of the London School of Economics, 1919–37; Master of University College, Oxford, 1937–45; Liberal MP, 1944–6. He was the author of the *Report on Social Insurance and Allied Services* ('the Beveridge Report'), 1942, which laid the foundations of the welfare state in Britain.

12. Ernest Bevin (1881–1951), trade union leader, instrumental in the amalgamation of fourteen unions into the powerful Transport and General Workers' Union in 1922. He vigorously opposed pacifism and early recognized the dangers of Nazism. He was a member of the War Cabinet from October 1940 and served as Minister of Labour and National Service, 1940–45. He was appointed Foreign Minister in the post-war Labour government, 1945–50. Much of the credit for the establishment of NATO falls to him. Recognizing the danger of Soviet attacks on Britain in the United Nations and by surreptitious means, he authorized the setting up of the Information Research Department of the Foreign Office in 1948 (see XX/*3590A* and *B*; also *Orwell and Politics* in this series). He steadfastly refused all honours.

13. An old name for a size of printing type. It was between what was then called Long Primer and Brevier, being about 9 point, so giving 8½ vertical lines to the inch. It may have been named after a French printer or typefounder.

14. The two nations derives from Disraeli's novel, *Sybil, or The Two Nations* (1845); Matthew Arnold described a division into three: Barbarians, Philistines and Populace in ch. 3 of *Culture and Anarchy* (1869). See *Orwell and the Dispossessed* in this series.

15. The Elementary Education Act of 1870 (not a Bill of 1871) provided for universal basic education organized through local School Boards. Fees could be charged but these were almost completely abolished in 1891.
16. The first ten Penguin books were published in May 1935. Orwell reviewed the third batch of ten on 5 March 1936 (X/*290*).
17. Orwell refers not so much to the small teashops operated by Messrs J. & L. Lyons, but to the multi-storey 'Corner Houses' first opened in London in 1908. They were extremely popular from the twenties to the forties and offered very good value.
18. Orwell gives an example of bêche-de-mer (South Seas English) in the last paragraph of 'As I Please', 80, 4 April 1947; see XIX/*3208*.
19. Orwell was influenced by Jonathan Swift (1667–1745) and wrote an imaginary interview with him for a BBC broadcast (6 November 1942; XIV/*1637*). He here refers to the satire, *A Compleat Collection of Genteel and Ingenious Conversation* (1738). Among other essays by Swift that probably influenced Orwell are 'On Corruptions of Style' (1710) and *A Proposal for Correcting, Improving and Ascertaining the English Tongue* (1712).
20. Although not published until after 'Politics and the English Language' (completed 11 December 1945; reproduced in *Orwell and Politics* in this series and XVII/*2815*), *The English People* was completed by 22 May 1944, and it anticipates here the opening of that essay: 'Most people who bother with the matter at all would admit that the English language is in a bad way', but it goes on: 'it is clear that the decline of a language must ultimately have political and economic causes'.
21. Orwell shared in a concern at this time at the decline in the birth rate and its supposed long-term effects. In 'In Front of Your Nose', 22 March 1946 (XVIII/*2940*), he suggests (granting that the figures are uncertain) that in seventy years (i.e. 2016), 'our population will amount to about eleven millions, over half of whom will be Old Age Pensioners'. He probably derived this calculation from *The Population of Great Britain* (1945) by Mark Abrams (see the review of his *The Conditions of the British People*, below), which he discusses in 'As I Please', 78, 21 March 1947 (XIX/*3196*). He concludes by asking, whether, in 1970, 'the Old Age Pension will stay at the equivalent of £1 a week when one person in three is in receipt of it'.
22. T. S. Eliot (1888–1985), poet, critic and a director of the publishing house Faber & Faber, in which capacity he rejected *Down and Out in Paris and London* and *Animal Farm*. He made a number of broadcasts to India under Orwell's aegis, and Orwell reviewed *The Four Quartets* (XVI/*2559*); he concluded his review by saying, 'There are very few writers now alive who are better worth taking trouble over', and although readers might find this poem disappointing, it might lead 'to the discovery of "Prufrock", or "The Waste Land", or "Sweeney Agonistes" '. Alfred Noyes (1880–1958), poet, novelist and dramatist, now out of fashion. Nevertheless, his poem 'Spring and the Blind Children' still has a power to move. Orwell reviewed his *The Edge of the Abyss* on 27 February 1944 (XVI/*2425*). Noyes's thesis 'is that western civilisation is in danger of actual destruction' by economic maladjustments and 'the decay of the belief in absolute good and evil'. Noyes argues that highbrows, 'our pseudo-intellectuals', as he calls them, are largely responsible for this. Orwell begins the review: 'Incoherent and, in places, silly though it is, this book raises a real problem and will set its readers thinking, even if their thinking only starts to be useful at about the place where Mr Noyes leaves off.'

23. The first giant panda, a native of China, to be brought to the West was exhibited in the United States in 1936. It aroused enormous interest and led to the mass-production of toy bears of the teddy-bear variety, a product still with us. When a giant panda appeared in London a little later, the *Daily Mail* referred in April 1939 to the 'sickly sentimental panda plague' that had infected the populace of England, though most people so affected would not actually see a giant panda. In January 2001, Washington Zoo acquired two pandas.

As Charles Humana, in Freedom *(18 October 1947), pointed out,* The English People *was generally very favourably reviewed: 'Strangely enough, despite the party line of the various journals, they were all unanimous on this occasion. Nationalism had transcended all.' Humana's review, while not quite coming down hard, did provide most perceptive comments. He would have preferred to ignore this book, 'coming so soon after the profundity of* Animal Farm, *as a natural weakening to temptation despite the promptings of higher reason'. But, had the reviewers connived or been fooled, and also the editor (W. J. Turner) of this 'prestige building series'? He went on,*

> *Orwell has cleverly produced out of his top hat a definite political pamphlet. The message that goes hand in hand with his carefully compiled lists of virtues and faults of the English people is one that he has been peddling in his more obvious political writings.*

That message was, briefly, 'that of Britain leading a European bloc in the face of the Russo-American stalemate'. Nevertheless, Humana thought 'a little fresh air should be allowed into the stuffy basement' and invoked Henry Miller. For all the claims to gentleness, not killing one another inordinately, being considerate and peace-loving, one should recall, as did Orwell, 'the traditional faults of the Englishman . . . hypocrisy and line shooting'. We should remember 'that even a Nigerian bushman will lose his suspicion in the face of kindness and become sullen and unfriendly when exploited'. Nor, concluded Humana, should we forget 'the example of progressive writers who, temporarily we hope, fail to remember all this'. In his notes for his literary executor written in the last year of his life, Orwell asked that The English People *be one of four of his works that should not be reprinted (see* XX / 3728*). The last line is echoed in* Nineteen Eighty-Four*: 'If there was hope it* must *lie in the proles'* (IX/72)*.*

[2484]

'Survey of "Civvy Street"'

Observer, *4 June 1944*

The surveys undertaken by Mass-Observation[1] from the beginning of the war onwards have revealed many different moods, but nearly all have suggested that Britain suffers from too little government rather than too much. Cheque after cheque has been drawn on the accumulated good will of the British people, but very little positive guidance has been given. They know what they are fighting against, but they have not been clearly told what they are fighting *for* or what the post-war world will probably be like. The new survey, like some previous ones, gives warning that their patience and hopefulness may not be inexhaustible.

Although specifically concerned with demobilisation, it also deals with re-employment and reconstruction. It reveals not only widespread cynicism about 'after the war' but also a surprising vagueness. Thus, when a cross-section of the public were asked in November, 1943, 'whether the Government had announced any policy of post-war reconstruction', only 16 per cent thought it had. The corresponding percentage had actually been higher two years earlier. Most disquieting is the return to the 1918 frame of mind. Great numbers are convinced that 'it will be just like last time', and, as their memories of last time are not happy ones, the effects on morale are potentially bad.

Disbelief in the future is especially strong in the armed forces and among the Civil Defence workers. The soldiers (this is somewhat less marked in the women's services) want above all things to get out of uniform as soon as the war is over, and a number of people even think that there will be great discontent if demobilisation is not achieved rapidly. They know that the process of demobilisation is complicated, but are not confident that it will be done fairly or intelligently (memories of 'last time' are a heavy liability here), and, even more serious, they have no clear idea as to how long it ought to take. Meanwhile countless soldiers cherish a private dream that they, as individuals, will somehow be able to get out of it when the fighting stops. The possible effects of this kind of thing in the immediate post-war period are obvious. They can only be countered by a clear statement from the Government which will let people know just how long they will be expected to stay in uniform, and why.

So also with post-war employment. According to the Mass-Observers' findings, a majority still expect large-scale unemployment after the war – another legacy from 'last time'. At the same time there is a growing consciousness that unemployment is an unnecessary evil. It is probably significant that the number of people expecting unemployment to return has not markedly altered over several years: there is no strong belief that our economic system will be radically changed. In general the feeling seems to be that most of our problems are soluble, but that the mysterious and all-powerful 'They' will prevent anything from being done. The result is increasing apathy and a determination – of course accentuated by sheer fatigue as the war continues – to sit back and have a good rest as soon as the guns stop firing.

It is a sign of the general lack of confidence in the future that in 1943, out of a random sample of Londoners, 46 per cent thought that there would be another world war after this one, and 19 per cent thought there might be. The majority of these thought that this new war would happen within 25 years. Faith in all the main political parties has dwindled, and there is a confused desire for more vigorous leadership combined with more genuine democracy.

Yet how ready for effort and sacrifice most people are, when they are given a good reason, can be seen in their attitude towards war-time controls. Nearly all of these have been accepted readily: even the withdrawal of white bread was approved by a four to one majority.[2] Other more drastic measures, not actually put into force, would be generally approved. For example, the Mass-Observers found a ten to one majority in favour of Government ownership of essential industries, and seven to one in favour of nationalisation of the mines.

Controls are even welcomed for their own sake, as having an equalising effect. On the whole, whenever the Government acts positively and explains what it is doing, even if what it is doing is to take something away, the people seem to respond. Certain events, such as the delay about 'Beveridge',[3] and even the release of Mosley, have deeply shaken public confidence, but it is the failure to explain, to give a picture of the future, that apparently does the most harm.

It is unfortunate that much of the work done by Mass-Observation should have to be financed by a private body which naturally only wants reports on a rather limited range of subjects. The present survey has one very serious omission: this is that it makes no reference to the war against Japan. The subject of demobilisation[4] is complicated by the fact that Japan will almost certainly go on fighting, perhaps for years, after Germany is defeated. But the main conclusions reached by the Mass-Observers can hardly be questioned.

Political consciousness has expanded greatly during the war, while belief in the existing leadership has shrunk. The belief that planned reconstruction is *possible* has grown, while the belief that it is *likely* has made no headway. There is a gap between the leaders and the led, and the deadly word 'They' saps confidence and encourages anarchic individualism. It is important that that gap should be closed before the war ends. For, as the Mass-Observers point out, it will need as great an effort to win the peace as to win the war, and the people may shrink from making it unless they have a better notion than at present of where they are going.

1. This article was prompted by *The Journey Home* by Mass-Observation, published for the Advertising Service Guild by John Murray. Mass-Observation was described by one of its founders, Tom Harrisson, as 'the science of ourselves'. The Movement, initiated in 1937, organized detailed observation of the masses. It depended upon large numbers of amateur 'observers' in order to compile and publish accurate accounts of the state of contemporary Britain. Its first and most famous report was *May the Twelfth* (1937), the day George VI was crowned king. This was republished in 1987 by Faber & Faber. It was prepared by more than 200 observers and edited by Humphrey Jennings (1907–50), later a distinguished documentary film-maker, and Charles Madge. Madge (1912–96) was born in South Africa and came to England after his father's death in the First World War. He was encouraged as a poet by T. S. Eliot who helped him find work as a journalist. He worked for Mass-Observation from 1937–40 and then for the National Institute of Economic and Social Research; later he moved to political and economic planning. He became Professor of Sociology (although he had no first degree) at Birmingham University in 1950. Observers did not hesitate to disguise themselves or even pretend to be drunk in order to make their observations unnoticed. Mass-Observation Diaries were still being compiled in 1981.

2. During the Second World War, to conserve imports of wheat, a National Loaf was concocted in 1941, and, except in the training of future bakers, was the only bread allowed to be made. It was stodgy and brownish and had a high roughage and chalk content. Bread was never rationed during the war but in March 1946 the wheat content was further reduced; in April the size of loaves was reduced; and in June it was rationed, partly to allow grain to be diverted to Continental Europe to alleviate near-starvation there. In *Nineteen Eighty-Four*, Winston Smith finds he has only 'a hunk of dark-coloured bread' to eat but has to save it

for the following morning (IX/7); this is a reflection of the immediate post-war conditions.
3. 'Beveridge' = *Report on Social Insurance and Allied Services*, or 'the Beveridge Report', 1942, the starting point for the Welfare State. For Beveridge, see n. 11, p. 331.
4. Some men called up in 1944 were not demobilized until 1948, three years after the war's end.

[2530]

Extract from 'As I Please', 37 [The colour bar]

Tribune, *11 August 1944*

A few days ago a West African wrote to inform us that a certain London dance hall had recently erected a 'colour bar', presumably in order to please the American soldiers who formed an important part of its clientele. Telephone conversations with the management of the dance hall brought us the answers: (a) that the 'colour bar' had been cancelled, and (b) that it had never been imposed in the first place; but I think one can take it that our informant's charge had some kind of basis. There have been other similar incidents recently. For instance, during last week a case in a magistrate's court brought out the fact that a West Indian Negro working in this country had been refused admission to a place of entertainment when he was wearing Home Guard uniform. And there have been many instances of Indians, Negroes and others being turned away from hotels on the ground that 'we don't take coloured people'.

It is immensely important to be vigilant against this kind of thing, and to make as much public fuss as possible whenever it happens. For this is one of those matters in which making a fuss can achieve something. There is no kind of legal disability against coloured people in this country, and, what is more, there is very little popular colour feeling. (This is not due to any inherent virtue in the British people, as our behaviour in India shows. It is due to the fact that in Britain itself there is no colour problem.)

The trouble always arises in the same way. A hotel, restaurant or what-not is frequented by people who have money to spend and who object to mixing with Indians or Negroes. They tell the proprietor that unless he imposes a colour bar they will go elsewhere. They may be a very small minority, and the proprietor may not be in agreement with them, but it is difficult for him to lose good customers; so he imposes the colour bar. This kind of thing cannot happen when public opinion is on the alert and disagreeable publicity is given to any establishment where coloured people are insulted. Anyone who knows of a provable instance of colour discrimination ought always to expose it. Otherwise the tiny percentage of colour-snobs who exist among us can make endless mischief, and the British people are given a bad name which, as a whole, they do not deserve.

In the nineteen-twenties, when American tourists were as much a part of the scenery of Paris as tobacco kiosks and tin urinals, the beginnings of a colour bar began to appear even in France. The Americans spent money like water; and restaurant proprietors and the like could not afford to disregard them. One evening, at a dance in a very well-known café, some Americans objected to the presence of a Negro who was there with an Egyptian woman. After making some feeble protests, the proprietor gave in, and the Negro was turned out.

Next morning there was a terrible hullabaloo and the café proprietor was hauled up before a Minister of the Government and threatened with prosecution. It had turned out that the offended Negro was the Ambassador of Haiti. People of that kind can usually get satisfaction, but most of us do not have the good fortune to be ambassadors, and the ordinary Indian, Negro or Chinese can only be protected against petty insult if other ordinary people are willing to exert themselves on his behalf.

[2637]

'The French Believe We Have Had a Revolution'

Manchester Evening News, *20 March 1945*

Orwell went to France as a war correspondent for the Observer *on 15 February 1945. In place of his regular book reviews for the* Manchester Evening News *he contributed articles of which this was the third. The titles for his articles are possibly not his but those supplied by the newspaper. Like many journalists, when in Paris he stayed at the appropriately named Hôtel Scribe. During this stay his wife, Eileen, had to undergo an operation on 29 March 1945 and died under the anaesthetic; her last letter to her* *husband (*XVII/2647*) was left unfinished. Orwell returned to England and arranged for the funeral and for his son, Richard, to be looked after while he completed his tour of duty on the Continent.*

So far as one can judge from casual conversations and from the press, Britain's reputation has never stood higher in France than it does now. The attitude of the average man is not only friendlier than General de Gaulle's speeches would lead one to suppose but it is also far friendlier than one would infer from what might be called the mechanics of the situation.

For four years France was subjected to a barrage of anti-British propaganda, some of it extremely skilful, and at the same time Britain was driven by military necessity to bomb French cities, sink French ships and commit other acts of war which the average man could hardly be blamed for resenting at the time when they happened. But on top of this, the invasion and the subsequent campaigns have seriously disrupted the economic life of the country. It is generally agreed that in the later period of the occupation France was better off in a physical sense than she is now, in spite of the huge-scale looting practised by the Germans.

The transport system has not yet recovered from the invasion, and the heaviest fighting took place in some of the best agricultural areas, upsetting first the hay harvest, then the grain harvest, and resulting in enormous losses of livestock. One gets some idea of what this means when one sees butter, almost unobtainable in any legal way, being black-marketed at something over £2 a pound. It is the same with many other foodstuffs, and thanks to the lack of locomotives the fuel situation in the big towns is catastrophic. Paris shivered through the winter of 1940, under the Germans, and shivered again through the winter of 1944, under the Anglo-Americans. Moreover it is realised that the food crisis has been accentuated in recent months by the diversion of Allied shipping to the Pacific.

Yet there seems to be remarkably little resentment. No doubt the forces that supported Vichy are still there, under the surface, but the only body of expressed opinion that could be possibly called anti-British is that of the Communists. The Communists are to some extent politically hostile to Britain because they see in Britain the likeliest leader of the 'western bloc' which it is the object of Soviet policy to prevent. The ordinary man is pro-British both personally and politically, and if asked why, he gives two reasons, one rather trivial, the other more serious and possibly containing in it the seeds of future misunderstanding.

The first reason is that the British troops have on the whole been better ambassadors for their country than the Americans. The comparison is not really a fair one, because the British are here in comparatively small numbers. The bulk of the British forces are in Belgium, and the vast majority of the soldiers who throng the streets of Paris are Americans. Most of them have come from several months in the unbearable conditions of the front line, and they have a large accumulation of pay in their pockets and only a few hours in which to spend it. But the other reason for the present friendly attitude of the French towards Britain is a flattering but somewhat exaggerated estimate of British political achievement during the war.

Frenchmen are much impressed not only by the obstinacy with which Britain continued the struggle in 1940 but by the national unity she displayed. They say with truth that in the moment of crisis Britain had no fifth column and not even any great bitterness of feeling between classes. But to a surprising extent they are inclined to mistake the surface changes of war-time Britain for an actual social revolution, accomplished by common consent. The word 'revolution' is used again and again in connection with Britain's present-day development, both in conversation and in print.

Frenchmen who might be expected to take a more cynical view are to be heard saying that class privilege is no longer rampant in England, that large incomes have been taxed out of existence, and that private capitalism has in effect given way to a centralised economy. And they remark with admiration that all this has been achieved without bloodshed, almost without friction, in the middle of a struggle for existence.

To anyone who knows how little real structural change has taken place in Britain during the war, these eulogies are rather disconcerting. Curiously enough they are repeated by Frenchmen who have visited war-time Britain, and perhaps spent several years there. The mistake made, in many cases, seems to be to confuse patriotism with social enlightenment. Without a doubt the general *behaviour* in Britain during the war has been good. All classes have been willing to sacrifice either their lives or their comfort, rationing has been equitable and efficient, profiteering and black-marketing have never been a major problem, industrial production has soared in spite of every kind of difficulty, and women have flung themselves into the war effort to an unprecedented extent. Frenchmen compare these phenomena with the much more discouraging things that have happened in their own country, and are apt not to realise that the essential social structure of Britain has remained almost unchanged and may reassert itself when the danger has passed.

There are other current misconceptions – in particular, the failure of nearly all Frenchmen to grasp the British attitude towards Germany and the peace settlement. Few Frenchmen realise how unwilling the British people will be to maintain a permanent army of occupation in Germany, or to support any settlement that would make such an army necessary. Not many Frenchmen understand the extent to which Britain's policy is conditioned by her close association with the U.S.A., and hardly any realise that Britain can never act internationally without considering the Dominions.

The present relations between France and Britain are good, but the possible sources of discord are many, and they could do with more illumination than they are getting at present.

France looks hopefully towards Britain as the land of true democracy, the country that has been able to recover from its past mistakes without civil disturbance, without dictatorship, and without infringing intellectual liberty. This picture is not altogether false, but it could be the cause of serious disappointment, and it would be well if more Frenchmen were able to distinguish between the real social changes that have taken place in Britain and the temporary expedients that have been forced upon a country fighting for its life.

[2482]

'Just Junk – But Who Could Resist It?'

Saturday Essay, Evening Standard, *5 January 1946*

Which is the most attractive junk shop in London is a matter of taste, or for debate: but I could lead you to some first-rate ones in the dingier areas of Greenwich, in Islington near the Angel, in Holloway, in Paddington, and in the hinterland of the Edgware-road. Except for a couple near Lord's – and even those are in a section of street that happens to have fallen into decay – I have never seen a junk shop worth a second glance in what is called a 'good' neighbourhood.

A junk shop is not to be confused with an antique shop. An antique shop is clean, its goods are attractively set out and priced at about double their value and once inside the shop you are usually bullied into buying something.

A junk shop has a fine film of dust over the window, its stock may include literally anything that is not perishable, and its proprietor, who is usually asleep in a small room at the back, displays no eagerness to make a sale.

Also, its finest treasures are never discoverable at first glimpse; they have to be sorted out from among a medley of bamboo cake-stands, Britannia-ware dish-covers, turnip watches,[1] dog-eared books, ostrich eggs, typewriters of extinct makes, spectacles without lenses, decanters without stoppers, stuffed birds, wire fire guards, bunches of keys, boxes of nuts and bolts, conch shells from the Indian Ocean, boot trees, Chinese ginger jars and pictures of Highland cattle.

Some of the things to look out for in the junk shop are Victorian brooches and lockets of agate or other semi-precious stones.[2]

Perhaps five out of six of these things are hideously ugly, but there are also very beautiful objects among them. They are set in silver, or more often in pinchbeck, a charming alloy which for some reason is no longer made.

Other things worth looking for are papier-mâché snuffboxes with pictures painted on the lid, lustre-ware jugs, muzzle-loading pistols made round about 1830 and ships in bottles. These are still made, but the old ones are always the best, because of the elegant shape of the Victorian bottles and the delicate green of the glass.

Or, again, musical boxes, horse brasses, copper powder-horns, Jubilee mugs (for some reason the 1887 Jubilee produced much pleasanter keepsakes than the Diamond Jubilee ten years later) and glass paper-weights with pictures at the bottom.

There are others that have a piece of coral enclosed in the glass, but these are always fantastically expensive.[3] Or you may come across a scrap book full of Victorian fashion-plates and pressed flowers or even, if you are exceptionally lucky, the scrap book's big brother, a scrap screen.

Scrap screens – all too rare nowadays – are simply ordinary wooden or canvas screens with coloured scraps cut out and pasted all over them in such a way as to make more or less coherent pictures. The best were made round about 1880, but if you buy one at a junk shop it is sure to be defective, and the great charm of owning such a screen lies in patching it up yourself.

You can use coloured reproductions from art magazines, Christmas cards, postcards, advertisements, book jackets, even cigarette cards. There is always room for one more scrap, and with careful placing anything can be made to look congruous.

Thus, merely in one corner of my own scrap screen,[4] Cézanne's card-players with a black bottle between them are impinging on a street scene in medieval Florence, while on the other side of the street one of Gauguin's South Sea islanders is sitting beside an English lake where a lady in leg-of-mutton sleeves is paddling a canoe. They all look perfectly at home together.

All these things are curiosities, but one does find useful things in the junk shop as well.

In a shop in Kentish Town, since blitzed, I once bought an old French sword-bayonet, price sixpence, which did four years' service as a fire-poker. And during the last few years the junk shop has been the only place where you could buy certain carpentering tools – a jack plane for instance – or such useful objects as corkscrews, clock keys, skates, wine glasses, copper saucepans and spare pram wheels.

In some shops you can find keys to fit almost any lock, others specialise in pictures and are therefore useful when you need a frame. Indeed, I have often found that the cheapest way of buying a frame is to buy a picture and then throw away the picture.[5]

But the attraction of the junk shop does not lie solely in the bargains you pick up, nor even in the aesthetic value which – at a generous estimate – 5 per cent of its contents may possess. Its appeal is to the jackdaw inside all of us, the instinct that makes a child hoard copper nails, clock springs and the glass marbles out of lemonade bottles. To get pleasure out of a junk shop you are not obliged to buy anything, nor even to want to buy anything.

I know a shop in Tottenham-Court road where I have never, over a period of many years, seen anything that was not offensively ugly and another, not far from Baker-street, where there is nearly always something tempting. The first appeals to me almost as strongly as the second.

Another shop, in the Chalk Farm area, sells nothing but rubbishy fragments of old metal. For as long as I can remember the same worn-out tools and lengths of lead piping have been lying in the trays, the same gas stoves have been mouldering in the doorway. I have never bought anything there, never even seen anything that I contemplated buying. Yet it would be all but impossible for me to pass that way without crossing the street to have a good look.

1. A turnip was a slang term for a large silver watch popular in the nineteenth century.

2. This essay has points in common with the description of Mr Charrington's shop in *Nineteen Eighty-Four.* For this paragraph, compare 'Only on a small table in the corner was there a litter of odds and ends – lacquered snuff-boxes, agate brooches and the like – which looked as though they might include something interesting' (IX/98).

3. The description of the paperweight is closely followed in *Nineteen Eighty-Four.* Winston Smith asks what is the 'strange, pink, convoluted object that recalled a rose or a sea anemone', and is told, 'That's coral, that is . . . It must have come from the Indian Ocean. They used to kind of embed it in the glass.' It would once have been expensive: 'that would have fetched eight pounds . . . it was a lot of money.' Winston paid four dollars 'and slid the coveted thing into his pocket' (IX/99).

4. Orwell's screen can be seen in some of the photographs showing him with Richard. Just the top is visible in Crick, plate 23; rather more is visible, much out of focus, in Lewis, 105; and it is to be seen more clearly in plate 69 of *The World of George Orwell,* edited by Miriam Gross (1971).

5. The floor-space of Charrington's shop 'was very restricted, because all round the walls were stacked innumerable dusty picture-frames' (*Nineteen Eighty-Four,* IX/98).

[2629]

'Poetry and the Microphone'

Written Summer 1943?; The New Saxon Pamphlet, *No. 3, March 1945*

As Orwell indicates, this essay is the product of his work as a Talks Producer in the Indian Section of the BBC's Eastern Service, 18 August 1941 to 24 November 1943. Although he was purportedly engaged in propaganda, even Orwell's News Commentaries were reasonably objective, and he devoted *much time to broadcasting cultural programmes of which Radio Three today would not be ashamed. He ran a series on drama production for Indians, which proved very fruitful, and he attempted (not too successfully) to create with others (including E. M. Forster) a new kind of radio story in which each contributor carried on from where his or her predecessor had left off. More successful, at least artistically, was 'Voice: A Magazine Programme'. Orwell acted as editor and the first number, broadcast on 11 August 1942, started with an Editorial by Orwell (*XIII/*1373). The succeeding numbers, all published in Volume XIV (though the text of No. 5 is lost) were devoted to War Poetry, Childhood, American Literature, Oriental Influences on English Literature (in which T. S. Eliot read 'What the Thunder said', Part V of* The Waste Land*) and Christmas. The discussions had to be scripted in advance to be passed by the security and policy censors, so the discussions were inclined to be stilted. Orwell's wish that poets should, wherever possible, read their own poems would not now seem unusual.*

It is probable that the essay was written eighteen months to two years before it was published in The New Saxon Pamphlet, *No. 3. This became, for Nos. 4 and 5,* The New Saxon Review, *and that was edited by John Atkins (1916–). He had been literary editor of* Tribune *before Orwell and he read Henry Treece's poems in 'Voice, 1' in the absence of Treece on war service. Atkins wrote one of the earliest books on Orwell:* George Orwell: A Literary and Biographical Study *(1954).*

About a year ago I and a number of others were engaged in broadcasting literary programmes to India, and among other things we broadcast a good deal of verse by contemporary and near-contemporary English writers – for example, Eliot, Herbert Read, Auden, Spender, Dylan Thomas, Henry Treece, Alex Comfort, Robert Bridges, Edmund Blunden, D. H. Lawrence. Whenever it was possible we had poems broadcast by the people who wrote them. Just why these particular programmes (a small and remote outflanking movement in the radio war) were instituted there is no need to explain here, but I should add that the fact we were broadcasting to an Indian audience dictated our technique to some extent. The essential point was that our literary broadcasts were aimed at the Indian university students, a small and hostile audience, unapproachable by anything that could be described as British propaganda. It was known in advance that we could not hope for more than a few thousand listeners at the most, and this gave us an excuse to be more 'highbrow' than is generally possible on the air.

If you are broadcasting poetry to people who know your language but don't share your cultural background, a certain amount of comment and explanation is unavoidable, and the formula we usually followed was to broadcast what purported to be a monthly literary magazine. The editorial staff were supposedly sitting in their office, discussing what to put into the next number. Somebody suggested one poem, someone else suggested another, there was a short discussion and then came the poem itself, read in a different voice, preferably the author's own. This poem naturally called up another, and so the programme continued, usually with at least half a minute of discussion between any two items. For a half-hour programme, six voices seemed to be the best number. A programme of this sort was necessarily somewhat shapeless, but it could be given a certain appearance of unity by making it revolve round a single central theme. For example, one number of our imaginary magazine was devoted to the subject of war. It included two poems by Edmund Blunden, Auden's 'September 1, 1939',[1] extracts from a long poem by G. S. Fraser ('A Letter to Anne Ridler'), Byron's 'Isles of Greece' and an extract from T. E. Lawrence's *Revolt in the Desert.* These half-dozen items, with the arguments that preceded and followed them, covered reasonably well the possible attitudes towards war. The poems and the prose extract took about twenty minutes to broadcast, the arguments about eight minutes.

This formula may seem slightly ridiculous and also rather patronising, but its advantage is that the element of mere instruction, the textbook motif, which is quite unavoidable if one is going to broadcast serious and sometimes 'difficult' verse, becomes a lot less forbidding when it appears as an informal discussion. The various speakers can ostensibly say to one another what they are in reality saying to the audience. Also, by such an approach you at least give a poem a context, which is just what poetry lacks from the average man's point of view. But of course there are other methods. One which we frequently used was to set a poem in music. It is announced that in a few minutes' time such and such a poem will be broadcast; then the music plays for perhaps a minute, then fades out into the poem, which follows without any title or announcement, then the music is faded [in] again and plays up for another minute or two – the whole thing taking perhaps five minutes. It is necessary to choose appropriate music, but needless to say, the real purpose of the music is to insulate the poem from the rest of the programme. By this method you can have, say, a Shakespeare sonnet within three minutes of a news bulletin without, at any rate to my ear, any gross incongruity.

These programmes that I have been speaking of were of no great value in themselves, but I have mentioned them because of the ideas they aroused in myself and some others about the possibilities of the radio as a means of popularising poetry. I was early struck by the fact that the broadcasting of a poem by the person who wrote it does not merely produce an effect upon the audience, if any, but also on the poet himself. One must remember that extremely little in the way of broadcasting poetry has been done in England, and that many people who write verse have never even considered the idea of reading it aloud. By being set down at a microphone, especially if this happens at all regularly, the poet is brought into a new relationship with his work, not otherwise attainable in our time and country. It is a commonplace that in modern times – the last two hundred years, say – poetry has come to have less and less connection either with music or with the spoken word. It needs print in order to exist at all, and it is no more expected that a poet, as such, will know how to sing or even to declaim than it is expected that an architect will know how to plaster a ceiling. Lyrical and rhetorical poetry have almost ceased to be written, and a hostility towards poetry on the part of the common man has come to be taken for granted in any country where everyone can read. And where such a breach exists it is always inclined to widen, because the concept of poetry as primarily something printed, and something intelligible only to a minority, encourages obscurity and 'cleverness'. How many people do not feel quasi-instinctively that there must be something wrong with any poem whose meaning can be taken in at a single glance? It seems unlikely that these tendencies will be checked unless it again becomes normal to read verse aloud, and it is difficult to see how this can be brought about except by using the radio as a medium. But the special advantage of the radio, its power to select the right audience, and to do away with stage-fright and embarrassment, ought here to be noticed.

In broadcasting your audience is conjectural, but it is an audience of *one.* Millions may be listening, but each is listening alone, or as a member of a small group, and each has (or ought to have) the feeling that you are speaking to him individually. More than this it is reasonable to assume that your audience is sympathetic, or at least interested, for anyone who is bored can promptly switch you off by turning a knob. But though presumably sympathetic, the audience *has no power over you.* It is just here that a broadcast differs from a speech or a lecture. On the platform, as anyone used to public speaking knows, it is almost impossible not to take your tone from the audience. It is always obvious within a few minutes what they will respond to and what they will not, and in practice you are almost compelled to speak for the benefit of what you estimate as the stupidest person present, and also to ingratiate yourself by means of the balleyhoo known as 'personality'. If you don't do so, the result is always an atmosphere of frigid embarrassment. That grisly thing, a 'poetry reading', is what it is because there will always be some among the audience who are bored or all-but frankly hostile and who can't remove themselves by the simple act of turning a knob. And it is at bottom the same difficulty – the fact that a theatre audience is not a selected one – that makes it impossible to get a decent performance of Shakespeare in England. On the air these conditions do not exist. The poet *feels* that he is addressing people to whom poetry means something, and it is a fact that poets who are used to broadcasting can read into the microphone with a virtuosity they would not equal if they had a visible audience in front of them. The element of make-believe that enters here does not greatly matter. The point is that in the only way now possible the poet has been brought into a situation in which reading verse aloud seems a natural unembarrassing thing, a normal exchange between man and man: also he has been led to think of his work as *sound* rather than as a pattern on paper. By that much the reconciliation between poetry and the common man is nearer. It already exists at the poet's end of the aether-waves, whatever may be happening at the other end.

However, what is happening at the other end cannot be disregarded. It will be seen that I have been speaking as though the whole subject of poetry were embarrassing, almost indecent, as though popularising poetry were essentially a strategic manoeuvre, like getting a dose of medicine down a child's throat or establishing tolerance for a persecuted sect. But unfortunately that or something like it is the case. There can be no doubt that in our civilisation poetry is by far the most discredited of the arts, the only art, indeed, in which the average man refuses to discern *any* value. Arnold Bennett was hardly exaggerating when he said that in the English-speaking countries the word 'poetry' would disperse a crowd quicker than a fire hose. And as I have pointed out, a breach of this kind tends to widen simply because of its existence, the common man becoming more and more anti-poetry, the poet more and more arrogant and unintelligible, until the divorce between poetry and popular culture is accepted as a sort of law of nature, although in fact it belongs only to our own time and to a comparatively small area of the earth. We live in an age in which the average human being in the highly-civilised countries is aesthetically inferior to the lowest savage. This state of affairs is generally looked upon as being incurable by any *conscious* act, and on the other hand is expected to right itself of its own accord as soon as society takes a comelier shape. With slight variations the Marxist, the anarchist and the religious believer will all tell you this, and in broad terms it is undoubtedly true. The ugliness amid which we live has spiritual and economic causes and is not to be explained by the mere going-astray of tradition at some point or other. But it does not follow that no improvement is possible within our present framework, nor that an aesthetic improvement is not a necessary part of the general redemption of society. It is worth stopping to wonder, therefore, whether it would not be possible even now to rescue poetry from its special position as the most-hated of the arts and win for it at least the same degree of toleration as exists for music. But one has to start by asking, in what way and to what extent is poetry unpopular?

On the face of it, the unpopularity of poetry is as complete as it could be. But on second thoughts, this has to be qualified in a rather peculiar way. To begin with, there is still an appreciable amount of folk poetry (nursery rhymes, etc.) which is universally known and quoted and forms part of the background of everyone's mind. There is also a handful of ancient songs and ballads which have never gone out of favour. In addition there is the popularity, or at least the toleration, of 'good bad' poetry, generally of a patriotic or sentimental kind. This might seem beside the point if it were not that 'good bad' poetry has all the characteristics which, ostensibly, make the average man dislike true poetry. It is in verse, it rhymes, it deals in lofty sentiments and unusual language – all this to a very marked degree, for it is almost axiomatic that bad poetry is more 'poetical' than good poetry. Yet if not actively liked it is at least tolerated. For example, just before writing this I have been listening to a couple of B.B.C. comedians doing their usual turn before the 9 o'clock news. In the last three minutes one of the two comedians suddenly announces that he 'wants to be serious for a moment' and proceeds to recite a piece of patriotic balderdash entitled 'A Fine Old English Gentleman', in praise of His Majesty the King. Now, what is the reaction of the audience to the sudden lapse into the worst sort of rhyming heroics? It cannot be very violently negative, or there would be a sufficient volume of indignant letters to stop the B.B.C. doing this kind of thing. One must conclude that though the big public is hostile to *poetry*, it is not strongly hostile to *verse*. After all, if rhyme and metre were disliked for their own sakes, neither songs nor dirty limericks could be popular. Poetry is disliked because it is associated with unintelligibility, intellectual pretentiousness and a general feeling of Sunday-on-a-weekday. Its name creates in advance the same sort of bad impression as the word 'God', or a parson's dog-collar. To a certain extent, popularising poetry is a question of breaking down an acquired inhibition. It is a question of getting people to listen instead of uttering a mechanical raspberry. If true poetry could be introduced to the big public in such a way as to make it seem *normal*, as that piece of rubbish I have just listened to presumably seemed normal, then part of the prejudice against it might be overcome.

It is difficult to believe that poetry can ever be popularised again without some deliberate effort at the education of public taste, involving strategy and perhaps even subterfuge. T. S. Eliot once suggested that poetry, particularly dramatic poetry, might be brought back into the consciousness of ordinary people through the medium of the music hall; he might have added the pantomime, whose vast possibilities do not seem ever to have been completely explored. *Sweeney Agonistes* was perhaps written with some such idea in mind, and it would in fact be conceivable as a music-hall turn, or at least as a scene in a revue.[2] I have suggested the radio as a more hopeful medium, and I have pointed out its technical advantages, particularly from the point of view of the poet. The reason why such a suggestion sounds hopeless at first hearing is that few people are able to imagine the radio being used for the dissemination of anything except tripe. People listen to the stuff that does actually dribble from the loudspeakers of the world, and conclude that it is for that and nothing else that the wireless exists. Indeed the very word 'wireless' calls up a picture either of roaring dictators or of genteel throaty voices announcing that three of our aircraft have failed to return. Poetry on the air sounds like the Muses in striped trousers. Nevertheless one ought not to confuse the capabilities of an instrument with the use it is actually put to. Broadcasting is what it is, not because there is something inherently vulgar, silly and dishonest about the whole apparatus of microphone and transmitter, but because all the broadcasting that now happens all over the world is under the control of governments or great monopoly companies which are actively interested in maintaining the status quo and therefore in preventing the common man from becoming too intelligent. Something of the same kind has happened to the cinema, which, like the radio, made its appearance during the monopoly stage of capitalism and is fantastically expensive to operate. In all the arts the tendency is similar. More and more the channels of production are under the control of bureaucrats, whose aim is to destroy the artist or at least to castrate him. This would be a bleak outlook if it were not that the totalitarianisation which is now going on, and must undoubtedly continue to go on, in every country of the world, is mitigated by another process which it was not easy to foresee even as short a time as five years ago.

This is, that the huge bureaucratic machines of which we are all part are beginning to work creakily because of their mere size and their constant growth. The tendency of the modern state is to wipe out the freedom of the intellect, and yet at the same time every state, especially under the pressure of war, finds itself more and more in need of an intelligentsia to do its publicity for it. The modern state needs, for example, pamphlet-writers, poster artists, illustrators, broadcasters, lecturers, film producers, actors, song-composers, even painters and sculptors, not to mention psychologists, sociologists, biochemists, mathematicians and what-not. The British government started the present war with the more or less openly declared intention of keeping the literary intelligentsia out of it; yet after three years of war almost every writer, however undesirable his political history or opinions, has been sucked into the various Ministries or the B.B.C., and even those who enter the armed forces tend to find themselves after a while in Public Relations or some other essentially literary job. The Government has absorbed these people, unwillingly enough, because it found itself unable to get on without them. The ideal, from the official point of view, would have been to put all publicity into the hands of 'safe' people like A. P. Herbert or Ian Hay:[3] but since not enough of these were available, the existing intelligentsia had to be utilised, and the tone and even to some extent the content of official propaganda have been modified accordingly. No one acquainted with the Government pamphlets, A.B.C.A. lectures,[4] documentary films and broadcasts to occupied countries which have been issued during the past two years imagines that our rulers would sponsor this kind of thing if they could help it. Only, the bigger the machine of government becomes, the more loose ends and forgotten corners there are in it. This is perhaps a small consolation, but it is not a despicable one. It means that in countries where there is already a strong liberal tradition, bureaucratic tyranny can perhaps never be complete. The striped-trousered ones will rule, but so long as they are forced to maintain an intelligentsia, the intelligentsia will have a certain amount of autonomy. If the Government needs, for example, documentary films, it must employ people specially interested in the technique of the film, and it must allow them the necessary minimum of freedom; consequently, films that are all wrong from the bureaucratic point of view will always have a tendency to appear. So also with painting, photography, script-writing, reportage, lecturing and all the other arts and half-arts of which a complex modern state has need.

The application of this to the radio is obvious. At present the loud-speaker is the enemy of the creative writer, but this may not necessarily remain true when the volume and scope of broadcasting increase. As things are, although the B.B.C. does keep up a feeble show of interest in contemporary literature, it is harder to capture five minutes on the air in which to broadcast a poem than twelve hours in which to disseminate lying propaganda, tinned music, stale jokes, faked 'discussions' or what-have-you. But that state of affairs may alter in the way I have indicated, and when that time comes serious experiment in the broadcasting of verse, with complete disregard for the various hostile influences which prevent any such thing at present, would become possible. I don't claim it as certain that such an experiment would have very great results. The radio was bureaucratised so early in its career that the relationship between broadcasting and literature has never been thought out. It is not certain that the microphone is the instrument by which poetry could be brought back to the common people and it is not even certain that poetry would gain by being more of a spoken and less of a written thing. But I do urge that these possibilities exist, and that those who care for literature might turn their minds more often to this much-despised medium, whose powers for good have perhaps been obscured by the voices of Professor Joad and Doctor Goebbels.[5]

1. Orwell gave the title as *September*, 1941.

2. T. S. Eliot had some direct knowledge of the music hall. He wrote an essay on the great music-hall comedienne, Marie Lloyd (1870–1922), shortly after her death. This is more appreciative than accurate: she was not the only performer with a 'capacity for expressing the soul of the people', and, in claiming 'no objector would have dared to lift his voice' against her, he was unaware that she had been booed off the stage by 'her own people' at the Paragon in the East End of London. Orwell's suggestion that *Sweeney Agonistes* (published 1932) was 'conceivable as a music-hall turn' is correct. Dusty's telephone conversation, which includes the telephone's 'Ting a ling ling' four times, actually precedes the act made popular from 1934 by Jeanne de Casalis (b. 1897) as Mrs Feather, whose scatterbrained telephone conversations were a popular music-hall turn for many years.

3. Alan Patrick Herbert (1890–1971; Kt., 1945; CH, 1970), humorist, novelist, dramatist and author of light poetry. From 1935 he represented Oxford University in the House of Commons until 1951, when university constituencies were abolished. He took his parliamentary duties seriously and he introduced the Matrimonial Causes Bill (enacted 1937), which made significant changes to the divorce laws. He served in the Royal Naval Division, 1914–17. Ian Hay (John Hay Beith; 1876–1952), novelist and dramatist. He wrote such successful plays as *A Safety Match* (1911), *The Middle Watch* (1931) and *The Housemaster* (1936). He collaborated with P. G. Wodehouse on the plays *A Damsel in Distress* (1928) and *Baa, Baa, Black Sheep* (1929). He also wrote histories of World War I.

4. The Army Bureau of Current Affairs organized lectures for servicemen on topical issues, for example, the Welfare State, the Atom Bomb.

5. Professor C. E. M. Joad (1891–1953), philosopher and writer. From 1930 until his death he was head of the Department of Psychology and Philosophy, Birkbeck College, University of London. He achieved popular fame as a member of the BBC's radio programme 'The Brains Trust', which discussed questions posed by listeners. Orwell's reference to (Paul) Joseph Goebbels has typically ironic implications. Goebbels (1897–1945) mastered Nazi propaganda in the press and on radio; he was a fierce anti-Semite. He died by his own hand in Hitler's bunker in Berlin. However, he had graduated from Heidelberg University in 1921

with a doctorate in German philology. There is a bitter contrast between his doctorate in the humanities and his inhuman policies, something not lost on Orwell, especially because Orwell had a particular interest in philology.

[2862]

Review of The Condition of the British People, 1911–1945 *by Mark Abrams*

Manchester Evening News, *17 January 1946*

Statistics by themselves are not lively reading, but Mr. Abrams's little book,[1] in which comparative lists of figures take up almost as much space as the letterpress, manages to give a remarkably interesting and convincing picture of developments in Britain during the past generation.

This study was prepared for the Fabian Society, and the dates, 1911–1945, were not chosen at random. This period coincides with a set of processes which Mr. Abrams calls the Edwardian Revolution, and which have now, he considers, finally run their course.

The Edwardian Revolution started early in this century with such events as the passing of the National Insurance Act, the introduction of Old Age Pensions and the beginning of rehousing on a big scale.

Its more or less conscious aim was to ameliorate the conditions of the poorer classes without upsetting existing property relations, and the method it followed was generally in the direction of redistributing the national income rather than increasing the gross total of the nation's wealth. The war has set a whole series of new processes going, and Mr. Abrams's main purpose is to compare the conditions of 1938 with those of 1911. Even without his explanations the sets of figures that he gives make clear the pattern of national life during these years.

If one had to sum up the development in one phrase, one might do it by saying that Britain has become suburbanised. To begin with, there has been a steady movement of population away from the old industrial areas of Scotland, Wales and the North of England and towards London and the Home Counties.

In London and in nearly every big town there has been a movement away from the centre into newly built and relatively convenient houses on the edge of the country. There has been a decline of the old staple industries such as coal and cotton, and a corresponding growth in the new light industries, mostly situated in the South of England.

There has been a startling decline in the birth-rate with a corresponding fall in the size of the average family. And though the actual increase of wealth has not been very great, the standard of living of the working-class, especially if one takes the shorter working hours into consideration, has risen notably. In 1938, Mr. Abrams considers the average person in this country was approximately 20 per cent better off than he had been in 1911.

Apart from the rising standards of the working class proper, the developments of the inter-war years brought into being a new class whose existence had not been foreseen in the nineteenth century. This class consists of the salaried white-collar workers who cannot be accurately classified either as bourgeois or proletarian. Mr. Abrams considers in any case that this classification is becoming obsolete.

Apart from the tendency to even out incomes by means of taxation – at this moment, in theory, even a millionaire has not an income of much more than £4,000 a year – there has been a tendency for more and more of the population to become property owners through the agency of building societies.

These societies were not active in a large way until about 1924. Now, however, there are about four million people in England who own their own houses – a block of the population potentially as important as the owner-peasants of a European country.

In general the picture is one of rising standards and diminishing class-distinctions, but it is by no means all rosy. To begin with, the economic system was never able to eliminate mass-unemployment, nor to save a quite considerable section of the population – 10 per cent to be exact – from acute poverty. The atrocious over-crowding and filthy living-conditions which used to exist in all big towns have improved in very recent years, because the population has not risen rapidly, while there was very extensive building of new houses in the last five years before the war.

But malnutrition persisted to such an extent that approximately 20 per cent of working-class children were born into families which could not afford the British Medical Association's minimum diet. Throughout the inter-war years there was always an average of from one to two million people unemployed, and the rates of benefit paid were such that the family of an unemployed man was inevitably under-nourished.

The other equally disquieting symptom of this period was the drop in the birth-rate. This appears to have been due partly to the general rise in standards and the greater regard paid to children, with consequent unwillingness on the part of parents to bring into the world a large brood of children who would necessarily start off in dire poverty.

Hitherto the dropping birth-rate has tended to benefit the average family, because it meant that wages and household accommodation had to be divided among fewer people; but the future effects on industry of a falling off in the number both of consumers and of young adaptable workers may be very serious. During the war years the birth-rate has risen steadily, but it is not yet certain whether this represents a real change of trend.

In 1938 the national 'real' income was about 20 per cent higher than it had been in 1911. The effect of the destruction and wasted labour of the war has been to push it back almost to the 1911 level. This of itself is sufficient to indicate the magnitude of the task we have ahead of us.

Writing just before the General Election, Mr. Abrams concludes: 'To-day it is clear that the methods of the Edwardian Revolution, even when pushed to their limits, are by themselves inadequate to accomplish all its purposes. The step that has been missed so far is the development of an overall economic strategy, designed to provide full employment and to raise substantially the productivity of British industry.'

In his postscript, written just after the election, he appears hopeful that the Labour Government will do what half a dozen preceding Governments have failed to do, and we may trust that he is right. The book has an interesting introductory chapter comparing the conditions of life in 1913 with those of today, and also a short foreword by G. D. H. Cole.[2]

1. Dr Mark Abrams (1906–94) was Director of the Research Unit, Age Concern, 1976–85. He worked for the Overseas Department of the BBC, 1939–41, and Orwell might have heard about him or even met him there. He then joined the Psychological Warfare Board, 1941–6, and the Metrication Board, 1969–79. Orwell discusses his *The Population of Great Britain* (1945), with its dire forecasts, in 'As I Please', 78, 21 March 1947 (XIX/*3196*), and

see pp. 322–3, above. Abrams did not include this book in his list of publications in *Who's Who* in the late 1980s.

2. G. D. H. Cole (1889–1959), Chichele Professor of Social and Political Theory, University of Oxford, and a Fellow of All Souls; socialist and prolific writer. His *The Intelligent Man's Guide to the Post-War World* (1947) was influential. Orwell referred to it as Cole's 'last 1143-page compilation' (XIX/*3254*).

[2900]

'Decline of the English Murder'

Tribune, *15 February 1946*

It is Sunday afternoon, preferably before the war. The wife is already asleep in the armchair, and the children have been sent out for a nice long walk. You put your feet up on the sofa, settle your spectacles on your nose, and open the *News of the World.* Roast beef and Yorkshire, or roast pork and applesauce, followed up by suet pudding and driven home, as it were, by a cup of mahogany-brown tea, have put you in just the right mood. Your pipe is drawing sweetly, the sofa cushions are soft underneath you, the fire is well alight, the air is warm and stagnant. In these blissful circumstances, what is it that you want to read about?

Naturally, about a murder. But what kind of murder? If one examines the murders which have given the greatest amount of pleasure to the British public, the murders whose story is known in its general outline to almost everyone and which have been made into novels and re-hashed over and over again by the Sunday papers, one finds a fairly strong family resemblance running through the greater number of them. Our great period in murder, our Elizabethan period, so to speak, seems to have been between roughly 1850 and 1925, and the murderers whose reputation has stood the test of time are the following: Dr. Palmer of Rugely, Jack the Ripper, Neill Cream, Mrs. Maybrick, Dr. Crippen, Seddon, Joseph Smith, Armstrong, and Bywaters and Thompson. In addition, in 1919 or thereabouts, there was another very celebrated case which fits into the general pattern but which I had better not mention by name, because the accused man was acquitted.

Of the above-mentioned nine cases, at least four have had successful novels based on them, one has been made into a popular melodrama, and the amount of literature surrounding them, in the form of newspaper write-ups, criminological treatises and reminiscences by lawyers and police officers, would make a considerable library. It is difficult to believe that any recent English crime will be remembered so long and so intimately, and not only because the violence of external events has made murder seem unimportant, but because the prevalent type of crime seems to be changing. The principle *cause célèbre* of the war years was the so-called Cleft Chin Murder, which has now been written up in a popular booklet;[1] the verbatim account of the trial was published some time last year by Messrs. Jarrolds with an introduction by Mr. Bechhofer Roberts.[2] Before returning to this pitiful and sordid case, which is only interesting from a sociological and perhaps a legal point of view, let me try to define what it is that the readers of Sunday papers mean when they say fretfully that 'you never seem to get a good murder nowadays'.

In considering the nine murders I named above, one can start by excluding the Jack the Ripper case, which is in a class by itself. Of the other eight, six were poisoning cases, and eight of the ten criminals belonged to the middle class. In one way or another, sex was a powerful motif in all but two cases, and in at least four cases respectability – the desire to gain a secure position in life, or not to forfeit one's social position by some scandal such as a divorce – was one of the main reasons for committing murder. In more than half the cases, the object was to get hold of a certain known sum of money such as a legacy or an insurance policy, but the amount involved was nearly always small. In most of the cases the crime only came to light slowly, as the result of careful investigations which started off with the suspicions of neighbours or relatives; and in nearly every case there was some dramatic coincidence, in which the finger of Providence could be clearly seen, or one of those episodes that no novelist would dare to make up, such as Crippen's flight across the Atlantic with his mistress dressed as a boy, or Joseph Smith playing 'Nearer, my God, to Thee' on the harmonium while one of his wives was drowning in the next room. The background of all these crimes, except Neill Cream's, was essentially domestic; of twelve victims, seven were either wife or husband of the murderer.

With all this in mind one can construct what would be, from a *News of the World* reader's point of view, the 'perfect' murder. The murderer should be a little man of the professional class – a dentist or a solicitor, say – living an intensely respectable life somewhere in the suburbs, and preferably in a semi-detached house, which will allow the neighbours to hear suspicious sounds through the wall. He should be either chairman of the local Conservative Party branch, or a leading Nonconformist and strong Temperance advocate. He should go astray through cherishing a guilty passion for his secretary or the wife of a rival professional man, and should only bring himself to the point of murder after long and terrible wrestles with his conscience. Having decided on murder, he should plan it all with the utmost cunning, and only slip up over some tiny, unforeseeable detail. The means chosen should, of course, be poison. In the last analysis he should commit murder because this seems to him less disgraceful, and less damaging to his career, than being detected in adultery. With this kind of background, a crime can have dramatic and even tragic qualities which make it memorable and excite pity for both victim and murderer. Most of the crimes mentioned above have a touch of this atmosphere, and in three cases, including the one I referred to but did not name, the story approximates to the one I have outlined.

Now compare the Cleft Chin Murder. There is no depth of feeling in it. It was almost chance that the two people concerned committed that particular murder, and it was only by good luck that they did not commit several others. The background was not domesticity, but the anonymous life of the dance-halls and the false values of the American film. The two culprits were an eighteen-year-old ex-waitress named Elizabeth Jones, and an American army deserter, posing as an officer, named Karl Hulten. They were only together for six days, and it seems doubtful whether, until they were arrested, they even learned one another's true names. They met casually in a teashop, and that night went out for a ride in a stolen army truck. Jones described herself as a strip-tease artist, which was not strictly true (she had given one unsuccessful performance in this line), and declared that she wanted to do something dangerous, 'like being a gun-moll'. Hulten described himself as a big-time Chicago gangster, which was also untrue. They met a girl bicycling along the road, and to show how tough he was Hulten ran over her with his truck, after which the pair robbed her of the few shillings that were on her. On another occasion they knocked out a girl to whom they had offered a lift, took her coat and handbag and threw her into a river. Finally, in the most wanton way, they murdered a taxi-driver who happened to have £8 in his pocket. Soon afterwards they parted. Hulten was caught because he had foolishly kept the dead man's car, and Jones made spontaneous confessions to the police. In court each prisoner incriminated the other. In between crimes, both of them seem to have behaved with the utmost callousness: they spent the dead taxi-driver's £8 at the dog races.

Judging from her letters, the girl's case has a certain amount of psychological interest, but this murder probably captured the headlines because it provided distraction amid the doodle-bugs and the anxieties of the Battle of France. Jones and Hulten committed their murder to the tune of V1, and were convicted to the tune of V2.[3] There was also considerable excitement because – as has become usual in England – the man was sentenced to death and the girl to imprisonment. According to Mr. Raymond, the reprieving of Jones caused widespread indignation and streams of telegrams to the Home Secretary: in her native town, 'She should hang' was chalked on the walls beside pictures of a figure dangling from a gallows. Considering that only ten women have been hanged in Britain in this century, and that the practice has gone out largely because of popular feeling against it, it is difficult not to feel that this clamour to hang an eighteen-year-old girl was due partly to the brutalising effects of war. Indeed, the whole meaningless story, with its atmosphere of dance-halls, movie-palaces, cheap perfume, false names and stolen cars, belongs essentially to a war period.

Perhaps it is significant that the most talked-of English murder of recent years should have been committed by an American and an English girl who had become partly Americanised. But it is difficult to believe that this case will be so long remembered as the old domestic poisoning dramas, product of a stable society where the all-prevailing hypocrisy did at least ensure that crimes as serious as murder should have strong emotions behind them.

1. *The Cleft Chin Murder* by R. Alwyn Raymond.
2. *The Trial of Jones and Hulten*, edited with a foreword by C. E. Bechhofer Roberts (1945), reviewed by Orwell, 1 November 1945 (XVII/*2779*).
3. The V-1 and V-2 were two types of German 'Revenge Weapons' (*Vergeltungswaffe*). The V-1 was pilotless and it and the V-2 each carried about a ton (900 kg.) of high explosive. The first V-1 was fired on the night of 13–14 June, seven days after D-Day. It was nicknamed the buzz-bomb, or doodlebug, arising from its sound before the engine cut out and it made

its descent to earth where it exploded. It was visible from the ground and of 9,251 fired at southern England (more or less the limit of its range), 4,621 were destroyed, 630 being shot down by the RAF. Orwell describes one approaching in 'As I Please', 32, 7 July 1944 (XVI/*2501*). The V-2 was a long-range rocket and simply arrived. The first was fired at Paris on 6 September 1944; on 8 September the first of some 3,000 were fired at England and a similar number were aimed at Belgium. It is the 'steamer' of *Nineteen Eighty-Four*. Far from being 'revenge weapons', their research began secretly in 1936, long before the war. They were designed to terrorize civilians, no precise targeting being possible. The Crown Film Unit made a short film of the V-1 called *The Eighty Days* (edited by the present editor).

[*3190*]

Extract from 'As I Please', 77 [Scrapping the British system of weights and measures]

Tribune, *14 March 1947*

Another thing I am against in advance – for it is bound to be suggested sooner or later – is the complete scrapping of our present system of weights and measures.[1]

Obviously you have got to have the metric system for certain purposes. For scientific work it has long been in use, and it is also needed for tools and machinery, especially if you want to export them. But there is a strong case for keeping on the old measurements for use in everyday life. One reason is that the metric system does not possess, or has not succeeded in establishing, a large number of units that can be visualised. There is, for instance, effectively no unit between the metre, which is more than a yard, and the centimetre, which is less than half an inch. In English you can describe someone as being five feet three inches high, or five feet nine inches, or six feet one inch, and your hearer will know fairly accurately what you mean. But I have never heard a Frenchman say, 'He is a hundred and forty-two centimetres high'; it would not convey any visual image. So also with the various other measurements. Rods and acres, pints, quarts and gallons, pounds, stones and hundredweights, are all of them units with which we are intimately familiar, and we should be slightly poorer without them. Actually, in countries where the metric system is in force a few of the old measurements tend to linger on for everyday purposes, although officially discouraged.

There is also the literary consideration, which cannot be left quite out of account. The names of the units in the old system are short homely words which lend themselves to vigorous speech. Putting a quart into a pint pot is a good image, which could hardly be expressed in the metric system. Also, the literature of the past deals only in the old measurements, and many passages would become an irritation if one had to do a sum in arithmetic when one read them, as one does with those tiresome versts[2] in a Russian novel.

> The emmet's[3] inch and eagle's mile
> Make lame philosophy to smile:

fancy having to turn that into millimetres!

1. Orwell's expectations came to pass. European Community Directive 89/617 phased out British imperial measures and Parliament's Units of Measurement Regulations, 1995, changed the existing Act of Parliament to accord with the Directive. It is now illegal to sell goods by imperial measure. Those who do face heavy fines. Thus, the Beamish Museum's recreation of a 1913 sweet shop has been forced to metricate traditional labels, an appeal to retain them having being rejected; a child asking for a quarter of sweets must be sold 113 grams-worth.
2. A verst is about two-thirds of a mile.
3. An emmet is an ant.

[3409]

'Such, Such Were the Joys'

1939?–June 1948?

It is well-nigh impossible to assign a date – or dates – to the composition and completion of Orwell's essay on his time at St Cyprian's preparatory school. Its position here is dictated by the belief that the essay was finally revised by about midsummer 1948.

Orwell attended St Cyprian's, Eastbourne, from September 1911 to December 1916. The essay refers to 'All this' being 'thirty years ago or more', suggesting that he was writing between 1941 and 1946, or later. Since his statement comes immediately after his reference to having left St Cyprian's, his 'thirty years ago or more' might reasonably imply 1946 to 1948. It could also – and probably did – refer only to the final revision of the essay.

Orwell must have written the essay after 1938, the year Cyril Connolly's

Enemies of Promise *was published, and to which, he told Fredric Warburg, it was 'a sort of pendant'; see* XIX/*3232. When Orwell wrote that, on 31 May 1947, a version of the essay had been completed, but the surviving typescript shows that it was subjected to final revision in 1948, probably in Hairmyres Hospital, Glasgow, after Orwell had sent the typescript of* Nineteen Eighty-Four *to Fredric Warburg. The title is from William Blake's poem, 'The Echoing Green', one of the* Songs of Innocence *(1789).*

This degree of revision, especially at a time when Orwell was much preoccupied with writing Nineteen Eighty-Four, *given that he was well aware that 'it is really too libellous to print' (see 3232) indicates how important this essay was to him. He realized it could not be published until some of those most concerned were dead. It would seem that 'Such, Such Were the Joys' had for Orwell comparable importance to* Nineteen Eighty-Four – *which is* not *to say (as have some critics) that the two works are related in content and attitude.*

Earlier printings of 'Such, Such Were the Joys' have shown changes of names to avoid giving offence to those then living. The text given here is that revised by Orwell but with the original names. It is hoped that, after all this time, no hurt will be sustained by anyone mentioned.

For a detailed account of the genesis of 'Such, Such Were the Joys', see XIX/*3408, and also Crick, 58–80; Shelden, 26–53, 58–62; S&A,* Unknown Orwell, *38–83; and three essays by Robert Pearce: 'Truth and Falsehood: George Orwell's Prep School Woes',* Review of English Studies, *ns, XLIII (1992), 367–86; 'The Prep School and Imperialism: The Example of Orwell's St. Cyprian's',* Journal of Educational Administration and History *(January 1991), 42–53; and 'Orwell and the Harrow History Prize',* Notes & Queries, *235 (ns 37) (December 1990), 442–3. For reminiscences, see Cyril Connolly,* Enemies of Promise, *ch. 19, 'White Samite';* Orwell Remembered, *32–6 (which includes an excerpt from Connolly);* Remembering Orwell, *4–11 (which includes John Wilkes, son of Mr and Mrs Wilkes). Wilkes's memory of life at St Cyprian's, as Stephen Wadhams puts it, 'is as benign as Orwell's is harsh'. Orwell and the Wilkeses' son were later fellow students at Eton and John Wilkes recalls him as 'a boy with a permanent chip on the shoulder' but 'very well read' (*Remembering Orwell, *11).*

An edition of this kind is not the place for a critical commentary, but a couple of points might be made. First, the essay is certainly not 'a true historical record', as Robert Pearce reveals. Second, what may have motivated Orwell's determination to write the essay, and work over it so much when he was seriously ill and anxious to get Nineteen Eighty-Four *completed, though he knew it could not be published in his lifetime, was his concern that if England was to be reformed, then it was its education system that must be tackled first, even before setting up a National Health Service. Tosco Fyvel, a close friend of Orwell, recalls that when Orwell resumed his 'As I Please' column in 1946, he wanted to attack the Labour Government, including his friend Aneurin Bevan, for being 'diverted into enlarging the National Health Service and the public sector and into measures of nationalization'. Orwell wished to write that if 'socialists had really wanted to change British society, they should have done three things: abolish public schools, abolish all titles and abolish the House of Lords'. Fyvel persuaded him not to write in this vein, but later regretted that he had done so: 'Orwell was of course right, as he so often was' (T. R. Fyvel,* George Orwell: A Personal Memoir *(1982), 146–7). That said, Orwell* did *decide to enter his son, Richard, for Westminster School (see 3645,* XX/113*), though he did not go there.*

Thirdly, as Robert Pearce shows, certain facts are wrong and there are clear exaggerations (though Orwell might have expected the judicious reader to spot those). One incident will suffice here. It seems Orwell was never beaten for bedwetting and that the person who was, Bobby Foote, became a very distinguished soldier who won the VC. There is no record of a riding crop being used for beating (see Robert Pearce's, 'Truth and Falsehood', as above, 373; and see n. 1, below). Thus, if one is looking for a factual account for life at St Cyprian's, this is not the place to seek it. What Orwell has done is put himself in Foote's place. He has written an imaginative account of how the experience felt, with the implication that he didn't want this system perpetuated. In that sense, and aware of what is not correct and what is exaggerated, the experience Orwell described strikes me, from my experience at a more modest level, twenty years later, as totally convincing. Although Orwell is often praised for his documentary-like characteristics, he was also an imaginative writer and that is sometimes forgotten. It would be wise to bear in mind when reading this essay something Orwell explained in 'The Prevention of Literature': 'The journalist is unfree, and is conscious of unfreedom, when he is forced to write lies or suppress what seems to him important news: the imaginative writer is unfree when he has to falsify his subjective feelings, which from his point of view are facts. He may distort and caricature reality in order to make his meaning clearer, but he cannot misrepresent the scenery of his own mind: he cannot say with any conviction that he likes what he dislikes, or believes what he disbelieves' (2792, XVII/375).

Soon after I arrived at St. Cyprian's (not immediately, but after a week or two, just when I seemed to be settling into the routine of school life) I began wetting my bed. I was now aged eight, so that this was a reversion to a habit which I must have grown out of at least four years earlier.

Nowadays, I believe, bed-wetting in such circumstances is taken for granted. It is a normal reaction in children who have been removed from their homes to a strange place. In those days, however, it was looked on as a disgusting crime which the child committed on purpose and for which the proper cure was a beating. For my part I did not need to be told it was a crime. Night after night I prayed, with a fervour never previously attained in my prayers, 'Please God, do not let me wet my bed! Oh, please God, do not let me wet my bed!', but it made remarkably little difference. Some nights the thing happened, others not. There was no volition about it, no consciousness. You did not properly speaking *do* the deed: you merely woke up in the morning and found that the sheets were wringing wet.

After the second or third offence I was warned that I should be beaten next time, but I received the warning in a curiously roundabout way. One afternoon, as we were filing out from tea, Mrs Wilkes, the headmaster's wife, was sitting at the head of one of the tables, chatting with a lady of whom I know nothing, except that she was on an afternoon's visit to the school. She was an intimidating, masculine-looking person wearing a riding habit, or something that I took to be a riding habit. I was just leaving the room when Mrs Wilkes called me back, as though to introduce me to the visitor.

Mrs Wilkes was nicknamed Flip, and I shall call her by that name, for I seldom think of her by any other. (Officially, however, she was addressed as Mum, probably a corruption of the 'Ma'am' used by public schoolboys to their housemasters' wives.) She was a stocky square-built woman with hard red cheeks, a flat top to her head, prominent brows and deepset, suspicious eyes. Although a great deal of the time she was full of false heartiness, jollying one along with mannish slang ('*Buck* up, old chap!' and so forth), and even using one's Christian name, her eyes never lost their anxious, accusing look. It was very difficult to look her in the face without feeling guilty, even at moments when one was not guilty of anything in particular.

'Here is a little boy,' said Flip, indicating me to the strange lady, 'who wets his bed every night. Do you know what I am going to do if you wet your bed again?' she added, turning to me. 'I am going to get the Sixth Form to beat you.'

The strange lady put on an air of being inexpressibly shocked, and exclaimed, 'I-should-*think*-so!' And here there occurred one of those wild, almost lunatic misunderstandings which are part of the daily experience of childhood. The Sixth Form was a group of older boys who were selected as having 'character' and were empowered to beat smaller boys. I had not yet learned of their existence, and I mis-heard the phrase 'the Sixth Form' as 'Mrs Form'. I took it as referring to the strange lady – I thought, that is, that her name was Mrs Form. It was an improbable name, but a child has no judgement in such matters. I imagined, therefore, that it was *she* who was to be deputed to beat me. It did not strike me as strange that this job should be turned over to a casual visitor in no way connected with the school. I merely assumed that 'Mrs Form' was a stern disciplinarian who enjoyed beating people (somehow her appearance seemed to bear this out) and I had an immediate terrifying vision of her arriving for the occasion in full riding kit and armed with a hunting whip. To this day I can feel myself almost swooning with shame as I stood, a very small, round-faced boy in short corduroy knickers, before the two women. I could not speak. I felt that I should die if 'Mrs Form' were to beat me. But my dominant feeling was not fear or even resentment: it was simply shame because one more person, and that a woman, had been told of my disgusting offence.

A little later, I forget how, I learned that it was not after all 'Mrs Form' who would do the beating. I cannot remember whether it was that very night that I wetted my bed again, but at any rate I did wet it again quite soon. Oh, the despair, the feeling of cruel injustice, after all my prayers and resolutions, at once again waking between the clammy sheets! There was no chance of hiding what I had done. The grim statuesque matron, Margaret by name, arrived in the dormitory specially to inspect my bed. She pulled back the clothes, then drew herself up, and the dreaded words seemed to come rolling out of her like a peal of thunder:

'REPORT YOURSELF to the headmaster after breakfast!'

I put REPORT YOURSELF in capitals because that was how it appeared in my mind. I do not know how many times I heard that phrase during my early years at St. Cyprian's. It was only very rarely that it did not mean a beating. The words always had a portentous sound in my ears, like muffled drums or the words of the death sentence.

When I arrived to report myself, Flip was doing something or other at the long shiny table in the ante-room to the study. Her uneasy eyes searched me as I went past. In the study Mr Wilkes, nicknamed Sambo, was waiting. Sambo was a round-shouldered, curiously oafish-looking man, not large but shambling in gait, with a chubby face which was like that of an overgrown baby, and which was capable of good-humour. He knew, of course, why I had been sent to him, and had already taken a bone-handled riding-crop out of the cupboard, but it was part of the punishment of reporting yourself that you had to proclaim your offence with your own lips. When I had said my say, he read me a short but pompous lecture, then seized me by the scruff of the neck, twisted me over and began beating me with the riding crop. He had a habit of continuing his lecture while he flogged you, and I remember the words 'you dir-ty lit-tle boy' keeping time with the blows. The beating did not hurt (perhaps, as it was the first time, he was not hitting me very hard), and I walked out feeling very much better. The fact that the beating had not hurt was a sort of victory and partially wiped out the shame of the bed-wetting. Perhaps I was even incautious enough to wear a grin on my face. Some small boys were hanging about in the passage outside the door of the ante-room.

'D'you get the cane?'

'It didn't hurt,' I said proudly.

Flip had heard everything. Instantly her voice came screaming after me:

'Come here! Come here this instant! What was that you said?'

'I said it didn't hurt,' I faltered out.

'How dare you say a thing like that? Do you think that is a proper thing to say? Go in and REPORT YOURSELF AGAIN!'

This time Sambo laid on in real earnest. He continued for a length of time that frightened and astonished me – about five minutes, it seemed – ending up by breaking the riding crop. The bone handle went flying across the room.

'Look what you've made me do!' he said furiously, holding up the broken crop.[1]

I had fallen into a chair, weakly snivelling. I remember that this was the only time throughout my boyhood when a beating actually reduced me to tears, and curiously enough I was not even now crying because of the pain. The second beating had not hurt very much either. Fright and shame seemed to have anaesthetised me. I was crying partly because I felt that this was expected of me, partly from genuine repentance, but partly also because of a deeper grief which is peculiar to childhood and not easy to convey: a sense of desolate loneliness and helplessness, of being locked up not only in a hostile world but in a world of good and evil where the rules were such that it was actually not possible for me to keep them.

I knew that the bed-wetting was (a) wicked and (b) outside my control. The second fact I was personally aware of, and the first I did not question. It was possible, therefore, to commit a sin without knowing that you committed it, without wanting to commit it, and without being able to avoid it. Sin was not necessarily something that you did: it might be something that happened to you. I do not want to claim that this idea flashed into my mind as a complete novelty at this very moment, under the blows of Sambo's cane: I must have had glimpses of it even before I left home, for my early childhood had not been altogether happy. But at any rate this was the great, abiding lesson of my boyhood: that I was in a world where it was *not possible* for me to be good. And the double beating was a turning-point, for it brought home to me for the first time the harshness of the environment into which I had been flung. Life was more terrible, and I was more wicked, than I had imagined. At any rate, as I sat snivelling on the edge of a chair in Sambo's study, with not even the self-possession to stand up while he stormed at me, I had a conviction of sin and folly and weakness, such as I do not remember to have felt before.

In general, one's memories of any period must necessarily weaken as one moves away from it. One is constantly learning new facts, and old ones have to drop out to make way for them. At twenty I could have written the history of my schooldays with an accuracy which would be quite impossible now. But it can also happen that one's memories grow sharper after a long lapse of time, because one is looking at the past with fresh eyes and can isolate and, as it were, notice facts which previously existed undifferentiated among a mass of others. Here are two things which in a sense I remembered, but which did not strike me as strange or interesting until quite recently. One is that the second beating seemed to me a just and reasonable punishment. To get one beating, and then to get another and far fiercer one on top of it, for being so unwise as to show that the first had not hurt – that was quite natural. The gods are jealous, and when you have good fortune you should conceal it. The other is that I accepted the broken riding crop as my own crime. I can still recall my feeling as I saw the handle lying on the carpet – the feeling of having done an ill-bred clumsy thing, and ruined an expensive object. *I* had broken it: so Sambo told me, and so I believed. This acceptance of guilt lay unnoticed in my memory for twenty or thirty years.

So much for the episode of the bed-wetting. But there is one more thing to be remarked. This is that I did not wet my bed again – at least, I did wet it once again, and received another beating, after which the trouble stopped. So perhaps this barbarous remedy does work, though at a heavy price, I have no doubt.

II

St. Cyprian's was an expensive and snobbish school which was in process of becoming more snobbish, and, I imagine, more expensive. The public school with which it had special connections was Harrow, but during my time an increasing proportion of the boys went on to Eton. Most of them were the children of rich parents, but on the whole they were the unaristocratic rich, the sort of people who live in huge shrubberied houses in Bournemouth or Richmond, and who have cars and butlers but not country estates. There were a few exotics among them – some South American boys, sons of Argentine beef barons, one or two Russians, and even a Siamese prince, or someone who was described as a prince.

Sambo had two great ambitions. One was to attract titled boys to the school, and the other was to train up pupils to win scholarships at public schools, above all at Eton. He did, towards the end of my time, succeed in getting hold of two boys with real English titles. One of them, I remember, was a wretched, drivelling little creature, almost an albino, peering upwards out of weak eyes, with a long nose at the end of which a dewdrop always seemed to be trembling.[2] Sambo always gave these boys their titles when mentioning them to a third person, and for their first few days he actually addressed them to their faces as 'Lord So-and-so'. Needless to say he found ways of drawing attention to them when any visitor was being shown round the school. Once, I remember, the little fair-haired boy had a choking fit at dinner, and a stream of snot ran out of his nose onto his plate in a way horrible to see. Any lesser person would have been called a dirty little beast and ordered out of the room instantly: but Sambo and Flip laughed it off in a 'boys will be boys' spirit.

All the very rich boys were more or less undisguisedly favoured. The school still had a faint suggestion of the Victorian 'private academy' with its 'parlour boarders',[3] and when I later read about that kind of school in Thackeray I immediately saw the resemblance. The rich boys had milk and biscuits in the middle of the morning, they were given riding lessons once or twice a week,[4] Flip mothered them and called them by their Christian names, and above all they were never caned. Apart from the South Americans, whose parents were safely distant, I doubt whether Sambo ever caned any boy whose father's income was much above £2,000 a year. But he was sometimes willing to sacrifice financial profit to scholastic prestige. Occasionally, by special arrangement, he would take at greatly reduced fees some boy who seemed likely to win scholarships and thus bring credit on the school. It was on these terms that I was at St. Cyprian's myself: otherwise my parents could not have afforded to send me to so expensive a school.

I did not at first understand that I was being taken at reduced fees; it was only when I was about eleven that Flip and Sambo began throwing the fact in my teeth. For my first two or three years I went through the ordinary educational mill: then, soon after I had started Greek (one started Latin at eight, Greek at ten), I moved into the scholarship class, which was taught, so far as classics went, largely by Sambo himself. Over a period of two or three years the scholarship boys were crammed with learning as cynically as a goose is crammed for Christmas. And with what learning! This business of making a gifted boy's career depend on a competitive examination, taken when he is only twelve or thirteen, is an evil thing at best, but there do appear to be preparatory schools which send scholars to Eton, Winchester, etc. without teaching them to see everything in terms of marks. At St. Cyprian's the whole process was frankly a preparation for a sort of confidence trick. Your job was to learn exactly those things that would give an examiner the impression that you knew more than you did know, and as far as possible to avoid burdening your brain with anything else. Subjects which lacked examination-value, such as geography, were almost completely neglected, mathematics was also neglected if you were a 'classical', science was not taught in any form – indeed it was so despised that even an interest in natural history was discouraged – and even the books you were encouraged to read in your spare time were chosen with one eye on the 'English paper'. Latin and Greek, the main scholarship subjects, were what counted, but even these were deliberately taught in a flashy, unsound way. We never, for example, read right through even a single book of a Greek or Latin author: we merely read short passages which were picked out because they were the kind of thing likely to be set as an 'unseen translation'. During the last year or so before we went up for our scholarships, most of our time was spent in simply working our way through the scholarship papers of previous years. Sambo had sheaves of these in his possession from every one of the major public schools. But the greatest outrage of all was the teaching of history.

There was in those days a piece of nonsense called the Harrow History Prize, an annual competition for which many preparatory schools entered. It was a tradition for St. Cyprian's to win it every year, as well we might, for we had mugged up every paper that had been set since the competition started, and the supply of possible questions was not inexhaustible. They were the kind of stupid question that is answered by rapping out a name or a quotation. Who plundered the Begums? Who was beheaded in an open boat? Who caught the Whigs bathing and ran away with their clothes? Almost all our historical teaching was on this level. History was a series of unrelated, unintelligible but – in some way that was never explained to us – important facts with resounding phrases tied to them. Disraeli brought peace with honour. Hastings[5] was astonished at his moderation. Pitt called in the New World to redress the balance of the Old. And the dates, and the mnemonic devices! (Did you know, for example, that the initial letters of 'A black Negress was my aunt: there's her house behind the barn' are also the initial letters of the battles in the Wars of the Roses?) Flip, who 'took' the higher forms in history, revelled in this kind of thing. I recall positive orgies of dates, with the keener boys leaping up and down in their places in their eagerness to shout out the right answers, and at the same time not feeling the faintest interest in the meaning of the mysterious events they were naming.

'1587?'

'Massacre of St. Bartholomew!'

'1707?'

'Death of Aurangzeeb!'[6]

'1713?'

'Treaty of Utrecht!'

'1773?'

'Boston Tea Party!'[7]

'1520?'

'Oo, Mum, please, Mum –'

'Please, Mum, please, Mum! Let me tell him, Mum!'

'Well! 1520?'

'Field of the Cloth of Gold!'

And so on.

But history and such secondary subjects were not bad fun. It was in 'classics' that the real strain came. Looking back, I realise that I then worked harder than I have ever done since, and yet at the time it never seemed possible to make quite the effort that was demanded of one. We would sit round the long shiny table, made of some very pale-coloured, hard wood, with Sambo goading, threatening, exhorting, sometimes joking, very occasionally praising, but always prodding, prodding away at one's mind to keep it up to the right pitch of concentration, as one might keep a sleepy person awake by sticking pins into him.

'Go on, you little slacker! Go on, you idle, worthless little boy! The whole trouble with you is that you're bone and horn idle. You eat too much, that's why. You wolf down enormous meals, and then when you come here you're half asleep. Go on, now, put your back into it. You're not *thinking*. Your brain doesn't sweat.'

He would tap away at one's skull with his silver pencil, which, in my memory, seems to have been about the size of a banana, and which certainly was heavy enough to raise a bump: or he would pull the short hairs round one's ears, or, occasionally, reach out under the table and kick one's shin. On some days nothing seemed to go right, and then it would be: 'All right, then, I know what you want. You've been asking for it the whole morning. Come along, you useless little slacker. Come into the study.' And then whack, whack, whack, whack, and back one would come, red-wealed and smarting – in later years Sambo had abandoned his riding crop in favour of a thin rattan cane which hurt very much more – to settle down to work again. This did not happen very often, but I do remember, more than once, being led out of the room in the middle of a Latin sentence, receiving a beating and then going straight ahead with the same sentence, just like that. It is a mistake to think such methods do not work. They work very well for their special purpose. Indeed, I doubt whether classical education ever has been or can be successfully carried on without corporal punishment.[8] The boys themselves believed in its efficacy. There was a boy named Hardcastle, with no brains to speak of, but evidently in acute need of a scholarship. Sambo was flogging him towards the goal as one might do with a foundered horse. He went up for a scholarship at Uppingham, came back with a consciousness of having done badly, and a day or two later received a severe beating for idleness. 'I wish I'd had that caning before I went up for the exam,' he said sadly – a remark which I felt to be contemptible, but which I perfectly well understood.

The boys of the scholarship class were not all treated alike. If a boy were the son of rich parents to whom the saving of fees was not all-important, Sambo would goad him along in a comparatively fatherly way, with jokes and digs in the ribs and perhaps an occasional tap with the pencil, but no hair-pulling and no caning. It was the poor but 'clever' boys who suffered. Our brains were a gold-mine in which he had sunk money, and the dividends must be squeezed out of us. Long before I had grasped the nature of my financial relationship with Sambo, I had been made to understand that I was not on the same footing as most of the other boys. In effect there were three castes in the school. There was the minority with an aristocratic or millionaire background, there were the children of the ordinary suburban rich, who made up the bulk of the school, and there were a few underlings like myself, the sons of clergymen, Indian civil servants, struggling widows and the like. These poorer ones were discouraged from going in for 'extras' such as shooting and carpentry, and were humiliated over clothes and petty possessions. I never, for instance, succeeded in getting a cricket bat of my own, because 'Your parents wouldn't be able to afford it'. This phrase pursued me throughout my schooldays. At St. Cyprian's we were not allowed to keep the money we brought back with us, but had to 'give it in' on the first day of term, and then from time to time were allowed to spend it under supervision. I and similarly-placed boys were always choked off from buying expensive toys like model aeroplanes, even if the necessary money stood to our credit. Flip, in particular, seemed to aim consciously at inculcating a humble outlook in the poorer boys. 'Do you think that's the sort of thing a boy like you should buy?' I remember her saying to somebody – and she said this in front of the whole school; 'You know you're not going to grow up with money, don't you? Your people aren't rich. You must learn to be sensible. Don't get above yourself!' There was also the weekly pocket-money, which we took out in sweets, dispersed by Flip from a large table. The millionaires had sixpence a week, but the normal sum was threepence. I and one or two others were only allowed twopence. My parents had not given instructions to this effect, and the saving of a penny a week could not conceivably have made any difference to them: it was a mark of status. Worse yet was the detail of the birthday cakes. It was usual for each boy, on his birthday, to have a large iced cake with candles, which was shared out at tea between the whole school. It was provided as a matter of routine and went on his parents' bill. I never had such a cake, though my parents would have paid for it readily enough. Year after year, never daring to ask, I would miserably hope that this year a cake would appear. Once or twice I even rashly pretended to my companions that this time I *was* going to have a cake. Then came teatime, and no cake, which did not make me more popular.

Very early it was impressed upon me that I had no chance of a decent future unless I won a scholarship at a public school. Either I won my scholarship, or I must leave school at fourteen and become, in Sambo's favourite phrase 'a little office boy at forty pounds a year'. In my circumstances it was natural that I should believe this. Indeed, it was universally taken for granted at St. Cyprian's that unless you went to a 'good' public school (and only about fifteen schools came under this heading) you were ruined for life. It is not easy to convey to a grown-up person the sense of strain, of nerving oneself for some terrible, all-deciding combat, as the date of the examination crept nearer – eleven years old, twelve years old, then thirteen, the fatal year itself! Over a period of about two years, I do not think there was ever a day when 'the exam', as I called it, was quite out of my waking thoughts. In my prayers it figured invariably: and whenever I got the bigger portion of a wishbone, or picked up a horse-shoe, or bowed seven times to the new moon, or succeeded in passing through a wishing-gate without touching the sides, then the wish I earned by doing so went on 'the exam' as a matter of course. And yet curiously enough I was also tormented by an almost irresistible impulse *not* to work. There were days when my heart sickened at the labours ahead of me, and I stood stupid as an animal before the most elementary difficulties. In the holidays, also, I could not work. Some of the scholarship boys received extra tuition from a certain Mr Knowles,[9] a likeable, very hairy man who wore shaggy suits and lived in a typical bachelor's 'den' – booklined walls, overwhelming stench of tobacco – somewhere in the town. During the holidays Mr Knowles used to send us extracts from Latin authors to translate, and we were supposed to send back a wad of work once a week. Somehow I could not do it. The empty paper and the black Latin dictionary lying on the table, the consciousness of a plain duty shirked, poisoned my leisure, but somehow I could not start, and by the end of the holidays I would only have sent Mr Knowles fifty or a hundred lines. Undoubtedly part of the reason was that Sambo and his cane were far away. But in term-time, also, I would go through periods of idleness and stupidity when I would sink deeper and deeper into disgrace and even achieve a sort of feeble, snivelling defiance, fully conscious of my guilt and yet unable or unwilling – I could not be sure which – to do any better. Then Sambo or Flip would send for me, and this time it would not even be a caning.

Flip would search me with her baleful eyes. (What colour were those eyes, I wonder? I remember them as green, but actually no human being has green eyes. Perhaps they were hazel.) She would start off in her peculiar, wheedling, bullying style, which never failed to get right through one's guard and score a hit on one's better nature.

'I don't think it's awfully decent of you to behave like this, is it? Do you think it's quite playing the game by your mother and father to go on idling your time away, week after week, month after month? Do you *want* to throw all your chances away? You know your people aren't rich, don't you? You know they can't afford the same things as other boys' parents. How are they to send you to a public school if you don't win a scholarship? I know how proud your mother is of you. Do you *want* to let her down?'

'I don't think he wants to go to a public school any longer,' Sambo would say, addressing himself to Flip with a pretence that I was not there. 'I think he's given up that idea. He wants to be a little office boy at forty pounds a year.'

The horrible sensation of tears – a swelling in the breast, a tickling behind the nose – would already have assailed me. Flip would bring out her ace of trumps:

'And do you think it's quite fair to *us*, the way you're behaving? After all we've done for you? You *do* know what we've done for you, don't you?' Her eyes would pierce deep into me, and though she never said it straight out, I did know. 'We've had you here all these years – we even had you here for a week in the holidays so that Mr Knowles could coach you. We don't *want* to have to send you away, you know, but we can't keep a boy here just to eat up our food, term after term. *I* don't think it's very straight, the way you're behaving. Do you?'

I never had any answer except a miserable 'No, Mum', or 'Yes, Mum', as the case might be. Evidently it was *not* straight, the way I was behaving. And at some point or other the unwanted tear would always force its way out of the corner of my eye, roll down my nose, and splash.

Flip never said in plain words that I was a non-paying pupil, no doubt because vague phrases like 'all we've done for you' had a deeper emotional appeal. Sambo, who did not aspire to be loved by his pupils, put it more brutally, though, as was usual with him, in pompous language. 'You are living on my bounty' was his favourite phrase in this context. At least once I listened to these words between blows of the cane. I must say that these scenes were not frequent, and except on one occasion they did not take place in the presence of other boys. In public I was reminded that I was poor and that my parents 'wouldn't be able to afford' this or that, but I was not actually reminded of my dependent position. It was a final unanswerable argument, to be brought forth like an instrument of torture when my work became exceptionally bad.

To grasp the effect of this kind of thing on a child of ten or twelve, one has to remember that the child has little sense of proportion or probability. A child may be a mass of egoism and rebelliousness, but it has no accumulated experience to give it confidence in its own judgements. On the whole it will accept what it is told, and it will believe in the most fantastic way in the knowledge and powers of the adults surrounding it. Here is an example.

I have said that at St. Cyprian's we were not allowed to keep our own money. However, it was possible to hold back a shilling or two, and sometimes I used furtively to buy sweets which I kept hidden in the loose ivy on the playing-field wall. One day when I had been sent on an errand I went into a sweetshop a mile or more from the school and bought some chocolates. As I came out of the shop I saw on the opposite pavement a small sharp-faced man who seemed to be staring very hard at my school cap. Instantly a horrible fear went through me. There could be no doubt as to who the man was. He was a spy placed there by Sambo! I turned away unconcernedly, and then, as though my legs were doing it of their own accord, broke into a clumsy run. But when I got round the next corner I forced myself to walk again, for to run was a sign of guilt, and obviously there would be other spies posted here and there about the town. All that day and the next I waited for the summons to the study, and was surprised when it did not come. It did not seem to me strange that the headmaster of a private school should dispose of an army of informers, and I did not even imagine that he would have to pay them. I assumed that any adult, inside the school or outside, would collaborate voluntarily in preventing us from breaking the rules. Sambo was all-powerful, and it was natural that his agents should be everywhere. When this episode happened I do not think I can have been less than twelve years old.

I hated Sambo and Flip, with a sort of shamefaced, remorseful hatred, but it did not occur to me to doubt their judgement. When they told me that I must either win a public-school scholarship or become an office-boy at fourteen, I believed that those were the unavoidable alternatives before me. And above all, I believed Sambo and Flip when they told me they were my benefactors. I see now, of course, that from Sambo's point of view I was a good speculation. He sank money in me, and he looked to get it back in the form of prestige. If I had 'gone off', as promising boys sometimes do, I imagine that he would have got rid of me swiftly. As it was I won him two scholarships when the time came, and no doubt he made full use of them in his prospectuses. But it is difficult for a child to realise that a school is primarily a commercial venture. A child believes that the school exists to educate and that the schoolmaster disciplines him either for his own good, or from a love of bullying. Flip and Sambo had chosen to befriend me, and their friendship included canings, reproaches and humiliations, which were good for me and saved me from an office stool. That was their version, and I believed in it. It was therefore clear that I owed them a vast debt of gratitude. But I was *not* grateful, as I very well knew. On the contrary, I hated both of them. I could not control my subjective feelings, and I could not conceal them from myself. But it is wicked, is it not, to hate your benefactors? So I was taught, and so I believed. A child accepts the codes of behaviour that are presented to it, even when it breaks them. From the age of eight, or even earlier, the consciousness of sin was never far away from me. If I contrived to seem callous and defiant, it was only a thin cover over a mass of shame and dismay. All through my boyhood I had a profound conviction that I was no good, that I was wasting my time, wrecking my talents, behaving with monstrous folly and wickedness and ingratitude – and all this, it seemed, was inescapable, because I lived among laws which were absolute, like the law of gravity, but which it was not possible for me to keep.

III

No one can look back on his schooldays and say with truth that they were altogether unhappy.

I have good memories of St. Cyprian's, among a horde of bad ones. Sometimes on summer afternoons there were wonderful expeditions across the Downs to a village called Birling Gap,[10] or to Beachy Head, where one bathed dangerously among the chalk boulders and came home covered with cuts. And there were still more wonderful midsummer evenings when, as a special treat, we were not driven off to bed as usual but allowed to wander about the grounds in the long twilight, ending up with a plunge into the swimming bath at about nine o'clock. There was the joy of waking early on summer mornings and getting in an hour's undisturbed reading (Ian Hay, Thackeray, Kipling and H. G. Wells[11] were the favourite authors of my boyhood) in the sunlit, sleeping dormitory. There was also cricket, which I was no good at but with which I conducted a sort of hopeless love affair up to the age of about eighteen.[12] And there was the pleasure of keeping caterpillars – the silky green and purple puss-moth, the ghostly green poplar-hawk, the privet hawk, large as one's third finger, specimens of which could be illicitly purchased for sixpence at a shop in the town – and, when one could escape long enough from the master who was 'taking the walk', there was the excitement of dredging the dew-ponds on the Downs for enormous newts with orange-coloured bellies. This business of being out for a walk, coming across something of fascinating interest and then being dragged away from it by a yell from the master, like a dog jerked onwards by the leash, is an important feature of school life, and helps to build up the conviction, so strong in many children, that the things you most want to do are always unattainable.

Very occasionally, perhaps once during each summer, it was possible to escape altogether from the barrack-like atmosphere of school, when Sillar,[13] the second master, was permitted to take one or two boys for an afternoon of butterfly hunting on a common a few miles away. Sillar was a man with white hair and a red face like a strawberry, who was good at natural history, making models and plaster casts, operating magic lanterns, and things of that kind. He and Mr Knowles were the only adults in any way connected with the school whom I did not either dislike or fear. Once he took me into his room and showed me in confidence a plated, pearl-handled revolver – his 'six-shooter', he called it – which he kept in a box under his bed. And oh, the joy of those occasional expeditions! The ride of two or three miles on a lonely little branch line, the afternoon of charging to and fro with large green nets, the beauty of the enormous dragon flies which hovered over the tops of the grasses, the sinister killing-bottle with its sickly smell, and then tea in the parlour of a pub with large slices of pale-coloured cake! The essence of it was in the railway journey, which seemed to put magic distances between yourself and school.

Flip, characteristically, disapproved of these expeditions, though not actually forbidding them. 'And have you been catching *little butterflies*?' she would say with a vicious sneer when one got back, making her voice as babyish as possible. From her point of view, natural history ('bug-hunting' she would probably have called it) was a babyish pursuit which a boy should be laughed out of as early as possible. Moreover it was somehow faintly plebeian, it was traditionally associated with boys who wore spectacles and were no good at games, it did not help you to pass exams, and above all it smelt of science and therefore seemed to menace classical education. It needed a considerable moral effort to accept Sillar's invitation. How I dreaded that sneer of *little butterflies*! Sillar, however, who had been at the school since its early days, had built up a certain independence for himself: he seemed able to handle Sambo, and ignored Flip a good deal. If it ever happened that both of them were away, Sillar acted as deputy headmaster, and on those occasions, instead of reading the appointed lesson for the day at morning chapel, he would read us stories from the Apocrypha.

Most of the good memories of my childhood, and up to the age of about twenty, are in some way connected with animals. So far as St. Cyprian's goes, it also seems, when I look back, that all my good memories are of summer. In winter your nose ran continually, your fingers were too numb to button your shirt (this was an especial misery on Sundays, when we wore Eton collars), and there was the daily nightmare of football – the cold, the mud, the hideous greasy ball that came whizzing at one's face, the gouging knees and trampling boots of the bigger boys. Part of the trouble was that in winter, after the age of about ten, I was seldom in good health, at any rate during term time. I had defective bronchial tubes and a lesion in one lung which was not discovered till many years later. Hence I not only had a chronic cough, but running was a torment to me. In those days however, 'wheeziness', or 'chestiness', as it was called, was either diagnosed as imagination or was looked on as essentially a moral disorder, caused by over-eating. 'You wheeze like a concertina,' Sambo would say disapprovingly as he stood behind my chair; 'You're perpetually stuffing yourself with food, that's why.' My cough was referred to as a 'stomach cough', which made it sound both disgusting and reprehensible. The cure for it was hard running, which, if you kept it up long enough, ultimately 'cleared your chest'.

It is curious, the degree – I will not say of actual hardship, but of squalor and neglect, that was taken for granted in upper-class schools of that period. Almost as in the days of Thackeray, it seemed natural that a little boy of eight or ten should be a miserable, snotty-nosed creature, his face almost permanently dirty, his hands chapped, his nails bitten, his handkerchief a sodden horror, his bottom frequently blue with bruises. It was partly the prospect of actual physical discomfort that made the thought of going back to school lie in one's breast like a lump of lead during the last few days of the holidays.

A characteristic memory of St. Cyprian's is the astonishing hardness of one's bed on the first night of term. Since this was an expensive school, I took a social step upwards by attending it, and yet the standard of comfort was in every way far lower than in my own home, or, indeed, than it would have been in a prosperous working-class home. One only had a hot bath once a week, for instance. The food was not only bad, it was also insufficient. Never before or since have I seen butter or jam scraped on bread so thinly. I do not think I can be imagining the fact that we were underfed, when I remember the lengths we would go in order to steal food. On a number of occasions I remember creeping down at two or three o'clock in the morning through what seemed like miles of pitch-dark stairways and passages – barefooted, stopping to listen after each step, paralysed with about equal fear of Sambo, ghosts and burglars – to steal stale bread from the pantry. The assistant masters had their meals with us, but they had somewhat better food, and if one got half a chance it was usual to steal left-over scraps of bacon rind or fried potato when their plates were removed.

As usual, I did not see the sound commercial reason for this underfeeding. On the whole I accepted Sambo's view that a boy's appetite is a sort of morbid growth which should be kept in check as much as possible. A maxim often repeated to us at St. Cyprian's was that it is healthy to get up from a meal feeling as hungry as when you sat down. Only a generation earlier than this it had been common for school dinners to start off with a slab of unsweetened suet pudding, which, it was frankly said, 'broke the boys' appetites'. But the underfeeding was probably less flagrant at preparatory schools, where a boy was wholly dependent on the official diet, than at public schools, where he was allowed – indeed, expected – to buy extra food for himself. At some schools, he would literally not have had enough to eat unless he had bought regular supplies of eggs, sausages, sardines, etc.; and his parents had to allow him money for this purpose. At Eton, for instance, at any rate in College, a boy was given no solid meal after mid-day dinner. For his afternoon tea he was given only tea and bread and butter, and at eight o'clock he was given a miserable supper of soup or fried fish, or more often bread and cheese, with water to drink. Sambo went down to see his eldest son at Eton and came back in snobbish ecstasies over the luxury in which the boys lived. 'They give them fried fish for supper!' he exclaimed, beaming all over his chubby face. 'There's no school like it in the world.' Fried fish! The habitual supper of the poorest of the working class! At very cheap boarding-schools it was no doubt worse. A very early memory of mine is of seeing the boarders at a grammar school – the sons, probably, of farmers and shop-keepers – being fed on boiled lights.

Whoever writes about his childhood must beware of exaggeration and self-pity. I do not want to claim that I was a martyr or that St. Cyprian's was a sort of Dotheboys Hall. But I should be falsifying my own memories if I did not record that they are largely memories of disgust. The over-crowded, underfed, underwashed life that we led *was* disgusting, as I recall it. If I shut my eyes and say 'school', it is of course the physical surroundings that first come back to me: the flat playing-field with its cricket pavilion and the little shed by the rifle range, the draughty[14] dormitories, the dusty splintery passages, the square of asphalt in front of the gymnasium, the raw-looking pinewood chapel at the back. And at almost every point some filthy detail obtrudes itself. For example, there were the pewter bowls out of which we had our porridge. They had overhanging rims, and under the rims there were accumulations of sour porridge, which could be flaked off in long strips. The porridge itself, too, contained more lumps, hair and unexplained black things than one would have thought possible, unless someone were putting them there on purpose. It was never safe to start on that porridge without investigating it first. And there was the slimy water of the plunge bath – it was twelve or fifteen feet long, the whole school was supposed to go into it every morning, and I doubt whether the water was changed at all frequently – and the always-damp towels with their cheesy smell; and, on occasional visits in the winter, the murky sea-water of the Devonshire Baths, which came straight in from the beach and on which I once saw floating a human turd. And the sweaty smell of the changing-room with its greasy basins, and, giving on this, the row of filthy, dilapidated lavatories, which had no fastenings of any kind on the doors, so that whenever you were sitting there someone was sure to come crashing in. It is not easy for me to think of my schooldays without seeming to breathe in a whiff of something cold and evil-smelling – a sort of compound of sweaty stockings, dirty towels, faecal smells blowing along corridors, forks with old food between the prongs,[15] neck-of-mutton stew, and the banging doors of the lavatories and the echoing chamberpots in the dormitories.

It is true that I am by nature not gregarious, and the W.C. and dirty-handkerchief side of life is necessarily more obtrusive when great numbers of human beings are crushed together in [a] small space. It is just as bad in an army, and worse, no doubt, in a prison. Besides, boyhood is the age of disgust. After one has learned to differentiate, and before one has become hardened – between seven and eighteen, say – one seems always to be walking the tightrope over a cesspool. Yet I do not think I exaggerate the squalor of school life, when I remember how health and cleanliness were neglected, in spite of the hoo-ha about fresh air and cold water and keeping in hard training. It was common to remain constipated for days together. Indeed, one was hardly encouraged to keep one's bowels open, since the only aperients tolerated were Castor Oil or another almost equally horrible drink called Liquorice Powder. One was supposed to go into the plunge bath every morning, but some boys shirked it for days on end, simply making themselves scarce when the bell sounded, or else slipping along the edge of the bath among the crowd, and then wetting their hair with a little dirty water off the floor. A little boy of eight or nine will not necessarily keep himself clean unless there is someone to see that he does it. There was a new boy named Bachelor, a pretty, mother's darling of a boy, who came a little while before I left.

The first thing I noticed about him was the beautiful pearly whiteness of his teeth. By the end of that term his teeth were an extraordinary shade of green. During all that time, apparently, no one had taken sufficient interest in him to see that he brushed them.

But of course the differences between home and school were more than physical. That bump on the hard mattress, on the first night of term, used to give me a feeling of abrupt awakening, a feeling of: 'This is reality, this is what you are up against.' Your home might be far from perfect, but at least it was a place ruled by love rather than by fear, where you did not have to be perpetually on your guard against the people surrounding you. At eight years old you were suddenly taken out of this warm nest and flung into a world of force and fraud and secrecy, like a goldfish into a tank full of pike. Against no matter what degree of bullying you had no redress. You could only have defended yourself by sneaking, which, except in a few rigidly defined circumstances, was the unforgivable sin. To write home and ask your parents to take you away would have been even less thinkable, since to do so would have been to admit yourself unhappy and unpopular, which a boy will never do. Boys are Erewhonians: they think that misfortune is disgraceful and must be concealed at all costs. It might perhaps have been considered permissible to complain to your parents about bad food, or an unjustified caning, or some other ill-treatment inflicted by masters and not by boys. The fact that Sambo never beat the richer boys suggests that such complaints were made occasionally. But in my own peculiar circumstances I could never have asked my parents to intervene on my behalf. Even before I understood about the reduced fees, I grasped that they were in some way under an obligation to Sambo, and therefore could not protect me against him. I have mentioned already that throughout my time at St. Cyprian's I never had a cricket bat of my own. I had been told this was because 'your parents couldn't afford it'. One day in the holidays, by some casual remark, it came out that they had provided ten shillings to buy me one: yet no cricket bat appeared. I did not protest to my parents, let alone raise the subject with Sambo. How could I? I was dependent on him, and the ten shillings was merely a fragment of what I owed him. I realise now of course, that it is immensely unlikely that Sambo had simply stuck to the money. No doubt the matter had slipped his memory. But the point is that I assumed that he had stuck to it, and that he had a right to do so if he chose.

How difficult it is for a child to have any real independence of attitude could be seen in our behaviour towards Flip. I think it would be true to say that every boy in the school hated and feared her. Yet we all fawned on her in the most abject way, and the top layer of our feelings towards her was a sort of guilt-stricken loyalty. Flip, although the discipline of the school depended more on her than on Sambo, hardly pretended to dispense strict justice. She was frankly capricious. An act which might get you a caning one day, might next day be laughed off as a boyish prank, or even commended because it 'showed you had guts'. There were days when everyone cowered before those deepset, accusing eyes, and there were days when she was like a flirtatious queen surrounded by courtier-lovers, laughing and joking, scattering largesse, or the promise of largesse ('And if you win the Harrow History Prize[16] I'll give you a new case for your camera!'), and occasionally even packing three or four favoured boys into her Ford car and carrying them off to a teashop in town, where they were allowed to buy coffee and cakes. Flip was inextricably mixed up in my mind with Queen Elizabeth, whose relations with Leicester and Essex and Raleigh were intelligible to me from a very early age. A word we all constantly used in speaking of Flip was 'favour'. 'I'm in good favour', we would say, or 'I'm in bad favour'. Except for the handful of wealthy or titled boys, no one was permanently in good favour, but on the other hand even the outcasts had patches of it from time to time. Thus, although my memories of Flip are mostly hostile, I also remember considerable periods when I basked under her smiles, when she called me 'old chap' and used my Christian name, and allowed me to frequent her private library, where I first made acquaintance with *Vanity Fair*. The high-water mark of good favour was to be invited to serve at table on Sunday nights when Flip and Sambo had guests to dinner. In clearing away, of course, one had a chance to finish off the scraps, but one also got a servile[17] pleasure from standing behind the seated guests and darting deferentially forward when something was wanted. Whenever one had the chance to suck up, one did suck up, and at the first smile one's hatred turned into a sort of cringing love. I was always tremendously proud when I succeeded in making Flip laugh. I have even, at her command, written *vers d'occasion*, comic verses to celebrate memorable events in the life of the school.

I am anxious to make it clear that I was not a rebel, except by force of circumstances. I accepted the codes that I found in being. Once, towards the end of my time, I even sneaked to Sillar about a suspected case of homosexuality. I did not know very well what homosexuality was, but I knew that it happened and was bad, and that this was one of the contexts in which it was proper to sneak. Sillar told me I was 'a good fellow', which made me feel horribly ashamed. Before Flip one seemed as helpless as a snake before the snake-charmer. She had a hardly-varying vocabulary of praise and abuse, a whole series of set phrases, each of which promptly called forth the appropriate response. There was '*Buck* up, old chap!', which inspired one to paroxysms of energy; there was 'Don't *be* such a fool!' (or, 'It's path*e*tic, isn't it?'), which made one feel a born idiot; and there was 'It isn't very straight of you, is it?', which always brought one to the brink of tears. And yet all the while, at the middle of one's heart, there seemed to stand an incorruptible inner self who knew that whatever one did – whether one laughed or snivelled or went into frenzies of gratitude for small favours – one's only true feeling was hatred.

IV

I had learned early in my career that one can do wrong against one's will, and before long I also learned that one can do wrong without ever discovering what one has done or why it was wrong. There were sins that were too subtle to be explained, and there were others that were too terrible to be clearly mentioned. For example, there was sex, which was always smouldering just under the surface and which suddenly blew up into a tremendous row when I was about twelve.

At some preparatory schools homosexuality is not a problem, but I think that St. Cyprian's may have acquired a 'bad tone' thanks to the presence of the South American boys, who would perhaps mature a year or two earlier than an English boy.[18] At that age I was not interested, so I do not actually know what went on, but I imagine it was group masturbation. At any rate, one day the storm suddenly burst over our heads. There were summonses, interrogations, confessions, floggings, repentances, solemn lectures of which one understood nothing except that some irredeemable sin known as 'swinishness' or 'beastliness' had been committed. One of the ringleaders, a boy named Cross,[19] was flogged, according to eyewitnesses, for a quarter of an hour continuously before being expelled. His yells rang through the house. But we were all implicated, more or less, or felt ourselves to be implicated. Guilt seemed to hang in the air like a pall of smoke. A solemn, blackhaired imbecile of an assistant master, who was later to be a Member of Parliament, took the older boys to a secluded room and delivered a talk on the Temple of the Body.[20]

'Don't you realise what a wonderful thing your body is?' he said gravely. 'You talk of your motor-car engines, your Rolls-Royces and Daimlers and so on. Don't you understand that no engine ever made is fit to be compared with your body? And then you go and wreck it, ruin it – for life!'

He turned his cavernous black eyes on me and added sadly:

'And you, whom I'd always [believed][21] to be quite a decent person after your fashion – you, I hear, are one of the very worst.'

A feeling of doom descended upon me. So I was guilty too. I too had done the dreadful thing, whatever it was, that wrecked you for life, body and soul, and ended in suicide or the lunatic asylum. Till then I had hoped that I was innocent, and the conviction of sin which now took possession of me was perhaps all the stronger because I did not know what I had done. I was not among those who were interrogated and flogged, and it was not until after the row was well over that I even learned about the trivial accident which had connected my name with it. Even then I understood nothing. It was not till about two years later that I fully grasped what that lecture on the Temple of the Body had referred to.

At this time I was in an almost sexless state, which is normal, or at any rate common, in boys of that age; I was therefore in the position of simultaneously knowing and not knowing what used to be called the Facts of Life. At five or six, like many children, I had passed through a phase of sexuality. My friends were the plumber's children up the road, and we used sometimes to play games of a vaguely erotic kind. One was called 'playing at doctors', and I remember getting a faint but definitely pleasant thrill from holding a toy trumpet, which was supposed to be a stethoscope, against a little girl's belly. About the same time I fell deeply in love, a far more worshipping kind of love than I have ever felt for anyone since, with a girl named Elsie at the convent school which I attended. She seemed to me grown up, so I suppose she must have been fifteen. After that, as so often happens, all sexual feeling seemed to go out of me for many years. At twelve I knew more than I had known as a young child, but I understood less, because I no longer knew the essential fact that there is something pleasant in sexual activity. Between roughly seven and fourteen, the whole subject seemed to me uninteresting and, when for some reason I was forced to think of it, disgusting. My knowledge of the so-called Facts of Life was derived from animals, and was therefore distorted, and in any case was only intermittent. I knew that animals copulated and that human beings had bodies resembling those of animals: but that human beings also copulated I only knew, as it were, reluctantly, when something, a phrase in the Bible, perhaps, compelled me to remember it. Not having desire, I had no curiosity, and was willing to leave many questions unanswered. Thus, I knew in principle how the baby gets into the woman, but I did not know how it gets out again, because I had never followed the subject up. I knew all the dirty words, and in my bad moments I would repeat them to myself, but I did not know what the worst of them meant, nor want to know. They were abstractly wicked, a sort of verbal charm. While I remained in this state, it was easy for me to remain ignorant of any sexual misdeeds that went on about me, and to be hardly wiser even when the row broke. At most, through the veiled and terrible warnings of Flip, Sambo and all the rest of them, I grasped that the crime of which we were all guilty was somehow connected with the sexual organs. I had noticed, without feeling much interest, that one's penis sometimes stands up of its own accord (this starts happening to a boy long before he has any conscious sexual desires), and I was inclined to believe, or half-believe, that *that* must be the crime. At any rate, it was something to do with the penis – so much I understood. Many other boys, I have no doubt, were equally in the dark.

After the talk on the Temple of the Body (days later, it seems in retrospect: the row seemed to continue for days), a dozen of us were seated at the long shiny table which Sambo used for the scholarship class, under Flip's lowering eye. A long, desolate wail rang out from a room somewhere above. A very small boy named Duncan, aged no more than about ten, who was implicated in some way, was being flogged, or was recovering from a flogging. At the sound, Flip's eyes searched our faces, and settled upon me.

'*You see,*' she said.

I will not swear that she said, 'You see what you have done,' but that was the sense of it. We were all bowed down with shame. It was *our* fault. Somehow or other we had led poor Duncan astray: *we* were responsible for his agony and his ruin. Then Flip turned upon another boy named Clapham. It is thirty years ago, and I cannot remember for certain whether she merely quoted a verse from the Bible, or whether she actually brought out a Bible and made Clapham read it; but at any rate the text indicated was:

'Whoso shall offend one of these little ones that believe in me, it were better for him that a millstone were hanged about his neck, and that he were drowned in the depth of the sea.'[22]

That, too, was terrible. Duncan was one of these little ones; we had offended him; it were better that a millstone were hanged about our necks and that we were drowned in the depth of the sea.

'Have you thought about that, Clapham – have you thought what it means?' Flip said. And Clapham broke down into snivelling tears.

Another boy, Hardcastle, whom I have mentioned already, was similarly overwhelmed with shame by the accusation that he 'had black rings round his eyes'.

'Have you looked in the glass lately, Hardcastle?' said Flip. 'Aren't you ashamed to go about with a face like that? Do you think everyone doesn't know what it means when a boy has black rings round his eyes?'

Once again the load of guilt and fear seemed to settle down upon me. Had *I* got black rings round my eyes? A couple of years later I realised that these were supposed to be a symptom by which masturbators could be detected. But already, without knowing this, I accepted the black rings as a sure sign of depravity, *some* kind of depravity. And many times, even before I grasped the supposed meaning, I have gazed anxiously into the glass, looking for the first hint of that dreaded stigma, the confession which the secret sinner writes upon his own face.

These terrors wore off, or became merely intermittent, without affecting what one might call my official beliefs. It was still true about the madhouse and the suicide's grave, but it was no longer acutely frightening. Some months later it happened that I once again saw Cross, the ringleader who had been flogged and expelled. Cross was one of the outcasts, the son of poor middle-class parents, which was no doubt part of the reason why Sambo had handled him so roughly. The term after his expulsion he went on to Eastbourne College, the small local public school, which was hideously despised at St. Cyprian's and looked on as 'not really' a public school at all. Only a very few boys from St. Cyprian's went there, and Sambo always spoke of them with a sort of contemptuous pity. You had no chance if you went to a school like that: at best your destiny would be a clerkship. I thought of Cross as a person who at thirteen had already forfeited all hope of any decent future. Physically, morally and socially he was finished. Moreover I assumed that his parents had only sent him to Eastbourne College because after his disgrace no 'good' school would have him.

During the following term, when we were out for a walk, we passed Cross in the street. He looked completely normal. He was a strongly-built, rather good-looking boy with black hair. I immediately noticed that he looked better than when I had last seen him – his complexion, previously rather pale, was pinker – and that he did not seem embarrassed at meeting us. Apparently he was not ashamed either of having been expelled, or of being at Eastbourne College. If one could gather anything from the way he looked at us as we filed past, it was that he was glad to have escaped from St. Cyprian's. But the encounter made very little impression on me. I drew no inference from the fact that Cross, ruined in body and soul, appeared to be happy and in good health. I still believed in the sexual mythology that had been taught me by Sambo and Flip. The mysterious, terrible dangers were still there. Any morning the black rings might appear round your eyes and you would know that you too were among the lost ones. Only it no longer seemed to matter very much. These contradictions can exist easily in the mind of a child, because of its own[23] vitality. It accepts – how can it do otherwise? – the nonsense that its elders tell it, but its youthful body, and the sweetness of the physical world, tell it another story. It was the same with Hell, which up to the age of about fourteen I officially believed in. Almost certainly Hell existed, and there were occasions when a vivid sermon could scare you into fits.

But somehow it never lasted. The fire that waited for you was real fire, it would hurt in the same way as when you burnt your finger, and *for ever*, but most of the time you could contemplate it without bothering.

V

The various codes which were presented to you at St. Cyprian's – religious, moral, social and intellectual – contradicted one another if you worked out their implications. The essential conflict was between the tradition of nineteenth-century asceticism and the actually existing luxury and snobbery of the pre-1914 age. On the one side were low-church Bible Christianity, sex puritanism, insistence on hard work, respect for academic distinction, disapproval of self-indulgence: on the other, contempt for 'braininess' and worship of games, contempt for foreigners and the working class, an almost neurotic dread of poverty, and, above all, the assumption not only that money and privilege are the things that matter, but that it is better to inherit them than to have to work for them. Broadly, you were bidden to be at once a Christian and a social success, which is impossible. At the time I did not perceive that the various ideals which were set before us cancelled out. I merely saw that they were all, or nearly all, unattainable, so far as I was concerned, since they all depended not only on what you did but on what you *were*.

Very early, at the age of only ten or eleven, I reached the conclusion – no one told me this, but on the other hand I did not simply make it up out of my own head: somehow it was in the air I breathed – that you were no good unless you had £100,000. I had perhaps fixed on this particular sum as a result of reading Thackeray. The interest on £100,000 would be £4,000 a year (I was in favour of a safe 4 per cent), and this seemed to me the minimum income that you must possess if you were to belong to the real top crust, the people in the country houses. But it was clear that I could never find my way into that paradise, to which you did not really belong unless you were born into it. You could only *make* money, if at all, by a mysterious operation called 'going into the City', and when you came out of the City, having won your £100,000, you were fat and old. But the truly enviable thing about the top-notchers was that they were rich while young. For people like me, the ambitious middle class, the examination passers, only a bleak, laborious kind of success was possible. You clambered upwards on a ladder of scholarships into the [Home][24] Civil Service or the Indian Civil Service, or possibly you became a barrister. And if at any point you 'slacked' or 'went off' and missed one of the rungs in the ladder, you became 'a little office boy at forty pounds a year'. But even if you climbed to the highest niche that was open to you, you could still only be an underling, a hanger-on of the people who really counted.

Even if I had not learned this from Sambo and Flip, I would have learned it from the other boys. Looking back, it is astonishing how intimately, intelligently snobbish we all were, how knowledgeable about names and addresses, how swift to detect small differences in accents and manners and the cut of clothes. There were some boys who seemed to drip money from their pores even in the bleak misery of the middle of a winter term. At the beginning and end of the term, especially, there was naïvely snobbish chatter about Switzerland, and Scotland with its ghillies and grouse moors, and 'my uncle's yacht', and 'our place in the country', and 'my pony' and 'my pater's touring car'. There never was, I suppose, in the history of the world a time when the sheer vulgar fatness of wealth, without any kind of aristocratic elegance to redeem it, was so obtrusive as in those years before 1914. It was the age when crazy millionaires in curly top hats and lavender waistcoats gave champagne parties in rococo houseboats on the Thames, the age of diabolo and hobble skirts, the age of the 'knut'[25] in his grey bowler and cutaway coat, the age of *The Merry Widow*, Saki's novels, *Peter Pan* and *Where the Rainbow Ends*, the age when people talked about chocs and cigs and ripping and topping and heavenly, when they went for divvy weekends at Brighton and had scrumptious teas at the Troc. From the whole decade before 1914 there seems to breathe forth a smell of the more vulgar, un-grown-up kinds of luxury, a smell of brilliantine and creme de menthe and soft-centre chocolates, – an atmosphere, as it were, of eating everlasting strawberry ices on green lawns to the tune of the Eton Boating Song. The extraordinary thing was the way in which everyone took it for granted that this oozing, bulging wealth of the English upper and upper-middle classes would last for ever, and was part of the order of things. After 1918 it was never quite the same again. Snobbishness and expensive habits came back, certainly, but they were self-conscious and on the defensive. Before the war the worship of money was entirely unreflecting and untroubled by any pang of conscience. The goodness of money was as unmistakable as the goodness of health or beauty, and a glittering car, a title or a horde of servants was mixed up in people's minds with the idea of actual moral virtue.

At St. Cyprian's, in term time, the general bareness of life enforced a certain democracy, but any mention of the holidays, and the consequent competitive swanking about cars and butlers and country houses, promptly called class distinctions into being. The school was pervaded by a curious cult of Scotland, which brought out the fundamental contradiction in our standard of values. Flip claimed Scottish ancestry, and she favoured the Scottish boys, encouraging them to wear kilts in their ancestral tartan instead of the school uniform,[26] and even christened her youngest child by a Gaelic name. Ostensibly we were supposed to admire the Scots because they were 'grim' and 'dour' ('stern' was perhaps the key word), and irresistible on the field of battle. In the big schoolroom there was a steel engraving of the charge of the Scots Greys at Waterloo, all looking as though they enjoyed every moment of it. Our picture of Scotland was made up of burns, braes, kilts, sporrans, claymores, bagpipes and the like, all somehow mixed up with the invigorating effects of porridge, Protestantism and a cold climate. But underlying this was something quite different. The real reason for the cult of Scotland was that only very rich people could spend their summers there. And the pretended belief in Scottish superiority was a cover for the bad conscience of the occupying English, who had pushed the Highland peasantry off their farms to make way for the deer forests, and then compensated them by turning them into servants. Flip's face always beamed with innocent snobbishness when she spoke of Scotland. Occasionally she even attempted a trace of Scottish accent. Scotland was a private paradise which a few initiates could talk about and make outsiders feel small.

'You going to Scotland this hols?'

'Rather! We go every year.'

'My pater's got three miles of river.'

'My pater's giving me a new gun for the *twelfth*.[27] There's jolly good black game where we go. Get out, Smith! What are you listening for? You've never been in Scotland. I bet you don't know what a black-cock looks like.'

Following on this, imitations of the cry of a black-cock, of the roaring of a stag, of the accent of 'our ghillies', etc., etc.

And the questionings that new boys of doubtful social origin were sometimes put through – questionings quite surprising in their mean-minded particularity, when one reflects that the inquisitors were only twelve or thirteen!

'How much a year has your pater got? What part of London do you live in? Is that Knightsbridge or Kensington? How many bathrooms has your house got? How many servants do your people keep? Have you got a butler? Well, then, have you got a cook? Where do you get your clothes made? How many shows did you go to in the hols? How much money did you bring back with you?' etc., etc.

I have seen a little new boy, hardly older than eight, desperately lying his way through such a catechism:

'Have your people got a car?'

'Yes.'

'What sort of car?'

'Daimler.'

'How many horse-power?'

(Pause, and leap in the dark.) 'Fifteen.'

'What kind of lights?'

The little boy is bewildered.

'What kind of lights? Electric or acetylene?'

(A longer pause, and another leap in the dark.) 'Acetylene.'

'Coo! He says his pater's car's got acetylene lamps. They went out years ago. It must be as old as the hills.'

'Rot! He's making it up. He hasn't got a car. He's just a navvy. Your pater's a navvy.'

And so on.

By the social standards that prevailed about me, I was no good, and could not be any good. But all the different kinds of virtue seemed to be mysteriously interconnected and to belong to much the same people. It was not only money that mattered: there were also strength, beauty, charm, athleticism and something called 'guts' or 'character', which in reality meant the power to impose your will on others. I did not possess any of these qualities. At games, for instance, I was hopeless. I was a fairly good swimmer and not altogether contemptible at cricket, but these had no prestige value, because boys only attach importance to a game if it requires strength and courage. What counted was football, at which I was a funk. I loathed the game, and since I could see no pleasure or usefulness in it, it was very difficult for me to show courage at it. Football, it seemed to me, is not really played for the pleasure of kicking a ball about, but is a species of fighting. The lovers of football are large, boisterous, nobbly boys who are good at knocking down and trampling on slightly smaller boys. That was the pattern of school life – a continuous triumph of the strong over the weak. Virtue consisted in winning: it consisted in being bigger, stronger, handsomer, richer, more popular, more elegant, more unscrupulous than other people – in dominating them, bullying them, making them suffer pain, making them look foolish, getting the better of them in every way. Life was hierarchical and whatever happened was right. There were the strong, who deserved to win and always did win, and there were the weak, who deserved to lose and always did lose, everlastingly.

I did not question the prevailing standards, because so far as I could see there were no others. How could the rich, the strong, the elegant, the fashionable, the powerful, be in the wrong? It was their world, and the rules they made for it must be the right ones. And yet from a very early age I was aware of the impossibility of any *subjective* conformity. Always at the centre of my heart the inner self seemed to be awake, pointing out the difference between the moral obligation and the psychological *fact.* It was the same in all matters, worldly or other-worldly. Take religion, for instance. You were supposed to love God and I did not question this. Till the age of about fourteen I believed in God, and believed that the accounts given of him were true. But I was well aware that I did not love him. On the contrary, I hated him, just as I hated Jesus and the Hebrew patriarchs. If I had sympathetic feelings towards any character in the Old Testament, it was towards such people as Cain, Jezebel, Haman, Agag, Sisera: in the New Testament my friends, if any, were Ananias, Caiaphas, Judas and Pontius Pilate.[28] But the whole business of religion seemed to be strewn with psychological impossibilities. The Prayer Book told you, for example, to love God and fear him: but how could you love someone whom you feared? With your private affections it was the same. What you *ought* to feel was usually clear enough, but the appropriate emotion could not be commanded. Obviously it was my duty to feel grateful towards Flip and Sambo; but I was not grateful. It was equally clear that one ought to love one's father, but I knew very well that I merely disliked my own father, whom I had barely seen before I was eight and who appeared to me simply as a gruff-voiced elderly man forever saying 'Don't'. It was not that one did not want to possess the right qualities or feel the correct emotions, but that one could not. The good and the possible never seemed to coincide.

There was a line of verse that I came across not actually while I was at St. Cyprian's, but a year or two later, and which seemed to strike a sort of leaden echo in my heart. It was: 'The armies of unalterable law.'[29] I understood to perfection what it meant to be Lucifer, defeated and justly defeated, with no possibility of revenge. The schoolmasters with their canes, the millionaires with their Scottish castles, the athletes with their curly hair – these were the armies of the unalterable law. It was not easy, at that date, to realise that in fact it *was* alterable. And according to that law I was damned. I had no money, I was weak, I was ugly, I was unpopular, I had a chronic cough, I was cowardly, I smelt. This picture, I should add, was not altogether fanciful. I was an unattractive boy. St. Cyprian's soon made me so, even if I had not been so before. But a child's belief in its own shortcomings is not much influenced by facts. I believed, for example, that I 'smelt', but this was based simply on general probability. It was notorious that disagreeable people smelt, and therefore presumably I did so too. Again, until after I had left school for good I continued to believe that I was preternaturally ugly. It was what my schoolfellows had told me, and I had no other authority to refer to. The conviction that it was *not possible* for me to be a success went deep enough to influence my actions till far into adult life. Until I was about thirty I always planned my life on the assumption not only that any major undertaking was bound to fail, but that I could only expect to live a few years longer.

But this sense of guilt and inevitable failure was balanced by something else: that is, the instinct to survive. Even a creature that is weak, ugly, cowardly, smelly and in no way justifiable still wants to stay alive and be happy after its own fashion. I could not invert the existing scale of values, or turn myself into a success, but I could accept my failure and make the best of it. I could resign myself to being what I was, and then endeavour to survive on those terms.

To survive, or at least to preserve any kind of independence, was essentially criminal, since it meant breaking rules which you yourself recognised. There was a boy named Cliffy Burton[30] who for some months oppressed me horribly. He was a big, powerful, coarsely handsome boy with a very red face and curly black hair, who was forever twisting somebody's arm, wringing somebody's ear, flogging somebody with a riding crop (he was a member of Sixth Form), or performing prodigies of activity on the football field. Flip loved him (hence the fact that he was habitually called by his Christian name), and Sambo commended him as a boy who 'had character' and 'could keep order'. He was followed about by a group of toadies who nicknamed him Strong Man.

One day, when we were taking off our overcoats in the changing-room, Burton picked on me for some reason. I 'answered him back', whereupon he gripped my wrist, twisted it round and bent my forearm back upon itself in a hideously painful way. I remember his handsome, jeering red face bearing down upon mine. He was, I think, older than I, besides being enormously stronger. As he let go of me a terrible, wicked resolve formed itself in my heart. I would get back on him by hitting him when he did not expect it. It was a strategic moment, for the master who had been 'taking' the walk would be coming back almost immediately, and then there could be no fight. I let perhaps a minute go by, walked up to Burton with the most harmless air I could assume, and then, getting the weight of my body behind it, smashed my fist into his face. He was flung backwards by the blow, and some blood ran out of his mouth. His always sanguine face turned almost black with rage. Then he turned away to rinse his mouth at the washing-basins.

'*All right!*' he said to me between his teeth as the master led us away.

For days after this he followed me about, challenging me to fight. Although terrified out of my wits, I steadily refused to fight. I said that the blow in the face had served him right, and there was an end of it. Curiously enough he did not simply fall upon me there and then, which public opinion would probably have supported him in doing. So gradually the matter tailed off, and there was no fight.

Now, I had behaved wrongly, by my own code no less than his. To hit him unawares was wrong. But to refuse afterwards to fight, knowing that if we fought he would beat me – that was far worse: it was cowardly. If I had refused because I disapproved of fighting, or because I genuinely felt the matter to be closed, it would have been all right; but I had refused merely because I was afraid. Even my revenge was made empty by that fact. I had struck the blow in a moment of mindless violence, deliberately not looking far ahead and merely determined to get my own back for once and damn the consequences. I had had time to realise that what I did was wrong, but it was the kind of crime from which you could get some satisfaction. Now all was nullified. There had been a sort of courage in the first act, but my subsequent cowardice had wiped it out.

The fact I hardly noticed was that though Burton formally challenged me to fight, he did not actually attack me. Indeed, after receiving that one blow he never oppressed me again. It was perhaps twenty years before I saw the significance of this. At the time I could not see beyond the moral dilemma that is presented to the weak in a world governed by the strong: Break the rules, or perish. I did not see that in that case the weak have the right to make a different set of rules for themselves; because, even if such an idea had occurred to me, there was no one in my environment who could have confirmed me in it. I lived in a world of boys, gregarious animals, questioning nothing, accepting the law of the stronger and avenging their own humiliations by passing them down to someone smaller. My situation was that of countless other boys, and if potentially I was more of a rebel than most, it was only because, by boyish standards, I was a poorer specimen. But I never did rebel intellectually, only emotionally. I had nothing to help me except my dumb selfishness, my inability – not, indeed, to despise myself, but to *dislike* myself – my instinct to survive.

It was about a year after I hit Cliffy Burton in the face that I left St. Cyprian's for ever. It was the end of a winter term. With a sense of coming out from darkness into sunlight I put on my Old Boy's tie as we dressed for the journey. I well remember the feeling of that brand-new silk tie round my neck, a feeling of emancipation, as though the tie had been at once a badge of manhood and an amulet against Flip's voice and Sambo's cane. I was escaping from bondage. It was not that I expected, or even intended, to be any more successful at a public school than I had been at

St. Cyprian's. But still, I was escaping. I knew that at a public school there would be more privacy, more neglect, more chance to be idle and self-indulgent and degenerate. For years past I had been resolved – unconsciously at first, but consciously later on – that when once my scholarship was won I would 'slack off' and cram no longer. This resolve, by the way, was so fully carried out that between the ages of thirteen and twenty-two or three I hardly ever did a stroke of avoidable work.

Flip shook hands to say good-bye. She even gave me my Christian name for the occasion. But there was a sort of patronage, almost a sneer, in her face and in her voice. The tone in which she said good-bye was nearly the tone in which she had been used to say *little butterflies.* I had won two scholarships, but I was a failure, because success was measured not by what you did but by what you *were.* I was 'not a good type of boy' and could bring no credit on the school. I did not possess character or courage or health or strength or money, or even good manners, the power to look like a gentleman.

'Good-bye,' Flip's parting smile seemed to say; 'it's not worth quarrelling now. You haven't made much of a success of your time at St. Cyprian's, have you? And I don't suppose you'll get on awfully well at a public school either. We made a mistake, really, in wasting our time and money on you. This kind of education hasn't much to offer to a boy with your background and your outlook. Oh, don't think we don't understand you! We know all about those ideas you have at the back of your head, we know you disbelieve in everything we've taught you, and we know you aren't in the least grateful for all we've done for you. But there's no use in bringing it all up now. We aren't responsible for you any longer, and we shan't be seeing you again. Let's just admit that you're one of our failures and part without ill-feeling. And so, good-bye.'

That at least was what I read into her face. And yet how happy I was, that winter morning, as the train bore me away with the gleaming new silk tie (dark green, pale blue and black, if I remember rightly) round my neck! The world was opening before me, just a little, like a grey sky which exhibits a narrow crack of blue. A public school would be better fun than St. Cyprian's, but at bottom equally alien. In a world where the prime necessities were money, titled relatives, athleticism, tailor-made clothes, neatly-brushed hair, a charming smile, I was no good. All I had gained was a breathing-space. A little quietude, a little self-indulgence, a little respite from cramming – and then, ruin. What kind of ruin I did not know: perhaps the colonies or an office stool, perhaps prison or an early death. But first a year or two in which one could 'slack off' and get the benefit of one's sins, like Doctor Faustus. I believed firmly in my evil destiny, and yet I was acutely happy. It is the advantage of being thirteen that you can not only live in the moment, but do so with full consciousness, foreseeing the future and yet not caring about it. Next term I was going to Wellington. I had also won a scholarship at Eton, but it was uncertain whether there would be a vacancy, and I was going to Wellington first.[31] At Eton you had a room to yourself – a room which might even have a fire in it. At Wellington you had your own cubicle, and could make yourself cocoa in the evenings. The privacy of it, the grown-upness! And there would be libraries to hang about in, and summer afternoons when you could shirk games and mooch about the countryside alone, with no master driving you along. Meanwhile there were the holidays. There was the .22 rifle that I had bought the previous holidays (the Crackshot, it was called, costing twenty-two and sixpence), and Christmas was coming next week. There were also the pleasures of over-eating. I thought of some particularly voluptuous cream buns which could be bought for twopence each at a shop in our town.[32] (This was 1916, and food-rationing had not yet started.) Even the detail that my journey-money had been slightly miscalculated, leaving about a shilling over – enough for an unforeseen cup of coffee and a cake or two somewhere on the way – was enough to fill me with bliss. There was time for a bit of happiness before the future closed in upon me. But I did know that the future was dark. Failure, failure, failure – failure behind me, failure ahead of me – that was by far the deepest conviction that I carried away.

VI

All this was thirty years ago and more. The question is: Does a child at school go through the same kind of experiences nowadays?

The only honest answer, I believe, is that we do not with certainty know. Of course it is obvious that the present-day *attitude* towards education is enormously more humane and sensible than that of the past. The snobbishness that was an integral part of my own education would be almost unthinkable today, because the society that nourished it is dead. I recall a conversation that must have taken place about a year before I left St. Cyprian's. A Russian boy, large and fair-haired, a year older than myself, was questioning me.

'How much a year has your father got?'

I told him what I thought it was, adding a few hundreds to make it sound better. The Russian boy, neat in his habits, produced a pencil and a small notebook and made a calculation.

'My father has over two hundred times as much money as yours,' he announced with a sort of amused contempt.

That was in 1915. What happened to that money a couple of years later, I wonder? And still more I wonder, do conversations of that kind happen at preparatory schools now?

Clearly there has been a vast change of outlook, a general growth of 'enlightenment', even among ordinary, unthinking middle-class people. Religious belief, for instance, has largely vanished, dragging other kinds of nonsense after it. I imagine that very few people nowadays would tell a child that if it masturbates it will end in the lunatic asylum. Beating, too, has become discredited, and has even been abandoned at many schools. Nor is the underfeeding of children looked on as a normal, almost meritorious act. No one now would openly set out to give his pupils as little food as they could do with, or tell them that it is healthy to get up from a meal as hungry as you sat down. The whole status of children has improved, partly because they have grown relatively less numerous. And the diffusion of even a little psychological knowledge has made it harder for parents and schoolteachers to indulge their aberrations in the name of discipline. Here is a case, not known to me personally, but known to someone I can vouch for, and happening within my own lifetime. A small girl, daughter of a clergyman, continued wetting her bed at an age when she should have grown out of it. In order to punish her for this dreadful deed, her father took her to a large garden party and there introduced her to the whole company as a little girl who wetted her bed: and to underline her wickedness he had previously painted her face black. I do not suggest that Flip and Sambo would actually have done a thing like this, but I doubt whether it would have much surprised them. After all, things do change. And yet —!

The question is not whether boys are still buckled into Eton collars on Sunday, or told that babies are dug up under gooseberry bushes. That kind of thing is at an end, admittedly. The real question is whether it is still normal for a schoolchild to live for years amid irrational terrors and lunatic misunderstandings. And here one is up against the very great difficulty of knowing what a child really feels and thinks. A child which appears reasonably happy may actually be suffering horrors which it cannot or will not reveal. It lives in a sort of alien under-water world which we can only penetrate by memory or divination. Our chief clue is the fact that we were once children ourselves, and many people appear to forget the atmosphere of their own childhood almost entirely. Think for instance of the unnecessary torments that people will inflict by sending a child back to school with clothes of the wrong pattern, and refusing to see that this matters! Over things of this kind a child will sometimes utter a protest, but a great deal of the time its attitude is one of simple concealment. Not to expose your true feelings to an adult seems to be instinctive from the age of seven or eight onwards. Even the affection that one feels for a child, the desire to protect and cherish it, is a cause of misunderstandings. One can love a child, perhaps, more deeply than one can love another adult, but it is rash to assume that the child feels any love in return. Looking back on my childhood, after the infant years were over, I do not believe that I ever felt love for any mature person except my mother, and even her I did not trust, in the sense that shyness made me conceal most of my real feelings from her. Love, the spontaneous, unqualified emotion of love, was something I could only feel for people who were young. Towards people who were old – and remember that 'old' to a child means over thirty, or even over twenty-five – I could feel reverence, respect, admiration or compunction, but I seemed cut off from them by a veil of fear and shyness mixed up with physical distaste. People are too ready to forget the child's *physical* shrinking from the adult. The enormous size of grown-ups, their ungainly, rigid bodies, their coarse, wrinkled skins, their great relaxed eyelids, their yellow teeth, and the whiffs of musty clothes and beer and sweat and tobacco that disengage from them at every movement! Part of the reason for the ugliness of adults, in a child's eyes, is that the child is usually looking upwards, and few faces are at their best when seen from below. Besides, being fresh and unmarked itself, the child has impossibly high standards in the matter of skin and teeth and complexion. But the greatest barrier of all is the child's misconception about age. A child can hardly envisage life beyond thirty, and in judging people's ages it will make fantastic mistakes. It will think that a person of twenty-five is forty, that a person of forty is sixty-five, and so on. Thus, when I fell in love with Elsie I took her to be grown-up. I met her again, when I was thirteen and she, I think, must have been twenty-three; she now seemed to me a middle-aged woman, somewhat past her best. And the child thinks of growing old as an almost obscene calamity, which for some mysterious reason will never happen to itself. All who have passed the age of thirty are joyless grotesques, endlessly fussing about things of no importance and staying alive without, so far as the child can see, having anything to live for. Only child life is real life. The schoolmaster who imagines that he is loved and trusted by his boys is in fact mimicked and laughed at behind his back. An adult who does not seem dangerous nearly always seems ridiculous.

I base these generalisations on what I can recall of my own childhood outlook. Treacherous though memory is, it seems to me the chief means we have of discovering how a child's mind works. Only by resurrecting our own memories can we realise how incredibly distorted is the child's vision of the world. Consider this, for example. How would St. Cyprian's appear to me now, if I could go back, at my present age, and see it as it was in 1915? What should I think of Sambo and Flip, those terrible, all-powerful monsters? I should see them as a couple of silly, shallow, ineffectual people, eagerly clambering up a social ladder which any thinking person could see to be on the point of collapse. I would no more be frightened of them than I would be frightened of a dormouse. Moreover, in those days they seemed to me fantastically old, whereas – though of this I am not certain – I imagine they must have been somewhat younger than I am now. And how would Cliffy Burton appear, with his blacksmith's arms and his red, jeering face? Merely a scruffy little boy, barely distinguishable from hundreds of other scruffy little boys. The two sets of facts can lie side by side in my mind, because those happen to be my own memories. But it would be very difficult for me to see with the eyes of any other child, except by an effort of the imagination which might lead me completely astray. The child and the adult live in different worlds. If that is so, we cannot be certain that school, at any rate boarding school, is not still for many children as dreadful an experience as it used to be. Take away God, Latin, the cane, class distinctions and sexual taboos, and the fear, the hatred, the snobbery and the misunderstanding might still all be there. It will have been seen that my own main trouble was an utter lack of any sense of proportion or probability. This led me to accept outrages and believe absurdities, and to suffer torments over things which were in fact of no importance. It is not enough to say that I was 'silly' and 'ought to have known better'. Look back into your own childhood and think of the nonsense you used to believe and the trivialities which could make you suffer. Of course my own case had its individual variations, but essentially it was that of countless other boys. The weakness of the child is that it starts with a blank sheet. It neither understands nor questions the society in which it lives, and because of its credulity other people can work upon it, infecting it with the sense of inferiority and the dread of offending against mysterious, terrible laws. It may be that everything that happened to me at St. Cyprian's could happen in the most 'enlightened' school, though perhaps in subtler forms. Of one thing, however, I do feel fairly sure, and that is that boarding schools are worse than day schools. A child has a better chance with the sanctuary of its home near at hand. And I think the characteristic faults of the English upper and middle classes may be partly due to the practice, general until recently, of sending children away from home as young as nine, eight or even seven.

I have never been back to St. Cyprian's. Reunions, old boys' dinners and such-like leave me something more than cold, even when my memories are friendly. I have never even been down to Eton, where I was relatively happy, though I did once pass through it in 1933 and noted with interest that nothing seemed to have changed, except that the shops now sold radios. As for St. Cyprian's, for years I loathed its very name so deeply that I could not view it with enough detachment to see the significance of the things that happened to me there. In a way, it is only within the last decade that I have really thought over my schooldays, vividly though their memory has always haunted me. Nowadays, I believe, it would make very little impression on me to see the place again, if it still exists. (I remember hearing a rumour some years ago that it had been burnt down.)

If I had to pass through Eastbourne I would not make a detour to avoid the school: and if I happened to pass the school itself I might even stop for a moment by the low brick wall, with the steep bank running down from it, and look across the flat playing field at the ugly building with the square of asphalt in front of it. And if I went inside and smelt again the inky, dusty smell of the big schoolroom, the rosiny smell of the chapel, the stagnant smell of the swimming bath and the cold reek of the lavatories, I think I should only feel what one invariably feels in revisiting any scene of childhood: How small everything has grown, and how terrible is the deterioration in myself! But it is a fact that for many years I could hardly have borne to look at it again. Except upon dire necessity I would not have set foot in Eastbourne. I even conceived a prejudice against Sussex, as the county that contained St. Cyprian's, and as an adult I have only once been in Sussex, on a short visit. Now, however, the place is out of my system for good. Its magic works no longer, and I have not even enough animosity left to make me hope that Flip and Sambo are dead or that the story of the school being burnt down was true.[33]

1. That this beating was not suffered by Orwell is referred to in the headnote. An autobiographical story by a friend of Orwell's, George Garrett (1896–1966), might also be relevant. Garrett was a Liverpool man, unemployed much of his life but who worked on the docks, as a seaman (hence one of his pen-names, Matt Low – *matelot*, a term used by Royal Naval seamen to describe themselves), an aspiring writer, and actor. He participated in the industrial troubles in Liverpool, 1921–2, and in the Hunger March of winter 1922, and he wrote about these. Orwell met him when he travelled north in 1936 and told Sir Richard Rees that he was 'greatly impressed by him' (X/*288*). Garrett's autobiographical story, 'The Apostate', was published in *Left Review*, March 1936. It describes his experiences at St Vincent's Roman Catholic School and a particularly memorable scene is the fierce beating the boys received from the priest. 'When one cane broke, another was produced, for there was always a supply kept handy for this purpose.' The priest knocked the boy representing Garrett to the ground with his fist, and, wishing to beat him further, but considering a cane 'useless for his purpose, tossed it aside, and picked up a long ebony ruler' (*The Collected George Garrett*, ed. Michael Murphy (1999), 107 and 111). Orwell met Garrett on 27 February 1936 so it is likely that 'The Apostate' came to his attention, especially as the title was also that of a story by Jack London which Orwell greatly admired (and spoke about in a BBC broadcast on 8 October 1945; see *2761*, XVII/299–301). Of course, the ebony ruler and the bone-handled riding crop may have only coincidental similarities, but there looks like imaginative representation of 'the scenery' of Orwell's mind here.

2. John Raphael Wentworth Savile, Viscount Pollington (1906–80) succeeded his father as 7th Earl of Mexborough, 1945. His education continued at Downside and Cambridge. He served in the Intelligence Corps and was in India, 1941–5. Cyril Connolly annotated his

copies of *The Orwell Reader* (introduced by R. H. Rovere; New York, 1956) and *CEJL* (in which 'Such, Such Were the Joys' appeared in 1956 and 1968). This name (misspelt) was one such annotation.

3. Parlour boarders at a boarding-school lived with the family who ran the school and had privileges not shared by the less-favoured. The term dates from 1777 and was common in the nineteenth century.

4. Connolly annotated this in *The Orwell Reader*: 'This was an "extra" for which they paid, including myself. Milk & biscuits were "medical".'

5. The typescript for the essay has Clive [of India] and Clive appears in some editions. However, Orwell crossed through Clive and wrote in Hastings. Connolly annotated against Clive in *The Orwell Reader*: 'Warren Hastings'.

6. In March 1943, Orwell asked T. S. Eliot to broadcast to India on a play by Dryden which he mistakenly called *The Indian Empress* (XV/*1953*). He then realized he meant *The Indian Emperor*, which was a sequel to *The Indian Queen* (performed 1664 and 1665). However, Orwell's error was more serious. He thought *The Indian Emperor* was set in India but then realized it was set in Mexico. He asked Eliot if he could tie his talk to India by 'just mentioning even if only in one sentence that Dryden wrote a play about Aurungzib, or however it is spelt'. *Aureng-Zebe*, Dryden's last play in verse, was performed in 1675. It was based, very loosely, on contemporary events in India. Aurengzebe wrested the Moghul Empire from Shah Jehan and his brothers. Orwell may have selected this from many possible dates because of the confusion he had got himself into; if so it would be an example of one of the 'private jokes' of which Orwell was fond.

7. '1773 . . . Party!' was added by Orwell as an afterthought; it is an interlinear insertion in his hand.

8. Connolly annotated *The Orwell Reader*: 'see Dr. J'. Dr Samuel Johnson, when asked by Boswell 'how he had acquired so accurate a knowledge of Latin . . . said, "My master whipped me very well. Without that, Sir, I should have done nothing"' (*The Life of Samuel Johnson*, 'His School-Days'); Orwell had a copy of the *Life* (see XX/*3734*).

9. Orwell's typescript has Knowles but *The Orwell Reader* and *CEJL* have Batchelor. Connolly annotated both texts 'Knowles'.

10. Birling Gap is close to the shore on a minor road west of Eastbourne.

11. For Ian Hay, see n. 4 to 'Poetry and the Microphone', above. Orwell wrote about or was influenced by the other three authors. His essay, 'Oysters and Brown Stout' (XVI/*2592*), discusses William Makepeace Thackeray (1811–63) and he regarded the short story 'A Little Dinner at Timmins's' as one of the best comic short stories ever written (XVI/500). He wrote a long and important essay on Rudyard Kipling (1865–1936) as a review of T. S. Eliot's *A Choice of Kipling's Verse* (1941; XIII/*948*) and he included the short story 'Baa, Baa, Black Sheep' (coincidentally with the same title as the Wodehouse/Hay farce, but a grim tale based on Kipling's unhappy childhood when sent away from home, a story relevant to 'Such, Such Were the Joys') in the same list as the Thackeray story mentioned on another occasion (*750*, XII/372). H. G. Wells (1866–1946) is discussed in 'Wells, Hitler and the World State' (XII/*837*) and Orwell dramatized Wells's short story, 'A Slip Under the Microscope', for the BBC (XV/*2297*). When a boy he read Wells's *A Modern Utopia* (1905) and became so attached to it that the father of his childhood friend, Jacintha Buddicom, gave him a copy. She recalled that when Orwell was between eleven and thirteen he told

her he would write a book like that, an early moment in the genesis of *Nineteen Eighty-Four* (see *A Literary Life*, 8–9).

12. See above for Orwell's review of Edmund Blunden's *Cricket Country*.

13. Sillar is given as Brown in *The Orwell Reader* and *CEJL*. Connolly annotated *CEJL* 'Siller' (with an 'e'). This was Robert L. Sillar. He taught geography and drawing and enthusiastically led the boys on nature-study field-trips, which Orwell greatly enjoyed. See Shelden, 47–8.

14. 'draughty' was typed as 'dreadful'. It was emended by Orwell in a rather wavering hand, perhaps when he did his final revision in Hairmyres Hospital, Glasgow.

15. 'prongs' has against it, in an unfirm hand, Orwell's note, 'tines?'.

16. Although Stansky and Abrahams repeated Cyril Connolly's assertion that he and Orwell both won the Harrow History Prize (*Unknown Orwell*, 72), Robert Pearce has shown that neither did. See his 'Orwell and the Harrow History Prize', *Notes and Queries*, vol. 235 (December 1990), 442.

17. 'servile' was typed as 'senile' but amended in Orwell's hand.

18. Connolly annotated against this, 'Pacheco'.

19. *The Orwell Reader* and *CEJL* have Horne. Connolly annotated *CEJL* 'Hardcastle'.

20. Connolly annotated both texts 'Loseby'. Captain Charles Edgar Loseby, MP (1881–1970), schoolmaster then barrister. He was wounded at Cambrai and awarded the MC in 1917. He became a Coalition National Democratic and Labour MP, 1918–22, and was a barrister in Hong Kong from 1945 until his retirement.

21. 'believed' is an interlinear insertion in the typescript in a hand other than Orwell's.

22. Matthew 18:6.

23. Orwell inserted 'physical' after 'own' and then heavily crossed it out.

24. 'Home' is an interlinear insertion in Orwell's hand.

25. A 'Knut' is a variant of 'Nut' (perhaps slang for the head) and, with a 'K', dates from 1911. It refers to a smart, man-about-town. In the music-hall song, sung by Basil Hallam, 'Gilbert the Filbert' (picking up the reference to 'nut'), the 'K' was pronounced: 'I'm Gilbert the Filbert, the Colonel of the K-nuts'.

26. Connolly annotated *CEJL* against this line, 'Kirkpatricks'.

27. The Twelfth of August – first day of the grouse-shooting season.

28. Cain: first son of Adam and Eve and the first murderer (of his brother, Abel; Genesis 4:1 and 8, and 1 John 3:12); Jezebel: wife of Ahab, King of Israel, who led him to worship pagan gods (1 Kings 16:31) and who killed the prophets (1 Kings 18:4 and 21:7–13), she herself was killed by being thrown from a window (2 Kings 9:33); Haman the Agagite: 'the Jews' enemy' (Esther 8:1), at first preferred but later hanged by King Ahasuerus, who reigned from India to Ethiopia (Esther 8:7); King Agag the Amalekite: spared by King Saul but when later he came before Samuel 'delicately', he was hewn in pieces by Samuel because his sword had made women childless 'so shall thy mother be childless' (1 Samuel 15:32–3); Sisera: Captain of the King of Canaan's army, killed by a nail driven through his head by Jael, wife of Heber, while he slept (Judges 4:2–21). Ananias: when accused by Peter of lying to men and to God, 'fell down and gave up the ghost' (Acts 5:1–5); Caiaphas: High Priest, who condemned Christ for blasphemy (e.g. Matthew 26:57–66); Judas Iscariot: the traitorous apostle who betrayed Christ with a kiss for thirty pieces of silver and then hanged himself (Matthew 26:47–9 and 27:3–5); Pontius Pilate: Roman Governor of Judea who condemned Christ to Crucifixion but washed his hands declaring, 'I am innocent of the blood of this

just person' (Matthew 27:24). In 1946 Orwell suggested he prepare a script for the BBC defending Pontius Pilate but it came to nothing (XVIII/*3059*).

29. From George Meredith's poem 'The Woods of Westermain', published in *Poems and Lyrics of the Joy of Earth*, 1883.

30. *The Orwell Reader* and *CEJL* printed Johnny Hale; Connolly annotated *CEJL* 'Clifford Burton'.

31. Orwell attended Wellington College for nine weeks of the first term of 1917. He joined Eton College in May 1917 as a King's Scholar. Crick notes: 'He did not like Wellington at all. He found the militaristic spirit of this famous army school abhorrent' (96).

32. Henley-on-Thames, where the family lived, 1904–12 and 1915–17. Orwell's parents were then at home, but on 13 September 1917 his father was commissioned as a 2nd Lieutenant and posted to the 51st (Ranchi) Indian Pioneer Company at Marseilles. He was reputed to be the oldest second lieutenant in the army. His mother then moved to London to work for the Ministry of Pensions.

33. The school burnt down in May 1939. There was one casualty, a sixteen-year-old servant, Winifred Higgs (Shelden, 62). The school was not rebuilt but the headmaster's house still stands and a plaque lists the names of five of those who were pupils there and later became famous: Sir Cecil Beaton, photographer and designer; Cyril Connolly, writer and journalist; Henry C. Longhurst, journalist and MP; Gavin Maxwell, naturalist and writer; and George Orwell.

Further Reading

The principal source for this volume is *The Complete Works of George Orwell*, edited by Peter Davison, assisted by Ian Angus and Sheila Davison, 20 vols. (1998); 2nd paperback edition from September 2000. Reference might also usefully be made to *The Collected Essays, Journalism and Letters of George Orwell*, edited by Sonia Orwell and Ian Angus, 4 vols. (1968; Penguin, 1970) and to the volumes *Orwell and the Dispossessed* and *Orwell and Politics* in this series. Left Book Club publications are well worth examination, especially Wal Hannington, *The Problem of the Distressed Areas* (1937; reviewed above); Ellen Wilkinson, *The Town that was Murdered: The Life Story of Jarrow* (1939); F. Zweig, *Labour, Life and Poverty*, with Preface by Lord Beveridge (1948). See also Margery Spring Rice, *Working-Class Wives* (1939), and Maud Pember Reeves's pioneering study, *Round About a Pound a Week* (1913; reprinted 1979 onwards), advertised, correctly, in 1994 as 'The classic account of working lives before the First World War'. The following highly selective list might prove helpful:

Correlli Barnett, *The Audit of War: The Illusion and Reality of Britain as a Great Nation* (1986)

Michael Carney, *Britain in Pictures: A History and a Bibliography* (1995)

Audrey Coppard and Bernard Crick, eds., *Orwell Remembered* (1984)

Bernard Crick, *George Orwell: A Life* (1980; 3rd edn 1992)

Andy Croft, *Red Letter Days: British Fiction in the 1930s* (1990)

Valentine Cunningham, *British Writers of the Thirties* (1989)

Peter Davison, *George Orwell: A Literary Life* (1996)

Benjamin Disraeli, *Sybil, or The Two Nations* (1845), ed. Sheila M. Smith (1981, 1998)

Tosco Fyvel, *George Orwell: A Personal Memoir* (1982)

Charles Garrett, *The Collected George Garrett*, ed. Michael Murphy (1999)

Miriam Gross, ed., *The World of George Orwell* (1971)

Rayner Heppenstall, *Four Absentees* (1960)

Robert Hewison, *Under Siege: Literary Life in London, 1939–45* (1978)

Graham Holderness, Bryan Loughrey and Nahem Yousaf, *George Orwell*, Contemporary Critical Essays (1998)
Humphrey Jennings and Charles Madge, eds. *May the Twelfth: Mass-Observation Day-Surveys, 1937* (1937; reprinted with a new Afterword, 1987)
Peter Lewis, *George Orwell: The Road to 1984* (1981)
Jeffrey Meyers, ed., *George Orwell: The Critical Heritage* (1975)
—, *Orwell: Wintry Conscience of a Generation* (2000)
Janet Montefiore, *Men and Women Writers of the 1930s: The Dangerous Flood of History* (1996)
Malcolm Muggeridge, *The Thirties* (1940); reviewed by Orwell, 25 April 1940 (XII/*615*)
David Christie Murray, *A Novelist's Note Book* (1887)
John Newsinger, *Orwell's Politics* (1999)
Christopher Norris, ed., *Inside the Myth: Orwell: Views from the Left* (1984)
Alok Rai, *Orwell and the Politics of Despair* (1988)
Sir Richard Rees, *For Love or Money* (1960)
—, *George Orwell: Fugitive from the Camp of Victory* (1961)
Patrick Reilly, *George Orwell: The Age's Adversary* (1986)
John Rodden, *The Politics of Literary Reputation: The Making and Claiming of 'St George Orwell'* (1989)
Michael Shelden, *Orwell: The Authorised Biography* (1991)
Ian Slater, *Orwell: The Road to Airstrip One: The Development of George Orwell's Political and Social Thought from* Burmese Days *to* 1984 (1985)
Peter Stansky and William Abrahams, *The Unknown Orwell* (1974)
—, *Orwell: The Transformation* (1979)
John Thompson, *Orwell's London* (1984)
Richard J. Voorhees, *The Paradox of George Orwell* (1961)
Stephen Wadhams, ed., *Remembering Orwell* (1984)
George Woodcock, *The Crystal Spirit: A Study of George Orwell* (1967)
David Wykes, *A Preface to Orwell* (1987)

Volumes of *CW* in which items will be found:

X: 1–355
XI: 355A–582
XII: 583–843
XIII: 844–1434
XIV: 1435–1915
XV: 1916–2377
XVI: 2378–2596
XVII: 2597–2831
XVIII 2832–3143
XIX: 3144–3515
XX: 3516–3715A

Vol. XX also includes in Appendix 15 the following supplementary items: 2278A, 2278B, 2420A, 2451A, 2563B, 2593A, 2625A, 3351A and 3715A. Each volume is indexed and vol. XX has a Cumulative Index, indexes of topics, and an index of serials in which Orwell's work appeared.

D. G.

Selective Index

There are references to poverty and the poor throughout this volume; Orwell's epigraph to *Down and Out in Paris and London,* Chaucer's 'O scathful harm, condicion of poverte!', might well apply to this compilation. Thus there are no dedicated entries to these topics, nor indeed, to England and Britain except for pp. 259 and 278 where he briefly contrasts these words. Discussions of 'class' are very important in this volume and a generous selection of references is indexed, all under 'Class' but with sub-headings, such as 'Working Class'. '*Bourgeoisie*' is similarly treated. Bracketed explanations are often given after line references to books and authors (e.g., 'rev.' for Orwell's reviews), and the practice is taken much further in this index than in those for the other three volumes in the series. *The Road to Wigan Pier* is fairly fully indexed; because the book only has Orwell's footnotes, many references are dated in the index if these are not given in the notes to the rest of the volume. This has been done because, although the first part of *The Road to Wigan Pier* is plainly rooted in the time when it was written, it is not, perhaps, as apparent how closely the second part is related to what Orwell was then reading. The relationship is often subtle and sometimes insignificant. An example which cannot be indexed will illustrate this. The last six lines of p. 193 are closely related in content, phrasing and time to a review Orwell wrote of Peter Fleming's *News from Tartary,* published in *Time and Tide* on 15 August 1936 (X/*322A*). Both refer to the nomad, however much discomfort he suffers, 'living while he is travelling', but that rapid travel by luxury liner or train or car is kind of 'temporary death' (the quoted words are identical in both texts). Anyone who has flown from Los Angeles or Sydney to Heathrow will have experienced such a 'temporary death'. Sources within footnotes are not usually indexed although there are exceptions if it is thought these would help the reader. Page numbers for the text are given in roman type (e.g., 57, 168); footnotes are in italic (e.g., *33*, *284*); bold italic is used for biographical and fuller details (e.g., ***44***, ***357***).

READ MORE IN PENGUIN

In every corner of the world, on every subject under the sun, Penguin represents quality and variety – the very best in publishing today.

For complete information about books available from Penguin – including Puffins, Penguin Classics and Arkana – and how to order them, write to us at the appropriate address below. Please note that for copyright reasons the selection of books varies from country to country.

In the United Kingdom: Please write to *Dept. EP, Penguin Books Ltd, Bath Road, Harmondsworth, West Drayton, Middlesex UB7 ODA*

In the United States: Please write to *Consumer Sales, Penguin Putnam Inc., P.O. Box 12289 Dept. B, Newark, New Jersey 07101-5289.* VISA and MasterCard holders call 1-800-788-6262 to order Penguin titles

In Canada: Please write to *Penguin Books Canada Ltd, 10 Alcorn Avenue, Suite 300, Toronto, Ontario M4V 3B2*

In Australia: Please write to *Penguin Books Australia Ltd, P.O. Box 257, Ringwood, Victoria 3134*

In New Zealand: Please write to *Penguin Books (NZ) Ltd, Private Bag 102902, North Shore Mail Centre, Auckland 10*

In India: Please write to *Penguin Books India Pvt Ltd, 11 Community Centre, Panchsheel Park, New Delhi 110017*

In the Netherlands: Please write to *Penguin Books Netherlands bv, Postbus 3507, NL-1001 AH Amsterdam*

In Germany: Please write to *Penguin Books Deutschland GmbH, Metzlerstrasse 26, 60594 Frankfurt am Main*

In Spain: Please write to *Penguin Books S. A., Bravo Murillo 19, 1° B, 28015 Madrid*

In Italy: Please write to *Penguin Italia s.r.l., Via Benedetto Croce 2, 20094 Corsico, Milano*

In France: Please write to *Penguin France, Le Carré Wilson, 62 rue Benjamin Baillaud, 31500 Toulouse*

In Japan: Please write to *Penguin Books Japan Ltd, Kaneko Building, 2-3-25 Koraku, Bunkyo-Ku, Tokyo 112*

In South Africa: Please write to *Penguin Books South Africa (Pty) Ltd, Private Bag X14, Parkview, 2122 Johannesburg*

BY THE SAME AUTHOR

Inside the Whale and Other Essays

In 'Politics and the English Language' Orwell puts the case for political writers to use plain English. The rest of this hard-hitting and wide-ranging volume of essays perfectly illustrates what he had in mind. 'England Your England', written during the Blitz, was described by Arthur Koestler as 'one of the most moving and yet incisive portraits of the English character'. 'Inside the Whale' uses the work of Henry Miller as a peg for a sharp survey of a whole generation of writers in English, while the other essays on language and literature consider *Gulliver's Travels*, Tolstoy and *King Lear*, boys' weeklies and freedom of speech. Two more personal and political pieces describe life 'down the mine' and shooting an elephant in Burma – a touching and beautifully concise critique of colonialism. All remain intensely stimulating, enriched by Orwell's unique combination of first-hand observation, decency, compassion and supreme clarity of expression.

'George Orwell has many of the traits of the best English pamphleteers: courage, an individual mind, vehement opinions, and an instinct for stirring up trouble … he writes in a lucid conversational style which wakes one up suddenly like cold water dashed in the face' V. S. Pritchett

Homage to Catalonia

'Every line of serious work that I have written since 1936 has been written, directly or indirectly, *against* totalitarianism and *for* democratic Socialism as I understand it'. Thus wrote Orwell following his experiences as a militiaman in the Spanish Civil War, chronicled in *Homage to Catalonia.* Here he brings to bear all the force of his humanity, passion and clarity, describing with bitter intensity the bright hopes and cynical betrayals of that chaotic episode.

'An unrivalled picture of the rumours, suspicions and treachery of civil war' Anthony Beevor

BY THE SAME AUTHOR

Down and Out in Paris and London

'It is the white-hot reaction of a sensitive, observant, compassionate young man to poverty, injustice and the callousness of the rich' writes Dervla Murphy, introducing Orwell's record of a period in the late Twenties when he lived among the tramps, dregs and *plongeurs* of London and Paris. 'It offers insights rather than solutions; but always insights have to precede solutions ... No one has ever claimed *Down and Out* is its author's best book, yet many of his admirers describe it as their *favourite* Orwell. Its flaws are numerous, but oddly endearing.'

'Written with so much simple force ... the result is curiously beautiful' Compton Mackenzie

'An excellent book and a valuable social document' J. B. Priestley

The Road to Wigan Pier

Commissioned by the Left Book Club in 1936, George Orwell set out to report on working-class life in the bleak industrial heartlands of Yorkshire and Lancashire. The experience profoundly changed him, and in *Wigan Pier* he unleashed a brilliant and bitter polemic that has not lost its force with the passage of time.

'It is easy to see why the book created and still creates so sharp an impact ... Above all, it is a study of poverty and, behind that, of the strength of class-divisions' Richard Hoggart

'For Orwell social injustice was a physical pain; it smelt, it hurt like a tooth, like a gangrene ... As a writer, he was a sort of missing link between Swift and Kafka' Arthur Koestler

BY THE SAME AUTHOR

George Orwell: Essays

This outstanding collection brings together Orwell's longer, major essays and a fine selection of shorter pieces. With great originality and wit Orwell unfolds his views on subjects ranging from the moral enormity of Jonathan Swift's strange genius, a revaluation of Charles Dickens to the nature of Socialism, a comic yet profound discussion of naughty sea-side picture postcards and a spirited defence of English cooking. Displaying an almost unrivalled mastery of English plain prose style, Orwell's essays challenge, move and entertain.

'Anyone who wants to understand the twentieth century will have to read Orwell' Timothy Garton Ash, *New York Review of Books*

also published:

Animal Farm
Burmese Days
A Clergyman's Daughter
Coming Up For Air
The Complete Novels
Keep the Aspidistra Flying
Nineteen Eighty-Four

and the collections of his essays:

Orwell and the Dispossessed
Orwell and Politics
Orwell in Spain